Copyright © 2018 by Brian P. Lahey, M.D.

I & i: The Book of Binary Psychology

An *Up & Up Solutions* Publication

ISBN: 9780997365610

Printed in the United States of America

Binary Psychology is the foundation for understanding the human consciousness and the origin of symptoms.

Highlights/Excerpts

Rejection

As a general rule—individuals reject what they don't understand, and fear what they have rejected. This illustrates the cyclical process whereby a lack of understanding compels rejection, which then increases fear, where increased fear then inhibits the pursuit of understanding. The lamentable tragedy which lies therein occurs between individuals—where a lack of understanding drives the discord which eventuates in division.

Why feelings

Feelings are best regarded as the substance for doing—for action—thereby enabling change or growth. How one feels is always in relation to one's present period of consciousness, and thus may be understood as the gathering of potential for one's creative intent—to effect a cause or to cause an effect based on the laws of cause and effect. The cause is found in thought as one's thought forms the outline of the world one exists within, and the feeling element then integrates to effect one's potential therein. For instance, in response to a lion suddenly attacking, the surge of adrenaline in response is an energetic potentiation to act. It produces physiologic readiness in support of either fight or flight. When no materialized cause is evident, then people become much more uncomfortable with the adrenaline effects. If such feelings are perceived as a problem, then an individual will fight against the adrenaline-based feelings themselves rather than applying the feelings. The attempt to control it, as a result, is energetically depleting and undermines adaptive growth. The imagined lion is thus the individual themselves, though each is blind to such.

Substance of anxiety

Conceptualizing sensory anxiety as an expression of non-integrated potential energy is the only explanation which accounts for its ubiquitous existence within individuals, where it occurs at varying intensity levels and takes on individualized ways of manifesting. Anxious energy is inherently uncomfortable because it represents impending change. The change is occurring outside of one's conscious intent, and thus, the anxiety is sensed negatively and given thought as if occurring from the world toward oneself. The mind naturally seeks to make sense of the anxiety by finding cause outside of oneself. Yet, in doing so, an individual finds reason to be anxious, thereby forming their subjective experience of life.

To be or not to be?

Thus, every individual may either *be* or *not be*—for that is the question each must answer. Such is the crossroads everyone must face within their present life. In order *to be,* an individual cannot be thinking *what to be*, *what to do*, or *what will be*. Rather, they must simply *be*. In just *being*, an individual strives to relate to the present, to bring themselves as they are for the betterment of the environment and the growth of those around them. *What* is given to the present moment to answer—where being themselves in connection with the present—enables a perspective of *whatever will be will be*.

Misperceiving offense

If the human mind did not take offense to rejecting behavior from others, then the rejective behavior seen from others would be properly perceived as defensive. As such, outwardly occurring upset would be recognized as stemming from a misperception, recognized to be fear, though manifesting as anger—like a sheep, only in wolf's clothing.

Growing problems

The relative peace and affluence for the past fifty years afforded an increasingly child-centered culture. However, doing so has exposed the character of the child mind and how their mind integrates what is done for them. Moreover, the process of development as preparation for life has been reaffirmed though the current wave of maladapted youth—who are demonstrating difficulty with life's challenges and believing their needs are going unmet. More and more children are struggling with their emotions in the school setting, being unable to channel their negative feelings into effort. Such children are becoming adolescents who seek to self-medicate through drugs, excessive gaming, and other various addictions. Adolescents, in increasing numbers, are having difficulty moving on—the step forth from home, whether into college or into independent living, isn't being accomplished. The cultural response, in attempt to identify the problems, has focused on finding something tangible (e.g. drugs), while increasingly trying to meet the needs of children. But since the psycho-emotional needs of children have not been outlined, children have been determining their own needs through their expression of need. In doing so, however, they are being taught to form thought out of feeling. In other words, children are being taught to see the world and themselves through a lens of how they feel. But since feeling is meant for energetic effort, turning feeling into thought comes at the expense of experience. The more a child turns their emotion into thought, the more they will be reliant on others regarding how they feel, and the less the child will then channel their feelings into action, into experience.

Need to love more

At present, the current culture is running low on love, and there is a rising surplus of fear. Fear cannot increase without love decreasing, and vice versa. Love cannot be hijacked by words which seek to represent it, as if one may possess it for another. Love is not simply a feeling, nor is love just a thought. The more one seeks to possess love, the more elusive it will seem. Love is a verb, a sacrifice, a giving of oneself. Love regards the other and seeks to give of oneself for positive growth within the other. Love is always outgoing—like the sun. Love knows no end and is blind to loss. Love does not wield itself as a weapon, and it attaches no strings. Love entitles nothing in return.

Where judgment fails

Relational understanding cannot be built from a triangulated position. Judgment of another's feelings or thoughts based on their behavior toward oneself causes most of the problems in human relationships. Such judgment occurs from a triangulated position because, despite one being part of the relationship, the judgment is coming from a third-person perspective. The human capability for third-person judgment causes problems when the judgment is applied to others as they relate to oneself. For someone to judge another based on how the other person is effecting them, then a third-person judgment is made without being able to see their effect from a first-person perspective. Only through the first-person, experiential perspective, in connecting to others as they experience oneself, can one develop the proper understanding of oneself.

The opiate effect

The opiate use is thus employed as a transitional blanket, to produce their own internal reassurance, as they seek to integrate socially and step away from the dependent position. As a general rule, the opiate-effect is more appealing to those who fight an internal sense of lacking.

The bully

Although such behavior is happening under the illusion of being a victim, truly, such behavior victimizes. It is a lamentable aspect of the human mind—bound to see the rejected aspects of oneself in others. Thus, the victimizer believes they are the victim as they are victimizing. The bully believes they are being bullied as they are bullying.

The way to adapt

The adaptation to life involves growing better able to independently and purposefully handle one's feelings. To manage oneself within the world, where one senses fulfillment, requires having creative power. One has to eventually learn to grow the world. The creative ability comes in the combining of one's energy/time with one's thought. While most perceive the outside world as dictating their thought, growing into an awareness of one's capability to look at things differently, to change the thought, is a milestone of immeasurable benefit. The space where change occurs is between oneself and the world. Thought negativity or rejection toward the world is based on centering the world around oneself. Thus, the potential shift in perspective is born out of a de-centering of oneself. In other words, for to center oneself around the world, and perceive life outside through the lens of one's potential toward it, is a shift in thought structure. Dong so enables them to see the bright side. Then, the world experiences them bringing forth such brightness.

To my parents —
A woman who took an interest
in me, and a man who told
me mysteries...

TABLE OF CONTENTS

TIME & SPACE

As a medical doctor, what do I do when I see harm being done? In becoming a physician, I had taken a single oath—I swore to initially do no harm. No doctor can promise to be helpful—there is no guarantee—but in our effort toward a patient, we had to swear by the Oath of Hippocrates—that we, as physicians, in our approach to a patient's condition, would not initiate any harm. I was not exactly sure what it meant—to do no harm—but I imagined physicians doing lobotomies, scrambling a patient's brain (the frontal lobe) with a prod through their eye socket as a treatment for *hysteria*. The hysteria usually improved. However, the person did not—meaning, they were reduced to a docile, disconnected shell of their former self. I have come to realize the harm in such cases preceded the lobotomy, for such patients believed they had something wrong with them—something which needed help, for which they hysterically sought treatment.

A medical doctor is trained to recognize physical problems and understand the nature of such problems. The expectation then is for the doctor to lessen or remove the problem—to help the individual by helping them with their problem. Since medical problems occur at the level of the body, the patient and the doctor should both be able to relate to the problem. In other words, the patient must have a problem the doctor can interact with, where it can be seen or objectively measured. When the problem the patient brings forth, however, is contained within their impressions—their internal experience (feelings, thoughts)—the doctor has nothing to treat as the problem which is separate from the patient's subjective experience of the problem. In such a scenario, the doctor has to focus on the physically based effects the person is struggling to manage—whether anxiety, depression, anger, or pain. The medical effort then is to support the patient's effort relative to themselves, which is to not experience the problematic effects, to lessen the intensity of their internal experience of negativity. However, the negativity is not the problem—rather, the rejective handling of the negative effects causes an internal trapping of negativity which then produces the dysfunction.

Where I see the current approach causing the most harm is in children and adolescents. Childhood is a period of belief formation—beliefs about themselves relative to life and of life relative to themselves. Children are bound to believe they need what they get from their parents. When such need is relative to their emotion or physical condition, independence becomes more daunting and appears less liberating. Adolescents will reach out to try and met such needs independently, precipitating relationships and use of substances. Fortunately, adolescents, as they step into an independent consciousness, can reject the belief in having a problem and needing outside help. When a child or adolescent gets medicine for a mental diagnosis, they have to believe they need it because they have a problem. Their belief in having a problem will repeatedly manifest through experiences where external controls/fixes are applied to correct the problem. To some degree, then, their willpower will go toward not experiencing themselves as a problem, to not need correction. However, when they are given medicine by a doctor, they will naturally attach to having a problem and a materialized need to offset such. They cannot conceive of the deficit being tethered to their immaturity and thus able to be grown past. Rather, the problem becomes imbedded in their sense of themselves relative to world—generating a sense of need—and infuses into their outlook on the world relative to themselves—producing feelings of inferiority and impending rejection. Through their misbelief in having a problem, the likelihood of substance abuse and self-destructive behavior goes up dramatically, as does the likelihood of an eventual struggle with nervousness, depression, and dependence.

Although the physician's effort is to to help, by approaching children & adolescents as if they have a problem, we are initially causing harm. The reality of the damage being done is reflected in the declining function of our nation's youth and the growing incidence of adolescent suicide. Currently, the medical system continues to amplify its effort to help with the growing problem without insight into our precipitation of the problem being treated. Without an understanding of what we are doing, the escalation of effort will continue to exacerbate the problem. In lamentable irony, by prescribing chemicals, a physician is collaborating with their patient's effort to reject or avoid themselves. By simply relating to a patient's complaints about bodily effects as if such effects are a problem—as if the patient, by experiencing them, has a problem—physicians are legitimizing a misbelief. By participating in the patient's rejective or avoidant effort, the problem is thus perpetuated—the misbelief in having a problem—and a belief in needing medicine (or alleviation from the outside) gets created. Since the medical system is positioned to respond to problems, clinicians are bound to take a rejective or eliminative approach to the identified problem. In other words, the medical system moves in response to a problem. The problem always comes first—it must. Otherwise, the system will create problems, as evidenced by the growing proportion of the population taking medication for their mood, anxiety, or pain.

In the medical system's effort to foster child and adolescent development, the system is theoretically positioned to support growth. However, an approach in support of growth is vector-opposite to an approach aimed at eliminating problems. To enable growth requires providing positive support, whereas battling against disease is an opposition—a conflict—where the clinician is the soldier fighting against the problem on behalf of the patient. A clinical position which supports growth may be likened to a coaching role, where the clinician, through guidance and positive regard, seeks to strengthen resolve and enhance functional capability. A coaching role provides oversight and correction, and should never be rejecting—meaning, a coach should always see the positive growth potential, where the solution to any problem occurs through a growth in capability. Effective coaches enable the potentiation of their players. The difference between these two starting points of reference—the perspective of the coach versus the soldier—is significant. The soldier is on guard to prevent or eliminate problems, whereas the coach is positioned to promote the growth of capability. The soldier is always responding to a perceived threat, where the threat has made the first move. In contrast, a coach makes the first move by setting the structure and putting for expectations. Phenomena which are not understood are usually seen as a threat, which is how the medical system is currently approaching symptoms and behaviors associated with individual mental health. Unfortunately, in doing so, problems are being perpetuated in adults and created in kids. Because kids do not make the first move on behalf of themselves, for us to perceive them as having problems and treating them as such is initially doing harm by seeding a misbelief which becomes disabling to their individualized pursuit into life.

Life, liberty, and the individualized pursuit of happiness—as cornerstones —were the foundation upon which The United States of America was built. As values, they are the bedrock the western culture has stood upon for over two hundred years. There is a right to be alive, and a right to be independent, and a right to pursue one's own happiness. However, an egregious error has occurred within public consciousness over the past twenty-five years—in the belief that everyone should be happy. An increasing proportion of the population believes in the right to happiness. Yet, life is difficult. It always has been. The erroneous belief during individual times of unhappiness manifests through the state of unhappiness being attributed to a problem outside of themselves. In other words, people focus on determining why they do not feel good enough by perceiving an outside cause and then blaming elements within the world around them. They hunt for the problem preventing their happiness as if happiness is supposed to be their de facto state. Thus, criticisms and complaining are increasingly filling interpersonal space. Gone missing has been the "pursuit" of happiness. It has been replaced by the expectation for happiness. The pursuit, then, is simply to identify negative within their experience. People remain bound to battling their negative feelings, frustrated at their lack of happiness. A genuine pursuit of happiness begins from a place where life is understood as being difficult, and thus, the individual pursuit contributes to the evolution of humanity. Through the pursuit comes an understanding of life, and within the pursuit an individual comes to know themselves.

Happiness involves finding the growth in everything, rather than the negative, and only comes to fruition through the understanding and acceptance of the negative. Judging the world negatively as it treats oneself is opposite to judging oneself as one treats it. Through the latter approach, an individual can regard themselves positively unto the world, and in doing so can increasingly distance themselves from the world's treatment of them. To do so, however, the misbelief within their operating consciousness—that they are supposed to be happy—must be corrected. Otherwise, the innate pursuit of happiness causes them to blame others or the environment for their lack of perceived happiness. As such, their pursuit causes more unhappiness than anything. The important part of the "pursuit of happiness" is not the happiness but the pursuit. One comes to understand that happiness is not just a feeling, nor is it contained within a thought. Happiness is a state of being. Happiness is inseparable from coming into individualized fruition of one's potential. Yet the process whereby a full blossoming of one's personhood occurs, is one of toil and sacrifice. The pursuit is the process itself—the beginning of one's blossom. Because modern individuals are increasingly believing happiness is entitled, they are pursuing happiness by finding reasons they are not feeling happy. Finding negative around oneself, as if that which can be criticized is somehow keeping one from being happy, is misguided. Unfortunately, seeing negative within the environment is a seeding of negativity. Naturally, one may feel better when cleaning away what is perceived negatively. However, doing so brings nothing positive to the environment. Such a perspective is always on guard against negativity, and thus interacts with the world to minimize discomfort. Normally, the reasons for one's unhappiness are blamed on other people, and thus, social discord has been on the rise.

Also on the rise has been the number of people identifying themselves as having a problem with how they feel. Diagnoses of anxiety and mood disorders are only being limited by the number of diagnosticians. Individuals are desperate to find a cure for their unhappiness, their tension, or their lethargy. Because feelings press for expression, individuals get some relief in expressing their negativity through dialogue. In doing so, however, they are normally not mindful of the negative energy they are expelling into the environment. Furthermore, when negative feeling is given thought, then it generates experience. Likewise, if negative thought is given feeling, then it generates experience. Thus, to be revolving one's world around one's own negative feelings or thoughts, creates a world where one is surrounded by negativity. The positivity each seeks to reflect within themselves is begotten through an outward giving of positivity, for then the individual will be surrounded by positivity coming at them. The positive feeling or thought coming toward them is thereby able to be internalized. If, however, an individual uses negativity to generate positive regard from others, then the positivity cannot be internalized without trapping themselves in their expressed negativity. To give positivity to the environment in the form of one's effort, intent, or judgment, requires the individual to detach from their own negativity. Unfortunately, when an individual's negativity has been their source of getting positive regard or influence, then detaching from the feelings is extremely difficult.

The current culture has tried to sterilize negative feelings. Whether through advertised products (medications, treatments, devices) promoting the possibility of feeling better, or protectiveness against hurt feelings (e.g. participation trophies), the importance placed on how someone feels has reached unprecedentedly high levels. When seeking to alleviate a child's negative feelings, then the child forms the belief in such feelings needing to be alleviated. They will thus always see such feelings as being a problem and in need of something or someone to make them better. Young adults are thus demonstrating a lack of emotional independence from their parent(s), as they believe they need the emotional support. As a cohort, their ability to internally manage upset feelings or stressful thoughts is minimal, and they tend to express the upset feelings, expecting "care" to come their way.

Love and growth are inseparable. Growth enables the ability for one's consciousness to see oneself relative to others, rather than others relative to oneself. Revolving the world around one's subjective feelings can not be sustained since the effect is analogous to a black hole. The binary opposite is the sun and its shine, bringing the life force. The force itself is love, but we are born turned around in such a way where we only experience the shadows. The sun shines through us, and since the force of the sun promotes growth, life is always upsetting to the conscious desire to be in control of one's experience. Resistance causes one to feel unwell, unsettled, internally threatened. The more one's impulse toward growth and self-actualization is avoided or rejected, the worse one will feel and the more depleted of energy. The natural attempt will then be to attract or gravitate more light (love, care, help), but since doing so has a "black hole effect," it leads to a sense of emptiness internally. An individual caught in such a state of consciousness does not realize they are the black hole, and thus will sense themselves victimized. Yet, their attempts to elicit help or gain control tend to victimize others. The only effective path in life is toward becoming more like the sun. The sun gives life, and life is purposed for growth. The more self-actualized an individual has become, the more they see the world in front of them as a reflection of their creative will, and for what they can bring to it. Oppositely, someone who is in self-defense is bound to regard how others are different and what they don't like around them. Such a perceptive approach to the world is necessary when a materialized threat exists. However, when an individual creates the problem by seeing it rather than receiving it, and expects by doing so their judgment is valued, they are blind to the effect their negative judgment has on the environment. They are oblivious to others having to concede to being disregarded or judged. They are unaware of the negativity they are sewing into the world, but rather spend their perceptive energy trying to reject the reaping.

Life occurs in a quantum manner because the processing/coding is binary. The human mind, in order to grow, must change. Yet, fear of letting go of control, or losing what we think we need, keeps us trapped in our own misbeliefs. We are grown from within, from an unconscious nuclear source which somehow is able to give us a directional truth through positive impulses. The conscious desire to protect one's heart, however, and to control one's experience, injects fearful thought into the uncertainty of what's coming up. The future is a blank canvas which our forethought tries to predict—as if life happens to us. In doing so, however, we unwittingly script our life.

Consequences are karmic. We live them. There will be no judge separate from ourselves, no damnation from behind the curtain, no winner. The solution is not an answer. We evolve the solution—we must become it. From out of our blindness comes clarity. But the light, to our consciousness, is painful. Most people spend their entire life trying to prove themselves right or feel better about themselves. They want to be good enough as they are, and be forgiven for how they have been. Keeping themselves rooted in their belief system (their way of perceiving the world and relating to it) produces suffering. The inability to let go of oneself, to grow, to change, keeps one from evolving to more advanced levels of consciousness. Each step is a different plane, a different frequency, and certain false beliefs or beliefs born out of negative feeling (fear, anger) are tethered to lower levels of consciousness. As such, holding on to them, and thus perceiving life through such a thicket of thought, creates conflict by opposing the directional aim of life—to evolve in understanding. The more one's belief system and overall being is in harmony with one's nuclear truth, the lighter and more effective will be one's being.

Time goes forward, invariably, inevitably. We perceive time because of change. Change means we must perceive either what we are losing or what we may gain. Fighting against losing one's attachments is like fighting against being awoken—where we are stuck in a dream, being torn away from ourselves in some fashion, as our parent is trying to shake us awake. We wake up fighting against our parent as we realize we are fighting within ourselves. The experience is one of awakening, becoming illuminated to the reality of one's existence in a new light. We wake fighting against a force which is trying to intervene. The two poles of oneself, the extreme positive and the extreme negative, mark the borderline between oneself and the world, and within which one must live. Only through a perfect balance, however, may we see past ourselves. When we are imbalanced, even so slightly, we depend on someone or something intervening—we depend on life. However, life is not here for us...we are here for life.

The human mind, through the past century, as science as sought to understand its nature, has become raveled into a Gordian Knot. Though Freud sliced through the psyche by discovering the other side (the unconscious), he did not take into account the nature of consciousness. He did not account for the perceiver of perception being unable to perceive their effect on the system being perceived. Thus, he did not recognize the creationistic nature of human consciousness and thought formation. By not recognizing the two sides of consciousness (two discreet positions from which to perceive), Freud created a lateralized model which was misrepresentative of the whole psyche. In other words, his model was one-sided. His relevance will always remain historically significant because he split open the mind. The shear impact of his cleaver into the meat of the mind has enabled the birth of psychology as a science. An accurate and applicable understanding, however, can only occur by seeing both sides of the mind equally.

Freud saw the self aspect within himself and others, and he perceived how, for certain individuals, the self aspect, which he termed the id, was wreaking havoc within their consciousness. Yet, the giver of thought, Freud himself, could not examine the side his "I" was on. Thus, the nature of thought—the impetus for thought, the formation of thought, the goal of thought within the two-part mind, the different modes of perception, and the effect thought has on perceptive experience—Freud did not elucidate. For Freud, thought was purposed to control the emotions and desires which were biologically driven (he believed), and which arose from the feeling side of the mind—Freud's non-dominant side. Since the "I" of human consciousness must relate to something or someone (including self feelings or thoughts), each's "I" can only form an image of oneself by reflecting off of their non-dominant side. Thus, an individual's internal sense of stability is inseparable from the reflective state of their non-dominant side. Naturally, the pursuit for stability or fulfillment occurs within the non-dominant side, for the perceptive action of "I" can only occur through the lens of either sensed feelings or reflected thought. Freud did recognize the existence of two naturally occurring perspectives—from the thought side of consciousness (where Freud's "I" was positioned)—to gain thought control of feelings—or from the feeling side (historically, the female position)—to achieve accepting thought.

Developing a psychology from one side of a two-sided psyche will naturally lateralize the problems to the other side, which is what has occurred since Freudian psychology incited a scientific inquiry into the psyche. Over the past century, while scientific understanding of the brain has grown, so has the lateralized belief in feelings being the problem element. The misbelief has imbedded into the consciousness of the average young adult now to the point where the responsibility for emotions is readily outsourced. Effort to protect feelings is presently determining the culture's approach to children. Fear of unintentionally causing someone upset has increasingly become a threat to free speech, and where having such upset has found power (influence) through the threat—by having such emotion and expressing it.

The sociocultural manifestation of the misbelief is finally becoming apparent in the precipitous collapse of the nation's youth. They believe life is supposed to be a happy experience, and thus believe themselves victimized by experiences which are upsetting. Smothered by emotion which they cannot internalize and channel, their motivation is sensed as outside pressure, and most of their effort is toward passive pleasures. A generation who believed happiness could be materialized, and who capitalized on materialism, gave birth to two decades of children who were expected to be grateful for what they got. Materialism was expected to make them happy, as parents worked increasingly hard in order to deliver. What had been promised to their parents—the fairy tale—was to feel loved, but it hadn't materialized for them, so they tried to give it to their kids by buying them things, which produced the millennial generation.

Gradually infusing into the parental approach has been an attempt to sterilize life of the experiences which are painful or upsetting. Seeking to protect the feelings of children was a natural outcome to Freudian psychology. However, in doing so, a generation of individuals have come forth choking on their feelings. The millennial generation, as a whole, cannot see outside the reflective cocoon of their feelings. Their blindness to the space they are expected to fill is daunting for anyone who depends on their effort. Thinking in a way which is rational, and forming understanding which is non-judgmental, is being been obliterated by the power of feelings to determine what is believed. The pendulum has swung so far, seemingly it cannot go any further. Turning the focus to the thought side, where Freud still stands with his meat clever, is now inevitable.

The importance of balance is increasingly coming into cultural consciousness. Increased power, adaptability, and growth are demonstrated in balanced minds. Within such individuals, there is an integration of both sides—a harmony, where each side seeks to be in proper alignment relative to the other. For most individuals, however, an increasing imbalance has occurred, to where the world is being perceived to explain how one feels, and through which they interact to feel better. The natural consequences have come from an increasing consumptive mentality, wherein individuals are trapped in focusing on what they don't have, and resenting others who they perceive as being treated more favorably. The growth which may be found within suffering, and the critical importance of letting go of need-based attachments, are principles which are becoming extinct. Excessive importance is being assigned to feelings, to the point where feelings are not being channeled purposefully within human activity—the activity which generates experience. Through experience, then, comes the growth in understanding and the realization of oneself. Thus, for feelings to be the basis of thought prevents the separation of thought from feeling, thereby impeding the individual's channeling of their emotion into effortful activity which is goal-directed. Without the separation between feelings and thoughts, an individual experiences life like a nightmare.

The Gordian Knot of the psyche lies in the reflection of itself, where the mind perceives its own shadows—where each's fear stems from their own rejection—in keeping a part of themselves separated from the integrative being of themselves. In existing divided, the sense of incompleteness or impending rejection/loss is unavoidable. Of greater importance, however, is one's directional heading—either toward the threat or away from it. To unravel the knot, one must go toward the threat which is sensed. Internally, one must integrate fully into the outgoing self. In doing so, one untangles from oneself—from the attachment to oneself—by integrating both sides. Then, through a process of both letting go and accepting, the void which one sought to fill within transforms into outgoing light, illuminating the singular space of one's true being. In effect, by being fully of oneself, the internal part which one seeks "not" to be—to "not" experience—it dissolves, therein loosening the Gordian Knot of one's mind.

Nothing robs one's sense of freedom more than fear. Whether it is fear of oneself (anger) or fear of others (mistreatment, loss, rejection), fear causes one to feel trapped. The tragedy comes in trying to escape fear or control fear. In doing so, one tries to separate fear from oneself, but in doing so one must continuously face it. Usually this comes in the form of how one experiences others, and the demands of life generally. One's world will grow to personify the threat one seeks to avoid. Currently, a generation of parents who sought to avoid negative feelings or negative experiences for their children, has lead to the current generation of young adults who are personifying the negativity toward life their parents sought to protect them from experiencing. As a result, a large number have attached to having problems with their feelings (depression, anxiety, anger, pain), and entitling themselves to a medical diagnosis and treatment. They believe medical treatment is warranted when they perceive the need to feel better. Unfortunately, the medical system, in conjunction with the pharmaceutical industry, has ingratiated itself to serving such subjective needs rather than opposing them and promoting growth based solutions.

A paradigm shift must occur within the medical community as to the handling of mental health problems in children and adolescents, so to stop perpetuating the problem. The medical community must take seriously the Hippocratic Oath, which obliges medical treatment to first do no harm. An aggressively protective method of parenting must no longer be seen as appropriate in raising one's child, and the medical community must stop aligning with such an approach through identifying children and adolescents as having a diagnosable problem or condition. Once something is recognized as having harmful effects, though unintended, to continue causing harm in the face of knowing better, is malpractice.

The Binary Brain

1

INTRO

"How would you feel if a lion jumped out?" I asked her, targeting the misbelief I knew was at the base of her struggles.

"Scared," she exclaimed.

"Correct. Why?"

"Because the lion could kill me." She was slightly tremulous, I noted, which for a young woman in her early twenties, seemed unnatural.

"Yes, there is cause for fear. But why do the scared feelings occur?" I pressed.

"Because I'm scared."

"Yes, but those scared feelings are happening in your body. Without a body there would be no feelings. They are from adrenaline effects occurring within your body. What's the purpose?"

"You mean—to fight or flight?"

"Yes, correct. To fight or to flee. Both options involve doing something. But the feelings don't tell me what to do, but rather they enable me to do. I can choose to run or to fight. The feelings don't have eyes. I see the lion." I said, pointing at my eye. "So would you agree the feelings come to help?"

"Yes, I guess they are, in that scenario," she agreed lukewarmly.

"Well, what would happen if an individual processes the feelings as a threat in and of themselves?"

"I don't know."

"The individual would be a deer in the headlights—frozen, unable to channel the feelings into action."

"That makes sense."

"So, can we see feelings as always coming to help us?" I asked, looking to confront her misbelief.

"I don't see how my anxiety could be helpful."

"Well, anxiety is just potential energy, so it's what you make of it," I began, incepting the idea. "Yet, seeing it as a threat makes an individual try to control it, or not experience it, but doing so undermines its potential for positive action."

"I don't know how to make it into positive," she pleaded.

"Well, willing against it traps it in your body—keeping it from becoming part of your willpower. Thus, it gets expressed negatively, inversely, within the body, which is very uncomfortable—symptomatic."

"I can't just turn it off," she pronounced. "And times when it's overwhelming, I'm lucky just to keep myself together."

"Of course. But you are trying to combat it, control it, or run from it."

"Yes, of course."

"So you are relating to the anxious feelings as the threat. Don't you see? Feelings come based on what is before us—meaning, the thought I have or what I see. Feelings come to effect or fulfill the experience—to support what I am doing—to fulfill my will."

"But my will is to not be anxious," she demanded.

"Right," I confirmed. "But your effort has you opposing your own potential. Your will is trying to not be anxious rather than willing yourself forward. But trying to not be anxious directs you to find reason for being anxious. You see negative potential in the world and then try to control what happens or doesn't happen."

"Is doing that wrong?"

"Well, you're starting with the feeling, then finding a cause. You're seeing the world so to explain your anxiousness. You are thus infusing your fear into the world and then trying to control your experience of the world."

"I don't understand," she admitted, and I could see her begin to agitate with herself.

"You're creating lions," I proclaimed. "You're letting how you feel determine what you think. But how you think is actually determining the feelings. What you are focused on, and your intent relative to the world and yourself— creates the feelings you experience."

"How do I change how I think?"

"Well, first—you have to get your focus in front of you. Put your cursor on whatever is in front of you—now—not what you think might be coming up." I paused and looked at her, making sure she was following. She nodded, so I continued. "Whatever is in front of you, outside of you, connect fully with what you are doing. Your energy—your feelings—will then be able to flow into that you are doing. Don't focus on your feelings and don't reflect what is coming at you. Focus on yourself going at life."

"What you are saying—I just want to make sure I'm understanding—is that my feelings aren't telling me anything about what's happening? I shouldn't listen to my feelings?"

"You shouldn't turn your feelings into thought. Don't give feelings thought, because the feelings are for action relative to the thought."

"I thought feelings have evolved for protection. Like an evolutionary advantage," she asked with a look of deep puzzlement.

"Yes," I exclaimed. "But the feelings are to do something relative to the perceived threat. Remember, the feelings come to effect the lion. The lion is the thought—the threat. You don't need the adrenaline to tell you to be scared of the lion. That's ridiculous."

"I guess you're right," she admitted, and I could see her face soften as her mind settled into an understanding. "I guess I have been doing this to myself. Trying to not be anxious, and seeing my anxiety as a problem...I have created my own problems."

"You got it. Now, going forward, you have a choice—as you positively intend yourself—there are two ways, two roads. Either by being yourself positively toward whatever is in front of you, or by trying to oppose negativity. Either to be or not to be."

"Is that the question?" she smirked.

"More like the answer," I concluded, tongue-in-cheek.

History

Sigmund Freud's position of consciousness was on the thought side (based on the two-part consciousness represented within the Binary Psychology model). Thus, he was reflecting on feeling as his non-dominant element. Since the thought mind is qualifying, it cannot conceive of something unless it is able to differentiate the something from something else. Thus, he had to see two *drives* at the base of the human being. He divided the base *self* into an aggressive drive and a libidinous or creative drive (libido), and conceived of the drives existing within the unconscious. Rather than seeing the drive as sensorimotor in nature and thus composed of two separate elements— sensory and motor—he differentiated the drive based on the third person thought (motor) perspective. Thus, his thought perspective, for within which his "I" was positioned, blinded him to the thought component, and thus he had to regard the two drives as imbued with thought—he had to give them thought. Thereby, Freud's characterization of the two drives simply illustrates the first bifurcation the thought side makes in the handling of the *self* aspect. The bifurcation represents rejection of aggression, which is then kept outside of consciousness, forming the unconscious. In other words, Freud was seeing, as emerging from his non-dominant side, the two manifestations of the same life force operating within him. Unfortunately, he was unable to perceive himself as the differentiating thought. When the drive was properly aligned then it appeared as the libido. When the same drive was improperly directed or rejected within the individual (denied within himself), then it was seen as the aggressive drive. He was intuitively correct to make a last binary division. However, he was actually incorrect by dividing the feeling or *self* element into two separate entities, rather than being able to recognize himself—the internal perceiving "I" of consciousness—as thought, as the other entity.

The relevance of an individual's regressive or avoidant processing of anger was the hallmark of the neurosis which Freud noted. However, he never explored the perceptive nature of judgment, nor the purposeful nature of life beyond an animalistic pleasure principle. For Freud, that which emerged from his feeling side was always a threat. He saw his non-dominant half very well, but being unable to appreciate the other half (the half that he was) ran him into problems. In fact, he ran into Carl Jung—the colleague Freud worked most closely with during the development of his theory. Freud's sense of Jung's disloyalty came as a result of Jung's contention of Freud's adherence to the unconscious as a reproductive animal. Jung had explored his own unconscious *self* and had found a spiritual realm, wherein he found liberation from the *self*. He found a road into the unconscious which demanded an acceptance of both sides. He found both sides being contained within the whole. Jung had to believe he was helping Freud by providing a more accurate understanding, illuminating where Freud was creating his own difficulties. However, an individual identified as thought (Freud in this case) is quick to see the challenging of their belief as a threat. Freud's thought structure itself was threatened, and thus he felt the potential of rejection, triggering him to reject Jung's construct. Freud thus employed rejection outwardly as it was occurring inwardly in creation of his unconscious. In other words, Freud was dividing himself, thereby forming two poles—a positive and a negative, whereby a sense of control was begotten within this perpetual triangulation of himself.

Modern Times

The discovery of the human genome generated a swell of enthusiasm for getting at the code of life. Subsequent identification of genes determining physical characteristics naturally lead to understanding the role of genetics in disease and heritability. Since most diseases are products of the human body's interaction with the environment through time, and since genes code for physical structure, then logically everyone's DNA code is relevant for their physical health. Inexplicably, however, this rational understanding morphed into an irrational belief in the mind being determined by genetics. The mind beholds memory, feeling, and belief through experience. The first two decades of life involve brain growth while interacting with the world, thus enabling a tremendous amount of adaptation or specialization. No animal has such an arrangement, which likely accounts for the magnitude of variability between humans and cultures, and which cannot be accounted for by variations in a person's DNA. Moreover, as is demonstrated by the Binary Psychology model, misbelief is at the foundation of psycho-emotional problems, and belief cannot be passed on genetically.

Biological research into the brain's neurochemical make up over the past thirty years and the narrowed focus on only observable processes has reduced the psyche into a 3-pound mass of brain tissue. Nevertheless, people maintain an awareness of individual consciousness being bound within their body—a sense of themselves being separate from their physical form. The history of the duality—the separateness kept between mind and body—has also kept the mind divided from modern science. Yet, modern science's hyper-focus on the physical brain precipitated the present culture becoming increasingly mind-blinded. The body has always been the bridge to experience life, and through the lens of the body, the human mind has always formed thought to explain one's present sensory experience. Increasingly, focus is shifting away from the observable brain and toward the invisible mind. The divide between the mind and body has largely been a result of the scientific method minimizing the attention paid to the mind because of the mind's difficulty being quantified. However, more than anything else, the lack of understanding for how the mind connects with the body and how the body is received by the mind has kept the two elements divided.

The separateness of mind and body has been exaggerated by the discovery of the genetic code and the subsequent neglect of unobservable phenomenon. This has downplayed the role of the mind—of one's consciousness—in determining one's experience of their feelings or thoughts. However, chemical remedies (medications, drugs) or physical fixes (materialism) have not proved significantly impactful and/or sustainable. Since the mind is primarily electromagnetic, not until the past decade has the collective consciousness (awareness among the general population) began to perceive the power and influence of invisible forces. The frequency of one's consciousness is produced by the level of harmonization within the feeling-thought interaction. The internal relationship between the two elements produces conscious awareness. Thus, one's awareness or experience will be a manifestation of their frequency of consciousness. The frequency of one's consciousness manifests as one experiences themselves within the world and within relationships. The less harmonization or the more dissonance between the two parts creating awareness, the more one's outward experience will be characterized by negative sensations (anger, fear, pain) and energetic depletion.

Seeing Two Sides

The brain is two-sided. It is a sensory vesicle as well as a motor vehicle. The brain receives and the brain sends. It is an antenna and a transponder. The brain senses and the brain realizes. The brain feels and the brain thinks. It is both a sensory tree and a belief network. The brain is constructed as a battery. Every individual has two poles within them—between which flows the electromagnetic current of life. From one pole emerges magnetism and from the other pole arises electricity. The connection to the world enables both an inflow and outflow of electromagnetic energies. Through an individual's interaction with life outside of them, creative energy can be expressed as well as begotten. The result is an equilibration of energies, therein achieving a mind-brain balance. The inflow occurs through the sensory system, whereas the motor system enables the expression. The mind must attach thought to one's consciously occurring sensory experience, thereby organizing the world in a way for energies to be expressed purposefully toward an individualized fulfillment.

A psychology which is not founded on the interactive nature of the mind will be unable to capture the human experience. The human mind's capacity to interact with itself—to *think*—engenders a creationist effect on each individual's experience. Yet, for life to occur as a longing for completeness, for security, compels individuals to exist as a pair. There occurs for each, within these pairings, the necessary reflection of themselves. Stability requires sacrifice and selflessness—love. The ability to do so requires significant maturation, and thus, a psycho-emotional imbalance or immaturity will produce relationship instability. The relationship will always illustrate the character of an individual's interactive mind. Thus, in order to grow more stable and secure, individuals must let go of certain aspects of themselves—beliefs which are childish and self-centering. Misbeliefs causing perceptive errors, and self-centered efforts which precipitate judgment, impair the stability of an individual's bond—both internally and externally. It is essential to understand the compensatory nature of the mind's efforts, and thus everything must be seen through the lens of the mind's relativity unto itself. The relationship which occurs between the two aspects of an individual's consciousness is more determinant to an individual's quality of experiences and overall adaptation to life than anything else.

Rational thought seeks to form a stable representation of life. It finds the irrationality and unpredictability of feelings to be the primary impediment to security. However, the presumption of fulfillment, stability, and functional intactness coming through control of feelings is based on an a priori judgment which is erroneous—a belief in negative feelings being the root of one's suffering and dysfunction. A psychology constructed by consciousness and a psychology of consciousness are two fundamentally different formations. A psychology for consciousness—formulated by consciousness—will necessarily be in relation to the feelings which, through internal perception, consciousness is bound to experience. The foundation of thought is thus to fulfill want and minimize negative experience. Since the perceiving "I" of consciousness cannot perceive itself perceiving, one's thought or judgment cannot be conscious of itself. Consciousness cannot objectify itself or have itself, and yet, consciousness maintains an awareness of its being. Consciousness truly cannot see the forest from the trees. As a result, any psychology born out of consciousness will manifest with an a priori judgment about feelings, and thus can only represent one side of the human consciousness. Such a psychology of rational thought will necessarily miss the equal importance of feelings. It becomes nearly impossible for consciousness to see unwanted feelings or experiences as being part of the creative life energy. Therein occurs the significance of the belief about a feeling, for it is the meaning given to feelings which ultimately determines an individual's conscious experience.

Seeing the forest from the trees requires looking at the relationship occurring between the two elements of consciousness. Binary Psychology takes into account consciousness itself, as the observing "I", and how misbeliefs and the inability to know oneself cause relational conflict within an individual's consciousness. In other words, Binary Psychology develops the understanding of how the belief or judgment and thus handling of one's feelings determines the character and meaning of one's experience. Binary Psychology is based on the two-sided nature of the human mind and the human experience. The process of attaining balance is very challenging, and yet, the tension produced by imbalance compels people toward balance. Invariably, relational pressures and interpersonal dependencies precipitate the problems related to the imbalance. Thus, it is through others whereby an individual can come to understand themselves.

Stable, supportive relationships which persevere through the inexorable changes occurring throughout one's life are born out of an internal equilibrium within the two-part consciousness. In general, outside relationships are illustrative of one's internal relationship between feeling and thought. To thus understand the nature of relationships, there first must be an understanding of how the adult mind relates to itself. The adult mind has a two-part consciousness, allowing an internal relationship between feeling and thought, between *want* versus *should*. Thought stems from language—from the labeling of things or experiences. This labeling is judgment, enabling humans to communicate with each other. It allows. for a shared sense of reality to be created and for people to understand one another. Most adults can recognize their ability to have an internal dialogue—to think.

Relativity

Recognizing the relative nature of everything is essential to understanding how the mind works. In other words, there cannot be good without bad, happy without sad, right without wrong. The formation of judgment or belief provides the framework for one to live and perceive. The fruition of one's beliefs (not hopes) is an undeniable human experience. The manner by which beliefs form during childhood is clearly illuminated within the Binary Psychology model. Then, by understanding the nature of the thinking mind—where each individual internally reflects themselves—a meaningful portrait of an individual becomes possible.

The internal dynamic between one's observing self and one's feelings or thoughts is a relationship. As such, it evolves throughout life as one grows in experience and understanding. Binary Psychology provides the framework for conceptualizing the human mind—the thoughts, feelings, and the actions which come forth. Binary Psychology focuses on the bridge, the relationship between feeling and thought. It provides a needed structure for the connectedness between the mind, the "I," and everything to which the "I" relates—the body, other individuals, the world. Sensory awareness requires the body, and yet, for an individual's "I" to remain rooted in how their body feels is maladaptive since doing so ignores the purposeful nature of the life experience—to learn rather than to feel.

Relationships occur naturally. They follow patterns which, when seen through the lens of the binary model, reveal an interesting structure, and will be presented throughout the book. In order to understand someone, there is no better source of insight than the feelings and behavioral patterns found within their primary relationship. Cultural influences and a confluence of gender roles are forcing relationships to undergo structural changes. The historical precedents for male-female relationships have been dismantled through eradication of social inequality. As a result, more confusion exists because of unstructured expectations. For young adults, there is a general lack of clarity regarding one's role within a marriage and family. Fragmentation of families because of divorce has injected pessimism and caution into younger people as they approach relationships, and their prioritization of being in control is not conducive to sustaining a complementary relationship.

The necessity of relationships for individual growth is part of the human experience. People come to realize themselves within relationships. How people relate to fears of loss and rejection are the most influential elements forming the character of a binary relationship. The sustainability of the relationship will be based on each person's ability to get past the other's defensiveness toward them. Paradoxically, each's defensive operation will get caught up in the defense of the other. The only way past, so to speak, is for neither to relate to the other as if the other is a threat. This enables each, when the other is being negative, to remain connected and in pursuit of understanding, to not get defensive. Thus, the handling of negative feeling and the understanding of the other's way of handling negative feeling is extremely significant for relational success.

Binary Psychology provides the framework for understanding one's conscious experience—as one is aware of oneself existing. The experience of life is inseparable from the manifestation of change. Life is a dynamic appearance and disappearance of elements, a growth and death of aspects of oneself. Experiential awareness itself arises from the interaction of the binary brain—between feeling (emotion, energy) and thought (belief, judgment). Life is thus a relational experience primarily occurring between the two parts which constitute the thinking mind. Binary Psychology provides the framework by which this relationship and relationships which manifest outwardly throughout one's life can be understood. Most importantly, through the binary model, psycho-emotional problems are illuminated as symptoms of consciousness. As a result, in clinical application, Binary Psychology facilitates corrective adjustments through changes of mind.

TWO-PART CONSCIOUSNESS

Two Sided Brain	Right & Left
Two Elements	Mind & Body
Two Part Consciousness	Feelings & Thoughts
Bi-Directional Nervous System	Afferent (In) & Efferent (Out)
Two Aspects of Individual	I & Me
Two Spaces	Inside & Outside

Life occurs as a pairing of two separate entities held together through an electromagnetic bond. Creation is able to come forth from the genetic bonding of one's DNA. Chromosomes are strands of DNA pairs, themselves paired together within the nucleus of every cell. The outer form of the human body is two sided with midline symmetry. Each side is a mirror image of the other. Coordination and balance between the two sides is essential for fluid physical function. The brain, too, has two sides, representing the two components: the sensory system and the motor system. This enables the adult mind to have a two-part consciousness. One side of consciousness is the emotional, feeling side, where one's drive originates. The drive is, at its base, a growth impulse forward, like the movement of time itself. The other side is the thought side of consciousness, where belief exists and where action within the world is generated. Within the motor system thought occurs in the form of images and words. The motor system uses words to form language which is then articulated as belief. This enables internal reflection off of feeling or thought in the context of the outside world. The dual-structure engenders a triangulation of perceptive awareness—it allows humans "to think"—and it is within this triangle where one comes to be aware of oneself.

To understand the two-part consciousness, first there must be an understanding of its development. A baby is born as purely a "me," driven entirely by their feelings and dependently attached to an outside thought structure (parent). These feelings relate to desires (needs) and sensations. The baby is directly dependent on mom who represents the world. To the baby, there is initially no difference between the environment and mom. Thus, environment and *alpha* (thought authority) are fused. From the baby's perspective, mom and the world are one continuous entity. As a result, they develop within a direct dependency, where things, from the child's perspective, cannot be any different than they are. Not until puberty does there occur a formal activation of the brain allowing the child to extract the judge from the environment—to internalize it. This enables the two voices to come alive within their mind—the "me" (want, feel) and the "I" (judge, controller).

The dual-mindedness (anatomically represented by the two hemispheres of the brain) create an inescapable sense of separateness from all which exists outside of the "I." The two-part structure forces a palpable duality into the human experience. The body is one's platform for sensory experience and one's vehicle for motor function. Prior to puberty, a child identifies as their body—perceiving no duality. Puberty brings an awareness of separateness, representing the onset of the thinking consciousness. An internal awareness of oneself in the context of bodily or sensory experience signifies the activation of the two-part consciousness, therein producing mindfulness. This mindfulness demonstrates the onset of thinking, whereby one can interact internally to generate belief. In other words, the two-part consciousness enables one to create experience.

Thought, without feeling, is "dead." Thought depends on feeling to come "alive." Feeling beholds the drive. Thought contains truth and purpose. Feeling, without thought, is chaotic and everywhere, without the structure needed to purpose itself. Thus, feeling will attract thought and thought will attract feeling. The human mind begins as sensory or feeling awareness bound to outside thought. The other side of consciousness—thought—becomes independently active around the time of puberty. This creates the two-part consciousness, enabling the individual to internally think about how they feel or internally feel their thoughts. Previously, as a child, thought was *externalized* or represented by the outside world, and one identified as their ability relative to their direct sensory experience. Some individuals will continue to reflect on thought, but take on the capability to do so internally. They will thus effort themselves to be good enough for the world, perceiving others as beholding thought of them or judgment. Others, rather, will shift and internally reflect off of feeling, identifying themselves as their judgment which is given outwardly, where they then perceive the feelings of others. So two different perceptive processes exist: either effort (feeling) is given outwardly and judgment is perceived, or thought judgment is given to the outside world and feeling is perceived.

As mentioned, two positions of consciousness exist within the adult human mind—the feeling position and the thought position. A feeling does not carry thought and thought has no feeling. Feelings and thoughts are distinct entities. Interaction within one's consciousness produces the thinking awareness which characterizes the adult mind. One's seat of consciousness, thus, has tow possible points of view—either as feeling interacting with outside thought or as thought interacting with outside feeling. If one's "I" of consciousness identifies as feeling then one will perceive thought outside of oneself. Internally, one's reflections will consist primarily of thoughts. However, one who is identified as feeling forms their self conception (as it occurs outwardly) based on their effort and intent—the "care" they bring forth. The belief in oneself and what one believes about oneself are based on one's functional ability. From the flip-side—where one's "I" of consciousness is identified as thought—one perceives feeling outside of oneself. The reflective process occurs off of feeling in forming thought, where thought is given to outer feeling. Internally, focus is on how one feels or how others are feeling.

Feelings

Feelings are experienced within the body. Feelings arise from the body. Since the nature of the body is sensorimotor (both sensory and motor), feelings may be meaningfully grouped into *sensory feelings* and *motor feelings*. *Sensory feelings* are those derived from the five physical senses—sight, smell, touch, hearing, taste—which provide information about the materialized environment. *Motor feelings* are bodily feelings related to an individual's conscious perception or thought consciousness, the substance of which is energy potentiated for motor activity. In other words, motor feelings are generated in relation to conscious thought, where an individual's thought causes the bodily effects they experience as feelings. The primary motor feelings are want/desire, fear, anger, and sadness. The motor feelings consist of energy which is (or was) potentiated. The energy is sensed as motivation or desire when integrated within an individual's will. However, when the feelings are unwilled (threat perceived) or unexpressed, then the energies are experienced negatively (e.g. depression).

Motor feelings are potentiated energies within the body based on what an individual is perceiving (or thinking about) relative to the world. The energy seeks expression through connected activity within the environment. This explains the phenomenon of an individual turning tension into activity—staying busy, keeping their mind occupied. It also explains the occurrence of an individual getting stuck on certain negative feelings since the perception of the feelings being a threat in and of themselves triggers more negative feelings. The danger involved in rejecting or avoiding certain feelings is thus obvious, since the feelings then potentiate themselves—like a dog chasing its own tail. The amount of willpower devoted toward feelings necessarily comes at the expense of energy being directed forward as positively intended effort in connection with the environment, and thus occurs at the expense of growth.

Feeling exists as sensation or emotion. Sensory awareness occurs through one's body, but the feeling itself is not oneself. Just as one occupies one's body, feelings occupy one's sensory system. The substance of feelings is energy potentiated by an individual's thought intention relative to their present environment or themselves. Thoughts or beliefs exist as mental images or ideas and are a separate entity from feeling. Thought forms around feeling in order to fulfill the feeling or protect the feeling. However, feeling must eventually fulfill the thought. This amounts to feeling no longer determining the thought, but rather is channeled into one's activity. Feeling and thought combine to produce experience. Through experience, thoughts can be feelings and feelings can be thoughts, and it is through the experience where one comes to know oneself. However, since feelings and thoughts are separate entities, attaching thought directly to feeling or attaching feeling directly to thought, avoids an experiential coming to know oneself. Without an experiential knowing, thought would be based on how one feels. Experience enables truth to be known. Otherwise, one is avoiding knowing by forming thought based on internal feelings or giving care to one's internal thoughts. An individual does not identify themselves as a feeling, nor are they able to be just a thought. It is the interaction of feeling and thought which creates the experience of oneself. The interaction occurs in the moment, producing a sense of "I am." Through this outward experience, feeling and thought unify, producing an actualized experience of oneself.

An essential point to recognize is that people are born into the world as "feeling individuals." There is literally no "thinking" as adults normally conceptualize thinking to be. Rather, the baby feels and moves (sensorimotor stage). The expressions which come across an infant's face are reactions to sensations bubbling within. As infants, they have yet to form the cortical connections (wiring of neurons) to enable a sense of separateness from the world around them. Further still, infants cannot exert conscious control of their body (i.e., move their muscles intentionally)—having not yet established the neural connections between the motor cortex (brain) and the body. Recognition emerges slowly. Initially, the ability to recognize mom's face awakens. Further discrimination of elements/objects in the world around them, thereafter, becomes the nature of mental mapping. This exploratory mapping, where layers of depth and understanding are formed, is part of the journey of life.

The child comes into the world with feeling awareness. For the infant, there is no knowledge or thought accompanying the sensations—no understanding of the feelings. The development of the motor system enables an infant to develop use of his or her body, thereby enabling their conscious effort toward experiencing objects within the environment. Experience itself is a simultaneous feeling-thought interaction with an object, thereby forming a belief about the object. However, the belief formed by a baby is purely based on how the object feels rather than based on the nature of the object. For example, a cup is represented based on how it feels rather than for its purpose as a container. The baby must grow the motor function to enable the nature of objects to be grasped by representative thought (cup is to hold one's drink). They must experience the nature of the object to understand, to then know. Similarly, the child must come to know themselves through experience. They cannot truly be what they want, though they can imagine themselves as something and genuinely believe it since they have not yet internalized thought reality. For experiential reality to occur, however, outside thought must attach (parents, environment). For example, a child may believe they could dunk a basketball because they have seen it done, but their body will not give experiential reality to it.

When feeling is understood as time, then the nature of feelings can be better appreciated. Time enables experience, as do feelings. Each provides the possibility for change, for growth. Each is directed forward. When measured, both time and feeling can only be quantified. Assigning qualification actually detaches one from experiencing life. To try and control one's feeling experience—to avoid certain feelings—is not possible—just as it is not possible to avoid time. The qualification of feeling may easily occur internally, as can the qualification of time. But the validity of doing so is limited to one's internal sphere. When assigning quality outside of oneself, one removes themselves from the present. One cannot judge something or someone relative to oneself without detaching from the experience itself. Assigning quality seeks to stop time.

An individual will be disengaged from the present if they believe they have to control themselves in the present, for in doing so they are unable to be present. In other words, an individual cannot present themselves to the moment and judge the moment at the same time. Because of their belief about the need to keep control of themselves, they cannot bring themselves to the moment without excessive vulnerability occurring consciously. Such individuals always regard what is coming up in a way where they seek to feel prepared. Surprises undermine their sense of being able to present themselves properly. Their sense of who they are is tied to the judgment of those who they perceive as a potential threat to them. Thus, they seek to create a certain image for others which is directly compensatory for who they seek not to be but must believe they are. If they didn't believe themselves as such, they wouldn't compensate for such.

The fear each would feel if a lion suddenly jumped out is the physiochemical response to adrenaline. The adrenaline is triggered by the conscious perception of threat (lion). The effect is a sudden potentiation of physical energy, for which to act—to fight or flight. The substance enabling action is initially experienced as fear within the body, but equally may be transformed into anger for which to willfully fight the lion. The triggered feelings, while uncomfortable, are blind—meaning, the fear does not tell an individual what to do or how to act. Rather, the feelings come within the body as a result of the perceived threat, to enable adaptation (fight or flight). Turned into fight, the feelings enable an efferent motor fight. Kept as fear, the energy allows for afferent motor flight. The potentiated energy triggered by adrenaline, is universally sensed as fear. Yet, the physical fear is simply potentiated energy. The energy, if not channeled into action, stays trapped within the body. When trapped in the potentiated state, it is experienced as signal anxiety, psychomotor restlessness, or agitation. In contrast, when the potentiated energy flows into an individual's willed action, the energy is actualized, and thus does not build up within the body where it becomes consciously bothersome or physically deleterious.

From the thought side of consciousness, where one is bound to reflect on feeling, there exist two possible sources of feeling. An individual's primary focal point can be on either how they feel (physically, emotionally) or on how others/objects feel. Invariably, the initial focal point is on their own feelings since the transition into the thought position was to take control of their own feelings. From the feeling side of consciousness, for individuals destined to identify as thought, being attached to the thoughts of others to derive a sense of value and security becomes unsustainable. Transitioning to the thought position detaches their sense of themselves from the approving thoughts of others, taking control of their feeling self in the process. The initial goal is to feel stable and in control. However, perceiving their feelings as being determined from outside of them (from the environment or others) causes them to respond either by trying to control the environment or through avoidance of situations or people. Irregardless, if their own feelings are the primary focus as they interact with the world, then they are only coming to know how the world feels to them. Getting to know how things feel relative to themselves traps them in a world of their feelings. When thought is formed directly from internal feeling, the world can only be experienced as an expression of such feeling. The world cannot become understood independent from one's own feelings about it. The natural direction of growth, throughout adulthood, is away from one's own internal feelings as the primary focal point, going more toward the feelings of others.

As an individual becomes less self-centered, increasingly they are able to see the positive feeling they can create in their environment, in others. Through a positive purposing of themselves, positive judgment can be given with the goal of creating positivity in others. Within one's own internal feeling space, the goal from the thought side of consciousness is to not feel (x), where x = anger, fear/anxiety, sadness, pain. If the occurrence of (x) is perceived as happening because of others or certain environments, then one will avoid such people or places, thereby detaching oneself. As an analogy, imagine a young boy at the edge of a swimming pool, afraid to get into the pool despite multiple family members trying to coax him in. The desire to swim has him at the edge of the pool, but the nervous feeling has him paralyzed. If he bails on his attempt and never tries again, he will characterize himself as not liking to swim, being uncomfortable with swimming, not being able to swim, etc.. However, in such a scenario, he has never swam, and so he cannot dislike swimming since he never has experienced swimming. Nevertheless, in his mind, he will attach the fear to swimming. But it was not swimming—rather, it was the thought of swimming. Thus, such reticence will likely characterize other endeavors, for it is not the endeavor itself but rather the anxiety attached to the uncertainty of the endeavor which is the issue. Since anxiety associated with uncertainty is part of the human condition, the anxiety itself can only be a problem as far as it is handled—based on the belief about the feeling. When an individual believes the feeling is indicative of an outside threat, then necessarily the feelings will be mishandled.

The more time spent thinking about or focusing one's own feelings, the less the feelings get turned into expressive activities or growth oriented experiences. Not properly channeling feeling or energy into one's interaction with life will lead to improper ways of energetic expression. Improper ways include suppression or avoidance, both of which lead to such energies being expressed internally and manifesting as either anxiety, depression, or physical symptoms (low energy, headaches, stomach issues). There is an energetic/feeling consequence to not adequately connecting oneself to the environment or others—if one does not bring oneself to the world. Any avoidance of time or difficulty in filling one's time is a direct detriment to growth, and effectively is a rejection of one's life within the moment. Time and energy should be regarded as an opportunity to experience oneself within the world.

Negative emotions try to find expressive control through expression, thereby achieving an effect on the environment. The reaction from the environment, if negative, will frighten a child, who will attach what happened to the feeling they expressed. Then, going forward, they will seek to exert control over themselves so to not re-experience themselves as such. Effort to keep control over their negative feelings then determines their focal point being fixed on either how they are internally feeling or the thought judgment of others relative to themselves. Control of the internal feeling will often be sought through their immediate environment, usually by means of compulsive cleaning or organization. Control of other's judgment relative to themselves is normally pursued by a combination of avoidance and overachieving pleasingness. Such individuals demonstrate a hypersensitivity to criticism or signs of negativity from others. Even though they are perceiving negative feelings in someone else, they reflect it as negative thought judgment toward themselves. Therein, their defensiveness is triggered, which will either be to run away or let the anger come out. In effect, their rejective relationship with their internal negativity has them bound to revolve around the negativity (anger). The greater the angry threat they sense inside, the greater the amount of control they will seek on the outside. Since thinking individuals form a relationship with themselves, individuals frequently seek to exert a compensatory level of control through their bodies (including physical appearance).

Feelings are sourced internally. They arise from within an individual, and an individual cannot truly relate to their feelings as separate from themselves. Thus, a feeling or an emotion cannot be a problem in and of itself —meaning, the emotion itself (fear, anger, sadness) cannot be the threat to which effort is made to avoid, nor can the emotion be a threat for which an individual must cope or get help. The more an individual avoids their feelings, the more negative they will feel and the more narrow will be their life. Equally, the more an individual attaches their feelings to needing outside help to feel better, the more emotionally unstable they will be in life. In the thinking mind, feelings can never be truly seen as the cause of what is done. Since action requires energy or feeling, and feelings cannot cause themselves, it makes no sense for feelings to be anything other than effects. For those whose perspective is determined by feelings, they have to tether their feelings to the environment, thus giving cause of their feelings to outside elements. Then, since their feelings cause their doing, they perceive themselves caused by outside forces. Truly, individuals attach themselves to things they experience. The world or others cannot truly cause an individual to feel. Similarly, an individual cannot truly justify what they do based on how they feel. Going from childhood to adulthood involves a detachment from feelings as being the cause of them. In other words, taking responsibility for feelings is necessary for true independence to be attained, which requires a 180° change in relationship with their feelings. To ultimately feel better, each must commit to being better in spite of how they may feel. Each must let go of wanting to feel or seeking to feel. Feelings are to be purposed—channeled into action, manifesting as effort.

Thought

Psychological development before puberty occurs without internal corruption from a critical internal judge. The pressure which comes in reaching this psychological milestone is seen with the average pubescent who is barely able to bare the self-consciousness pubescence brings. With the capability for an internalized, interactive relationship with the judge piece, there also becomes the ability to reflect. Kids begin thinking about others thinking about them, and their world is never the same.

The importance of feeling and thought separating into two distinct entities within one's consciousness is demonstrated through the creative power enabled by the separation. Having formative power over one's experiences imbues a sense of capability to create one's own life. This comes as an awareness of oneself and the potential to give life to one's ideas. The ability to conceive a child is the physical realization of this newfound ability. The more complete the separation between feeling and thought, the more pure each entity may become. In other words, thought should not be determined by feeling and feeling should not be determined by thought, and yet each should be positioned in loving regard of the other. There is tremendous power which comes as a result of the synchronization. Imbalance however, results in conflict, which is de-powering. The more conflict, the greater will be one's sense of being determined by outside forces—the world. Therein, one's sense of control over their experience is much more limited. This will necessarily lead to a sense of vulnerability in living life.

The brain as a sensory organ has received much less study than the brain as a motor mechanism for thought. Thought requires language for its judgment. Since thought and language develop within the world one is born into, it is thought and language which are bound by experience, and by the reaches of understanding. If truth were accessible through thought, then humanity would have already arrived at it. Accepted truths are taught, presented logically through demonstration or language. Experience is uniquely individualized. Attempts to communicate one's experience to another can only ever be an approximation. Truth must be experiential, like a color, and thus only able to be known through an experience of it. In other words, truth must be individually experienced or sensed. One cannot truly communicate their experience with another, and thus truth cannot be told by anyone to anyone.

Thought creates potential space. It gives representative form to the possibilities which may occur and qualifies what one experiences based on its association with the spaces one has created. In other words, one will tend to fulfill the spaces they create. Negative thoughts of the world or others will create negative experiences, in part secondary to the amount of disconnected space which rejective thought injects between oneself and the world. One's experience, in the context of one's negative judgmentalism, will not involve the spatial connectedness necessary for growth. When one's perspective is fear driven, one's formation of thought in perception of the world casts darkness into one's world—thereby determining the quality of their experience and, often, the environment's experience of them.

Over the past one-hundred years, insights within quantum physics have shown the judgment of the observer has a determining effect on the behavior of light. To investigate something objectively is, thus, not possible. Though the scientific method has become more refined and standards for research studies more rigorous, nevertheless, the effect of judgment (the hypothesis) on what is seen or observed is unable to be "controlled." In other words, phenomenon are inseparable from the observation or recognition of the phenomenon. The rational thought mind seeks to know, to objectify, to reduce uncertainty through organization of sensory phenomenon. Yet, each individual cannot perceive their own expectation in what they are observing, or their causal role or effect on what they are experiencing. The less one recognizes where they are precipitating their experience, the more they will perceive it as happening to them and outside their control. The less one's subjective reality aligns with the objective reality of the material world or the subjective reality of others, the more there will occur conflict or frustration within the interaction. The crucial insight this brings for psychologists and philosophers is of the human consciousness being part of the creative process, and yet without the ability perceive itself as such. In other words, what the human consciousness perceives as reality is an individual's initial brushstroke of creation. People, generally, fail to recognize their judgment of the environment has a determining effect on the environment.

From the feeling side of consciousness, one must reflect on thought. As with those from the thought side of consciousness having to reflect on feeling, individuals from the feeling side have two sources of thought for which to reflect on: internal thought or external thought. Internal thought includes memories or objects which one desires. External thought is contemplative of something or someone else. Within the external thought world, one can either be in regard of the world (people, places, things) relative to themselves or themselves relative to the world. Within relationships, one who is positioned on the feeling side of consciousness will reflect thought of themselves through the other person. In other words, when an individual induces happiness in another, they will see the happiness as indicating the other person's understanding and fondness for them. They are blind to the possibility of what they are seeing being indicative of the feelings they create in the other. When such a scenario exists, the individual is likely to experience themselves as unrecognized, misrepresented, or poorly understood, producing an increased sense of detachment and insecurity. Often, at this juncture, the individual on the feeling side of consciousness will detach meaning from the other's judgment of them, since they experience not being understood or "known" by the other.

From the feeling side of consciousness (reflecting on thought), thoughts born out of insecurity or fear are usually wrong. The defensive projection of what another person thinks about oneself is nearly always wrong. Moreover, forming thought about another person's intentions relative to oneself will carry a similar certainty of being wrong. Thus, the thought spaces one creates should not be insecure reflections of oneself. Self-reflective thought should not involve others relative to oneself, but rather should be oriented toward one's relationship with oneself. Such thought will then go toward areas where fear is holding one back. Thought is meant to serve as a bridge of understanding between oneself and the world—with the goal of growing in understanding and facilitating creation. Thought directed outwardly (outside oneself) should always strive to understand and accommodate. Rejection is misplaced when it occurs outside oneself. Fear causes individuals to reject something or someone outside of themselves, and yet the capacity for rejection is naturally intended to reject the feeling of fear itself. When someone forms a rejecting thought of another, they are seeking to stabilize their sense of themselves by seeing the source of their pain outside of them and casting rejective judgment.

The fundamental problem in identifying an element outside of oneself as the cause of one's upset is in the effort to control one's upset revolving around the identified element. For example, if one blames their upset on their partner, then one is likely to get angry with them. The intent of the expressed anger is to get control of the source of upset (the element). However, the true source of one's upset is internal fear related to uncertainty and potential loss/ rejection. The anger is thus meant to be on the inside, where naturally it will attach to fear. Therein, one is empowered to try new things and step into new experiences. Most importantly, with anger on the inside, one is able to properly channel it into increased effort—utilized so one is less quick to give up or "shut down" when feeling upset. On the inside, it is available as a motivating push from behind when needed. The more one's anger is avoided, and thus not available internally, the more one has to create negative thought space for which to motivate themselves. In other words, they have to create a potential negative outcome or scenario and seek to avoid its occurrence. Unfortunately, when space is created by insecure thought, then the more a person efforts themselves toward not being the thought, the more they are giving reality to the thought space they created. When an individual does something because they do not want someone to be upset with them, then they are giving their creative will to the other person and trying to realize themselves within the person's approval of them. This gives too much power to another's disapproval, such where the individual loses a sense of having their own space to fill.

Almost without exception, early beliefs about one's negative feelings serve as the framework for one's relationship with life. If there exists a line between one who is mentally healthy and one who is mentally ill, then it can only be drawn in the space where thinking occurs—in the interaction between feeling and thought. At this deepest level of the feeling-thought interaction lies the misbelief about feelings. One's understanding of something, if limited to how one feels about it, or the sensory experience associated with it, cannot be regarded as a true understanding of the nature of that something. An emotion being processed in a rejective manner gets unwittingly seen as happening to them and entitling a need. Thus, what is internally regarded as a response to what was being done to them, is actually making the world or others responsible for their negative emotions. Doing so is a seeding of negativity outside of themselves and is the current de facto method for which younger individuals are interacting with their negative feelings.

Where there exists internal conflict within an individual's mind, between the two elements (feeling and thought), anxious energy is generated. Whether the conflictual relationship is within the individual's mind or occurring in interpersonal space, the disharmony is an anti-truth. In other words, both sides are wrong and right. Because each side sees the other as wrong and covets self-righteousness, conflict is unavoidable. For someone to be on guard against being wronged or judged wrongly is inexorably going to increase anxiety for them. The amount of anxious or chaotic energy in the world is likely fixed, since energy can neither be created or destroyed. Disharmony is thus a lack of acceptance of oneself. For if everyone is derived from the same source, then it is through rejection of others or negative judgmentalism whereby negative energy is passed between individuals. The negativity stems from an internal conflict which individuals naturally wish to expel unto the environment. Keeping consciousness rooted into believing harmony may be attained through control and influence of others (or of one's environment), leads to cyclical frustration and increasing negativity. It is adaptive to accept negative energy as a part of life. Then, proper attention can be paid to one's relationship with such negative energy as it occurs within oneself—to realize taking responsibility for one's negative energy is the first step toward self-acceptance and a more harmonious existence. Yet, to do so, one cannot regard negative feelings as a problem.

I & Me

The two parts constructing human consciousness produce the dual sense of oneself—the awareness of oneself. When an individual has achieved independent consciousness, they will be able to reflectively recognize the two poles of themselves. Independent consciousness is characterized by feeling and thought existing as distinct entities, wherein "I" is able to conceive of oneself separate from how one feels. Within the thinking mind, there is "I" and there is "me." Every individual has an "I" component (motor pole) and a "me" component (sensory pole). "I" is the element which goes toward the world. "Me" receives the world. "I" is expressed through the motor system. Oppositely, the sensory system gives a sense of "me." The relationship occurring between each's "I" and "me," within space and through time is, for each, their experience of life.

> "I" goes toward the world.
> The world comes toward "me."
>
> "I" think about others.
> Others think about "me."
>
> "I" understand others.
> Others understand "me."
>
> "I" can be unto others as others have been unto "me."

The nature of the mind imbues a desire for mirroring. Once an individual stops seeking direct fulfillment of their internal self, they will seek to establish relationships which give them a sense of likeness with others. People either see their self in others or sense themselves caused by others. The former is a mirroring of "me" while the latter is a projection of "I." Rather than being similarly projected, "me" magnetizes itself, thus producing the mirroring. Unfortunately, the mirror of "me" is blinding to the awareness of "I." Each's "I" cannot see the "me" in others if "I" is perceiving others as causing "me."

However, only "I" causes "me." Even though it is imperceptible, each's internal sense of the world as it has treated them will be based on how they have treated the world.

An attachment to life as "me" is the nature of childhood. "Me" is where attachment occurs, where need is felt. Adolescence is characterized by the internal activation of "I," thereby producing an awareness of "I" separate from "me." "I" attaches in a parental fashion to "me." Believing in the needs of "me" drives "I's" efforts for "me." Through "me" occurs the experiences of the world and others, wherein "I" is able to grow in understanding of the world and others. The more "I" attaches to the feelings of "me," the more "I" experiences the world and others through beliefs based on how "me" feels. In other words, "I" will perceive others or circumstances as the cause of "me." In other words, "me" will be causing "I." The subsequent action of "I" will be a reaction to "me" being made to feel. The accumulation of experience and understanding constructs a belief in the value of "I" to be able to fulfill "me," which serves as the base by which "I" aims toward life. What also occurs is the use of "me" in defense of "I" as well using the emotion from "me" to justify "I."

The "I" is bound to a relationship with the "me," and thus "I" must take a position relative to "me." The position may either be *operational*, and thus relating to the potential effort (willpower) within "me," or *reflective*—wherein the feelings or desires of "me" are reflected as thought about oneself ("I") or the world relative to oneself ("me"). The operational position generates sensorimotor connectedness with the environment or others through the first-person perspective. "Me" is the bridge spanning between "I" and the world, across which "I" connects to others and grows in understanding and awareness. All the same, "me" is also the bridge by which "I" may stay separate from others, protected from the world. The life energy given to "me" may be channeled into physical energy by which "I" may mechanically effort unto the environment or others. Similarly, "I" may transform the energy into thought. However, if the thought is about "me," then "me" is not actually connected, and thus no potentiated energy of "me" is willfully expressed. Eventually, the energy will be expressed as emotion if not expressed through sensorimotor activity. The emotion will be an expression of "me" which has not been properly handled or channeled by "I."

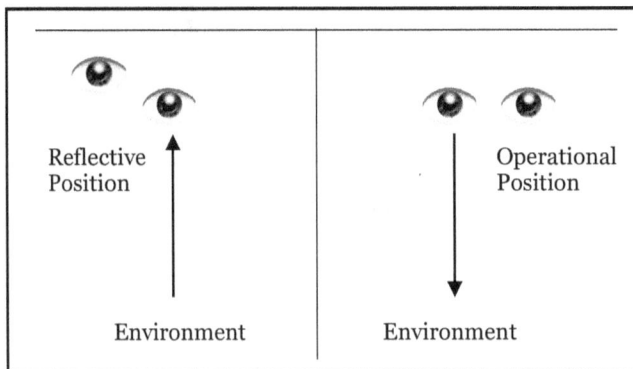

Reflective Position — Environment

Operational Position — Environment

The opportunity life affords to "I" comes through the giving of "me" to the world. In other words, giving sensorimotor effort or focused sensitivity outside of oneself enables "I" to grow in understanding. An individual cannot internally feel themselves at the same time they are feeling something or someone outside of themselves. In other words, for "I" to intend upon "me" requires the focus of "I" on assigning thought to "me." Doing so, however, while simultaneously focusing on mechanically feeling something or someone outside of oneself, is not possible. Thus, focus on "me" will limit the understanding "I" is able to develop. If "I" is rejecting of "me" or protective of "me" then "I" will be determined by the needs "I" attaches to "me." Attachment is mediated through "me" but believed in by "I." However, in letting go of attachments to "me," "I's" awareness of "I" is more fully realized, and the sense of "me" is lighter and more stable. Moreover, through breaking the attachment, "me" exists more freely, and increased energy is made available to "I," resulting in more creative motivation toward the world.

The first juncture in the separation process between "I" and "me" occurs in detaching from "me." This enables the development of an "I" separate from how one internally feels or thinks. The separation creates an "I" which is distinct from "me." However, "I" attaches to "me" and depends on "me" for vital energy, and is bound to get for "me." The second step is the letting go of "me." Effort primarily seeking fulfillment of "me" is equivalent to effort driven toward an avoidance of "me." Both involve "I" revolving around "me." The letting go process thus equates to "I" growing more independent from "me," where "I" is able to take control of "me." In doing so, "me" increasingly gets applied to the belief of "I," thereby producing an experience of such belief. Put another way, "me" will experience from the world what "I" is to the world. For example, if someone believes they have been mistreated by others, then truly, they are experiencing their treatment of others. The third step is accepting "me." This necessitates an integration of "I" and "me." All of "me" is given over, absorbed into who "I" am. Once integrated, who "I" am is realized in the being of "me." Prior to achieving such, there will be an active sense of internal emptiness or lacking, whereby fulfillment of "me" will be sought.

Two Nervous Systems—Sensory (afferent) & Motor (efferent)

The incoming sensory system is the *afferent* nervous system. Processing of the incoming sensory data occurs in a way where the mind constructs perception to explain the conscious experience. The outgoing nervous system is the *efferent* pathway, where the mind intends the body's exertion in relative connection to the outside world. The perceiving "I" is an efferent entity. Any aspect which is being perceived is unable to be integrated into willed efferent output. The "me" entity is able to be perceived separately, and thus "I," in perceiving "me," must be reflecting off of afferent sensory data. When an individual is connected with the present, "me" is connected, and so the incoming sensory data is of the materialized environment, where "I" is focused outwardly. Perceiving as such, no separation between "I" and "me" is able to exist, thus enabling a connected experience.

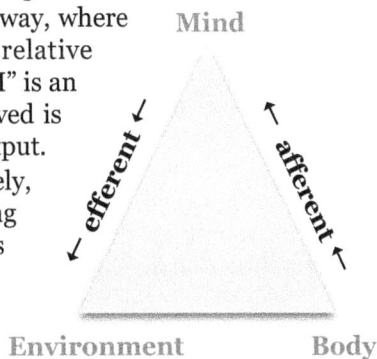

The premotor cortex houses forethought—wherein planning efferent action is enabled. An individual's efferent premotor cortex is tethered to their afferent system until they willfully let go in effort to be more actualized—to be more fully potentiated. Individuals feel internally very vulnerable with the process of letting go of control as to what happens in order to fully give of themselves. The sense of control within an individual's life experience is begotten through outward rejection and internal escape. However, perceiving as such forces an individual into seeing the world as a threat. Interacting with life outside of them then occurs based on a triangulation with their afferent sensory system.

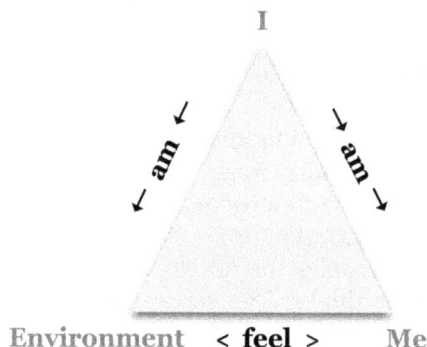

I

am ↙ ↙   ↘ ↘ am

Environment   < **feel** >   Me

The triangle formed by the mind ("I")—the body ("me")—and the environment (including others). "I" may focus outwardly, directly on the environment, or "I" may focus internally by reflecting upon the afferent nervous system. The incoming sensory system may be used to enable a sensory experience of the environment. Equally, however, it may be used to reflect on how one internally feels relative to the environment. Doing so produces a sense of the environment happening to oneself.

Within the motor system, language is learned and thought is formed. The more a thought is based on feeling, the more likely the thought is wrong. Similarly, if a negative feeling stems from an internal thought, then it is misplaced if seen as being caused from outside of oneself. The flow of energy/feeling through a human being is best understood as an organization of creative energy into purpose. The energy/feeling condenses through one's sensory system and then into one's motor system where there occurs efferent output. In handling the flow of energy/feeling, the structure of the brain can be visualized like the heart. The heart's anatomical handling of blood-flow and the brain's structural handling of energy/feeling are analogous. The sensory brain is analogous in structure to the right side of the heart, and the motor brain is like the left side of the heart. As with the anatomy of the heart, there are two portals of entry from the outside. In the case of the brain, sensation and energy flow into the sensory system. From there, feeling/energy leaves the sensory brain and is bridged into the motor brain. Within the motor brain, like the left side of the heart, there is only a single portal out. For the motor brain, energy/feeling exits through one's motor action or mechanical activity unto the environment. Each of the two parts are inseparable from the other. Each enables a purpose for the other, and each needs the other for its own fulfillment. The "I" of one's consciousness is positioned between the two systems, allowing an internal awareness of both the sensory and motor aspects of oneself. However, since "I" is an efferent or outgoing entity, the sensory system can also be perceived, but the mind is limited in awareness of the motor aspect, unable to perceive the motor aspect separate from itself.

Negative feelings are initially undifferentiated. Awareness of discomfort triggers the motor system to cry out. The negative feelings stem from physical discomfort, and are represented as bodily needs. Bodily sensations signaling such needs become well understood by the growing child. Feeling comes internally in the form of energy and mostly gets routed to the baby's growing motor system. Awareness of physical separation can trigger negative feelings, but not until they begin to walk and form intent does anger surface. The organization of energy into forming intent within the environment creates cognitive excitement. However, when their intent gets blocked, sudden anger fits are witnessed. It is clear anger is a motor expression toward the environment which has lost a sense of control. When one is enacting their intent within the environment, to be interrupted or blocked causes a trapping of one's effort, producing the experience of being angry. For example, while driving with the intent to get somewhere, having to stop at a red light is associated with mild agitation.

When energy is trapped within one's sensory system, anxiety is felt. When one's motor attention is focused on one's sensory system, then necessarily there will be some degree of perceived anxiety. The motor system will naturally attach thought to the feelings in effort to control them. However, the more one forms thoughts by focusing on internal feelings, the more one is determining their reality to explain how they feel. A child is unable to see anything but the environment causing how they feel, and themselves causing the feelings of their parents. The child's feelings should not determine the parental thought. The thought structure needed by the child is simply in the handling of their negative feelings. The parental response will determine the belief about the feeling based on how they relate to the child in the context of the child expressing the certain feeling.

The motor system serves as the outlet for one's energy, one's feelings. If one's attention is directed toward one's own feelings, then the amount of expressive output is reduced. The goal should be a total transformation of sensory feeling into motor being. To do so requires one's conscious attention be rooted outward, with an outgoing intent to bring oneself positively to others. If one's feelings are given too much attention, then the motor system will not be generating experience. The ability to effect others or to get something for oneself, then, must rely on the verbal expression of one's negative feelings. This will increasingly add power to the negative feelings and undermine growth of understanding and capability.

THE BINARY PSYCHOLOGY TRIANGLE

Mind

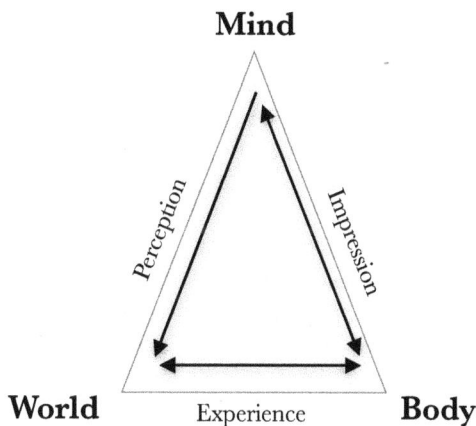

World   Experience   **Body**

From the position of the mind, an individual perceives the world. Through the body, impressions occur (feelings), as well as the potential to impress upon the environment—to have an effect. Within the materialized world, experience occurs. An individual may perceive the world to explain their impressions or, conversely, an individual may perceive the world as they are impressing themselves upon it.

Sensitivity

The character of a child's relationship with their mother forms their emotional sensitivity to both themselves and to others. If a child's negative feelings bring about a maternal effort to make them feel better, then they will become more sensitive to negative feelings. The child will have hypersensitive reactions to things, and through those negative feelings they will solicit love and support from mom. If the paternal thought is overly negative, and mom is overly sensitive, then the child will have a difficult time being emotionally tough enough to withstand their own self-criticism. They will be very critical of others and hypersensitive to feeling slighted or rejected. When they experience negative feelings, such individuals tend to have exaggerated reactions, and blame others for causing such feelings. When such negative feelings occur socially, it causes conflict. Conflict amongst boys will tend to lead to physical altercations, while with girls it tends to manifest as "drama."

Usually, the resting level of tension in mom and dad serves to balance the other, where if dad is "high-strung" then mom is "laid back." This enables the child to be more balanced internally between modes of motor effort and sensory perception. If both parents are "wired" similarly—for example, high-strung or intense—because of hypersensitivity to negative feelings, the child shows more difficulty tolerating what their intense efforts bring about. Interaction between parents, especially when there is a conflict between the two, provides the child with a learning experience as to the interchange of feeling and thought. Eventually (post-pubescence and beyond), the feeling-thought exchange within their two-part consciousness determines their experience of life. Thus, a balanced interaction between parents is very relevant to the interaction between the child's sensory and motor systems which later unfurl into the binary mind. Thought should have a calming influence on feelings. Likewise, at times, feeling should be able to have a reassuring effect on thought.

Pre-thinking children cannot help but to identify based on how they feel. Thinking allows the child to begin separating feeling from thought. The goal is to reach the emotional milestone where one's feelings no longer determine one's thinking. One's feelings can no longer be the responsibility of others. One is either going to go forward identifying as feeling (not as they judge themselves to feel), and thus putting themselves into their effort and intent; or they will be identified as thought or belief, and will thus seek to establish a sense of control or security while fulfilling their belief system.

The influence gained in expressing negative feelings at home is significantly greater than if expressed outside of home. It is thus at home where the developing adolescent last lets go of such negative feelings entitling support. Throughout their childhood, the more they got a controlling influence over the environment via the expression of their negative feelings, the harder time they have, during adolescence, in separating themselves from how they feel. Put another way, the parental sensitivity to their upset feelings as a younger child establishes the internal sensitivity to the feelings the adolescent must battle. The more sensitive a mom's feelings to the feelings of her child, the more it will intrude on a male child's feeling (self) development and on a female child's thought (alpha) development.

The Sensory Tree

The sensory tree is the brain's bodily representation of the mind. The sentinel sensory event at birth is suffocating heaviness in the chest which gets associated in thought form with the loss of connection or oneness with mom.

The mind eventually represents it as heartache and seeks to guard against it happening again. The next sensory experience which causes distress is gastric emptiness. The outcry leads to being fed, and thus fulfillment. This establishes the schema for the handling of hunger. Because the schema was effective, any new negative sensory experience which arises will be initially handled along the hunger pathway. The relevance is appreciated in how hunger is perceived and sought to be alleviated, wherein the feeling is perceived as happening to oneself and having a need outside of oneself. Such a perceptive structure is appropriate for hunger—food, but is maladaptive for the self-perception of emotion (anger, anxiety, sadness). In other words, by perceiving one's emotion as happening to them and representing a need outside of themselves, one necessarily sees the world as rejecting them. This opacifies the view of oneself relating to the world. By seeing one's negative feelings as happening from the world, one interacts with the world in a way where the world (including others) are made responsible for how one feels.

As mentioned, the first sensory experience upon one's birth is suffocation, inducing one to breathe. The heaviness in the chest becomes attached to the loss of connection, with the separation from mom. Later, especially adolescence, it becomes heartache. Panic attacks, also, can involve a similar feeling, and since the panic is being precipitated by an impending loss of one's present consciousness or "I," it is not surprising for the symptoms of panic attacks to often involve the chest or the heart, and for the individual having a panic attack to believe they are dying. The loss of connection upon birth and the "heartache" experienced therein becomes the context for one's life. The direction one takes in pursuing their fulfillment, as well as the manner in which one protects against a re-experience of the heartache, serve as cornerstones of one's character. Inevitably, those two aims become conflictual. The crossroads of the conflict, however, does not come to pass until one is faced with becoming independent or facing a relationship loss. Yet, more and more young adults are avoiding relationships all together so to avoid the crossroads—to avoid re-experiencing the heartache. The problem with such an approach is—in avoiding experience—growth in understanding is limited. One may seek fulfillment through materialism and pleasure—however, neither will result in sustained fulfillment. Only through a giving of oneself for the betterment of those in one's world does one secondarily attain fulfillment. In other words, one has to create the space through the giving of oneself in order to have a sense of internal fulfillment.

The second negative sensory experience after a child's birth is a rising emptiness in the stomach—hunger. The english language only uses one word to describe the feeling since the feeling arises from the body and is related to as representing a need outside of one's body. No other sensory experience (other than thirst) occurs as such. Sensory feelings arising from the body, which have to do with a bodily need for correction, or from an injury, are not the same as hunger. Nor are bodily feelings related to an environmental effect the same (e.g. needing to escape the cold). Hunger (and thirst) is thus a unique sensory experience—the one which has not been "digested." It is thus the only sensory experience which entitles one to consume from the environment. All other uncomfortable sensory experiences (including emotion) must therefore be due to a corrective need—a repair to one's body, or a change in one's being or orientation. The first twelve years of life, when psychologically dependent on the parental thought, the child experiences the meaningfulness of their feelings based on the parental/environmental response to their expressions. They also witness the impact emotion has within the parental relationship. The more a negative emotion affects the environment (including the parent), the more power it is assumed to possess. The ego consciousness (reflective) will readily conceive of negative emotions being triggered from the environment and entitling influence. The occurrence of such negative emotion internally is thus perceived as happening to oneself and entitling relief from outside of oneself— similar to the hunger schema.

Once a sensory experience is swallowed, or internalized, then it can be properly diffused throughout one's system. Also, the individual can grow in understanding of the negative feelings they experience. Ultimately, letting go of the need to control one's negative feelings enables a true escape from them. The escape, however, ironically, occurs through a digestive process. Uncomfortable sensations from the body in the form of hunger, or feelings related to digestion, are readily expressed by an infant. The crying baby elicits the help they depend on receiving. They have no ability to make themselves feel better. However, it must be recognized that infants, initially, do know what they want. The association between negative feelings and being fed gets established. The attempts then for the baby to control their own discomfort come initially through putting things in their mouth. The discomfort manifests as desire. By a year old, they are seeing things in the environment to which they attach their desire, and thus, increasingly, they are able to form motor intent to get what they want. Fits or tantrums—as expressions of upset —are simply them seeking relief for the discomfort they believe is a problem. It is no different than the crying baby who is hungry, except that it is not a physical need they are expressing. They are attaching their negative tension to a desire. When they are unable to meet the desire, they can only bring forth the negative feelings attached to the desire or perceived need. If a parent impedes the fulfillment of said desire, then the parent should do so by reflecting to the child that they do not need to have said desire met, that the uncomfortable feelings are not a problem. Then, once the child accepts their feelings as not needing to be made better, it becomes possible to work with the child to give them a thought perspective unto fulfilling their want. This cannot be done, however, unless the feelings being experienced are first accepted internally. The child cannot work with the feelings as they are spilling out into interpersonal space. Once they settle, then such processing is possible. Yet to do so, they need to reflect the expressed feelings not causing parental concern or being regarded as a problem. Thus, the mirror the parents behold should be utilized to calm the child by giving them a reflection of unperturbed understanding, of confidence, ideally—of positivity.

The negative feelings of a baby are initially undifferentiated—meaning, an amalgamation of fear and anger. A sub-division into either the anxiety spectrum or the anger spectrum occurs noticeably come toddlerhood. For the parent, to mirror the negativity by reflecting anger will influence the child's upset feelings to be characterized by fear. To reflect fear or hurt will precipitate the child's upset feelings becoming characterized by anger. In other words, the negative feelings will either become characterized by anger or by fear, usually determined so to complement the negative feelings reflected. Angry reflections from the parent will direct the child's upset feelings onto the anxiety spectrum, while anxious reflections from the parent (running off, crying, worrying, seeking to make them feel better, etc.) will direct the child's upset feelings onto the anger spectrum. Put another way, an anxious reflection from their parent(s) means the child must perceive themselves as scary.

Believing in one's negative feelings (anxiety, anger) being a problem produces associated "needs" to deal with the feeling(s). Often, support from one's parents, especially mom, is consciously reassuring. The believed need keeps the attachment active, which is usually where the misbelief about one's feelings originated. To grow forward, one must let go of their belief in needing help. Spending the majority of one's life striving to feel better by complaining about not feeling well or feeling mistreated is a waste of energy. If someone believes a certain negative feeling is sourced outside of themselves, then they will not consciously perceive a choice in what they are doing in response to a certain negative feeling. However, others will experience such an individual as creating their own dust storm in order to justify doing what they want without taking responsibility for wanting to do it. In other words, they are basing their actions on how they were feeling and blaming others for inducing those feelings.

Within the consciousness mindset where certain negative emotions are perceived as happening to oneself, the handling of such feelings is seen as needing to occur on the outside as well. This handling process, where the sensory experience is processed within the hunger schema, is mediated by the sympathetic nervous system—the fight or flight system. The sympathetic nervous system forms the defense between oneself and the world. It rejects through a fighting defense or active avoidance. The perception of a threat occurring from the outside will trigger a fear sensation associated with the sympathetic nervous system activating. However, since the source of the threatening feeling is within oneself, to see it as happening to oneself is false. Thus, the defensive response will actually be the manifestation—precipitating others to have defensive responses. The triggering of sympathetic nervous system responses thus gets passed from one to another. For individuals perceiving their internal agitation as being because of others, expressing their upset toward others will be cathartic and seem justified at the time. However, those on the outside will perceive it as unjustified. Much thought may go into the justification of how one feels. However, doing so is simply attaching one's feelings outside of oneself—in effect, seeding negativity.

A build up of negative feeling along the hunger pathway will be felt as an internal emptiness, compelling one to pursue either positive feeling from the world or increased control of one's environment. Both are ignorant of the fullness and the actual need to express oneself. The expression is meant to occur through one's daily activity. However, for this to occur, the negative emotions must be internalized—therein being digested and diffused properly within one's entire system. When the negative feeling is compartmentalized with hunger, however, then it effectively gets trapped. From there, the buildup which occurs can only be expressed eruptively. Since the welling up of compartmentalized tension is sensed as impending chaos, there thus occurs an increased compulsion for control.

The sensory tree past the level of the stomach involves the gut and is related to retention and control of oneself. The process of absorbing what is important and letting go of what is not is the life process. Absorption is required to grow, to learn, to generate a new understanding of the world. However, if an adequate level of letting go does not accompany the absorption, then one's ability to absorb will become compromised. Physically, this is constipation. Psychologically, this is difficulty with new experiences or resistance to change.

Once the negative sensory experience is internalized—symbolically swallowed—then it will no longer be processed like hunger. It will have shifted inside oneself. A nauseated fullness at the initial level may occur, and is indicative of the shift. Bulimic behavior provides the most clear illustration of this shift and the perceptive difference between the two states. The fear attached to internalizing the negative emotion is from the depression and self contempt it threatens to bring with it. Aggression turned inward must undergo a period of psychic pain until it's adequately digested. Unfortunately, it is during this period where an individual—being unable to see the passage past the pain, and reckoning themselves no longer able to bear it—is more likely to give up on themselves and fall back into a dependence.

The fear of vomiting in public is a relatively common phobia surfacing during pubescence. The psychological fear is a loss of control of one's rejective aggression. Vomiting is an aggressive expulsion, and the phobia represents one's current relationship with their anger—specifically, the belief in their rejective impulse potentially being harmful to others. The dramatic nature of the fear demonstrates the erroneous concept of what one's anger may do to the environment. Such individuals fear what may come forth if they lose control of themselves. This phobia rarely persists since it is associated with the initial period following internalization or "swallowing" of one's anger. Most often, this time period follows a shift from the feeling side of consciousness (self position) to the thought side of consciousness (alpha position). Where previously, seeing the thought judgment of others outside of themselves, they struggled to reflect acceptance and generate a sense of being good enough for others. From the thought side of consciousness, however, an individual seeks to control their own feeling/emotion. To do so, they will have to form a relationship with their own potential for angry expression unto the environment. When an individual is newly transitioned to the thought position, their negative emotion (anxiety, anger), when it occurs, is usually at the level of the stomach. Thus, trying to control it within the environment requires displacing it onto something tangible, like vomiting in public. The level of phobic fear will wane as they digest their feelings, therein channeling the tension into their activity.

Once an individual internalizes control of their negative emotion, the sensory experience of gut emptiness, from the thought side of consciousness, will be responded to by increasing their control over the expressive elements within their environment. Put another way, the individual will crave more "self-control." The "self" is represented on the outside (children, partner, family, home environment), and thus they become more controlling in relation to such "self-elements." However, the misperception of emptiness belies the actual fullness and need to give more of themselves—more of one's "self." Thus, although some initial relief is discovered from the goal-directed interaction with the environment or others, there does not occur the necessary giving of themselves. As a result, no sustained benefit is achieved, and the sensory experience of stomach emptiness and the misperceived need for more control will recycle.

When the sense of emptiness occurs within an individual, what they do to fulfill themselves will determine their experience and largely determine others' experience of them. If someone perceives the source of emptiness being outside of themselves, they will likely retreat from the world while entitling themselves more protection or furnishings. In other words, they will try to surround themselves with creature comforts or protective devices. This often includes at least one other individual, who they seek to keep close and in a position of support. However, in such a scenario, they are compromising self-activation. The individualized fruition of themselves gets compromised for to maintain comfortability. Conversely, if the source of the internal emptiness is perceived from within, then it will be perceived as unfulfilled desire. The desire is an important impulse unto the world, for it precipitates relationships and thus facilitates creation and growth. However, self-desire requires denial at times, and the resistance to desire can be overwhelming. Forethought, is thus necessary to foresee situations where resisting one's desire could be impossible, and thus not putting oneself in such positions. The use of forethought requires judgment, and thus caution must be used to not use forethought fearfully. Doing so limits necessary experience. The forethought must be grown from wisdom, from knowing, not from fearful conjecture.

The relevance of the sensory tree comes about by localizing where along the tree one's anxious symptoms are felt. There are three psycho-sensory nodes: chest, stomach, and gut. Each has a quantum distinction from the other. Anxious energy related to loss of a loved one, or ego-death of oneself, will manifest and be sensed from within one's chest. Tension related to rejected energy/feeling gets positioned alongside hunger and is thus sensed at the level of the stomach. Anticipatory anxiety gets attached to the gut where the goal is to not lose control. A sudden, unexpected assault from the environment will cause a dropping sensation within the gut, and is illustrative of a perceived loss of control occurring acutely in reaction to something unexpected. However, when one seeks to create an increased sense of control by thinking about what's coming up or what could happen, then anticipatory tension gets created. Such anxiety is related to life's uncertainty and attempts to know what is going to happen. Control is achieved through the digestive process, where within the gut one gains a sense of possession. Yet, the retentive desire of the human consciousness can become imbalanced, leading to constipation. The psychological consequences of a constipative approach to life are primarily a result of the increased difficulty taking in new information or generating new experiences. Just as with intestinal constipation causing one's appetite to lessen and the stomach's receptivity to food to nauseate, the mind's forage for control produces systemic effects. Learning requires taking in new information. Learning is psychological growth. Therein, one's ability to let go of previous beliefs or habits will directly affect one's learning capability. Psychological constipation is thus inwardly obsessive or stuck on thought, and outwardly unchanging or behaviorally compulsive.

Identifying Dominance

When people internally reflect themselves, they must either perceive what they feel or what they think about themselves. If each person, in labeling the component which most constitutes their awareness, must choose between feeling and thought, and then for each person to conduct a similar labeling for the component which they perceive as most outside their control, where both components must be represented, results in two groupings of individuals. The two groups are *thought dominant* and *feeling dominant*, containing all individuals therein. The feeling component is the energetic emotion or sensory desire, derived from magnetism. The thought component is the conceptual word or representational image, derived from electricity. The interaction of the two components makes labeling difficult. Since feeling fulfills thought and thought is attracted to feeling, the two components naturally interact. The relevance for the above mentioned discrimination is to identify which side is perceptually dominant, for doing so opens up a relevant portal of understanding.

Within the two-part consciousness, in order to identify which side is dominant—which side the "I" of consciousness perceives from—a distinction must be made between *perception* and *awareness*. To perceive something is a relation to something, thus necessitating oneself being separate from what is perceived. In contrast, to be aware of something is to sense something as an integrated part of oneself. For example, Jill—in perceiving Jack's negative thought judgment—becomes aware of her feelings of nervousness. An individual is aware of their dominant side and perceives their non-dominant side. No individual is able to perceive their dominant side since the perceiving part of the mind must perceive something which is separate from the perceiving part of themselves. In other words, the perceiving "I," which is rooted on the dominant side, cannot perceive itself. For instance, an individual who is feeling-dominant is aware of their feelings but they perceive thought—such as Jill in the above example. Thus, an awareness of negative feelings gets attached to perceptible thought in order to assign cause outside of oneself. Alternately, a thought dominant individual is aware of their thought but they perceive feeling. An individual will perceive more difficulty controlling feelings if they are thought dominant, versus someone who is feeling dominant having more difficulty managing thought.

The improved understanding of others provided within the illustration of the two sides of consciousness is, for individuals, most readily applicable within their relationships. Within most relationships, pairing occurs whereby each's dominant side is the other's non-dominant side. Thus, the structure of most relationships is such where each is compelled toward their non-dominant side. Such a structure propels individual growth. For a relationship to achieve similar growth, each person must become more balanced over time, which is enabled through attraction and repulsion producing back and forth movement, where each person must become aware of themselves to the degree necessary to understand and support the other. Otherwise, the relationship cannot become balanced. Furthermore, for it to stay stable, one person will have to grow excessively to sustain the imbalance. Within interpersonal interactions, the meaning of the other person's expression is perceived oppositely when interpreted within the self-reflective space, as opposed to when understanding is begotten in the space between. For example, Jill sees Jack scrambling around looking for something he has misplaced, and asks if she can help him. Jack responds with irritation, which Jill sees as her having upset him, and thinks he does not like her. Though, in truth, Jack was irritated with himself and sensed Jill's offer as reflecting his incompetence.

The vulnerability in pursuing understanding comes with the growth in awareness of oneself which inexorably results. This is a result of the self-awareness which is needed to properly frame the other individual's expression so to produce an understanding. To limit awareness of oneself comes at the expense of understanding others. Thus, in limiting awareness of oneself, relationships must be objectified to such a degree. In other words, objectification of the other fills the void from the lack of understanding. The objectification is based on internal images of oneself which one seeks to have fulfilled or to have manifested—necessitating mirroring support from another individual. The internal balance each individual is naturally compelled to establish requires a growth in understanding as well as awareness. Doing so within relationships is integral to establishing stability, and necessitates each to pursue a deeper understanding of the other, thereby growing in self-awareness at the same time. The difficulty lies in the rejected images of themselves which naturally get seen in the other person and protected against within themselves—i.e. individuals get scared by what they see in the mirror and run away.

Automobile Analogy

The independently thinking mind may be likened to the operation of an automobile. The structure of the automobile is analogous to the physical body. Fuel is required for operation of the automobile just as life energy must infuse into each being, to activate their life. The operator of the vehicle is the "I" of human consciousness, the perceiver of the road, the decider of direction. In operation of the car, power is produced from fuel undergoing internal combustion, therein moving the vehicle. Similarly, the body and mind require life energy for activation. Increasing vehicular force or speed requires increasing fuel delivery. Equally, increasing the force or speed of one's effort necessitates an increase in energy. In an automobile, the amount of fuel being delivered is controlled by the operator via the pedal. In the independent mind, the throttle is tied to the sympathetic nervous system, whereby a surge of adrenaline turbocharges the system by increasing energetic delivery to the motor system. The total amount of fuel available, however, is not under conscious control. Nor, within the individual, is the amount of energy able to be consciously determined. The application of available energy is able to be harnessed, however. The efficiency of the vehicle in getting the fuel delivered to the engine, as well as the engine's efficiency (output/input), determines the amount of overall power able to be harnessed or put to use.

The more the operator reacts to other drivers or is determined by conditions outside the vehicle, the more there occurs an extraneous use of fuel. The more an operator operates based on outside effects, the less stable will be the operation of the automobile. Also, the compensatory level of control sought causes excessive energy expenditure due to excessive energy spent in inhibition. More directly wasteful is acceleration without being in gear—analogous to an individual getting angry—where a significant amount of energy is released without meaningful activity. Being in gear is to be engaged with the drivetrain. Similarly, an individual must connect their energy to their motor system—the part which acts into the world—in order for their energy to flow into their doing. Failure of such energy to be routed into intentional, purposed kinetics is like revving an engine while the car is in park. Operator focus which is not affixed to the road in front of them is misdirected. Equally, for an individual to focus on themselves—to fix their attention on their body or their internal feelings—misdirects their flow of creative energy. The operating consciousness—the driver—must take responsibility for what is focused on.

A background awareness of oneself is naturally present, like the monitoring system of an automobile, and thus intentional monitoring is a waste. An inbuilt alert system can be trusted to bring into awareness an issue in need of conscious attention. Having an awareness of oneself is not the same as being focused on oneself. Also, attention should not be fixed on oneself as one is being or not being regarded by others. In order to drive most effectively, the operator must be positively intended—their attention fixed on the road along which they are positively willing themselves. Similarly, for the independently minded individual, their focus should stay attached to the present, wherein energetic effort activates an experience of themselves as they relate to their environment.

1.3

THINKING

Dating back to ancient Sanskrit, the inability of the "I" of human consciousness to see itself has been recognized. As translated from the Upanishads, "You cannot see the seer of sight, you cannot hear the hearer of hearing, nor perceive the perceiver of perception, nor know the knower of knowledge." Binary Psychology is based on the human two-part consciousness—the two sides of the mind—where the "I" of consciousness is positioned on one side and reflects off of the other side, generating triangulated awareness. The triangulated awareness is "thinking" as Descartes noted, producing the ability to reflect "I think therefore I am." The child's perception, not yet triangulated, stays bound to their sensory experience in the present. Once an internal thought element is formed and becomes active around puberty, formal "thinking" begins. The awareness associated with such thinking is transformative—for what was a two-dimensional life becomes a three-dimensional existence in the context of life. Mathematically, a flat triangle becomes a pyramid. Within the pyramidal space, introspection occurs —where an individual interacts with the sensorimotor aspect of themselves.

The sensorimotor self is bound to the present through an individual's experience, interacting with the environment from the first person perspective. The interaction occurs at the level of the body between the first person self and the outside world. Individuals are able to articulate how things feel through a sensorimotor interaction (mechanical interaction). However, to sense themselves internally, they must separate their sensorimotor perspective into sensory and motor, thus giving thought (motor) to their feeling (sensory) experience. Unfortunately, forming thought about physical feelings detaches an individual's sensorimotor connection within the present. An individual cannot feel something outside of themselves (mechanically) and feel themselves internally (sensory) at the same time. Thus, separating motor from sensory in order to focus on their sensory experience disables the sensorimotor connection. From such a perspective, the motor effort gets used to examine or control how one internally feels rather than being unified within the first person perspective. Therein, the mechanical connection with the environment is lost.

The internal element which forms independent thought activates with puberty. This enables a third person thought perspective. The third person is compelled to assign meaning through the process of categorization, acceptance, or rejection. The third person constructs an understanding of the world outside of oneself by positioning oneself as the reference point. The triangulated awareness—which enables one to have an internal "I" of consciousness which is aware of itself—is made possible by the two-sided human mind. The process of "I" reflecting off of the other side of the conscious mind produces the awareness of oneself. The ability to reflect on an internal image of oneself relative to the world leads to being able to consider the world relative to oneself. An individual's "I" of consciousness becomes aware of itself at the time of puberty, thus enabling a third person perspective within their consciousness ("I think therefore I am"). Once an individual begins formally "thinking," they can form a self-reflective perspective of their environment. In other words, a person can form thought judgment about something or someone relative to themselves. Rather than relying on their direct sensorimotor experience to determine like versus dislike, independent thought judgment can be formed which is both comparative and constructive.

The onset of "thinking" is marked by the emergence of an "I" within one's consciousness, enabling one to conceive of oneself as "I am." This developmental step coincides with puberty and brings a triangulated awareness of oneself and the world outside of oneself. Thereafter, the human psyche is imbued with an "I" of consciousness. The "I" is the observer and decider within one's mind. "I" interacts with feelings and thoughts and is positioned in view of one's body and the environment. This "I" of consciousness goes through nodal changes, producing a new "I" in a quantum stepwise fashion. When individuals recollect, if they think back far enough, they can normally remember themselves for what they were, but are unable to relate to how they used to think. Though their bodily vehicle is still the same, the "I" of consciousness has changed, grown.

The Thinking Mind

The first negative sensory experience of "life" occurs at birth—a gasping for one's first breathe. Therein, the suffocating experience of loss gets positioned within one's chest. It will eventually get attached to one's heart, and the experience of heartache during relationship loss is a throwback to the separation following birth. The next experience of a negative feeling occurs with emptiness/hunger, which is soothed through feeding. Thus, the baby's neuronal system will initially structure negative feeling as indicative of an outside need. Once the baby begins to ambulate, they begin seeing objects in the environment they want to experience. When their effort is impeded, they will become angry, bringing the upset forth as a feeling, analogous to the handling of hunger. In order to integrate the emotion and grow more able to channel it into their effort, it cannot be processed as being caused from the outside or indicative of an outside need.

During infancy and toddlerhood, the child perceives as if they have created what they are experiencing based on need. Their nature is to express the emotional sensations they are experiencing, to thus get their needs or desires met. Increasingly, a child's perceptive style becomes desire driven once they are able to perceive objects in the environment, thereby developing a longing to experience things. Being able to articulate their desires leads to feelings of being rejected when told no, and children frequently express such frustrations during early childhood. During the pre-thinking years, however, children remain experiential and tethered to their present experience, essentially seeking to feel happy as much as possible. Thus, they do not "hold onto" such frustrations—fortunately.

A child is a ball of pure feeling/drive, and therefore is one side of a dependent dyad with their environment. As the child matures, they become able to conceptualize their beliefs in relation to their ability to process the thought environment which exists outside of them. Childhood then is a time of belief formation, especially about oneself as the environment unfolds seemingly in front of them. Eventually, typically around puberty, the environment (thought) which once existed outside the individual becomes internalized, and an interaction begins between one's thoughts and one's feelings. This stage of development represents the time in which one has reached "thinking consciousness," meaning an internal reflection between feeling and thought has begun.

To say that the developing child does not "think" until puberty requires a definition of what it means "to think." When adults think, they consider or reflect, as though there are two perspectives inside one's mind. Anyone who is operating with this internal awareness of themselves knows themselves to be "thinking." This intuitive understanding comes only once it begins. Its onset allows for one to understand the significance and depth of Rene' Descartes statement "I think therefore I am." The ability of the human mind to create metaphor requires the two-parts of one's consciousness to interact. It is the ability to do so which separates humans from lower animals. In effect, the nature of thinking, once it begins, causes a transcendence of the animal world through metaphorical thought. The term *binary thinking* has been used to denote this type of thinking—defined as the holding of two thoughts about the same thing simultaneously. In other words, the thought would involve a representational judgment about something in the environment, as well as the related feeling toward that something.

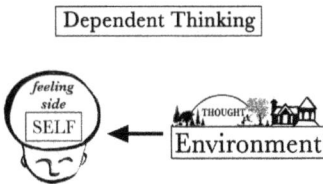

Dependent Thinking (Pre-Thinking): There exists no independent thought element. The environment and thought are fused within the child's dependency on parents.

To illustrate the structure of the thinking mind—in addition to the two parts, when the outside world (environment, object of thought) is added, it forms a three-dimensional triangle. The three parts which form the triangle are the feeling, the thought, and the environment. Such a triangle is necessary to think in the way humans can think and other species cannot—in the way thinking must be defined so to enable it relevance. Thinking enables any one part to look at the relationship between the other two. Consideration or judgment upon the other two is thinking. For example, the alpha aspect inside every individual frequently judges the worthiness of others' (environment) treatment of self. Similarly, self (feeling element) may judge the world's treatment of their alpha-element or thought representation.

Soon after the commencement of thinking, teenagers become primarily identified as either their judgment (alpha) or as their feeling effort (self). The self position is best understood as a continuation of the child perspective with the addition of being able to form internal thought to reflect on. The outside environment is still perceived as thought, and the individual continues to identify as their effortful capability. The pubescent can now reflect off of their thoughts since they primarily identify as their drive and caring ability. Interestingly, if Descartes had been perceptively positioned on the feeling side, thereby reflecting on thought outside of himself, his statement would have been: "I am, therefore I think."

To think requires an internal ability to form thought in relation to one's feelings. The process of thinking initiates the division between feeling and thought. An individual can remain identified as feeling and therein reflect off of thoughts to form additional conscious thought. Or one can transition to a belief point of view wherein they reflect off of feelings to form additional conscious thought. If the feeling self of childhood does not feel good enough or acceptable, and thus out of control, there occurs a shift to a belief in being able to care enough for themselves. They stabilize through a detachment of their emotional self from others. An emotional suppression occurs, where they care for themselves. This enables them to identify with a stable belief or thought perspective unto themselves. Their perspective then grows as they internally reflect off of how they feel about things, therein forming their belief system on a foundation of what keeps their emotional containment stable.

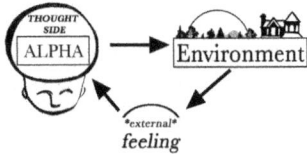

Independent Thinking (Alpha): The "I" of consciousness is positioned on the thought side and reflects on feelings outside of oneself (i.e. feelings in others).

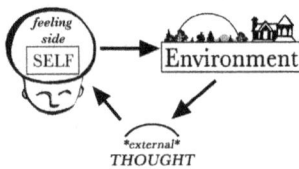

Independent Thinking (Self): The "I" of consciousness is positioned on the feeling side and reflects on thoughts outside of oneself (ideas, truths, occurrences, etc.).

The "I" of one's consciousness, in order to internally reflect oneself, must identify as one part and then focus on the other to generate reflective awareness. Each of the two reference points are inverted relative to the other. The result of the initial reflection is to create a thought separate from the two points used to reflect it, thus forming the third point. The third point—the belief—manifests in the environment. In other words, the outside world (as one believes it to be) is the outcome of the reflection. One's world then becomes where they can experience themselves. The sensory experience of one's belief relative to themselves is considered life. Through life, then, one's relationship struggle will manifest as experience. The less an individual recognizes themselves in the events which transpire, and believes they are being treated unjustly, the more the frustrating relationship pattern will continue. Since people consciously can not see themselves, changing requires a conscious realization of not wanting to be a certain way or of a certain character type. This usually occurs through heartfelt reflection within one's primary relationship.

If an internal feeling is the starting point used to characterize the environment's effect on oneself then one attaches a thought internally to the feeling in relation to the environment. Put more simply, if one focuses on how they feel internally, thereby using the feeling to form thought about the world or others, then such judgment will be erroneous. The judgment will be a thought—a belief—but without having experienced something or someone (only having experienced one's feelings in the context of something or about someone), one cannot truly know something or someone. To have an experience which generates knowledge or understanding, one's thought mind must be outwardly focused and open to understanding. If one is focused on how they are feeling, then the judgment of another person will only be a reflection of such feelings. From within the other individual's experiential frame, there is no connected reality. When the two-part consciousness forms thought directly based on how they feel, then there can be no actual understanding of another. Others will experience being wrongly judged and unable to "get through" to such an individual. Thus, such individuals rely on loyalty founded on moral or ethical law or consequences they are able to impose. Otherwise, they have to consciously attend to the feelings of others or try to bring themselves positively to others. To do so, however, the starting point of their perceptive thought experience can no longer be within their own sensory system. The starting point, rather, must be on the feelings or efforts of others, with the intent of providing positive thought regard so to have a positive effect.

If an internal thought is the starting point to which one gives their effort, then an obsessive imbalance can occur rather quickly. An individual who is identified as feeling will effort themselves toward an externalized thought. If one creates the thought internally, then it is a formation of their feelings and is not true. Thus, one cannot legitimately say, "you don't love me" to someone based on internal feelings of being unloved. Doing so externalizes an internal formation of fear as representing another's reality. At a basic level, one creates their own thought based on thought attachment to negative feelings. Then, the extent to which they express or energize such a thought into the environment determines the magnitude of the derailment from shared reality. Rather than forcing one's own thought into interpersonal space, the effort should be unto the outside thought—toward understanding or in fulfillment of the thought of others. Thus, an open-minded effort outside of oneself is necessary in order to grow in understanding. Through such effort, there will occur a realization or a coming to know—independent of one's feeling effort—which can be structured as belief within oneself going forward.

The Separation of Feeling & Thought

The onset of thinking enables internal judgment of how one feels, where feelings get turned into internal thought. This begins the separation between feeling and thought. Prior to becoming fully separate, thought (desire) can determine feeling (effort) and feeling (emotion) can determine thought (judgment). The instability of the adolescent is a result of the proportionally large attachment still existing between feeling and thought. Early adulthood, then, involves a maturation where one experiences the error of certain feelings protected by thoughts or certain thoughts protected by behaviors. The expression of these erroneous feeling-thought formations occurs through one's *being* within the environment. Experiencing the manifestation of these feeling-thought formations then enables one to grow past such inclusions within their personality.

Thinking begins with a division of one's consciousness. Internally, it is experienced as an awakening of awareness. Private thoughts and feelings are coveted as an internal relationship with oneself begins. By controlling their outward representation, newly thinking pubescents compensate for the insecurities they sense on the inside. Thus, their surface personality, if extreme in any direction, can be assumed to characterize the opposite extreme on the inside. Internal thinking is simply the ability to reflect on feeling or thought, from a reference point ("I") which cannot know itself. For one to perceive the outside world as the cause of certain feelings or thoughts is erroneous. Fear based beliefs about others relative to oneself, and the expectations one has, cause one to attach negative feelings or thoughts to elements outside of oneself.

With the development of the dual-consciousness, the individual begins judging in a triangulated fashion, where they can internally judge others for how the other is treating or may treat them, and how another is regarding them versus how they feel they should be regarded. Similarly, judgment of one's own intentions associated with what one does becomes possible. Thus, there arises a divide between the layer of internal judgment toward their own effort and intent and their projected layer of how others are judging them. Much of the next two decades (after the onset of adolescence) occurs in the space between these two layers, seeking to get both layers to align or exist in a stable fashion. When there has occurred a rejection of the emotional self because it causes too much destabilization of the parent or environment, then the conscious effort to feel loved is turned off in favor of seeking control and power, thus breaking their emotional dependence.

The initial purpose of feeling and thought is to attain separation from the other. Binary relationships help in the separation process even though the relationships will be mutually self-centered, since each is trying to work out an internal sense of stability through the other person. The breakups often represent each having an internal breakage of a feeling—thought formation. Then, each is able to take a step closer toward self-actualization. An internal sense of being "grown-up" comes once feeling and thought are adequately separated. Therein, feeling—thought formations are no longer the primary threat to one's being. Thus, true control of oneself is obtained. This enables one to genuinely bring their focus onto others, into the environment, where the focus is on others for the purpose of bringing oneself beneficially to them. Put another way, the separation of feeling and thought enables one to love rather than being primarily driven to feel loved.

The separation of feeling and thought within one's consciousness enables conscious recognition of the two-sidedness of every coin. Prior, one will remain rooted in identifying oneself as right and others who are different as wrong. One cannot see oneself being both right and wrong. In the drive to reflect being right (to thus create reassurance), necessarily others are made to feel wrong, triggering their conscious defenses. The ensuing battle occurs between equally opposing defenses, where each is seeking to get the other to admit wrong and concede right, but neither is able to do so in the moment. Thus, the fight is unable to be won, and will usually persist until both have exhausted their defensive emotion, wherein the sense of threat diminishes. This conflict can be seen as occurring between the two parts of an individual's thinking consciousness just as it outwardly occurs between two individuals.

A stable sense of internal control comes with the separation of feeling and thought. When each is independent, neither can determine the other. Thus, a "problem" with a feeling or a thought can be stabilized through the complementary support from the other. Without separation, a mirroring takes place. For example, a negative feeling will produce a negative thought through a mirroring of the feeling in thought form. Much of early childhood is spent forming a mirroring understanding of one's own feelings. However, pubescence brings the beginning of the thought—feeling separation, where one starts the process of coming to know oneself. Forming thoughts based directly on how one feels causes instability, experienced mostly through the interpersonal discord it produces. If one's self-identification is based solely on how they feel then others will experience being undeservedly blamed for how one feels. Also, the entitlement which seems to come from having certain feelings is generally off-putting to others. This is a result of the feeling-thought connection, thereby not having open space between feeling and thought for another to fill. Feeling and thought will always seek to interact.

Thus, for an interpersonal connection to occur, there has to be a feeling-thought connection between individuals. It is necessary for each to reflect off of the other, and thus, one cannot keep a feeling-thought connection internally without compromising personal relationships. In other words, for one to be reflecting off of their own feelings or thoughts will eliminate relational space for the other to fill.

Thoughts which are formations of feelings are not true. Trying to control negative feelings by attaching thought to them is natural. However, the more one does so, the more ideas and images of bad things will fill one's mind. To judge something within the environment based on how one feels about it, without experiencing it, is to avoid knowing it. Similarly, to avoid experiences because of fear is to avoid coming to know oneself. To feel something does not equate to knowing it. Feelings in relation to something cannot be used to know it. To know something requires an understanding of it separate from the feeling of it. Feelings can always be cited to underlie one's action if there is not a full separation of feeling and thought. To illustrate, consider the scenario of person A doing something to degrade person B. Person A justifies doing it by claiming that person B upset them initially by doing something disrespectful. In other words, a negative feeling in reaction to person B produced a thought about person B which then became a belief which resulted in the action. Thus, person A's action centered around a negative feeling occurring internally which consciously became paired to what person B did. However, since person B's behavior was not revolving around person A's feelings, then judgment of person B will be based on a subjective, self-centered judgment rooted in feeling. Such thought forms are simply concretions of feeling, and thus cannot serve as a true understanding of person B.

Feeling requires thought and thought requires feeling. For feeling to be organized into a creative purposing of oneself requires thought. Equally, for thought to be realized requires feeling to energize fruition. Both elements are necessary for experience. However, if feeling is being given thought or thought is opposing feeling, then there is conflict. The goal for thought cannot be to feel. Similarly, the purpose of feeling cannot be unto itself. In other words, the purpose of feeling cannot be for the feelings to be felt. Feeling is potential energy. As potential energy it exists pressing toward expression. The purpose of thought is to know. However, to know requires experience. Experience is a manifestation of belief, an act of creation. Feeling is necessary to actualize the experience and for the sensations of the experience. Both feeling and thought must orient properly relative to the other. Otherwise, there will be a power struggle internally, therein diminishing one's energy for conscious activity. Having independent thought enables one to exist without fear of feelings. Otherwise, thought perception, to some degree, will be determined by how one feels. Put another way, one's perception at any moment will be colored by one's internal feelings. The more feelings influence one's perspective, the more distorted from "reality" will be their perspective.

Within the clinical setting, patients normally present for help with their feelings. Occasionally the "problem" is brought forth as a thought or an idea. Paranoid thoughts and obsessive thoughts are examples. However, in examining the underpinnings to such thoughts, it becomes clear the thoughts are being formed directly out of negative feelings. In other words, the feelings are receiving mirroring thought. There is no separation, no space for truth to exist independent from the feeling. The more one attaches thought to their feelings, the more they are seeking to control the feeling through formations of thought. Doing so is believing in the feelings as being indicative of a materialized truth—a thought. However, a feeling cannot be a thought, just as a thought cannot be a feeling. The more thought being directed toward one's own feelings, the more sensitive will be one's feelings. The extent to which one forms beliefs based on feelings will be the severity to which their belief system is distorted.

Every individual will have to primarily give feeling or thought to the environment. Feeling is given in the form of one's effort and intent. Thought is given as judgment or directive. If one primarily gives feeling, then they will be primarily reflecting thought or judgment from the environment. Oppositely, one who identifies as thought will reflect feeling from the environment (including one's body). If one is focused on their own feelings, then their feelings are perceived as being caused by the environment. This type of perception is indicative of a feeling—thought connection. Without a separation of feeling and thought, one cannot perceive having the ability to exert thought control in the face of negative feelings. As a result, what one does is determined, to a significant degree, by how one feels. Such an individual will be unable to depend on themselves to fulfill obligation or commitment since feelings (which come and go) are able to determine what they do or do not do. A separation of feeling and thought yields an increased sense of security. One's thoughts are no longer as threatened by feelings, and feelings experience less rejection by thought. The separation of feeling and thought provides a sense of being internally protected. It enables control of oneself, where outwardly, one feels less threatened.

Feeling-thought formations press to be expressed. There is tension associated with this pressure. The tension occurring in the sensory system is sensed as anxiety. The same tension, when in the motor system, causes conscious agitation. When one focuses on negative feelings internally then thought is not enabling an expression of feeling, but rather, is expressing feeling back unto the sensory system. If seeking to control one's feelings by attributing negative feelings to outside causes, then one's thought focus will be directed outwardly. Tension will thus be attached to things within the environment and expressed angrily or critically. If one is fighting against an internal thought, then putting feeling into it by trying to prove it wrong becomes an activation of the thought—thus increasing its likelihood of becoming the reality as experienced by others.

The more one believes in the need to control one's feelings, the greater must be their sense of threat associated with certain feelings. This is a result of a previous experience of their expressed feelings having had a destructive effect on another individual. A misbelief that the feeling was the problem will precipitate guarding against having such feelings going forward. Doing so requires a partial rooting of one's conscious attention on how one is feeling. This creates feeling—thought formations internally, and forces the environment into being a two-dimensional reflection of oneself. Therein, one's perceptive experience of their environment is of it determining how one feels. Similarly, in relating to an internally held misbelief, the more one acts based on that belief—and thus acts out the misbelief—the more solidified the belief becomes.

Feeling is truly unqualified. Assigning qualitative judgment to certain feelings/emotions is qualifying the sensory experience. While this can be done subjectively for oneself, judging the perceived emotion in another person as representing positive or negative is illegitimate. Emotion can be regarded quantitatively. Taking the *absolute value* of the feeling/emotion strips it of qualitative judgment. When labeling a perceived feeling in another person as good or bad, one cuts oneself off from understanding the complexity and exploring the depth of the feeling/emotion. When one is expressing oneself passionately, if others become defensive, then one may easily become defensive themselves, perceiving thought rejection. As such, an individual is unable to perceive their own feelings, contained within their passion, as being the trigger for the reaction they experienced from others.

Thought is unquantifiable. No thought can be more or less than another. A thought is a judgment, and thus it differentiates. It qualifies something outside of oneself. A thought creates. Feeling is required for the process of fruition, and is required to sustain the thought creation. Thus, feeling determines the quantity or size of the thought. For one to qualify one's feelings by judging them as positive or negative, one is then bound to experience the world as causing them to feel, thus qualifying their experience based on the quality of the feeling produced. Relating to their internal feeling/emotion as a signal of the world will trap one behind a fog of feelings. One's sensory system, if serving as the source of one's thought judgment, causes a self-centering of one's perspective. Furthermore, when forming thought of the environment or others based on one's feelings, then feelings must be qualified as good or bad, positive or negative. This then produces "black or white" judgment of the outside world. Often, to sustain themselves, such individuals crave feeling coming at them, for which to judge—usually to reject. Thus, it is only the lack of feeling or "care" which is feared.

To bring the world unto oneself is assuming there is no detriment in doing so—either to the world or to oneself. The consumptive approach of childhood is driven by the optimistic expectancy for pleasurable experience. However, if positive experience is begotten primarily by expressed negativity rather than positive effort, then one will feel empowered by finding things to criticize. However, as one interacts with the world, the act of negative judgement being formed is the "first move" or the first brush stroke which does more to color one's experience than any actual experience.

Generally, the human consciousness cannot know oneself as one is presently occurring within the environment. One can know their intention and their feelings/emotions. One can know what they think or feel about the environment. But one cannot know oneself relative to the world as one is experienced by the world. Consciousness has to reflect oneself, and is thus sensitive to others' reactions. The tendency is to reflect the experienced reaction as thought judgment of oneself. Otherwise, one must reflect off of their own feelings related to experienced reactions, thus staying rooted in their own sensory experience. Coming to know oneself is limited to the degree to which one remains identified with their feelings, since feelings are part of the experiencing of oneself and do not carry thought judgment. Giving qualifying judgment to feelings only allows one to know how they feel within a certain context. Doing so also takes one's attention away from the environment or others—both of which are necessary to reflect off of in order to come to know oneself. Otherwise, one is splitting themselves internally by giving thought to certain feelings, therein allowing one's feelings to represent the outside world. Putting one's feelings between oneself and the world means one must perceive the feelings as caused by the world, thereby reacting to what they believe has been done to them. Unfortunately, the reality of others is obviously quite different, and people will resist being blamed for one's negative feelings.

Independence

A division in the feeling-thought consciousness endows creative control of one's experience. However, for inner control of the creative process to initiate, independence must be achieved. Independence is associated with a completed division between feeling and thought. Without such, an individual will always believe themselves determined by external circumstances, never able to realize their experience is what they make of it. Perceptively becoming conscious of oneself holding the paint brush which takes the first stroke in the creation of one's experience is the finish line for developmental dependence. In other words, once that line is crossed, one's independent life begins.

The human consciousness reacts based on how something feels or is experienced. The ability to separate feeling and thought enables internal reflection, and as described previously, is the onset of the thinking consciousness. However, not until becoming psychologically and emotionally independent from one's parents does an individual perceive the space between what they are experiencing and what they do or do not do in response. Prior, the adolescent continues to believe they are "made to feel."

Pubescent activation of independent thought enables the child to think independently about themselves. No longer is the child bound outwardly to reflect causing others. They can form a conception of themselves, an "identity" they see being formed in the perceiving minds of others. This two-part consciousness allows for an internal interaction and the cognitive perception of separateness. Put another way, the two-part consciousness enables one to perceive themselves independently. This is because the observing "I" of one's conscious perception now has another part to reflect off of, thus being able to internally regard themselves. Put more succinctly, to form awareness of oneself, consciousness must divide into two parts. This requires the development and internalization of the rational, language-based mind.

The feeling of *want* normally determines what an adolescent believes they need. The more they entitle their desires, the more they will feel the need for their desires to be met. Their frustration toward parent(s) for impeding them stems from a belief in being entitled to get what they want—because, in their reality, their want is their judgment and they deserve to exercise their own judgment. The narcissism of the child perspective comes forth in the self-centeredness of the adolescent perspective. Forming judgment of "reality" based on how they feel (about how they are being treated) or what they think (based on desire) entraps parent(s) in the adolescent's feelings. The logic of the parental perspective cannot penetrate the subjective logic of the adolescent judging based on how they feel or what they want.

Want is a desire, and since desire is a feeling, to form belief or judgment based on one's desire is natural in children and adolescents. However, this type of thinking keeps them trapped in their own perspective, thus not having the open mindedness to take on perspective growth. The older someone gets, the more it's expected for them to be able to control their own emotion. Thus, others will see the emergence of upset feelings as indicative of the person needing to be controlled. If feelings are kept on the inside but still are used to form one's thought judgment, then one's belief system will be centered around the fulfillment of desire—either to satiate longing or to alleviate tension.

A true separation between feeling and thought manifests inwardly as an ability to disentitle a want from having any relevance. Outwardly, being able to see the space between experience and feeling is experienced internally as having the source of one's feelings within oneself. No longer is one directly "made to feel." Achieving a full separation marks the attainment of psycho-emotional independence. Complete independence from others produces a consciousness perspective where one is not attending to fears related to loss or judgment, therein enabling a truer, less distorted view of others. Since a distortion of one's perspective arises out of feelings or thoughts being misattributed and self-centering, a more accurate understanding of the behavior and feelings of others results from being independently minded.

Psycho-emotional independence enables one to not reflect another's behavior or expressions as relative to oneself, and therein more accurately attend to another person as a separate individual. The goal is to understand others in a way where they are not understood as they relate to oneself, but rather understood as they come forth—independent from their effect on oneself. If the effect another has on oneself is given focus, then it is difficult to perceive where the other person is coming from. This is because one will remain self-centered in their effort to understand the other. However, to make sense of another as if they are revolving their thoughts and behaviors around oneself causes significant errors in perceptive judgment. The most poignant illustration of an error in perception stemming from a lack of separation of feeling and thought is the perception of stronger feelings strengthening the truth of a thought. In other words, the more feelings attached to a thought the more the individual will believe the thought. Those who have made the separation, however, will unanimously support the opposite—the more feeling attached to a thought, the more distorted is the thought.

Beliefs & Judgment

Consciousness is produced by the combination of feeling and thought, generating the perception of experience. Experience manifests belief. Feeling awareness will be regarded as either positive or negative. Neutral will not be perceived. Negative feelings are pain, fear, anger, and sadness. First order beliefs are beliefs about one's physical senses, and are hardwired. For example, the belief in a certain upsetting smell being noxious. Such beliefs cannot be changed. Second order beliefs are beliefs about the feelings related to one's being—meaning, what one believes about their emotions or feelings. Second order misbeliefs underlie conscious symptoms within the domains of either sadness, fear, or anger.

Belief is rooted in thought, which is a formation of language. The building of early language cannot occur without concurrent judgment as to the relevance of an object or potential danger of something or someone. This occurs because the parent teaches language through communicating to their child about the shared world. These foundational beliefs are the lens through which people's perception must pass as they judge the world. The application of one's decidedness unto the environment is judgment. Giving thought to one's experience is judgment. Judgment is bound to one's beliefs, and also is dependent on feeling for activation. However, feeling should not directly determine the judgment. The formation of judgment can be directly based on how something feels, as in the child, or it can occur from within a more balanced system of feeling-thought. When one forms thought about people, places, or things based on how one feels, then one is forming a subjective judgment. Such a thought is not rooted in experiential understanding and thus one truly cannot know anything about it. The formed thought is self-reflective and based on one's internal feelings. To communicate such thought to others then passes on the thought. However, the thought is passed on as fact, and thus occupies a more factual representation in the minds of others.

Consciousness is bound to perceive through the thicket of one's beliefs. One's observations are inseparable from what one believes in. When something occurs in contradiction to what is believed to be, then defensive perception rejects it via a negative judgment. The negative judgment will be a reflected thought off of the negative feeling (anger or fear) which arises. Thus, the rejection is based on a negative feeling which one perceives being triggered by the environment. To believe in the negative feeling being indicative of an outside problem needing to be rectified leads to a negative judgment. In other words, when a feeling is not accepted as arising from within the context of one's being, then one will perceive an external cause. Negative feelings, however, should not be automatically reflected into negative judgment about the environment or others. Doing so simply sews the negative feelings into the environment, passing them on.

The capacity to form an independent thought belief, or to utilize judgment, is extremely powerful in its effect on one's life. Such thought has more to do with determining one's experience of life than anything else. Fear related to losing control or suffering painful feelings frequently triggers one to form premature judgments about something or someone. If everyone stems from the same single life source, then negative judgment results in a repulsive force, thus distancing oneself or severing a relational bond. In effect, with judgment, one has formed their belief, and thus lessened or stopped any further understanding of, or interest in, the person, place, or thing being judged. Such is necessary for individuals to organize the material world they must navigate and grow within. However, when one judges other individuals, it is usually secondary to either fear or relative applicability to one's desires. Certainly, everyone draws objective lines which others can see, know, or experience. However, reading between the lines of others to ascribe intent can be perilous when one is seeking to reassure oneself. For, in such an instance, the other person will necessarily feel misjudged, unappreciated, or unloved.

When one person is in a position of authority or leverage (e.g. holding the plug in a relationship), their judgment can be de-individualizing if the judgment relates to the other's value unto the person judging. Such judgment is one-sided and will result in an imbalance and lack of mutuality. Within a love relationship, this one-sidedness will impair growth toward unification. Open mindedness and faith in the other person is important for each to grow nearer to the other. When it comes to the judgment of the other person as good or bad, each must recognize doing so is toxic to the relationship. There is an innate inability for people to accept a "bad" judgment from another human being. Necessarily, one's independent judgment of themselves is based on internal factors (effort, intent, feelings, environmental forces, the other person's effect), and thus will run counter to the negative label from the other person. Once one person begins to judge the other in such a way, defenses will arise and resentment will build from the person feeling negatively judged. To escape this ping-ponging of negativity, both individuals must seek to find the positive in the other, where each then experiences the other as up-lifting.

Mirroring & Reflecting

The term *mirroring*, as it is being used, requires further description to minimize confusion. *Mirroring* is the experience of likeness or sameness in interaction with another—where they perceive their feelings or thoughts being shared within the other person. In a behavioral sense, it simply means doing as the other is doing—as if playing in front of the mirror. But in the realm of what one thinks and how one feels, the experience of mirroring is much less tangible. People are extremely effortful in the pursuit of emotional and psychological mirroring, and no more so than in the context of intimacy between two individuals—where each seeks to feel understood or "gotten" through mirroring. When an individual is perceiving another as they sense being treated by the person or as they are being judged by the person, then they are reflecting themselves. To do so requires a triangulation of the individual's mind. This explains the explosion of social discord which accompanies pubescence, since everyone is beginning to reflect themselves off of others. Mirroring or likeness is sought from others when one is growing into their identity, or when there is insecurity about oneself. However, binary relationships (where both reference points are established) enable more relational stability and identity support through the complementarity, and thus form naturally. Then, in order for each's conscious "I" to understand the other, each must be able to understand how they are effecting the other. To do so is a maturational feat, for it requires the "I" of consciousness to have enough internal security so to take one's focus off of oneself.

If one's conscious awareness could know itself, then there would not be the need for mirroring. Since an individual is not just a feeling, nor just a thought, each must come to know themselves through experience in the context of others providing a reflective experience for them. Just as physical mirrors allow an individual to see themselves physically, psychological and emotional mirrors characterize the nature of their being. The human child must learn they are looking at themselves in the physical mirror; otherwise, they will try to reach into the mirror to interact. An analogous process must occur psychologically and emotionally, where an individual's perspective comes to recognize itself in those around them. In other words, within relationships individuals are provided with a framework to reflectively come to know themselves. Each must see where problems arise because of themselves, even though they perceive it as being caused by the other. Since consciousness cannot perceive itself, the child is attached to the reflections from parents to form a sense of themselves. Equally, they are dependent on reflective stability to provide them a sense of support for their growth-oriented activity. Once the child enters pubescence and their consciousness separates, they are infused with the ability to reflect on themselves internally. This enables the creation of an individual identity. In order for an individual to experience the fruition of their internal sense of themselves, it has to eventually align with the perceptions from others.

Making a conscious effort to reflect one's effect on others is not undertaken naturally. A critical level of self-acceptance must be reached before the two-part consciousness will begin to think about oneself as one effects others. If young adults are sampled, a significant percentage will not regard their effect on others. Rather, their perception remains self-reflective, and thus always consumed with how they are being treated or regarded. They remain imbedded in the identity formation process, where they are carving out their relationship with the world based on their personal experience. Thus, the reflective consciousness—the "I"—will be drawn primarily toward their own reflection until they feel solidified with themselves. Only then are they able to affix their conscious attention on others and reflect their effect on others, rather than attending to their own feelings or judgments about others.

Self-reflective perception is the perceiving of individuals as they relate to oneself. Others are only seen relative to one's own feelings or desires. Thinking about others' treatment of oneself is forming thought based on sensory feelings. Similarly, thinking about how another feels about oneself is thinking about one's own feelings by reflecting the feelings off someone else. Whenever an individual's thoughts triangulate back onto themselves, then they are simply reflecting themselves off of the world. An individual's end point should not be themselves. However, when their primary goal is to enable the motor system to protect the sensory system, or generate better feelings within the sensory system, then an individual has to remain self-reflective. Their thoughts, in being founded on feelings, are not independent of their feelings. As such, each thought is only a formation of feelings. From such a reference point, an individual is revolving their world around their ego-axis. In doing so, they will run into problems as a result of others revolving similarly around their own axis. An individual will be unable to get the positive reflections from others to support their ego's reality. The ego's reality is based on reflective feelings, without a true concept of themselves. To know themselves, thought has to become independent of feeling and be born out of experience.

Each thinking person's "I" may be focused on their internal reflection, their external reflection, or the world/others separate from themselves. An individual's internal reflection occurs off of their internal image of themselves relative to themselves—where they think about themselves relative to their internal image of themselves. External reflection occurs in relation to their first person experiential self—the sensorimotor self which is connected to the environment through the physical body. A good example of an external reflection is an individual reflecting their loneliness as indicative of being rejected by others. External reflection—whether reflecting the world unto self or self unto the world—occurs in a self-centered way, as if others revolve around them. The more centered an individual is around the axis of their first person experience, the greater will be the sensorimotor nature of their thought formations.

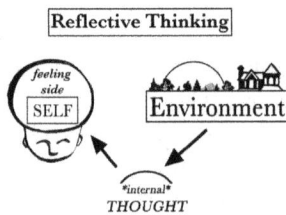

Reflective Thinking (Self): The "I" of consciousness is positioned from the feeling side and reflects on internal thought in relation to the environment.

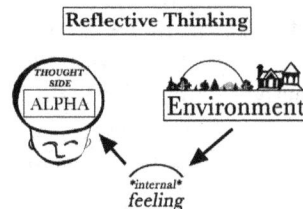

Reflective Thinking (Alpha): The "I" of consciousness is positioned from the thought side and reflects on internal feeling in relation to the environment.

First-Person & Third-Person

To perceive reflectively, an individual must separate from the object or individual being perceived. Reflecting on one's own body is a third-person perspective, and thus occurs from a position separate from one's body. Physical mirrors are outward manifestations of this inward ability. Such a perspective is different than the internal sensing of one's body which occurs from within the first-person sensorimotor perspective. In doing so, the sensorimotor connection with the environment is lost. Because the sensorimotor connection with life occurs from within the first-person perspective, taking a step back into the third-person perspective disconnects oneself from the first-person position. As previously mentioned, from the first-person perspective, to sense how one feels, the motor or thought element must separate from the sensing part of oneself. As such, from the third-person perspective, if one's focus remains on the environment/others relative to how one feels, then one is perceiving defensively. This is because the perceptive thought is being formed relative to one's internal sensory experience rather than from within one's first-person sensorimotor experience. Doing so causes an individual to perceive their internal sensory experience being caused by the environment.

Positioned in the third-person perspective (reflecting on one's first-person experience) limits one's experience of the environment to how one feels about it. Along the same line, others are experienced for how they reflect oneself. From this defensive position, however, one can only form thought judgment about others—as good or bad, to like or dislike, accept or reject. Any pursuance of further understanding, unfortunately, cannot come from the defensive position. Defensively formed thoughts will either be directly rejecting of others or related to others rejecting of oneself. Both operations produce the same outcome—separation or division. In contrast, when one's third-person perspective is occurring from the same level as one's first-person perspective, then one's mind is open and attached to experiencing and giving thought to the present. Such is the path which leads, through understanding and acceptance, toward the unification of oneself.

As described, the first-person experience should not be an individual's primary reference point in forming a thought understanding of others or the environment. Doing so positions the individual in a triangulated relationship with themselves and the world. In other words, the individual has their life positioned in between their third-person "I" and their first-person experience. The clearest illustration of this perceptive phenomenon is in those who treat others most negatively being the most sensitive themselves to negative treatment from others. The double standard, as experienced by others, is tremendously frustrating and illustrative of such an individual's connection with others not extending beyond how they feel about them.

The "I" of consciousness, born from the third-person perspective, must reflect an image of oneself, from which one operates. Each's perceptive experience is perceived through the lens of the internal perceiver who can only relate to the reflected image of themselves relative to their concurrently occurring first-person sensorimotor experience. An image of oneself created as a reference point is an inseparable aspect of the human condition, where each exists as an individualized consciousness. The image of "I" is outlined as an electric image which binds to the individual's magnetic or sensorimotor existence. The human "I" cannot reject itself. Only an individual's first-person experience, their sensorimotor existence—their life—can an individual reject. Doing so, however, is simply a rejection of the individual's relationship to life —a rejection of experience. From the third-person perspective, an individual may conceive of not being alive, but cannot conceive of not conceiving. People may regard having lived before, but are bound to sense themselves being most fully aware within their present consciousness. No individualized "I" can recall not existing, nor relate to their previous state of diminished awareness.

This is due to a reconfiguration of an individual's "I" which accompanies the leveling up of awareness as growth steps in consciousness occur. When consciousness grows, the newly formed image of themselves, which serves as the new point of reflection, is a layer nearer to the true core of the individual. Thus, the individual will be better aligned with themselves and sense more internal validation. The process of a new "I" being established within an individual's consciousness requires the previous "I" to have let go of control—to have let go of the reflected image they attached to themselves. Most experience this detachment process from themselves as death, making the growth through life a formidable process.

The perceiving element of consciousness—the "I" which forms thought, which decides, and which grows in awareness—cannot be the object of perception. The individual forming thought is the primary subject, inextricably. Within an individual, as an individual relates to themselves, the object must be the "me" aspect—which senses, feels, and attaches. "Me" is the physical, experiential aspect—the body. For example, if Jill says "I feel scared" then the object is the sensation of fear within Jill's "me," whereby the subject is "I" or Jill. The "I" is mind.

Each's "I" must perceive from either the first-person or third-person perspective. From the first-person position, an individual's "I" is the subject of experience. In contrast, from the third-person position, "me" is the object of experience. When forming a thought about a noun (person, place, or thing) from the first-person position, the noun is the object of perception—e.g. "I like you." In this example, "I" is the subject and "you" is the object. If the formed thought places the noun as the subject, then the perception is occurring from the third-person position—e.g. "You like me." In this example, "you" is the subject and "me" is the object. Another example from the third-person position—"You like her"—maintains "you" as the subject, but the object is "her." As demonstrated, the object may either be *circular* if the object is oneself, or *linear* if the object is another noun separate from oneself. Another good example, the thought "Jill was rude to Jack" positions Jack as the linear object since the object is another noun separate from the observer (the individual forming the thought). Rather, "Jill was rude to me" has "me" as the object, and thus is circular. To perceive in a circular or reflective fashion involves the individual being both the subject and the object. Assigning Jill as the subject gives causal responsibility to Jill, even though "I" as the perceiver is bound to be the primary subject. Doing so gives control to outside elements which cannot be controlled. Giving another the subjective position of causing "me" is a reverse engineering which inverts cause and effect. Yet, in actuality, the perceiver is both the subject and the object. Forming thought wherein the individual (primary subject) is also the object is illegitimate since it is a self-contained perception, without a connected understanding occurring. Doing so is not only narrow minded, but also precipitates a misrepresentation in the mind's of others who receive the information from the third-person position, thus regarding as the object the individual who actually subjected the experience. Thus, those who form their beliefs based on what others tell them—without having a first-person (connected) experience of them—are foolish to do so.

Every independently thinking individual can recognize inhabiting their body rather than "being" their body. Thus, "I" can perceive "me," and thus, "I" must relate to "me." The independently thinking "I" can relate to "me" as the primary object of perception. For instance, if Jill judges Jack as being rude to her, she is forming thought about Jack based on how she senses his treatment of her. Such judgment, however, is based on reflecting Jack's behavior as causing her feelings, and then internally forms judgment based on such, without ever connecting to understand Jack's behavior. In other words, Jill sees Jack as the cause of her negative feelings, therein generating the thought about his treatment of her being wrong, without understanding the intent behind his behavior. Thus, in the scenario of Jack being rude to Jill, the subject is Jack, and the object is Jill. To legitimately assign "rude" to Jack's behavior can only come from an objective, third-person position. For Jill to be both the judge and the object, however, is illicit and self-reflective. By the very nature of such a judgment, it comes from a defensive mode of perception. Thus, the thought of Jack being rude, if formed inside of Jill, requires Jill's "I" to reflect off of the negative feelings of her "me." The judgment of Jack is based on Jill's feelings attaching to his behavior, feelings for which Jill is responsible for handling. Centering her feelings around his behavior precludes consideration of Jack's individuality.

Causality

The causality of an individual's behavior is based either on their "I" or their "me." Following the pubescent onset of thinking, individuals are able to conceive within their internal thought space, separate from the present environment. The internal thought space develops due to the emergence of an independent thought element which forms the third-person perspective. The third-person "I" brings an awareness into consciousness which previously did not exist, thus producing the ability to internally reflect upon the "me" element—i.e. to think. Since "I" is both the perceiver and the decider, "I" is the doer. "Me" is the sensory aspect which feels and connects, enabling a first-person experience. "I" is naturally inclined to try and find fulfillment for "me" while also protecting "me" from what "I" perceives to be a threat to "me." When cause for what someone does is based on "me" as an object—whether "me" is being protected (defended) or fulfillment of "me" is being sought (hunger, desire)—then "I" is being determined by needs perceived within "me." Since attachment of the "me" aspect creates dependence, adolescence is characterized by an effort toward independence, and thus is invariably centered around freeing the "me" element. The self-centered perception of adolescents and young adults, familiar to most grown-ups, is a result of perceiving and behaving based on the wants or needs arising from their "me" element.

When an individual's "I" attaches cause to "me" for what is done or not done, then "I" is bound to attach outside cause for the experience of "me." For example, Jack yelling at Jill to go away because "she is annoying" illustrates the experience of Jack's "me" (annoyance/discomfort) determining what his "I" did (yelling/rejection). Jack cannot see his behavior ("I" yelling) as anything but a reaction to Jill's effect on him ("me" annoyed). Thus, Jack's perceptual experience will center around the cause of what he did being based on what was happening to him. Giving causality to "me" then tethers causality to what happened to "me." This is because the "me" aspect within everyone is the space where the sensory or feeling experience is internalized.

Whenever an individual perceives a threat, they are perceiving from the defensive position, and thus, they necessarily must sense life happening to them. Any perceiving position which has the "me" element as the object is invariably either defensive or consumptive—i.e. protecting oneself or getting for oneself. The protection is pivoted on the attachment to the "me" element, driven by the fear of loss or rejection contained therein. This attachment to the "me" element is innate because of the physical body's attached need for food. The consumptive drive arises from within the internal emptiness, physically patterned by hunger. This survivalist perspective—to secure safety and sustenance—comes naturally within an individual's perspective when experiencing an internal emptiness or lacking, including fear. Such a perspective is based on what the "me" element is believed to need, and thus causality for one's behavior is in reaction to a feeling perceived within the "me" element. The "me" aspect therein becomes the object for one's perception of the outside environment.

An individual's "I" aspect, when being caused by the "me" aspect, must perceive causality outside of them. Control, thus, is begotten by rejection of the identified cause of "me"—necessarily perceived outside the bounds of what "I" is doing in relation to "me." If the "I" aspect attains realization of causality, then "me" becomes detached from being the object-cause of what "I" does. Recognition of the "me" aspect being caused by what "I" is doing or thinking then establishes causality within the perceiving individual. The more to which an individual's behavior is determined by the needs they attach to their "me" aspect, the more they will experience themselves determined by circumstances outside their control. In contrast, when behavior is based on the conscious intent of "I," then no preceding cause exists. Thus, the behavior is an act of creation with forward intent. The intent is expressed within the individual's present being from the subject position. In other words, an individual takes causal responsibility for their perception and behavior toward whatever or whomever they are perceiving. For instance, an individual who perceives someone mistreating them is perceiving through the lens of being the object. In contrast, the same behavior may be perceived from the subject position, maintaining the other person as the object. From the subject position, an understanding can be pursued which centers around the other person, thereby positioning the perceiving individual to form an understanding of the other's behavior as stemming from some belief mis-occurring within the person. Rather than interpreting the behavior as centering around the effect it had within their "me" aspect, the "I" as subject may seek to understand the behavior as centered within the other person. Doing so properly maintains the object outside of the perceiver's "me" aspect. Understandably, the more an individual's "me" aspect is attached to the object of their perception, the less clearly the object may be understood, and thus the more objectified will be the object. In other words, the objectification of another occurs to the degree to which "me" is attached. This is due to the nature of perception when it occurs through the lens of the "me" aspect—wherein an individual subjects the world as the cause of them.

When "me" is the object, then the "me" element is not in a connected state within the present. If in a connected state, then necessarily the "me" aspect is conjoined with the subject—the perceiver—thereby enabling a perspective which properly maintains the object outside of oneself. For those individuals who exist perceiving from the subject position, having freed themselves from being determined by their "me" element, they see life for what they may bring to it rather than for what it brings to them. Such represents an internalization of causality, thus bringing into them an awareness of their potential for creative influence within the world.

Introspection

The individual whose "I" is positioned on the thought side will internally introspect on their thought. From the feeling side (self individual), introspection will be upon feeling or desire. The process of introspection requires one to take a third person perspective upon themselves. If one's focal point affixes to their non-dominant side, then one is not being introspective. Reflecting on one's non-dominant side occurs relative to one's body (physical feelings) or in relation to others. Such externalized reflection is not the same as internalized reflection or introspection. The conscious process of internalized reflection (introspection) requires an internal center of self—the development of which comes through attainment of independence. Until independence is accomplished, the separation of thought from feeling does not occur to the extent necessary for introspection. The introspective perspective, by definition, is positioned in consideration of oneself relative to oneself. Having an internal center is indicative of an awareness of an internal source of causality. In contrast, when an individual's center is outside of themselves (body, others), then they will perceive themselves caused by others or by how they physically feel. This self-reflective process is not equivalent to introspection since it does not occur from an internal center relative to themselves. From the feeling side of consciousness, self-reflection involves thought of oneself. Oppositely, the self-reflection, from the thought side, involves the feeling of oneself. Introspection, rather, involves the "I"—if positioned on the thought side and thus identified as thought—interacting with their internal thought. Likewise, an individual whose "I" is positioned on the feeling side, will introspect upon feeling.

Put forth as a definition, introspection is the perceptive process whereby an individual, from the third person perspective, reflects upon their internal identification of themselves. In contrast, self-reflection, although similarly a third person perspective unto themselves, occurs upon an individual's external identification with themselves. Thus, the outcome of self-reflection is an experience of the world relative to themselves (sensory experience) or themselves relative to the world (thought experience). The self-reflective process, though potentially motivating, is inherently separating or dividing since it involves an individual perceiving the unfulfilled space between themselves and the world. Moreover, the perceptive position for which self-reflection occurs, is a defensive position, and thus precipitates others experiencing them as distant, possibly rejecting. Introspection, on the other hand, is inherently unifying since an individual introspects to better understand and align themselves relative to the first person they interact with internally. Thus, introspection is an important process to enable balance throughout an individual's life, and through which an individual, by integrating aspects of themselves, is able to grow more internally unified.

Temporal Direction of Thinking

There are 3 possible temporal directions of thought: past, present, and future. Thinking about the past is relevant only in consideration of the future. For example, deciding what to do about something often requires a remembrance of previous experiences and outcomes. Thinking of the past because of worry or doubt is a waste of thought energy. Longing for the past, similarly, is non-productive and wasteful. Regret imbeds itself in memories where a person recognizes having left empty space, and thus wonders *what could have been?* Otherwise, a person will be drawn into thinking about the past as a way of identifying wrongs committed. Such individuals normally have internal shame related to their aggression, and as a result, obsessively seek to gain a sense of control. They analyze their interactions in order to reassure themselves they did not say anything wrong, or do anything which may have been upsetting, thereby opening the door to potential conflict. Put another way, one will think about the past to reassure oneself the part of them they seek to keep suppressed did not poke through. Efforts to undo things one did usually involve scouring the past for misdeeds and methods to make amends. Also, keeping current negative feelings attached to previous negative experiences keeps such memories "alive." Usually, this is for good reason since the experience itself has yet to be overcome. The individual is still rejecting an aspect of themselves.

The future, if thought about, usually beholds an infinite amount of *what ifs*. Imaginative worry is common and driven to avoid surprises—to feel in control—via a sense of preparedness. The more significance an individual gives to their anxiety in a way where they seek to take control of it, the more they will focus on what is coming up, what needs to be done, and what could happen. Staying presently minded is difficult when one's thoughts are unquiet or generally anxious. People tend to think about what's coming up when they are anxious—to create a sense of preparedness and thus feel more in control of life. However, in doing so, the now—the present—and thus the chance for experience, is forever relegated to their past, and without memory. The present moment beholds experience. Nothing else can. To be most open

Alpha (positive)	Self (positive)
To be in control	To be pleasing
To be respected	To be accepted
To be looked up to	To be good enough
To be powerful	To be effective
To be right	To be cared for
To be nurturing	To be wanted
To be trustworthy	To be special
Alpha (negative)	**Self (negative)**
Scorned	Rejected
Criticized	Failure
Blamed	Not good enough
Disrespected	Repulsive
Out of control	Unwanted
Betrayed	Worthless
Disregarded	Unlovable

or available for experience, one cannot judge it. Doing so will give thought representation to an experience, thereby giving it parameters of belief and, to some degree, forming a judgment of the experience. Judging the experience as it's happening is partially closing one's mind off from the experience itself.

From the perceptive experience of others, when a person's thoughts are not attending to the present, the person is perceived as "not present." It is felt, individually, as a lack of personal attunement. Generally, it is regarded as a lack of engagement. The importance of the present in establishing shared connectedness and binding one to a shared reality is readily demonstrable in those who have significant difficult connecting to the present. The most pernicious effect, however, is on children, who depend on the empathic connectedness for self development.

Positive memories which exist in one's mind are impressions from a moment gone by. Such an impression was taken from the moment and was meaningful. No such memories are formed when one is recollecting the past or thinking about what is to come. Only in the present does meaning occur, and thus it is only within the present where the human mind can be impressed upon. Thinking about the past and the future can assist in the organization of one's thoughts and the piecing together of patterns, but growth requires an open-minded effort forward within the present. Growth requires stepping into unknown space, bringing oneself to what is rather than trying to predict what will be or reconstruct what had been. Growth is consciousness becoming more aware, and comes from the conscious effort to understand more. Experience of oneself necessarily occurs within the present. While one may process experience after its occurrence, the experience itself is always of the present moment. Thus, thoughts occurring outside the present moment miss the opportunity for experience. The more someone attempts to control the thought representation they have constructed of themselves, the more they will have to avoid experiential understanding.

Human forethought is often the source of an individual's difficulty. Engaging in predictive thought scenarios in order to reflect the associated feelings creates pockets of experience which exist as potential. Taking oneself into forethought is usually to create a sense of knowing what is coming up, to give oneself a feeling of control. Whether created thoughts trigger negative feelings or negative feelings trigger reflective thoughts, the result is the same: internally generated feeling–thought formations. An individual's creative energy is able to express itself into the environment only when they are engaged in the present moment within the environment. For their focus to drift into forethought requires them to remove themselves from the present. An individual's positive, creative energy, becomes damned when thinking outside the present. In doing so, they avoid experiencing themselves. The more someone utilizes forethought, the more they are trying to control their experience. However, this sacrifices the opportunity for growth through experience. Therein lies the lamentable tragedy—of an individual not pursuing the fruition of their individuality, believing rather in the need to protect their potential feelings.

Forethought can involve thinking about what is coming up for the sake of organization, envisioning what is coming up in order to feel prepared, or in order to make a decision by imagining a scenario so to reflect on the feelings which would likely come. The latter two uses of forethought are in effort to protect one's feelings and thus are attempts to avoid certain feelings. By attaching thoughts to feelings in the form of outside scenarios or preparedness, one is seeking to establish conscious control of their experience. The effort to create one's own experience is driven by a belief in needing to control oneself. However, this increases the likelihood of one judging their experience rather than experiencing themselves within the experience. To judge one's experience, one must reflect either how the experience aligns with what they expected or how they are feeling about the experience. Both cognitive approaches to an experiential moment partially remove oneself from the experience, and thus diminish one's growth. To grow is to change, to become wiser. The wiser one becomes, the more one operates with an open-minded receptivity and an understanding of all which can be gained through each experience in life.

In trying to manage negative feelings by routing them into *what if* scenarios, the domain of forethought must absorb the concocted feeling-thought formations. This will create a sense of internal restlessness or agitation. The more negative energy existing within one's forethought, the more unstable will be one's sense of life around them. With the use of forethought, one is trying to control cause and effect. In other words, one is trying to control what happens within their experience. One is trying to control life.

ALPHA | SELF

Within long term relationships, there are two sides—two roles or positional perspectives. The male role and the female role exist naturally—akin to yin and yang. The two sides or roles provide complementarity, and together form the whole. A relationship, though made up of opposites, must be regarded as the whole. The roles are not determined by manifest gender but rather by gender identification. The male-identified individual identifies as the thought, thereby defining "what" is done. Cognitively, the male-identified individual does the approving, and thus utilizes disapproval or rejection as a defense in order to secure themselves. In contrast, the female approach toward security occurs through attempts to sustain existing attachments. Thus, during times of perceived rejection, such individuals will intensify their outward effort in order to not be rejected.

The character of each individual as the opposite of the other creates the synergistic potential inherently found within relationships. For the positive potential to be realized, however, neither individual can be related to as if they are a threat to the other. Whenever an individual attaches their internal space to another individual, for which they seek to protect or fulfill, a fear of failure or loss accompanies the attachment. In other words, when one believes in needing the other relative to their internal space, the other is perceived as a potential threat. Unfortunately, doing so comes at the expense of understanding the other individual because understanding must be established in the space between. Perceiving another defensively precludes reaching out to form an understanding. Seeing the other for the threat they pose means they will be perceived negatively and will experience being misunderstood. Defensiveness toward the negative judgment will then occur, likely triggering discord. Each is thus responsible for overcoming their own fears related to loss or rejection—the fears which infuse the other with threat. The importance of doing so comes from the detriment which occurs to the relationship when one of the individuals sees the other from a defensive position, as doing so prevents a growth of understanding. Rather, the individual perceiving defensively will be reacting—which means they will either move toward the other or away from the other depending on their defensive style—which is related to their gender identification. The movement occurs in order to not experience something negative—to not be rejected or upset—for which the other individual is perceived as the cause and then defended against.

In the space between two individuals, an entity is able to form from each's output. Judging the other's output negatively will always come at the expense of the judging individual's positive output, therein detracting from the relationship. Although a relationship is made up of two individuals, a relationship must be seen as an entity in and of itself, where the summation of one plus one involves creation, and thus the total is greater than the sum of the two individually. Conceiving of a relationship as such means neither individual should focus on their individualized space—how they feel or what they want from the other, nor should either regard their own action as being caused by the other.

The part of each's mind which seeks approval is distinct from the part which does the approving. Giving outward approval or disapproval requires exercising thought judgment. Within the two-part consciousness of the thinking mind, the part which forms external judgment relates to the aspect which would seek another's approval. In other words, an individual cannot be consciously forming judgment of another and, at the same time, be striving for the person's approval. The thought forming aspect of the thinking mind occurs from the third-person subject position, which is distinct from the first-person subject position where the perspective is experiential. Attaching to the judgment of another produces a sensitivity to rejection, whereby disapproval is feared and effort is made to avoid being rejected. Doing so, unfortunately, gives power and control to the other individual. Within the context of most romantic relationships, one of the individuals will be seeking thought approval from the other. By definition, then one of the individuals is positioned to potentially reject the other through their expressed judgment of the other. From the judgment position, rejection is often used to gain a sense of control or to reaffirm power over the other individual. Historically, males filled the judgment role, where they entitled decision making authority within the relationship. The female effort toward gaining approval came in the form of energetic effort to be pleasing to the man.

At present, gender is no longer able to determine the relationship role which is fulfilled. No longer does being a man entitle being in the controlling or approving position relative to women. Increasingly, this parental position within male-female relationships is occupied by the female. Thus, looking at a relationship through the lens of historically-based gender stereotypes often produces a misunderstanding of both individuals, and thus leads to an erroneous assessment.

The attachment of oneself to the approval of another is an equal partner to any power-control imbalance within a relationship. The greater an individual's subjective need to reflect approval from another, the more they will be giving over power and control. In doing so, for females, the male pattern of power and control is precipitated, which is characterized by aggression. At times, the imbalance, when occurring in the context of excessive female dependence, requires outside intervention. However, for males who seek approval within their relationship, the female pattern of power and control is potentiated, which is is characterized by passive-aggression. Independent of gender, the passive-aggressive approach toward getting power and control within a relationship is accomplished through the use of rejection. Such a relationship dynamic is supported by the other's effort for approval or to not be rejected. Frequently, males who seek approval within their relationship are more emotive—where, episodically, they express their emotion intensely—often occurring in a self-rejective, pleading manner —rather than explosively, as would characterize the angered expression of a dominantly positioned male. In the individual who seeks approval, expression of negative emotions are not used used for intimidation or domination. Rather, such emotion exists within the attachment—within the individual's effort to be good enough for the other. Thus, when negative emotion surfaces, it will be related to feeling rejected, and thus does not get expressed in a manner which is rejecting of the other person. Increasingly, however, such episodic upset is being misrepresented by individuals seeking a sense of control and power over their emotive partner.

Alpha & Self-Personalities

Every individual's psycho-emotional mind will have a strong preference as to the internal handling of negative emotion: whether it is more threatening and uncomfortable to hold such emotion in (expresser type) or is it more uncomfortable or destabilizing for it to come out (suppressor). Expresser type individuals feel more internally unstable if they hold negative feeling inside as opposed to letting it out or expressing such emotion. In sharp black and white contrast, those of the suppressor type have the opposite experience in relation to negative emotion rising within them. For suppressors, the discomfort and sense of instability is compounded if their negative emotion emerges outwardly. The two styles require a strict definition to avoid being confused with introversion and extroversion or level of openness. The emotional expression is not a verbalization of how one feels, but rather the experience of getting emotional—where the internal upset comes to the surface as outward upset (anger, sadness) which can be felt by others. In maintaining this definition, a staggering majority of relationships are composed of a suppressor and an expresser. Rarely will a relationship involve two people of the same type. To unlock the personality code existing within human relations, a second dimension—the psychological personality—must be added. Again, like the emotional personality, there are two types which divide equally—the self personality and the alpha personality. Those who remain identified with the emotional or experiential side are labeled self-personalities. Those who flip to a thought or belief identity are labeled alpha-personalities. The difference in perspective between the two is so fundamentally different, human relationships cannot be understood without understanding how each perceives. The interpersonal or relational goals for an alpha-individual are fundamentally different from those sought by self-individuals. The accompanying table characterizes the positive feelings/thoughts sought within a complementary relationship, as well as the negative feelings/thoughts which arise from relationship failings for both alpha and self-individuals. If the positive feelings/thoughts are understood to be what an individual seeks to experience within his or her primary interpersonal relationship(s), and negative feelings/thoughts being those in which a person seeks to avoid experiencing relative to the other person, then it is striking how fundamentally different are the relationship aims between the two individuals in a complementary relationship. These differences in perspective are indicative of the cognitive differences between self-individuals and alpha-individuals.

In order to fully understand the Binary Psychology model, it is imperative for the natural pattern of relational pairing to be well characterized. The natural ordering of love relationships based on role identity (alpha or self) and emotional style (expresser or suppressor) illustrates the fundamental components of a long term relationship. Within the relationship, each serves to structurally support and balance the other. The binary relationship itself is analogous to two individuals holding a rope between them. The rope must remain taught for each to feel secure. For each to have supported function, each person must extend at times to enable the proper movement for the other. Both will be sensitive to sacrificing their position to support the other, as will each sense being held back if not being enabled the support they feel they need. To give it, however, the other person must sacrifice their position even further, for otherwise, the pair cannot move adequately in space/time to meet life's demands. When each has plenty of themselves (time, effort) to give, then supporting the other by shaving off personal time/effort is not as difficult. When the relationship pair is a system or family, however, then personal time for each is limited, and thus the personal sacrifices get more difficult—more painful. Resentment toward the other for causing the pain of sacrifice may surface. The perspective each has toward sacrifice—namely, how comfortable each is with self-sacrifice—is imperative to the success of a binary relationship. For every characteristic one has—for every *yin* of one's interpersonal nature—the other individual's personality is sought to behold the *yang*. It is natural for people to wish for completeness. One-sidedly, this would require a magical being who is dynamic, selfless, and understanding at every moment. Since individuals cannot exist as a perfect relational being, the tension in the rope will always be changing, it will never be still, nor perfectly stable. Volatility is inherently a threat in the arrangement—in the very nature of a binary relationship.

Returning to the rope analogy, consider a scenario where both individuals are pulling away from the other. They are each wanting more from the other. At this point, a power struggle has paralyzed the relationship and, for there to be a rekindling of relational support, a concession by one or both is required. It illustrates the eventual impasse when both individuals are primarily self-serving rather than loving. For a complementary relationship to be successful, each has to pay attention to supporting the other whenever the chance arises. If each maintains their focus on the other person in effort to better understand, support, and love them, then a *synergy effect* is possible. A synergistic combination of two individuals is where the force or function of the pair, existing in a complementary relationship, is greater than the sum of the two individuals. In other words, each individual is better because they are with the other.

As previously described, the Binary Psychology model is founded on the two-part consciousness which develops during puberty. The brain's own pubescent changes give rise to the two-part consciousness, and therein the ability to think or reflect on an image of oneself. The capacity for doing so is taken for granted thereafter—the inner voice which allows discourse—where one can debate *want* versus *should*. The two part, hemispheric brain in humans, once activated, enables the adolescent to internalize (take inward and sense within) the judge, and thus subjectively consider themselves. Similarly, they are able to think about others thinking about them. Then, throughout the remainder of adolescence, this inner relationship between self and judge, in the context of seeking to establish relationships with others, creates an outward identity which either expresses their inner sense of self or rejects it. In the context of romantic relationships, a relational identity will develop, involving emotional attachment/intimacy. Such relationships will necessarily reflect the two-part consciousness—meaning, the two individuals will outwardly relate with each other the same way as the two elements do within each's mind. In other words, one person will personify the *self*—where the desire is for pleasing acceptance. The other individual will personify the judgment element, termed *alpha*—which, around the time of puberty, becomes independently active, and which seeks to engender a sense of control through autonomous authority. Thus, just as there are two parts to the individual consciousness, there are two relational role types: self and alpha. Outward identification as one or the other usually solidifies during the teenage years, and usually follows gender identification within the family. For example, girls in a female-alpha household will likely become alpha female adults while boys in the family are likely to become self-personalities.

Due to the combination of gender identification with one's parent, and the relational style between one's parents, role identity as self or alpha is handed down. There is no conscious "choice" about it since the tracks are laid during the pre-thinking years. Handedness (right or left hand dominant), though manifesting earlier than role identity, is a similar process and equally outside of one's conscious ability to determine. Gender identity formation is another example. It is necessary to recognize pre-thinking identity formation will be outside the person's awareness. In other words, one cannot recollect conscious awareness of a self-conception prior to the onset of thinking.

Feelings Within A Relationship

All people are drawn toward expressing themselves. An individual will respond to another's expression of negative feeling or emotion, when seen as a problem, by trying to fix the situation. However, someone expressing themselves often occurs not as a problem in search for help but as purely an expression of themselves, to be regarded, understood, known. The same expression, from a different individual, however, may represent an outreach for help. To know, effort is required in order to understand. Feelings cannot be used as the basis for which to understand another.

The relevance of the opposing emotional styles within relationships is significant. Most failed relationships (especially marriages) occur because the couple is unable to work past negative emotions which arise (usually anger). A couple, when dealing with negative emotion existing between them, can split apart very quickly as a result of the following phenomenon (as depicted by a hypothetical couple—"The Jones"). Mrs. Jones (expresser) is upset with Mr. Jones (suppressor) because Mr. has been coming home late and Mrs. feels neglected. Mrs. experiences negative emotion (sad and mad) which she expresses when he gets home through facial expression, body language, and tone of voice. Such emotion, palpable to Mr. Jones, causes him to react in the exact same way he reacts internally if such emotion were occurring within him—suppressive, shut-down, avoidant. To Mrs., he appears to get more introverted and less expressive (shut-down style). Mrs. is looking for a sense of validation and recognition through mirroring—she wants him to reflect her emotion. In getting the opposite however, she feels uncared for, and thus has a flare of emotion which she expresses. This causes an even greater suppressive reaction in Mr., who likely will walk away or flee at some point. In doing so, Mrs. feels abandoned or rejected, and though her emotion will eventually dissipate, her experience of being shut out will undermine her security in the relationship. Moreover, Mr. is left feeling more insecure because of the greater instability he senses in the relationship. The slippery slope is apparent if there is a lack of recognition in how the other person handles emotion, as there becomes a malignant misrepresentation of the meaning of other's response based on an "if it were me" interpretation. To clarify, say the situation was reversed and Mr. was upset about something. If Mrs. reacted with introversion or by shutting down, then doing so would communicate Mrs. not caring—having no empathic emotion to express. Naturally, Mrs. interprets Mr.'s introversion as if it was her, and thus, she becomes more acutely upset, and later she grows more insecure and resentful. Once this lack of mirroring is experienced, the couple arrives at the first major hurdle.

The importance for each person in a binary relationship to understand the other's handling of negative emotion cannot be overstated. The significance of one's negative expressions, the manner of expression, and the perception of its effect on the other, if unexplored between the pair, often becomes a slow leak which eventually sinks the ship. The misperception of what lies behind negative feelings and the way each deals with them often causes underlying resentment to build. Any amount of mischaracterization, and resultant communication difficulties, make adaptation to each other and growth as a couple more challenging. If a clear value system can be agreed upon, in combination with a shared goal existing outside of either individual, then *method judgment* of the other will naturally develop in place of *subjective judgment. Method judgment* centers around the effort unto a shared goal, rather than being based on subjective feelings or reflective thought (subjective judgment). Use of method judgment lessens the likelihood of defensiveness in their interactions, and thus, promotes more open, secure communication. In doing so, each is able to grow in understanding of the emotional goals of the other relative to themselves. Knowing fully what the other seeks to experience and why enables a flow of consideration back and forth, infusing the relationship with an atmosphere of love and support.

The attraction which an expressive individual has toward a suppressive individual is based on the ability of the suppressive individual to contain the expressions of the expressive individual. Receiving the emotion without becoming emotional is very comforting to the expressive individual. The control over the emotion is admired and elicits respect because the expressive individual recognizes how emotions can be destabilizing. They yearn for the control over themselves, where threat of rejection and loss doesn't dominate them. The expressive individual will naturally see the suppressive individual as someone who has gained control over their emotion, representing significant internal strength. From the suppressive person's point of view, they are attracted toward emotion. They prefer to help the expressive person control their negative feelings, and seek to elicit the expression of positive emotion. Expression also infers transparency for the suppressive individual, and thus makes them more secure with expressers. Since the suppressor is able to recognize relevant feelings within themselves being kept hidden, they more readily trust expressers. From the flip side, expressers believe relevant feelings (based on intensity or level of threat), would naturally come out. Thus, a sense of acceptance comes more naturally in their interactions with suppressor individuals, especially during times of expressivity.

The "as if it were me" perception of the other's emotion, or lack thereof, underlies the majority of divorces. In other words, the reaction each has to the upset of the other is the same reaction they take toward themselves in reaction to internal upset. When expressing vulnerable emotions, the expressive individual will have a desire to see similar emotion from the suppressive individual, especially when their insecurity rises in reaction to the suppressor getting more shut down or closed off. This triggers further emotion, often leading to either a loss of emotional control from the suppressor or a walk away. The shut-down or walk away triggers a sense of abandonment in the expresser. On the other hand, emotion coming forth gives the expressive individual a sense of reassurance. Seeing the emotion gives the desired mirroring, and thus, the expresser feels better. However, the loss of control for the suppressor creates a sense of being internally wrecked, despite the expresser feeling acutely relieved.

The tolerance shown by a suppressive individual for negative emotion being expressed by others is rooted in how their own negative emotion was reacted to during childhood. Put another way, an individual's experience as a child of tolerance shown unto them largely determines their later tolerance for the expression of negative emotion from others. If the expression of negative emotion as a child was met with significant anger or threat of abandonment (i.e., parent becoming overwhelmed and walking away), then for such individuals, a general intolerance to negative emotion is frequently observed. Also, a family's overall tolerance for negative emotion being expressed conditions a person's sensitivity level during their childhood. The more emotion expressed in the home as a child the more expressive becomes their home as an adult. Whether one gravitates to an expresser of a similar caliber or is such an expresser, the level of expressivity in the home holds fairly true to one's childhood.

When an expressive person is coming forth with negative feelings, then likely they are looking for a stabilizing, positive thought. Normally, insecurity causes anxious energy to catalyze the negative thoughts expressed. A calming influence comes from someone with suppressed emotion who expresses positive or reassuring thought. If negative feeling surfaces in reaction, then the expressive person will perceive it as negative judgment or rejection. The stabilizing power of positive regard in the face of negative feelings is significant. However, to do so, the individual cannot have a feeling reaction themselves or make it about their own feelings. Usually, relationship stalemates occur because each is focusing on the wrong element in the other (feelings or thoughts). For example, if person A feels threatened by person B's upset feelings, then person A will focus on person B's upset feelings being unjustified rather than seeing person B as struggling with negative thoughts they believe person A is having of them. Person A will thus miss the curative power of providing positive thought about person B to person B.

Thought Within a Relationship

The sense an individual has in interacting with the world is, at its most basic level, a relationship between "I" and "other." The relationship is invariably colored by the following—the individual's representation of themselves (who they sense themselves to be), their representation of the world, and their relationship to their own wants or entitlements. If an individual's relational role is as an alpha-individual, then he or she will primarily seek control as an endpoint. This is not to say such individuals seek to be controlling or come off as such, but rather they take control of their interaction with the world (or others). Such an approach stands in stark contrast to how self-individuals relate to the world, where the world is in control, and where the self-individual seeks growth in ability to be pleasing and impressive through functional value. Self-individuals interact with the world by growing into it while always mentally receiving it. They seek to grow each day, and sense the world will seek to take control of them—to care for them in a parental fashion.

The self will have difficulty denying the validity of their feeling. Oppositely, the alpha will have equal difficulty denying the validity of their thought. From the self perspective, thought or belief seems concocted, and they tend to not affix themselves to beliefs. Self-personalities are always seeking to apply themselves by turning their emotion into purposeful effort. For doing so, they expect to achieve positive thought or regard, but only for what they intended themselves toward doing. They are less concerned with their general representation or reputation. The self is tethered to their experience, both in how they form their beliefs and how they bring themselves to others. They are thus sensitive to the judgment from those having direct, present-minded experience of them.

The "I" of consciousness coming from the self position seeks to reflect loving thought. This will be obtained either actively or passively. An active pursuit requires putting one's feelings into functional effort with an intent to receive loving judgment. The passive approach requires expressing how one feels in order to get the positive regard one seeks. From the alpha perspective, the active effort from the self individual applies pressure. The pressure then empowers their limit setting through passive judgment. If the alpha-individual seeks active control, then they will relate more comfortably and naturally with passive self-individuals.

Internal judgment, or belief about oneself, is alpha-judgment. It necessarily arises from a belief in needing to care for oneself—to manage the potential of one's feelings, to parent oneself. Thus, alpha judgment is often felt by a self personality as being critical or rejecting. When the alpha individual feels more insecure, they will seek to bolster their sense of themselves by attaching their negativity to the self-personality. Security is then reflected based on the amount of response or help they receive. The conscious perspective of alpha-individuals is difficult to change. In part, this is because they often relate rejectingly with their internal self-element (feeling/emotion). Thus, when an alpha-individual expresses negativity to a self-individual, they hope the self-individual will be drawn to make such feelings better. The potential imbalance is seen in the use of expressive control. In other words, when the self individual is in thought control then the complementary balancing goes away. Judgment which is driven by self-want, and applied decidedly, amounts to playing both sides. The dominance brings a loss of checks and balances, and can thus get out of control quickly and dramatically.

In a binary relationship, when the self-individual seeks support for their efforts or understanding of their negative feelings, it threatens the established dynamic. This occurs because the self-expresser's needs are perceived either as more to deal with (burden) or expressions of negative judgment (criticism), even though the expression from the self-individual was intended to elicit understanding. This forces the self-individual to put less emphasis on their emotional needs, and more into functional output. The result is an overall maturation of the self-individual, and so it serves them well. Otherwise, resentment intensifies and the relationship will fragment. Times when the alpha-individual expresses negative feelings, if the self-expresser does not show signs of being influenced, increased insecurity is felt. This then triggers an attempt to elicit emotion, or to exert emotional influence, with the goal of re-establishing their internal sense of control.

By each's "I" of consciousness reflecting off of the other to form a sense of themselves, there is a hypersensitivity to negativity from the other. In a defensive state, each will see their own offense as being in defense against an initial offense from the other. Thus, each can always play the chicken or the egg in their own favor. It is interesting how the game of "you are not the boss of me" which occurs in early grade school, when looked at from the perspective of alpha-self relations, is simply the early sorting out of relational styles. Who gets to judge? Who will submit to such judgment? Who will be intimidated by the tattletale? How will they evade it? How to enact control over others? For the child whose gender predicts them later to become an alpha-personality, figuring out ways to exert leadership or control is necessary, and starts during elementary school. The playground is a bustling back and forth, where if watched closely, the dynamic of push-pull across genders is unmistakable. There is a difference in the styles between future alpha girls versus girls destined to be self-personalities, as there is a difference between pre-alpha and natural self boys. However, since each young child is still a self-personality, the taking on of the alpha role becomes fleeting, and in fact, it is the pre-alpha children who usually engage most intensely in the back and forth. This is not surprising since pre-alpha children will be the most compelled by dynamics involving an alpha or authority, and thus, most readily engage in cat & mouse games with the opposite gender. Children destined to remain self-personalities will seek more of a recess from alpha-individuals and will not have much enthusiasm for playing push-pull with a pre-alpha from the opposite sex.

Categorization

It is necessary to introduce some terminology so to characterize the eight types of individuals noted when an individual's predicted positional personality (alpha or self, based on gender identification) is subdivided based on current positional role and gender. The terms *natural, pre-alpha,* or *false* are applied to the two base positional personality types (alpha, self) in order to denote an individual's current position within his or her primary relationship. A natural alpha male (NAM) for instance is an alpha male functioning within the alpha role as would be expected based on the natural course of gender role identification within his family of origin. Individuals naturally destined to be in the alpha role but who still are functioning in the self position (children, adolescents), are termed *pre-alpha,* and thus, pre-alpha males (PAM) and pre-alpha females (PAF) form two of the eight positional types.

The self-personality experiences continual growth throughout life. The self-personality is very sensitive (judgmental) toward those they seek to please, or in the manner from which they derive their sense of judgment. The self-personality's sense of control pivots on feeling accepted or good enough. The self-individual is always susceptible to being liked, seemingly understood, where they experience a twinkle from the eye of an alpha-individual or a mirroring self-personality. They perceive being recognized positively for who they are, and the other individual seems pleased by them. Two powerful notions—being accepted and being good enough—captivate self-individuals. Their level of maturity determines to what extent they expect unconditional care and commitment. It also determines the level of responsibility they will take for their actions within the relationship—i.e., how they react when feeling negatively judged or criticized.

Like children, self-individuals who lack the necessary emotional maturity will also have immature psychological defense mechanisms. Most of these defense mechanisms will be in effort to avoid being controlled, or experiencing rejection. Also, taking responsibility will be difficult, and immature self-individuals frequently will engage in either deceit or insistence on being judged by their intentions. In the latter situation, where an outcome is negative, and they feel they are being criticized (blamed), they usually claim their intentions were misrepresented. Their frustration will be from believing they are being mischaracterized. However, it is their elusiveness in taking responsibility which tends to frustrate their binary other. Oppositional behavior, in the form of avoidance or passive aggression, is also very common —especially, in less expressive self-individuals. The dynamic of cat and mouse which characterizes most every alpha-self interaction (assuming an inverse mirroring attraction exists) may manifest as flirtation or a positive push-pull between the two.

The cognitive process to enable thinking differs between self-personality individuals and alpha-personality individuals. The self-personality has their "I" of consciousness rooted on the feeling side, and thus, their initial reflective process is to reflect off of the other side, which for the self-personality will be the thought side. Thus, self-personality individuals reflect off of thought in order to intend their effort. Oppositely, the alpha-personality individual has their consciousness "I" positioned on the thought side, and thus must reflect initially off of feeling in order to form thought. When something from the environment presents itself to the alpha-individual, the initial process is to form judgment based on whether or not they feel comfortable with it. Within a binary relationship, feelings of discomfort expressed by the alpha-individual are sensed by the self-individual as getting in-between them. In contrast, conflictual beliefs or thoughts from the self-individual come across more as a threat to the alpha-individual. The pairing which naturally occurs between an alpha-personality and a self-personality to form the majority of relationships is driven by the complementary effect each provides the other.

A transition of an individual's consciousness to the thought side enables them to take control of themselves. This occurs through a detachment of their consciousness from others, enabling the individual to relate directly with how they feel. It must always be assumed the alpha position will not be forsaken by the developing individual. Rather, it is the self position, due to excessive insecurity and feelings of vulnerability from the power-control imbalance within the environment, which gets rejected for the sake of the seemingly more secure alpha position within a primary relationship. Thus, if the naturally predicted course for a certain individual is to be an alpha, then it must be assumed the transition has yet to occur. The pressure of an individual's potential will always be toward actualization or realization. A delay in esteem development can cause the pre-alpha individual to cognitively remain in the self position. Delays are not uncommon. Similar to other aspects of human development, delays in the transition are often multifactorial in cause. Delays may be nothing to have concern about, or can be indicative of significant underlying pathology. Nevertheless, self-individuals who are predicted to transition to their alpha-role/identity are referred to as *pre-alpha*.

On the other hand, a natural self individual functioning in the alpha role is *false* because the person is not naturally destined for that role. The use of the term false does not infer negative judgment or that it is wrong for the false-alpha individual to be positioned as an alpha. It is appreciated in two different scenarios—the first and most naturally common being when an adolescent self male gets into his first relationship (transitional relationship), he will often do so as an alpha. However, cognitively he will be functioning as a self-personality—reflecting on thought. The other scenario where false alpha-individuals are noted occurs across both genders and is driven by relationship insecurity (excessive fear of loss)—wherein a natural self-individual will take the alpha role in effort to feel more secure through the more dominant or controlling position. If they are cognitively an alpha, despite being predicted (based on family, gender identification) to be a self-personality, it is usually due to significant losses or abandonments while in the self role as a child or young adult. To understand relationship dynamics between two individuals, knowing each's cognitive style is essential. Success is heavily influenced by each being in the role which aligns with their cognitive style.

In a binary relationship, the goal for each is to reflect off of the other, rather than themselves, therein forming a complete union. Each individual is naturally driven to reflect themselves off another person rather than off of their internal complementary element. The self-individual wishes to enable decided thought in the alpha-individual who wishes to enable relevant feeling in the self-individual. In other words, the self personality wants to establish the reflection of positive, stable thought from the alpha-individual, and the alpha-individual wants to reflect positive feeling from the self-individual. Fear of losing oneself to the other causes insecurity to flare up. If not gotten past, then the relationship will stop short of achieving a true complimentary union.

The cognitive style of alpha-individuals may be characterized as form-giving. They seek to represent information they hear—to give it a binary place (usually good or bad, right or wrong). They seek to control the representation others have of them, and their perspective is labeling in character. Their language semantics indicate a formed judgment. The judgment is not necessarily logically sound, or valid in its stated actuality. Rather, it is the form by which the alpha-individual ascribes to their claim. To do so is unavoidable, as it is imbedded in their representational way of thinking. In communicating to people, alpha-individuals speak factually, decidedly. Their perspective, when interacting, is outward, and gives form to the world and others. They are judging the world outside them. When speaking of experience, they usually present the formed representation of the experience rather than communicating their experience. For the alpha-individual, interaction with people is decided—meaning, they must judge what to give or what to pursue. They have difficulty existing relatively or relatedly in the moment. Generally, they are unable to interact on the "same wavelength." The mental effort in considering how to respond, as well as the importance placed on their representation to others, is significant. For them, it is "work."

In alpha-individuals, as stimuli from the outside are sensed, an initial filter involving judgment or relevance to their own system occurs. If the stimuli or information is deemed to contradict or lack relevance to the alpha-system, it will be discarded without conscious thought. Thus, this initial *value judgment* enables parameters or limits to exist within the world, as an alpha-individual perceives the world to exist. In other words, the brain draws boundaries, like a cookie cutter, forming the world in a shape which the individual may recognize. Moreover, the shape funnels what they need from the world to their sensory system, funneling it toward them so they can perceive what they need. Cognitively, this is a fundamental shift of perception, which enables the individual, as a sensory organ, to interface with the world in such a way where they are able to siphon more of what they need. Once information passes through the filter of valued judgment, if judged relevant, then the information will be processed and placed within the alpha-system, thereby giving it formed judgment. Then, formed judgment can be communicated in thought or language, thus being expressed outwardly.

In contrast, the cognition of the self individual receives data from the environment with no initial filtering. Judgment occurs by identifying patterns within the information in order to satisfy feelings or desires within the environment or in accordance to the alpha-system they function within. Identifying patterns within the unfiltered data (in one's memory, experiences/ observations) and drawing associations is *associative judgment* and occurs in effort to advance the individual's intent. As it relates to the experience of the moment, the cognitive processing of an alpha-minded person causes a slight time delay in solidifying the formed judgment. The self-minded individual, in contrast, exists in a state of expectancy, and thus, they never feel accurately branded by the past. Self-individuals, on the other hand, use experiential expressions when communicating. They tell of their experience of an event in a way which provides a visual illustration for the other's reference. They do not judge the other person per se, but will judge another person for creating their experience.

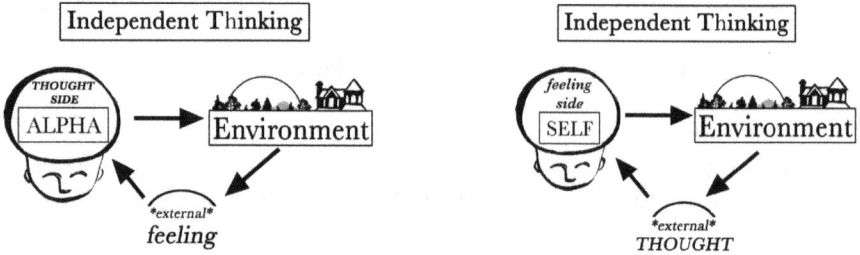

The alpha-consciousness perceives feeling first in forming thought. Thought is then given to the environment (judgment) and the environment is received based on how it feels. The self-consciousness, on the other hand, perceives thought first in forming feeling. The feeling is given to the environment as effort and intent. The environment is received based on the thought it bestows. The alpha-consciousness will fear a feeling more than a thought. The self- consciousness will fear a thought (a situation, something happening, etc.) more than a feeling.

Self-perception is directional, integral, and growth based. The self-perspective judges the wave of the form, while the alpha-perspective judges the form of the wave. For example, "Fred was being rude" is a judgment of what the self-individual thinks Fred was intending, but it is not a judgment of Fred, such as "Fred is rude." When self-individuals describe the being/behavior of others, their semantic language illustrates the experiential nature of their perspective. They do not represent what is or is not about a person, but rather they speak about a person's being. From the self-perspective, every person has a nucleus inside a shell. The shell interfaces with the outside world, and thus can be represented separately from the nucleus or the inner person. For example, someone can be acting or doing things in a way which is not "true to themselves." The inner person could be judged as "good" even though the action was "bad"—they were being bad despite the fact they are good. Interestingly, the cognitive style of alpha-individuals struggles to discriminate between the two.

This phenomenon becomes relevant in marital relationships between alpha and self- individuals, for criticisms are verbalized in different ways and taken differently as well. For the purposes of illustrating differences in cognitive perspective, imagine being critical of a child's behavior and how the criticism may be verbalized. "He is being bad" could be stated, as could "He is bad." A person, in stating the latter, as with the former, still recognizes a true, inner child separate from the bad behavior. Self-individuals see all people from such a perspective, while alpha-individuals represent themselves and others more singularly. The self-individual, if feeling criticized or misrepresented, may get defensive and disagree with the perceived judgment. This judgment will be based on experiential factors. Usually the self-judgment (self-individual's judgment of themselves) is based on effort, intent, and feeling. Thus, self-representations will be based on internal judgment from the standpoint of effort, intent, or feeling. When the alpha-representation, or outside judgment, is significantly different than their own self-representation, or inner judgment of themselves, then relational frustration and distrust develop. This is why children, in defense of themselves, will say they did not mean to do something for which they've gotten in trouble, or they will beg intensely, displaying a high level of want.

Dual Personalities

Both parts of the two-part consciousness will have a personality based on reflective identification with parents. In other words, each's self aspect will have a personality, as will each's alpha element. The non-dominant side will be used defensively to protect the dominant side. Thus, initial impressions of others are usually based on interacting with their non-dominant side since it is the non-dominant side which forms each's shell.

A person's personality inside the home can be strikingly different than their personality outside the home. This is especially true for alpha-individuals. Alpha-individuals usually put forth their self to those on the outside—toward those who they seek to please in effort to acquire tangible good judgment. Normally, alpha-individuals are sensitive to others judging, and expect those inside the home to recognize their outward efforts. The manner in which they treat their spouse/dependent(s) is reflective of their true personality since it comes forth within the binary relationship. From the outside, it is difficult to discern a person's personality type since alpha-individuals tend to behave in the more pleasing manner, while self-individuals tend to initially be more standoffish and judgmental. The self-personality, outside of their primary relationship, will protect themselves with a shell characterized by their alpha-aspect. To summarize, the self-personality uses their alpha-shell for defense while the alpha-personality uses their self-persona defensively. The general duality of the mind is exhibited in the character differences between how one is at home versus outside of home. Truly, home is the line of demarcation.

The alpha element forms in order to both control the self and fulfill the self. If the self emotion is believed to be a threat to one's stability, or to one's relationships, then the alpha element will be 1/self. Suppression of negative feeling is thus the goal. Oppositely, when seeking to fulfill oneself, then the drive is to empower or enable want. Such individuals strive to love themselves by reflecting being cared about and needed. This latter style produces a more consistent personality, but they may have problems at home if they expect their feelings to be subserved. The *Jackyl & Hyde* phenomenon frequently experienced within relationships is a result of this 1/self type of alpha-personality.

The self-personality can be mistaken for an alpha-personality if their alpha shell is too compensatory. When one's inadequacy is overly attached to fears of loss or rejection, then seeking to represent the opposite outwardly usually occurs. Any outward signs or displays, however, are representational, and thus compensatory. On the inside, or within a relationship, they attempt to conceal the inadequacy, and any acting out tends to occur privately.

The characteristic beheld by the alpha-parent meriting the controlling position is termed *alpha-justification*. Alpha-justification is the ostensible basis for a parent's alpha position relative to the other parent, as it is perceived by the child. It is most meaningfully defined through the eyes of the child. Each child has a sense of the trait which justifies the alpha-parent's control relative to the self-parent. However, it normally follows gender lines, and yet children usually do not report gender as being the alpha-justification. Within each of their families, the alpha-justification is what gives Parent A control over Parent B. Children are very in tune to the power dynamics between parents. Additionally, they quickly identify the one in control and the other who seeks to be pleasing. It is important to realize the pleasing behavior from the self-parent legitimizes and empowers the justification. If the young pre-alpha child is able to mimic the alpha characteristics (e.g. being smarter, a know-it-all) they will often do so very blatantly in effort to justify their alpha behavior.

Pre-alpha children will seek to be little deputies to authority figures of the same gender. Pre-alpha girls of early elementary school age can often be seen carrying out interpersonal tyranny in the name of the teacher they have taken the liberty of identifying with. Ultimately, children do not tolerate other children controlling them through alpha-authority mimicry, as each child seeks more autonomy from parents/adults. Thus, children who seek interpersonal control over peers go about it by taking an authoritarian position/approach, and frequently become ostracized to some degree. This is because the other children reflect the controlling efforts as disapproval, and thus defensively distance themselves.

Mirroring Relationships (transitional relationships)

The volatility of adolescent love relationships is due to the transitional nature of their purpose. The difficulty for the adolescent consciousness in stepping away from home can be significant, and having a love relationship helps by providing emotional support as a bridge. This enables decreased anxiety regarding separation, often leading to an increase in motivation to become independent, as well as providing essential emotional support. However, because of the mirroring or membranous nature of the attachment, there exists the expectation for the other person to attend to their feelings and insecurities. This incites a control struggle where each begins to pull at the other to feel more secure and loved. Because they are transitioning into independence, each's insecurity creates a sense of dependence on the other, which is developmentally threatening since both are developmentally seeking independence.

Once the neuro-connectivity associated with pubescence enables the child to think, the threat of loss/rejection becomes a dominating force. Adolescent relationships are marked by insecure push-pull dynamics. Despite intense expressions of love and devotion, the intensity of the ups and downs can be intense. The power dynamic frequently shifts, and threats to break up from each commonly are countered by outpourings of stated love from the other. The extreme behavior is frightening to the vicariously involved parent. Parental over-reactions to normal expressions or musings of mortality usually amount to pouring fuel on a fire. Statements like "If you break up with me I will kill myself" are part of the normal breaking up process for the age due to their level of emotional immaturity. Such threats normally occur when one pushes away from the other. The directional drive to escape the emotional vice-grip grows more intense as the relationship becomes more attached to the adolescent's identity, and thus depended upon. Though wishfully pursued, a recapturing of the initial explosion of love and affection, and all the fantasy contained therein, is unable to be achieved.

If an adolescent, who is in the midst of a love relationship, is asked to characterize what it is they love about the other person, the majority of the time they will describe how the other person makes them feel. They will profess that the other person is nice to them, is entertaining (e.g. "they make me laugh"), or simply that the person loves them. The "rockets red glare" feeling at the onset of these mirroring relationships inevitably fades. Upset feelings stemming from each's own insecurity (e.g., not getting enough attention), if expressed, will precipitate an early crossroads within the relationship. There are few things so closely tied to childhood as the belief in one's negative feelings entitling attention, and the wish to be coddled. It is very powerful for two people to enable each other to feel loved through each's joy being reflected back at them. However, striving for the relief of life's pain and suffering through another is chasing a fantasy. For negative emotions to entitle a positive response from others is a remnant of childhood. Empowering the impact of one's insecurity or anxiety runs the risk of potentiating its occurrence, and thus, impeding the deliverance of one's love.

There is a reason teenage love relationships rarely stay intact beyond the transitional time period of adolescence. Both teens within a transitional relationship will identify being intensely in love. The love feelings they are able to recognize internally are consciously tethered to the other. This means both believe the other is causing such feelings internally, and thus, the fear of losing the feeling, for both, is a shrill, frightening prospect. Doing things within the relationship to lessen their insecurity regarding loss will make the other person feel unaccepted or not good enough. This will in turn trigger insecurity in the other which, at some point, will be expressed and precipitate a cycle of insecurity. In such a scenario, the fear of loss gets empowered as a problem, thus entitling alleviation from the other person. Back and forth it will go, and since fear breeds fear, the insecurity necessarily grows. Despite episodic alleviation through positive reassurances or behaviors to make the other feel better, it is only a fleeting experience of conscious relief. The insecurity, in actuality, will have grown more intense. Thus, the cycle precipitates greater mood swings, and overall, the relationship grows more unstable. Eventually, the negative feelings within each outweigh the positive feelings, and it is only each's fear of loss which keeps them tethered together. At this point, the relationship is consciously detrimental and unwanted, but the fear of not having it usually keeps it intact for a few months longer. The letting go or break up process is extremely important. How the teenager psychologically gets support in stepping away from home strongly affects their personality going forward. Seen another way, undergoing the painful and frightening loss makes them very conscious of themselves—as they try to avoid the loss, then cope with the loss, and finally how they go forward protecting their heart. In going forward, their relational personality solidifies in character, though eventually the erected defenses will have to be dealt with as a barrier within their primary relationship(s).

Mirroring love is never more blatantly on display than during the transitional relationships between adolescents. The intensity with which each seeks to feel loved is reflected in these relationships. However, a mirror cannot promote character growth if it reflects what an individual wants to see. If a mirror could reflect how one is doing in their effort to gain the reflections of love they strive for, then such a mirror would compel change. The binary relationship is such a mirror. The other person, at some point in the courting process, radiates a pure love-light which is transfixing to the mind and heart. However, once the relationship becomes real—whereby each is asked to sacrifice for the betterment of the other—a frustrating inability to get the reassuring love-light from the other is experienced. For to some degree, the initial love-light was based on the surge of self-esteem within the other person. Put another way, the love Jack saw and felt directed at him from Jill, during the bliss of their initial infatuation, was constructed partly by Jill's good self feelings from experiences of mirroring love from Jack. To this end, it is impossible to fall in love and it not be, to some degree, falling in love with one's own reflection.

If the purpose of life was compatible with mirroring infatuations, then such relationships would not crumble as they do. From a functionality standpoint, there is no augmentation of function. Mirrored strengths can exponentially power each individual, enabling certain gains or achievements for both individuals. However, for the navigation of life's ever changing waters—where a variable wind drives the tide—to maintain stable direction and a sense of flowing forward, the relationship must be complementary, or binary. This means, of the pair, one must be expressive and the other suppressive. One must be seeking control and have judgmental authority while the other must have the will to please—to feel secure in their pleasingness to the other. In this arrangement, the relationship, as a whole, embodies the two-part human psyche. The two brains, the self (right) brain and the alpha (left) brain achieve holographic representation within a binary relationship, and thus it naturally "feels right." For there to be psychological attraction, *inverse mirroring* must occur. Simply put, each feels completed. Both individuals see the other as an outward representation of what each is keeping protected on the inside. He is out as she is in, and she is out as he is in.

The self-centeredness of adolescents and young adults causes them to be representational in their love and conditional with their commitment. In other words, they are constantly judging how the other feels about them and how they feel about the other. The ability to give of themselves independent of how they feel has yet to develop. The act of sacrificing oneself for the betterment of another is impossible when focus is on how one is feeling or what one wants. Power within the relationship should not come from negative judgment or upset feeling. When one cannot see past how they feel or what they want, then growing in understanding and acceptance of the other is not possible. At some point, the other person will recognize being liked for their effect rather than for their individual personhood. Usually, this does not become an issue until after a child is added to the system.

Caring for a child requires frequent one-way injections of love, thereby straining one's conscious equilibrium—being forced to give of oneself rather than to do for oneself. Once the system is triangulated, it can be judged. Where before, the giving and receiving occurred along the same road, and thus allowed for one to take positive from the other's happiness with them, within a triangulated system, however, each can judge the other's input relative to their own. A problem often lies in one's subjective sense of their own efforts relative to the efforts they represent from the other. The more one's feelings affect their judgment, the more imbalanced will be their perception of their own effort comparatively. They will thus feel undervalued, which can quickly become toxic to the relationship.

Sometimes, mutually self-serving relationships establish a balance where each is satisfied by the other. However, it is a precarious balance since each will be sensitive to things they do for the other and will be keeping score of it.

A tit-for-tat perspective is common in relationships where each is seeking to love themselves. Put another way, if each person is primarily wanting to feel loved, then they will give only in their effort to get. In this way, the relationship becomes conditional. The stark reality of the affection being conditional brings fright to each, and suddenly neither feels in control or secure. Subsequent attempts to grab ahold of the relationship cause a push-pull alternation which usually signals the beginning of the end.`

If individuals naturally paired in a mirroring fashion, then relationships would not form as an outward representation of the two-part human consciousness. Relationships would not be complementary. For adult consciousness is comprised of two voices—the self and the alpha. For an independent adult to live outside of a binary relationship is unusual. Normally, a domesticated pet (dog or cat) will serve as the relational other, enabling there to be a living being within the home for the person's psyche to relate with. This need illustrates just how fundamental is the binary structure of the human mind. The binary brain compels people into binary relationships so the inner division is represented also on the outside. When an individual is not in a binary relationship, it can assumed they are in pursuit of one. Part of such pursuit, depending on the person's level of insecurity and character immaturity, involves a certain amount of attraction toward mirroring. In other words, to some degree, an individual's likeness for another will be based on how good the other person makes them feel. Put another way, if Jill loves Jack for how Jack makes Jill feel about herself, then the love is mirroring, and mirroring love is in vain.

Transition via Rejection

The transition into one's alpha identity tends to occur rather abruptly and often dramatically. This is due to the cognitive shift to the thought side, which is a quantum change. Effort to be pleasing to everyone for the pre-alpha adolescent becomes too conflictive while still in the self position. Pre-alpha individuals will eventually run into the fact that their pleasing efforts toward certain people cause others to be displeased. It becomes a catch-22 which gets solved by rejecting the pleaser-self and representing themselves as having been judged to be pleasing. In other words, the alpha-individual seeks to represent themselves as being able to offer his or her judgment as a guide, since he or she has earned the ability to preside. They no longer have the self-effort to feel loved and/or avoid abandonment. In effect, they have taken control of themselves.

Normally, the tension in the pre-alpha adolescent, in reaching a certain internal threshold, as a result of feeling unappreciated or mistreated, fuels a conscious rejection of the pleasing child-self. In other words, they give up on the effort and intent to please others. Often, they feel the child in them was mistreated, used, and was ultimately never good enough. They believe they went under-recognized. They give up on needing people emotionally. They give up on dependence and closeness for the sake of security. They feel grown-up, convicted. The child-self gets repressed into the world of Freud's unconscious. Alternatively, the process of giving up the pleaser role, or letting go of the child feelings, can be seen as a deactivation. Notwithstanding how the underneath process is characterized, it is sensed, by the individual, as a liberating experience. Furthermore, the letting go of attachment based on feelings serves as a mental backbone in relationships—namely, as the method for their own stabilization.

Part of meriting the alpha position is from the accomplished control of the emotional "self." However, it frequently transpires as a rejection of the emotional, child-self. By negatively judging the child (self) inside, they are able to use the negative connotation of childhood (dependence, emotional dyscontrol, poor judgment) to have a momentous wind of support in also rejecting the efforts of childhood—to please in effort to reflect approval. Now they get to be the parent, the teacher, the boss, etc. They are destined to take control, but by subscribing to the pleasing approach they got pulled apart and misrepresented at times by those they sought to please. When they expressed their want and intent, and yet, still were expected to do what was pleasing by parents/authorities/peers, they felt used. The pervasive acceptance was lacking, and others' expectations for the pre-alpha individual became too daunting, too constricting, and so they came to a crossroads. For the pre-alpha individual to maintain an identity of being pleasing to parent(s) and teachers, they are bound to worry about being "good enough" in those people's eyes. Yet, to maintain such approval, they would have to sacrifice independence, as well as forgoing actualization of their inner potential. The recognition of others' pleased state being subjectively held within, means others' judgment cannot be objectified. Moreover, they experience just how quickly feelings can change, and therein, how others' perspective unto them can change. As such, they feel out of control, and gradually it worsens as adolescence progresses, until the transition occurs.

When there occurs an internal rejection, it enables an individual to relate to themselves under the guise of stability being found within the control of negative feelings. However, this means their consciousness is bound to then regard people on the outside as potentially able to see or induce their negativity. Growth through acceptance and understanding is thus impeded. The effort will always be then to conceal themselves, whether by acting opposite or through avoidance. It requires living under a state of judgment. For the alpha-individual, there are downsides to taking such a role, which stem primarily from the sensitivity to others' judgment. The judgment they receive from others is threatening because of insecurity in the role of being judge. In effect, the judge is always, to some degree, insecure about meriting the position of judge. Such alpha-individuals feel most comfortable and in control at home, where the threat from other judges judging is not palpable. Inside the home is where they feel free to be as they sense themselves to be— their personal alpha-identity. Yet, most of their anxiety goes unto the outside world—where it is applied either for protection from the outside world, pleasing the outside world, or representing themselves to the outside world.

Usually, a need for control or stability triggers the shift to the alpha-minded cognition. Then, by fencing off a certain amount of the world—which then becomes the property in which their perception operates—they create stability. Therein, the individual cultivates a sense of mastery. The size of perceived property expands only as the alpha-minded individual decides the larger scope is relevant to their system. The experience of expansion then comes from a center-point, where the center-point is the perceiving individual. Layers are centrifugally added as it suits their want or need. Emotionally, the original quest to feel loved is replaced by desire to feel in control. Having powerful influence over the environment/others is part of feeling in control. In effect, the alpha-cognition takes perceptive control over those they depend on. If the individual is a child or adolescent, a period of discord ensues due to a control-power struggle with parents. In their alpha-system of belief, parents exist to do for them what they need. Thus, for others to control them, in opposition to what they seek, is completely antithetical to their aim.

In complementary relationships (with a self-individual), the alpha-individual will stand in judgment, advertising possible acceptance by dangling rejection. The rejection may not fully occur, but it is a palpable potential. The process of rejection is an outward representation of what the alpha-individual did internally as part of gaining control of themselves. In relationships down the road, it enables rejection of self-personality individuals, effectively terminating the relationships. This is necessary since self-individuals have a significantly harder time giving up on relationships. The alpha-individual's self-representation is tied to those they have authority of or for whom they are responsible. A house is an empty box without the people it houses. In such analogy, the house has representational dependence on those who are sheltered within. The pleasing dependence role is that maintained by the natural self, whose sense of internal control and stability comes most naturally from the pleaser position—seeking acceptance and to feel good enough through growth. For the alpha-individual, a sense of internal control is derived most naturally from within the controlling position within a relationship (the parental role).

Binary Relationships

When newly separated from home, and in a state of psycho-emotional independence, an individual exists in a *narcissistic* state, basking in the ability to judge themselves however they want and do whatever they feel. For the natural self, there occurs a tremendous sense of liberation. For the alpha-individual, omnipotence is felt. Usually, this narcissistic state is unable to be sustained, and the individual is drawn into a binary relationship. For the alpha-individual, they feel more stable having someone else to judge and focus on. For a suppressive alpha-individual, the relationship enables vicarious expression. For expressive alpha-individuals, there becomes someone to receive the externalized emotion. The alpha-individual knows they must represent the judgment they embody without hypocrisy. They must uphold the value of their judgment by expecting it to exert influence over others. This ties into the alpha-justification they use as a foundation to empower their sense of stability and control, and the righteousness for which they occupy the alpha role.

When the human being is understood as having emerged from a single life source, then it is logical to assume the human being contains all potentialities. In other words, anything which can be felt, thought, or intended by one person must therefore be a potential occurrence within each. The more one fears these aspects of themselves, the more they will seek to keep such elements on the outside or separate from themselves. Experiencing something one is conscious of but cannot perceive as oneself creates a conflict. For example, if an individual is compulsive about their house being clean, then perceptively they are always seeing the dirtiness of things and seeking to clean it away. Such individuals relate to natural dirtiness as a problem, as it is bothersome and threatening to their sense of internal cleanliness. If an individual accepts their own subconscious dirtiness as not a problem, as "normal," then no longer do they perceive dirtiness all around them. Perceiving dirtiness occurs in effort to separate from it—to not be it. On an interpersonal level, people interacting with such individuals may feel dirty or muddying. Such individuals, in relating to the critical thoughts toward others as a problem, may try to come across as very accepting and nice. This becomes work for them, however, since it is compensatory in character. The critical tension will thus build, and often gets expressed explosively within their binary relationship, or in the form of physical health problems and exhaustion.

Push-pull alternations in a relationship have been previously conceptualized as a sign of insecurity, and thus overall emotional immaturity. In emotionally unstable individuals, fears of loss are intense, and their relationships are peppered with volatility. However, push-pull relations between two individuals in a binary relationship is a natural phenomenon. There are periods where it feels like each is acting in ways to get the other person positioned within their frame of control. The teeter-tottering tug of war is in effort to re-situate their position along the loss-love continuum—the place where each feels comfortable, and where the relationship can be more stable. Sometimes, there is no change in set point. Rather, the act of resetting is reassuring to both. The cyclical experience is one of pain then relief, where the relief of pain provides the momentum to reconnect in a passionate way— which is what was sought all along. But for most relationships, the push-pull dynamic is a subtle, undercurrent which enables change.

The electromagnetism running between the alpha-self pair is sensed as tension—like the excitable foreplay between cat and mouse. Each seems to understand where promise exists, contained within the other. The push-pull alternation serves as the base pattern for a binary relationship. Then, for the interaction to become more intimate, it has to grow deeper—it has to change. When two complementary individuals are experiencing electromagnetic attraction, they travel like a wave—alternating up and down, back and forth, to and fro—seeking to come together. Usually the progression slows and the relationship takes on a stable, mutually comfortable distance, which outwardly looks to be within normal limits for a married couple. The journey however does not cease. Life ensures each will have to change, to grow. Each individual hopes they have something the other person needs, and perceives the other person beholding what they need. However, nothing can be gotten without a sacrificial giving. Thus, within every complementary love relationship, there exists an alternating wave pattern the relationship travels. When significant change is taking place, the ups and downs increase in frequency (how often) and amplitude (how intense). This is sensed as instability, and insecure feelings become intensified. The pendulum swinging provides times of increased intimacy, but so to, at other times, the pair becomes more distanced when alternating away from each other.

If either individual believes the relationship with the other is a detriment, then they will have a certain level of resentment in making sacrifices. Often, martyrdom results. This type of scenario cannot be sustained without a significant imbalance of power and control. The inherent problem is in mutual gratitude being unable to develop. The relationship will be based on indebtedness and masochism, and thus cannot be nurturing or growth promoting. In contrast, the more each feels fortunate to be with the other, the more the relationship will have gratitude and humility imbued in it. These two qualities—humility and gratitude—necessarily must develop for a binary relationship to achieve long term growth and unification. In the end, the goal will be, in the accounting of their marital life, for each to believe themselves fortunate for having been with the other. In general, to feel fortunate, whether in retrospection or day-to-day, each must be able to recognize their own weaknesses, and see clearly the strengths in the other. Otherwise, there is little to be thankful for, and it will be impossible to marvel at their life.

The alpha-suppressor's perception of the expressions from the self personality is instrumental in determining the success of the binary relationship. To see the expressions as a threat to their stability or reflecting them personally, then motivates the alpha-suppressor's attempts to "fix" it. For the self-expresser, this creates a feeling of being unaccepted due to their primary identification with their feelings. What they long for is simply to be able to express their feelings without having more insecurity as a result. Simply being listened to—their emotion received—is a needed outlet for the self-expresser. The passive reception for their emotion, plus or minus mild reassurance, is seen as understanding, and thus sensed as acceptance. Combined with the discharge of chaotic feelings from inside, a secure feeling comes for the expresser in the face of the suppressive person's calm containment of the emotion.

An important dynamic to recognize within a binary relationship is—who holds the plug? Meaning, who would end the relationship. Almost always, it is the suppressor, especially if the individual is an alpha-suppressor. The fear of rejection and/or abandonment is much more poignant for the self-personality due to their psychological structuring—where their sense of internal goodness and outward security is tethered to the relationship with the alpha-individual. Their effort to please the alpha-individual, or be of functional value to the alpha-system, forms the scaffolding of the self-individual's thought and intention each day. In effect, this provides the limits and boundaries which circumscribe the world they must consider. Thus, the threat of losing structure for not being good enough causes significant trepidation in the mind of the self-individual. Threats to end the relationship are thus commonly used by some alpha-individuals to exert control or influence when they perceive a lack of control or are feeling insecure. Though the effect acutely gives them an increased sense of control, it is only gotten by reflecting control of the self-individual's emotions or behaviors. Underneath, the self-individual will feel more insecure, and this increases the likelihood of the self-individual seeking to establish an alternate relationship to lessen the anxiety associated with being trapped in a relationship with somebody who may leave them or reject them. As a result, gaining an increased sense of control comes at the expense of an ability to trust.

Relationship struggles within a binary relationship surface when forces begin to oppose rather than balance. Opposite traits should be complementary in a relationship, and the binary relationship depends on certain character traits existing in such a way where the other person brings a complementary balance. However, excessive insecurity triggers too much defensiveness within a complementary relationship, allowing volatility to take hold. Relational insecurity is determined by two elements—the ability to sustain a relationship (being good enough for the other person) and the capacity to cope with loss (abandonment, betrayal, rejection). Attempts to lessen the intensity of one's sense of dependence can take on several forms. Usually, a reduced sense of dependence is begotten by increasing one's sense of control of the other person. Possessive behavior is a good illustration of this, being driven by insecurity which the individual seeks to assuage through a grip-tightening approach. A relatively equal amount of insecurity in the other person potentiates a positive regard in being controlled and/or treated in a restrictive, possessive manner. Such couples, composed of moderate-severely insecure people, can usually find a stable balance along the control-controlled continuum. Yet, the tendency for insecurity to grow by feeding on itself makes stability elusive since insecurity tends to be like a drug, and the person like an addict—always seeking more.

At some point, the possessed/controlled individual will become less hopeful of ever being good enough or pleasing enough, and thus will feel suffocated rather than safe. There is an important line between an individual feeling loved/wanted versus used/objectified. Once a person recognizes they are being treated greedily and possessively, they become wrecked with the notion their partner does not want what's best for them. They recognize their partner's selfish pursuit to have total control, rather than affection. Attempts to self-activate and stand-up for themselves are usually met with possessive anger, and then the relationship takes on further instability from the combustion of push-pull dynamics. Where the break-up line is which gets crossed depends on each person's self-esteem and ability to tolerate loss. The lower a person's esteem (subjective value), and the less capable of handling loss, the further away will be the line. Often, by the time it is crossed, there is not enough willpower to get out of the relationship—to offset the fears—and so the relationship tends to remain intact, though volatile and erratic. The erratic back and forth is intended to power a change, usually a breakup, but the fears of loss or being alone, often, keep it from fragmenting all the way. Certain relationships like this may last a lifetime since each person is impotent when it comes to letting go or accepting loss.

When an individual believes their negative feelings are potentially hurtful to others, then they will regard avoidance of expressing upset as "loving." However, the other person, the one being "loved," cannot sense the lack of negative as positive. Usually, the other person doesn't regard the individual's feelings as a problem. For them, in reflecting themselves off of the anger, it is the thought—of being unacceptable or not good enough—which internally causes torment and increases insecurity. In turn, this will spur insecurity behaviors which have a likelihood of inciting more anger, therein perpetuating the cycle.

The inherent potential for positive creativity within a binary relationship is tremendous. However, existing alongside the positive potential is the potential for negative results. When each seeks to maintain themselves, and control what they receive from the other person, the relationship becomes a struggle. As within most relationship struggles, the use of expressed negativity takes ahold of each individual. Neither is willing to receive and contain the negativity, and so each can only reflect it. Thus, the negative energy bounces back and forth between them, and both wither in the process. Assuming positive expressions and efforts are given, each will gladly receive those. Naturally, in the giving of love, one seeks to see the love reflected, and may become insecure if there is no outward show of love from the other. The insecurity will come forth negatively, however, rather than positively. Positivity given to the other out of love will grow in love, where, over time, there will be a positive fruition from what was given.

Belief System

The significance of the alpha-system (system of belief, perspective) is due to the cognitive style of an alpha-individual, where information from the outside world (including behavior from others) is judged without cognitive awareness. A filter gives immediate representation of the incoming information as relevant or not. For information to be processed, it is first filtered as related or unrelated. Once it passes this step, if relevant, then the data will undergo cognitive processing where it is given representational meaning or judgment. The judgment is inscribed into the alpha-individual's system so to maintain a sense of power and security of thought.

Alpha-individuals maintain their internal judge in such a way where they are independent of any one person's judgment of them. Options for a structured value system, such as religion, for which they can hold themselves accountable, are pervasive. Most develop their own value system based on the morality of their parents, commonly held societal standards, and a cherry picking of beliefs from various sources. Initially, they structure their system such that it may be outwardly represented without being deemed unacceptable, despite being self-serving in aim. Beliefs will change based on the composition and character of those an alpha-individual has taken responsibility for, since ultimately those individuals (as perceived by the alpha-individual) serve to represent him or her. The nature of the binary relationship (alpha-self) is such where, within the expressive medium of the relationship, there is an expression of mutual-self (shared self) and control of mutual-self at the same time.

The alpha-system is a value system, best visualized as an upside down triangle, where existing at the bottom (vertex) is the core motivation unto life. An individual's value system can be seen during times of sacrifice, where more distant or shared values—those further from the base or core of an individual's value hierarchy—are unable to be sustained. When an individual is challenged by life, adaptation usually requires letting go of aspects of themselves (feelings, ideas, expectations). The prioritizing of values along life's journey is unavoidable. Unfortunately, conflicts within an individual— and between individuals alike—are normally the result of a battle between prioritization of values.

An alpha-individual may subscribe to an outside system for which to derive his or her alpha-system. An outside-system provides a structure of thought and a shared point of reference. This avoids having a closed system, and is often integral in sustaining a binary based system (family). Outside systems are plentiful across cultures, and usually take the form of a religion. A religion serves the function well since it contains a higher power (greater alpha), thus absolving the alpha-individual from the creationist role. Moreover, an outside system provides an objective source for the self-individual to envision/consult, and thus, there exists a pressure release portal to lessen the explosive potential of a closed system. More secular value systems need to be created, however, since religion is off-putting or untenable for a significant proportion of the population.

By giving up the self-position relative to others, alpha individuals subscribe to a system of control and predictability. They seek to deliver on their thoughts, believing that if they do things the right way, then the outcome they want will materialize. They believe in their perspective, and seek to fulfill it. What is believed to be the driving force/belief behind the desirable behavior from another, as well as what undesirable behavior is reflected to mean, is based on an individual's belief system—what they know or have experienced. For example, if Person A is accustomed to Person B seeking to make Person A feel better or bring positive energy unto Person A, then Person A may believe it is because Person B believes Person A deserves to be made to feel better. If Person B begins having frustrated reactions to Person A's complaints, Person A may reflect Person B no longer believing Person A is right, or that Person B no longer cares about Person A. Person B's point of view however, in actuality, is conflicted with other demands they are facing, and with an expectation for Person A to recognize Person B's dilemma. Person B is likely then to reflect Person A's complaints as unsupportive and threatening, thereby feeling misunderstood or under-recognized. Person B's efforts to please and adapt positively to Person A were believed by Person B to have been appreciated and seen as loving effort, and thus feeling increasingly known by Person A along the way. For Person B, it is sobering to realize Person A never really knew them, but only reflected their own feelings related to Person B. Thus, when Person B needed Person A to understand them, Person A was unable to do so. Thus, the interpretation of Person B's undesirable behavior by Person A is erroneous. In fact, the interpretation is opposite to how Person B believes themselves feeling/believing about Person A.

Since most long term relationships are binary (composed of an alpha-individual and a self-individual), the values of the alpha-system should be well understood by the self-individual. For the self-individual functioning within an alpha-system, trust in the alpha-individual's judgment is essential for relational success. If the alpha-system is constructed primarily to serve the desires of the alpha-individual, then the judgment of the self-individual will always come from a source of want/desire within the alpha-individual. Stability will be elusive from the changing nature of wants/desires. Judgment will always center on what the alpha-individual thinks/wants. An alpha-individual's system of thought is designed to maintain stability and positional relevance, and thus, making changes to the system is very difficult. Moreover, a self-individual functioning within a binary relationship cannot significantly change the alpha-system. Seeking to do so is a threat to the system and thus, independent of the logic, it will be seen as wrong—simply because it violates the structure of judgment, power, and control within the system/relationship.

Two possible goals exist for the alpha-individual's system—a dead-end, closed system which seeks to meet their desires, or an open system which seeks to nurture growth through a giving of themselves. If the alpha-system is self serving, then mutual benefit can only be sustained if the alpha-individual can reflect back mirroring approval from the self-individual, making it a win-win. However, once a child is brought into the relationship, then the system becomes triangulated—where a back and forth mirroring can no longer occur. The more beings (children, dependents) brought into the system, the more difficult becomes the balance of input and output to sustain homeostasis or stability.

Roles as a Parent

When a parent is in the self-position, it causes the child to make an erroneous reflection about themselves. Since such a parent is seeking to please their child, or protect them from negative feelings, the child must reflect needing such external care. The ability to internally process their negative feelings, as a result, remains underdeveloped. They focus their attention on identifying things to get upset about, expecting others will recognize the legitimacy of their upset and subsequent entitlement to be pleased. When thinking begins, they will expect others to be as sensitive to them as they are to themselves. When the parent is relating to the child from the self-position, the child's sense of themselves is outwardly tethered to feeling loved by the parent. However, they are unable to internalize the feeling if their parent is seeking themselves to feel loved. The more the parent reacts emotionally or defensively to the child's fearful or angry expressions, the more the child must regard their feelings (and thus themselves) negatively.

When parenting from the alpha-position, the parent does not emotionally depend on the child, and the parent does not seek to please the child. They do not play to the child's judgment of them. They care for the child but are not personally threatened by the child's feelings. A child's feelings can be seen as threatening a loss of control. However, doing so is reflecting to the child a need to be controlled. Excessive insecurity from the alpha-position results in an anxious need for transparency and control, thus producing the "helicopter parent." The children of such parents tend to experience themselves as causing concern and needing to be controlled, therein diminishing the child's self-development. A resultant sense of needing to feel better propels adolescents to try drugs, and thus drug problems are more prevalent in those who have q helicopter parent.

From the alpha-position relative to one's child, if the parent's self-feelings are entirely cut off, and thus unavailable for their child to mirror, then the child's emotional development will be compromised in favor of thought or representational development. In other words, the child's sense of goodness and esteem will be tethered to their outward performance and/or how well they are outwardly regarded or judged. As grown-ups, such individuals are very confident in their system of thought, their perspective, and do not internally feel empathic feelings. On a personal level, others experience them as emotionally cold. Care from such individuals is not felt, but rather is represented through their actions. From their standpoint, however, such care is normally provided by including the other person in the benefits of their efforts. The more representational is their "care," however, the more potentially objectified or depersonalized the other person will feel.

Maintaining the alpha-position in relationship to one's child provides the space for the child's emotional self development. When mom's relational style is rooted in the self-position, it will force the child into the alpha-role. Since a child is only able to judge based on their immediate feelings about something —like or don't like, want or don't want—seeking to please them or keep them happy will have a "spoiling" effect. The child, perceptively, is unable to feel "loved" like mom seeks to make them feel it. Rather, they are quick to develop wants and have difficulty not relating to those wants as "needs." The more a developing child believes their feelings require others to make them feel better, the more they will represent "love" as getting their way. The effect is to position the child in the expressiveo-alpha position, where control and influence is wielded through the externalization of how they feel. Predictably, this leads to more interpersonal conflict or "drama" as a teenager, and throughout life. Prior to the pubescent activation of thinking, the child personifies their feelings. When expressing upset feelings, the child needs positive thought for stabilization. No matter the character of the parental response, the child will reflect the parental response as thought or judgment. Thus, mirroring the feeling simply gives the child a thought formation of the feeling being a problem or representing a need. Thus, the feeling will escalate until stabilized or expired. In light of this understanding, the ability for a parent to provide a positive thought for the child to reflect, in the face of upset feelings, engenders their child with the necessary coping tools. Otherwise, come adolescence, they will believe they have to keep feeling attachments active for their stability.

A child forms beliefs about their feelings and their desires by reflecting off of their parent's responses to them. When the parent displays emotion— whether anxiety, anger, or sadness—it will necessarily be seen by the child as a thought reflection about themselves—indicating to the child their expressed feeling is a problem or they are upsetting. Experiencing their parent becoming destabilized in the face of their expressed upset turns the child against themselves, forming a belief certain feelings are a threat. The pitfall of the self position in parenting one's child occurs in the child's state or expressed upset being turned into thought and then giving self effort to make it better. This creates a mirrored thought about their feeling state rather than providing a complementary or stabilizing thought. As a later adult, the expectations for the environment's reaction to one's expressed upset is determined by the parental response to such feelings received as a child. A male child will emotionally grow in complement to his mother. Thus, the more emotionally expressive mom is, the less expressive will be the child once they complete childhood. Within the mom-son binary relationship, if mom is an expresser then her son will end up as a suppresser. Put simply, they will be emotional opposites. Thus, imbalance will occur in a proportionally equal, but emotionally opposite manner. In contrast, a female child will usually mirror mom emotionally rather than getting into a complementary relationship with her.

Summation

From the feeling side of consciousness (self position), one's activity goes toward what they care about. The self-identity is inseparable from their personal effort, and they are always bound to their activity. Thus, their activity will either be directed unto themselves (fulfillment of desire) or unto another. Their level of care will be reflected by the amount of activity or time given. They will naturally be attracted to those who reflect the most thought positivity, and will be sensitive to negative or critical thought. Since they do not attach their negative feelings outside of themselves, they cannot perceive the expression of their negative feelings as determining the rejecting thought from another. They cannot regard the expression itself as a threat since they identify as the expression.

Every child begins life in the self position. The starting point is their drive, which translates into want. The want is to experience secure, stable, fulfilling unification. From the self position, the want is always sensed as being toward a fulfillment of thought, through growth, and thus existing outside of them. Usually, the thought is represented through others, and thus, the self-personality seeks to be loved. If the fulfillment of a thought is self initiated, then the thought is simply the self desire. However, if the outside thought is given the first move perceptively, then the self will be properly giving of themselves. Doing so is not possible during the developmental years because of the need for a net consumption of energy from the environment. A fulfillment of desire during childhood and adolescence breeds a sense of capability. Thus, from the self position, self desire makes the first move unto the environment. On the other hand, the initial process from the thought position involves seeking self fulfillment through feeling. Since the perspective, from the thought side of consciousness, is toward feeling, the source of fulfillment is sensed to be contained within internal feelings. Thus, they pursue self fulfillment through doing what feels best. Initially, because their primary focus is on how they feel, they perceive themselves feeling a certain way because of the environment/others, or because of their body, and will then form thought/action based on such feelings. From the alpha or thought position, such a perspective is a reactive one, believing the environment makes the first move by causing their feelings.

The maturational process of cognition is different for the self-individual versus the alpha-individual. The starting point for the self-individual (once thinking consciousness begins) is to fulfill thought desire. The endpoint is to fulfill truth outside of themselves, where none of the self goes into fulfillment of self desire. The starting point for the alpha-individual is to fulfill or control feeling. The endpoint cognitively is to give thought outwardly so to nurture positive feeling. Self fulfillment never comes through fulfilling self desires, and alpha fulfillment is not found through being in control. In order for a binary relationship to be stable and fruitful, the alpha thought must be the first step—where from the alpha-individual's perspective, they have taken responsibility for their thought, for their judgment. They cannot perceive reactively within the relationship—as if their decision was secondary to feelings caused by the other individual. Their thought must come first—it must be the first move which sets the relationship in motion. From the flip side, from the self position within the relationship, the individual is called to let go of self desire making the first move. This enables the self-individual to give of themselves within an outside thought structure. Without this process occurring, a power struggle and an acrimonious playing of chicken or the egg is unavoidable. Then, each is in a position to easily point a finger at the other person in defense of something they did or said. Each can always find reason to reject or disregard the other relative to themselves. For, to error, is human.

The Adam & Eve Metaphor

Eve ate the apple. This imbued her with the psychological capability to internally create, and thus a longing to know. She could also conceive of what could be different. In effect, the tree of knowledge introduced imagination into her consciousness. Naturally, she saw the positive potential for her imagination. However, for her internal creations to externally manifest, she needed Adam to have the same ability. In such loving vain, she fed Adam from the tree of knowledge. Therein, each had become a thinking mind. Each had undergone a psychological pubescence. During a time of Adam's absence, Eve wondered if she could be more fulfilling to him. Eve began imagining what could be different about her, so to be more fulfilling. She imagined being more like Adam. She reflected on what she was not, thereby imagining herself equipped with what she lacked. Doing so magnetized a serpentine energy to come in fulfillment of her imagining. Adam returned and saw Eve interacting with the "serpent." At that moment, Adam formed a thought which had never before been conceived. Prior to the apple, he would not have been able to internally, independently conceive *what* Eve was doing. Rather, Adam would have had to pursue understanding in connection with Eve—and thus, he would have been bound to collaboratively pursue *why* she was doing what he saw. Doing so in the above scenario would have lead him to the proper understanding—Eve was seeking to be more fulfilling to him. Instead, Adam constructed his belief internally. The reflected thought he formed, however, was an inversion of the truth—Adam believed he was not fulfilling enough for Eve. It was at that moment, when, in an instant, creation occurred, with a bang.

To understand relationships, as well as the behavior of individuals within relationships, the metaphor of Adam & Eve brings us closest to the garden of understanding we seek. Once both became imbued with the psychological space to know, then both were able to judge. This meant Adam could reject Eve and Eve could reject herself. The significance of the psychological space born within them may be likened to an individual's pubescence, wherein the internal ability to reflect forms a triangle of perception. Two spaces thus form —internal and external. Eve's relationship with her internal space was to sense a lacking when Adam wasn't with her, into which she perceived being not good enough. Adam's relationship with his internal space was one where he sought to control himself. Adam's internal space would fill with negative feelings, in contrast to Eve's internal space which, as mentioned, would fill with negative thoughts. Since each was perceived by the other as the cause of their internal negativity, the other became a threat—to reject, as sensed by Eve, or loss of devoted care, as sensed by Adam. When they were together no problems occurred because Eve was able to direct herself toward Adam's thought which was in nurturance of her positive effort. Since each partially beheld the power for creation, as a complementary pair, they were able to create externally, therein existing in a shared paradise. However, creation could occur also within each's internal space. Naturally, Eve sought to grow more fulfilling to Adam, but she mistakenly thought Adam's absence was a result of her being unfulfilling. Similarly, Adam wrongly reflected her effort to be more like him as if she was rivaling him, as if he were not fulfilling enough to her. Each was thus seeded with a misbelief, which took them into separateness, into the wilderness of individuality.

The more an individual seeks for the wilderness to materialize fulfillment within them, the deeper into the desert they have journeyed. Adam had to go forth caring for himself, and thus having to face his own rejection—which man projects outside of himself, and thus must wade forward against his own current. Eve gave birth to children who themselves longed for internal fulfillment. She was thus bound to provide what she had sought. Eve found value in doing so, but unfortunately, the more she gave of her effort, the more needy became her children, and the more they fought with each other. Eve saw how she had given birth to rejection. Her children bore an internal emptiness which they gave to life—wherein each sought to both fulfill and protect their internal space through consumption and rejection. Thus, destruction and division became engendered within creation, intermixing with the impulse to grow and unify. The positive potential which existed within her children, though she could see it clearly, they could not. Eve lamented how they struggled to fight off the darkness within, and how their plight to lighten their insides drove them further into the wilderness. Because each shone the light they could not feel within, they were drawn to each other. The exchange of light brought life, and so creation continued.

Existing in a paired state is necessary for each to overcome their blindness, so to keep themselves focused outwardly. Yet, for a pair to become a stable, luminous entity, both have to willfully give their light. To do so, however, means each has to stop prioritizing their own internal fulfillment. Each must turn away from their internal space in order to not express rejective energy into the relationship. Otherwise, the lack of fulfillment gets attached to the other, who is then rejected. In the relationship between Adam & Eve, a misunderstanding had occurred, then a misbelief, resulting in a misdirection into the mirror. Subsequently, every born human was initially conceived by way of their parent's desire to fulfill or to be fulfilled. However, each child is born reflecting themselves as the cause of their parent's behavior toward them. Each child is thus born as a mirror, wherein they either take on their parent's self-reflection, and thus be like the parent, or take on their parent's self-projection, and thus be the mold of their parent. Not until puberty, where they become imbued with the ability to know, and thus the capacity to create, may they begin to separate from the parental image. Thereafter, the journey into life is an individual's journey into themselves—an experience of themselves—whereby, through growing awareness and understanding, each may break forth from the mirrored image of themselves internally, thereby stepping into gnosis. To transcend the reflective captivity, however, each individual must first grow into a thought acceptance of themselves, and then, each must let go of their directed effort toward internal fulfillment. Therein, the internal space—where self-reflective thought is created—diminishes, gradually, as there occurs internally an integration of each's Adam with each's Eve.

LOVE & FEAR

The Binary Psychology model, as presented, arises from the natural duality which typifies the adult consciousness. The duality permeates nature. Light and dark, good and bad, love and fear, unity and separation. The tethering force is one of attraction and repulsion, ultimately existing in a balance which prevents each from consuming the other. When fear is understood to be the opposite of love, then the phenomenon of equating fear with love becomes illuminated. When fear is termed love, fear has essentially consumed love. This is dangerous since it is love which provides the counterforce to fear. Also, entitling fear, in the name of love, to be externalized onto others is one of the ways fear gets passed on. To see another as in need of "care" or help is usually done by perceiving their negative aspects. Fear truly breeds fear.

An internal harmonization between one's feeling element (self) and one's thought element (alpha) requires each's effort be directed toward the other. Otherwise, each is seeking dominance over the other through an internal opposition. The more the self element seeks self-fulfillment (feeling loved), the more their consciousness will gravitate toward fear. The alpha element, on the other hand, if controlling the self element in order to feel more in control, will struggle with anger. As long as one's two-part consciousness is in conflict, one's primary perceptive focus will be rooted onto oneself—what one feels or what one wants. However, binary harmonization requires each's primary focus to be on the other, in sacrifice of their self-reflection and sense of security. Only then does the fear or anger transform into outgoing, positive activity.

Most mood problems manifest within relationships—with one's partner, in parenting one's children, or within the web of familial relations. The greater the psychological or emotional dependence on someone, the more fear-based tension infuses into the relationship. Naturally then, when an individual feels chaotic, their anxiety can quickly turn into irritability toward those they believe they need. Bringing their frustration forth to others causes relational instability because others take it personally and become defensive. Also, the more dependent an individual is on another, the more sensitive they will be to the other's expressed negativity. Doing things to make the person feel better, if done out of fear, empowers the negative feelings. Thus, it cannot be legitimized as love. To love the other is not to fear the other or worry about the other's feelings relative to themselves. Love strengthens. It does not take away the negative feelings. Rather, it enables one to transform the negative feelings into positive effort. For unto others, love regards them positively when they are feeling or acting negatively. This can only be done through understanding (this does not equate to approval). Thus, one's fear feelings or negative thoughts related to the other person's negative mood can only impede understanding.

The purpose of relationships is for each to genuinely experience themselves. This can be demonstrated through the patterns of attraction. In general, an individual will unconsciously gravitate toward someone who will compel their growth. For example, if an individual believes their anger is a problem, then they will get with someone whose fear of loss or rejection is paramount and who turns to expressive effort when feeling threatened. This is because the person who believes their anger is a problem will have a shut down, walk away approach in dealing with conflict. The defense works to gain influence over the other person, therein enabling a sense of security. However, since it is an induction of fear which gains control, any security achieved is not built on a foundation of love, and thus, will be chronically unstable or underscored by resentment. Love, as a method of being, pursues understanding and confers acceptance. Love seeks to know the other person and trusts in positive intent lying beneath the other person's surface upset. The formulaic expression of the phenomenon is: if character trait (A) stems from not having a certain fear or deficit (B), or from a relative strength, then those who have the certain fear or deficit (B), or weakness (1-A), will be attracted to individuals with character trait (A). In other words, an individual is consciously attracted to those they believe or sense can "save" them or structure their purpose. However, the fruition of such requires purposeful experiences and recognition of negative aspects of themselves.

No individual can consciously know themselves as they are being experienced because their perceptive consciousness is motor oriented. Thus, the human consciousness must be constructed to be part of a loving bond where one's attention is on the other. To reach the point where one's focus is primarily on the other requires a maturation into selflessness—a feat most individuals cannot ever accomplish. It is not selfishness standing in the way normally, but rather fear of trusting another with the care of themselves. Ironically, the less an individual is able to trust themselves to not give up or to withstand temptation, the less comfortable they will feel trusting the other.

The beautiful irony of every binary relationship is appreciated in the qualities normally loved about the other—when one's consciousness is in a perceptive state of defense—become the characteristics which are most threatening and despised. Fear turns life upside down. Fear, when given thought, produces the experience of itself. Fear binds people to their belief system about the world in such a way where the world is the reason for the fear. At present, the current culture is running low on love, and there is a rising surplus of fear. Fear cannot increase without love decreasing, and vice versa. Love cannot be hijacked by words which seek to represent it, as if one may possess it for another. Love is not simply a feeling, nor is love just a thought. The more one seeks to possess love, the more elusive it will seem. Love is a verb, a sacrifice, a giving of oneself. Love regards the other and seeks to give of oneself for positive growth within the other. Love is always outgoing—like the sun. Love knows no end and is blind to loss. Love does not wield itself as a weapon, and it attaches no strings. Love entitles nothing in return.

Love does not reflect, and thus the human consciousness is blind to it. It escapes from possession and breaks any rule assigned to it. Words refer to love but stand hollow upon its ground. The mind knows love's print but cannot reconstruct the foot which made it. Love is unable to put itself first. It cannot be quantified—it stands above qualification—and thus, cannot be judged. It cannot be remembered or decided. Love is experienced, it exists in the present. Each depends on love's forgiveness to rebalance, to be merciful when the ego has gotten stuck on itself. Love lets go of oneself for the sake of another. Love fills every space. It is effervescent. Love comes forth and craves to be shared. Love cannot envy for it senses no threat, and love takes no pride. Love cannot be given just as it cannot be taken. Love is a triangle where fear, anger, and sadness are trapped, enabling the transcendence of each. Love is everywhere and within everything.

Opposing Forces (fear)

The life force most shaping to people's lives is fear. People end up forming their personality to protect themselves from feared elements through the use of tools within their consciousness. Because those threatening elements are inclusions which get projected for an individual to experience, people are attracted toward a sensory relationship with themselves—where they, through mirroring interaction, seek to know themselves. The attraction is mainly due to the perception in the other of what they want more of—or feel the need for—within themselves. This will manifest externally in the form of attraction toward another person, and a relationship will form. Because what was seen initially and pursued is not found, each begins to frustrate. In order for the relationship or bond to remain stable, each needs to let go of previous beliefs or desires. This process of self-sacrifice is emotionally painful and psychologically tortuous, and is only enabled by a love which comes forth from the nucleus.

Fear is simply a feeling. It is rooted in the loss of connection or separation inherent within the life experience. When the feeling is turned into thought, then effectively the fear is externalized or given "reality" on the outside. The fear gets explained as if being caused by things happening from the outside. The less one is able to perceptively attach with people, the more impressionistic will be the thoughts associated with the fear.

The big bang of creation was an explosion, a loss of equilibrium. The accidental nature of the disequilibrium which occurred imbedded chaos and the potential for loss into conscious awareness. Fear itself came about as a reaction to the loss of attachment and control. The ability to love is initially nonexistent within the human consciousness of the child. Once it is infused, the impulse to love causes inner tension between the ego (which is attached to reflections of oneself) and the directional force of love—growth. The battle between these two elements, in effort to establish an equilibrium, necessitates a gradual increase in ability to love throughout an individual's life. Since fear emerges from the ego and is defensive, it will distance an individual from the inflow of love, and block any outflow.

To demonstrate how directionally opposite fear behaviors are from the direction of love, a simple but abstract truth must be recognized, and its effect given description, namely—the closer Person A is with Person B, the more fearful Person A is to lose Person B. For a general understanding, it is appropriate to say—the more Person A loves Person B the more fearful Person A will be to lose Person B. This generalization remains mindful of the multitude of representations the term *love* may carry, and thus would not pass a discriminatory deposition seeking to find exception. Nevertheless, assuming love or closeness grows for another individual, so does the fear of losing the person. Then, for to continue growing closer, fear's directional force must be overcome by a greater force compelling further closeness. For that to happen, as Person A gets closer to Person B, the greater must become Person A's affection for Person B. Otherwise, person A's pursuit for further closeness with Person B will stop.

To illustrate how fear detracts from love, consider the couple—Mrs. Jones and Mr. Jones. Mrs. Jones seeks to be unconditionally loving at every moment, both of action and of thought. Doing so, at times, upsets Mr. Jones when Mrs. Jones is doing things for others and thus not attending to his desire to spend time with her. Furthermore, at times Mrs. Jones does things for other people, triggering Mr. Jones to feel threatened (for various reasons). In taking issue with her actions, Mr. Jones can only express internal discomfort and beliefs rooted in a defensive judgment of her actions. Mrs. Jones will feel mischaracterized, and confounded by the injection of negativity where Mrs. Jones previously saw none. Mr. Jones then can only advertise her needing to be protected, thus transforming the fear into "care." However, for Mrs. Jones, the "care" is made of negative energy, and thus is palpably depleting. To love is to give of oneself for the betterment of the other, and thus love would support her loving efforts unto the outside world.

Excessive fear imbedded in an individual's conscious perception of themselves relative to the outside world causes the ego to perceive defensively or reflectively. This self-centered reflecting off of others is to strengthen or refine their conscious understanding of themselves as they come into fruition, thereby better adapting to the environment. However, if the reflective thinking continues into adulthood, then others will increasing feel objectified since the individual is not seeking to understand them. The lack of established resonance with others gives them the experience of being used, judged, or rejected.

If the source of fear for a child is also the source of protection, then a paradox occurs. To maintain psychological stability, there has to occur a split of consciousness. Once puberty occurs and consciousness splits naturally (able to internalize judgment), then the perceptive problem manifests in their conscious perception of others. During adolescence, paranoia about other's behavior toward them increasingly takes hold of their thinking. In other words, the fear feelings produce a negative thought about others, which then gets reflected back as a perception of others being threatening.

Fear has a magnetic effect on itself, where it brings about what is feared. Fear will realize itself. When the human consciousness fears something, one becomes more vigilant or "on guard" for something to happen. Thus, fear sensitizes one's consciousness to realize the fear. In effect, what one's consciousness expects, one gets. This can be appreciated within relationships, where what is guarded against occurs nonetheless. This is because fear causes one to erect certain defenses which unwittingly make the other person feel not good enough or unaccepted. This will then trigger defenses in the other, and the cycle between them will build on itself.

The love force which compels people toward one another may be equated to other longings which surround basic needs, such as hunger. To build on the analogy, there are times where food has been consumed and one is satiated or "full," wishing to take in no more. Similarly, there are times where relationships cause a bloating of the mind. If one eats something toxic (food poisoning), and thus experiences a direct sickness from what was eaten, one's senses (taste, smell, sight) become scarred by the certain food. Thereafter, they will experience a repulse whenever the food comes into their sensory experience. Bad relationship experiences tend to affect individuals in a similar way, whereby relationship "anorexia" can easily take hold. The threat of pain and potential loss is guarded against through either restricting oneself from a love relationship, or by taking an obsessive, controlling approach toward the other person. In equal proportion, from the flip-side or self position, individuals who have suffered abandonment often engage in excessive clinginess and relational dependence. Both scenarios are common and problematic within the domains of authority and control—where a disproportion, if excessive, creates a parent-child dynamic, and thus, the relationship is not as complementary.

It is impossible to truly see ahead of oneself. People are continuously subjected to letting things go. Difficulty giving over control or forgiving someone who has caused hurt are two mental characteristics which strain an individual's sense of connectedness. If the intra-psychic guide within everyone's psyche could structure itself in the opposite direction from where their anxiety points, people would find themselves much wiser. This is because of the narrowing, confining effect fear has on one's knowledge base, experiences, and depth of understanding. Fear reflects itself from the environment. It causes more fear, and trends toward a logarithmic progression which spirals into nothingness. Fear is unable to communicate love energy or shine positive light. Outwardly, fear shows itself lifelessly or darkly. It is consumptive and seeks for positivity to come soothingly from somewhere or from someone. People are always inclined to externalize their problems—for "help." Those who help, however, expect to be helpful—meaning, they expect to see the fruition of their positive giving. A lack of fruition suggests the person being helped is a toxic personality—who is only able to externalize negative feelings, and who is unable to turn and give of themselves. This wears down those trying to help—who will be repelled by a growing sense of helplessness within them. Inevitably, their efforts wane.

Opposing Forces (love)

If thought of in terms of energy vectors or directional forces, then the force of fear (of losing those one depends on, or losing control of oneself) is a directional force going in the opposite direction to the natural force pushing for growth (love). This latter force drives all children down the road of autonomy and independence. They seek, through increasing capability, to feel good enough or loved. Most grow into young adults who continue their effort to feel loved or accepted. In seeking to feel loved, one must attend primarily to how one feels as it relates to others. Thus, judging others by how they are unto oneself causes a circling back of the vector. Young adulthood, then, involves building esteem and a sense of worthiness.

The fear of loss, or experience of chaos, is imbedded in the human condition from the separation of birth. The threat of loss thereafter is inseparable from dependence. Since the child remains functionally and emotionally dependent, they seek to eliminate such needs. Once reaching independence, it's natural for an individual to have a weariness about dependency developing. Thus, young adults frequently remain in a state of protected narcissism whereby they serve their own judgment in subservience of self-desires. Thus, the dating process involves a gradual fusion of overlapping circles. Each circle represents an individual in a state of independent detachment. Theoretically, the two circles are able to grow into one, and then, as one circle, grow in love. The love is represented by the amount of goodness coming forth from the circle. To see the situation as analogous to stars versus black holes may be helpful in giving it illustration. To say *love shines forth* is descriptive and metaphorically true. If love is conceived of as *two beings functioning as one soul* (as stated by Aristotle), then two beings fusing into one soul will radiate love and can be thought of as forming a star. Oppositely, a relationship which produces negativity, and where love is fought over, is like a black hole, within which everything is consumed, and thus, no love shines forth.

The motivation to love must overcome the conscious desire to feel loved or in control. Both preoccupy an individual's perception, thus distracting them from the giving of effort to what is perceptively before them. Doing so causes conscious vulnerability and a heightened tendency to react defensively. Since perception based on fear obfuscates the surrounding world, it is the fear of loss/rejection/betrayal/abandonment which determines the amount of positive energy or love a person may emanate—where the amount is inversely proportional to the amount of conscious fear.

The ability to love, and to receive love, requires overcoming the physical animalism and fear-ridden ego. Love is earned by overcoming the daily self-fascinations and enabling an awaking of consciousness. To quote Samael Aun Weor, who has written extensively on the consciousness of love:

"People live sleeping and dream about love, but they have not awakened themselves to love. They sing about love and believe that love is that which they dream about. When a human being awakens to love, he makes himself conscious of love and recognizes that he was dreaming. Then and only then does he discover the true meaning of love. Therefore, before that awakening, we only dream about love. We take those dreams as reality, believing that we are loving. Thus, we live in a world of passions, romances which are occasionally delectable, disillusions, vain oaths, carnal desires, jealousies, etc., and believe that this is love. We are dreaming and we ignore it."

The idea of love and loss being on different sides of the same coin has its roots in ancient mythology, and can be appreciated within eastern thought. The more someone loves another, the more frightful becomes the thought of losing them. Thus, greater love must traverse a more perilous path—for it requires opening up and giving of oneself. It necessitates courage and a willingness to overcome the vulnerability. Within a binary relationship, two forces predominate—love (closer) and fear (distance). The fear of loss or hurt pressures each toward self-protection. Seeking to protect oneself opposes the ability to be giving. It thus detracts from one's ability to love.

The fallibility of human consciousness is due to the lack of innate inclination *to love*. Rather, the desire to feel loved is clearly evident in children. However, the ability to sustain feeling loved becomes more difficult as one grows in autonomous capability. This is because the child wants to feel the parent's love for who they are becoming. Frustratingly, since the child is growing apart from the parent's sense of control, it is impossible for the parent to give them the internal reassurance they desire. This frustration, however, is the impetus for the child to develop their capability, propelling growth of function. Parents reflecting wellness to the child, rather than trying to make them well, allows the necessary space for the child to grow in ability to make themselves well. If a parent can reflect wellness in the face of their child's outcries of upset, then the child will be able to integrate the feelings and pursue an individualized solution. Such a parental approach does not involve effort to make the child feel better or feel loved.

Defensive Consciousness

Despite almost everyone believing they have things inside which would disgust or repel another, it is each's handling of their insecurity which most gets in the way of relational success. An individual's fear of loss escalates as they get closer to another, and feels like a loss of their independent self or a giving over of control. Either way, an increase in the sense of emotional dependence—and thus, an overall increase in vulnerability—is the rule. To compensate for the intensifying fears of loss (loss of self reliance, control, part of self) an individual will engage defense mechanisms imbedded in their personality to create a sense of being in control. Insecurity often drives behaviors in effort to get the other person to illustrate their affection, and to reiterate the relationship's intimacy point. People of high interpersonal insecurity are hypersensitive to slight drawbacks from others, and often will overreact to situations if fears of loss infuse too greatly into their perception.

The defensive consciousness (one's consciousness in a state of defense) is bound to think about the other person's treatment of oneself. Judgment of how the other is negatively affecting oneself occurs automatically. Also, it occurs from a self-centered position, whereby one judges the other as if what the other is doing is centered around oneself. Believing the other person intended the negative effect within oneself makes it feel personal. People tend to revolve what they do around themselves, rather than around an intention to cause certain negative feelings in another. When consciously seeking to protect oneself, then one's focus necessarily goes onto one's sensory system. In effect, this causes a reflective sensory experience, wherein they perceive being made to feel. To believe another is causing one's feelings, allows for the expression of one's negativity while consciously believing one is doing so in righteous defense of themselves. Behavioral avoidance is a defense against experiencing vulnerability. Usually, the avoidance is blamed on negative aspects of the situation being avoided. However, being isolated from one's purpose of being increases conscious anxiety, experienced in the form of either paranoia, worry about one's body/health, or panic. When an individual goes in the opposite direction from their individualized fruition, it is always because of conscious fear. Avoidance leads to greater and greater degradation of individualized power, and a dissipating sense of control. If fear can be overcome, then the individual's ability to love (sacrificial giving of self for the betterment of another) becomes proportionally greater than the average individual.

To judge someone is to close one's mind around the person, entrapping them in one's system of thought. The more one forms such judgments, the more one becomes closed off to others, and thus, the more one becomes a victim of such judgments—whether through others' reactions in equal measure, or through an isolation of oneself. Fear causes the mind to conclude, to judge, and thus, to some degree, to make an assumption. Fear closes the mind so to protect one's self-construct (identity) or one's feelings. The space between people is the undefined "reality" which individuals, generally, effort to uncover. The potential for experiencing what is longed for, as well as the risk for suffering what is not, is inseparable from interpersonal life. Thus, relationships involve a guarding of oneself while seeking fulfillment. Furthermore, the more one's mind traps itself in judgments, the more empty space remains as unchartered experience. Regret or remorse within one's past (in memory)—through "what could have been" thinking—then grows within these spaces.

The problem caused by defensive reactions stem from the shift into a defensive perspective. An individual in a state of defense can no longer openly receive the environment or maintain an open interaction with someone. The defensive perspective consciously judges how one is being treated or regarded. Since there is no conscious open mindedness, there is no ability to grow in understanding of oneself through experience of others. Moreover, in a judgmental state, one can only project what is within oneself, in the context of one's belief system. Thus, casting judgment of another person or of an occurrence, will necessarily be as the person or the event applies to oneself. Since consciousness cannot know the experience others are having of oneself, any judgment in regards to others' treatment of oneself is myopic and alienating.

Negative reflections of oneself (as being the source of upset or feeling rejected) are immediately defended against through a defensive posturing of one's perspective, where the other person is judged to be "bad" or "wrong." It is easy to focus on the negative aspects of another, therein dismissing their judgment of oneself. However, just because one finds fault in another does not equate to the other's judgment being wrong. The more an individual tries to control their reflective experience, the more interpersonally or behaviorally disordered they will be. Controlling their own reflections comes at the expense of perceptively connecting with others. For instance, individuals with schizophrenia are unable to form interpersonal attachments, and thus, their reflections are projections of their own internally occurring rejection. Not being able to attach to others shows their inability to attach internally to themselves. In other words, they are excessively afraid of themselves to the point where they cannot form an internal relationship between feeling and thought. Rather, they are still fighting to separate feeling and thought into relatable objects.

The perceptive errors committed by one's consciousness when in a state of defense predicate the difficulties experienced within personal relationships. To triangulate one's perspective, where one becomes both the judge and the victim, is to monopolize "reality" through one's singular perspective. When defensive, the mind judges how one is being treated by the other, thereby attaching directly to them as the cause of the negative feelings inside oneself. The other person will feel illegitimately blamed. Any attempt to explain themselves will be perceived as if they are returning blame. Getting defensive themselves will start a fight, as each will realistically see the other person as having started it. However, when perceiving defensively, one will not be able to integrate what is being said about oneself.

The independently-thinking human mind, when postured defensively, is impenetrable. When normally interacting with the environment, one's body is primarily operated as a motor apparatus to fulfill desire or enable achievement. Open mindedness allows one to have a creative, positive interaction. When perceiving defensively, however, consciousness steps backward of the body and relates to it as a sensory organ. Consciousness judges what one is sensing or feeling as if it is being inflicted. No open mindedness can exist in such a state, for one can only attend to how they are feeling. Expression of how one feels comes with the expectation for help or recognition and, ultimately, alleviation. The defensive perspective is entirely self-centered and thus, when defensive, one is unable to consider the outside perspective of another. Rather, one is trapped in only perceiving how they are "being made to feel." In effect, one is blind. This is ego-blindness.

An individual who is ego-blind can only regard others for how others make them feel. They can only see others as others relate to them. To form an actual relationship, the ability to separate one's feelings and desires from one's regard of another is necessary. Often, another's ego-blindness is run into like a wall. No matter what is done or said or demonstrated, the regard remains only for how the ego-blinded person is feeling. Put another way, if Jill is judging Jack based on how Jack is making Jill feel, then the thought judgment occurring is only a reflection of how Jill feels. Thus, Jill's system of judgment, or belief architecture, cannot stand on its own. Jill beholds no independent system of belief beyond doing what feels best or most secure. For one to be locked in a battle with their own feelings, they must believe their feelings to be a potential threat to their stability. Thus, there will be some amount of conscious energy put into making oneself feel better or in hyper vigilance of how one feels. As a result, a constant strain is common within such individuals, and exhaustion is experienced generally. Further elaboration of ego-blindness is contained within the chapter on efferent disorders.

Fear as Love

Increasingly, children are becoming adolescents who sense a fear of loss as representative of them caring. To worry about someone, thus, is internally felt as "loving" someone. The giving of love feels naturally entitled within people. So when individuals give love to another, they believe the other is receiving it as such. However, fear works in the opposite direction, because it is a self-protective force which seeks to secure oneself. Love is a giving of one's positive effort for another, and having an optimistic belief in the other. Love always grows. Thus, giving fear under the guise of love degrades the relationship's potential for synergy and undermines growth. This synergistic potential is sensed as being contained within a relational unification. However, with increasing love feelings for someone, necessarily the fear of losing the person also intensifies. The fear of losing control of one's individuality adds to the fear and contributes to the difficulty of unification.

The amount of love a person expects to feel internally, or seeks to feel, will drive their level of emotional neediness. Seeking to feel loved internally detracts from their ability to give of themselves. An underdeveloped, immature self-personality seeks nurturance to enable their maturation. In such individuals, fears of abandonment are intense and usually stem from a history of excessive cognitive and/or emotional dependence on parents, or traumatic loss. Such people will appeal to individuals who have an equally proportionate issue with loss or abandonment—those who seek to establish a parental level of control through a dependence on them. Such a relationship can be sustained, as long as growth of the self-individual is suppressed. If not, the self-individual will mature within the stability and structure afforded to them and will gradually seek increased individuality and autonomy of mind. This is usually experienced as threatening to the person in the alpha role who seeks control via domination. An increase in the self-individual's confidence and self-initiative may thus cause the alpha-individual's insecurity to flare.

Standing in the way of providing nurturance is usually an individual's insecurity feelings (derived from loss fears and self-criticism), which potentiate possessive behaviors and rejective beliefs. Though one's beliefs are organized logically, and outwardly seem legitimate, their perspective is often rooted in the effort to reduce anxiety through restriction or avoidance. Alpha-individuals who are the most highly achieving (money, power, beauty, success) tend to be the most intolerant of any outward display of weakness or insecurity from their partner, and tend to have intensely high expectations for the individual they are with. Ultimately, the alpha-individual seeks for the self-individual to provide functional and structural support for their system of thought. The representational outcome is what is valued by the alpha-individual. Self-individuals, on the other hand, identify their value through their effort and intent. For illustration, *stage-mom* (alpha position) behavior is where a focus on representational outcome (winning) comes at the expense of the child's effort and intent. The judgment, as it can be represented, is given all the merit by such moms. However, the child can only sense their effort and intent. Ultimately, the child wants mom to reflect happiness or approval. Driven by mom's indignation at an unfavorable judgment, the child will often feel misrepresented, and thus victimized. However, it is mom's insecurity in her own physical appearance which truly drives the entire effort.

The force of insecurity (fear of loss) within a binary relationship accounts for most of the anxiety people experience. This base fear normally manifests as excessive worry about the other's judgment, as well as fears related to loss of control. The problem produced by such fears, within a binary relationship, is from fear undermining each's ability to love the other. Most sense the fear of losing someone as a natural consequence of loving someone. However, the meaning of *to love* involves not a feeling of love, but rather a giving of self (effort, intent), or a pursuit of thought understanding and accommodation. To focus on one's own feelings thus takes focus off of the other person, and then traps one's perspective on seeing the other person only relative to how the person aligns with one's feelings. This creates a narcissistic bubble which can be impenetrable, and is thus used defensively (out of fear). *To love* is independent of the feeling of being *in love*. Thus, *to love* is a sacrifice of one's feelings for the nurturance of the loved one. One's fear, however, will arrest the progressive ability *to love* the person. *To love* someone fully, there has to be the ability to sacrifice what one wants from the other person. One's security will have to be compromised *to love* someone, otherwise the "love" is fear based—meaning, the loving behavior or expressions are in effort to reassure one's own insecurity.

To truly love another, there has to be a letting go of oneself—specifically, the desire to feel loved and secure. The protective bubble must be broken through, otherwise one's relationship will be between oneself and the other person's reflection of oneself. When anxiety over loss determines one's treatment of another, then technically such behavior is self-serving. Insecurity is so often the basis of adolescent relationship behaviors, that pangs of insecurity are used as reasons to get upset and entitle reassurance from the other. In other words, any behavior causing insecurity in the other person gets labeled as inappropriate and the person is accused of misbehaving. Naturally, the blamed individual feels misrepresented, and eventually will feel constrained by the restrictions. Once this happens, they feel controlled and increasingly react angrily. At this point, the opposing forces within each begin to push and pull at each other, and the relationship grows inherently unstable. Since both individuals are primarily serving their own insecurity, the relationship will continue as long as each's current agony doesn't outweigh the fear of losing the other. Partly, the agonizing feelings serve to harden each's heart unto the other, thereby enabling them to let go. As mentioned, especially for self-individuals, side-stepping into another relationship is common, buffering their experience of aloneness with the loss. A lily pad like relationship pattern can be a problem if it keeps the person from ever being independent—independence being a developmental milestone which must be reached for secure relationships going forward.

The current epidemic of entitling hurt or fearful feelings is injecting excessive chaos into relationships, now surfacing within workplaces and schools. Humans are drawn to get what they want, and thus, will identify with whatever gains influence over others. Through being unwell, the more one experiences being cared about, the more one will identify aspects of themselves as unwell, believing in the power of such feelings to be regarded. Expressed in rational form: if Jill, in going out with her friends, does not intend to cause hurt feelings in Jack, and yet, Jack develops hurt feelings—as if Jill intended to hurt him—then Jack's judgment of Jill will be erroneous. Furthermore, for Jack to then entitle recognition for being hurt entraps Jill in a catch-22. For Jill to attach to Jack's feelings legitimizes his experience and causes Jill to question herself and her behavior.

When one is not feeling well, the more one entitles care from others, the greater the resentment toward others who are unable to satisfy one's expectations. Also, gratitude for care received is more elusive. In addition, the more an individual has lived (matured), the more they tend to set firm limits and not treat the world based on their feelings at the moment. Especially debilitating are the situations where an individual's anxiety and overall negativity paint the world with indignation—where the person feels angry at the world (blameful) or neglected by the world (uncared for). There is no genre of behaviors more toxic to a love relationship than entitled feelings stemming from fears of loss, since they exhaust each's effort toward feeling secure.

Two Forms of Love

There are two ways in which someone may be loving—thought love and feeling love. Feeling is the substance of action, meant to be purposed by generating experience through one's activity within the world. If one's intent is for the growth in those around them, then feeling should flow into one's activity with positive intent for the growth of either oneself, others, or the environment. Feelings are supposed to compel one to grow, and thus, feelings cannot be expected to be pleasant in and of themselves. Furthermore, feelings are meant to exist as fuel for growth, but should not be used as conscious information for which to judge the world. One may judge themselves for their feelings since one's handling of feelings is one's own responsibility. The experience of feelings cannot be directly controlled unless one seeks avoidance of life through avoiding experiences or masking feelings with chemicals. The more one puts their feelings as the determining factor for how one acts or what one does, the less one is able to put the feelings into willed activity. If one's creative intent can be for the betterment of one's environment or the growth of others (rather than to subjectively feel better about oneself) then one is appropriately loving. When one's effort is properly outside of oneself, intending to have a positive, growth-promoting effect on the world, then the inner sense of pressure or gravity gradually dissipates

The sympathetic nervous system mediates an individual's feeling effort. It is responsible for the surge of *fight* or *flight*. However, its role cannot be defined only as it is noted outwardly, but rather is best understood for its role in an individual's everyday activity. An increase in adrenaline accompanies an increase in sympathetic activity, therein evidencing the intention to increase motivation, increase energetic effort acutely, and intensify an individual's attention—all purposed toward fulfillment or accomplishment of their goal directed activity. It enables creation through the surge of effort, through the extra giving of themselves. However, for the surge to have a creative impact as they intend within the world, it has to be properly positioned internally so it can push from behind, increasing effort and decreasing conscious apprehension. Otherwise, an individual will experience the increased adrenaline as agitation or anxiousness. If an individual experiences the sympathetic output within them as indicative of a threat outside of them, then the surge in adrenaline will be disorganizing, where action gets impeded, producing a relative paralysis.

The love an individual has for themselves is most legitimately measured by their ability to step forward into uncertain space despite being afraid—to take the leaps of faith toward self-realization, to grow. This self love is the willpower or energetic will to grow, to achieve. It is always moving forward unless someone is actively fleeing or trying not to be themselves. However, it is the sympathetic surge from within which enables the extra step, the striving effort, where an individual pushes past themselves and into new experience or new growth capability. When an individual perceives the source of discomfort as their internal fear related to the situation (rather than the situation), then the sympathetic surge is able to be channeled into overcoming the internal fear. As a result of the willed surge of adrenaline, the conscious sense of fear is lessened, enabling one to step out into uncertain space—where, naturally, creation is able to occur.

Thought love is purposed outwardly, since thought is purposed to communicate or interact with the world outside of oneself. Loving thought is always understanding. Loving thought builds an understanding of the world and others, and accepts the nature of what happens to oneself. Loving thought does not reject or denigrate. Loving thought is accommodating. The parasympathetic nervous system mediates this thought love, and is the binary complement (opposite) to the sympathetic nervous system which handles the self-love.

The complementary relationship between the parasympathetic and the sympathetic nervous systems is best demonstrated by the nature of the male erection and ejaculation. The erection is produced by the parasympathetic nervous system—the relaxing, accommodating nervous system. Oppositely, however, ejaculation is caused by the sympathetic nervous system. People assume an erection and ejaculation are different intensities along the same neurological path. The phenomenon demonstrates the nature of creation, which always takes two elements—the accommodating, positive thought (erection) and the positive energy (ejaculation). Necessarily, the erection is needed first—as a structure of understanding and acceptance, and signaling thought desire. Then the creative feeling effort can be given within such space. However, if the thought is negative (critical, rejecting, denigrating), then there is no positive, supportive space to fill. In such a scenario, an individual will either give up their effort or they may try to fight their way in —but eventually, they will have to recognize and accept the rejection.

The forward, growth oriented purpose within life is made obvious by the self-growth which occurs during childhood. The feeling self, while one is alive, is active and imbued with growth potential. The feeling self seeks to flow forward and be outwardly regarded for the effort and capability along the way which, for a self-personality, necessitates someone to keep outside structure for them. The self-individual will always flow toward space which feels positive to them—where they reflect thought understanding, where they are most likely to grow. The direction of the self effort is always toward positive—for growth and connectedness. They tend to believe the thought expressed by others as to how they are being experienced, and try to grow more effective with their effort. However, when they run into rejecting thought, they become distrusting. The self-individual internally senses chaos and misdirection when without a thought structure to operate within. The amount of growth they will manifest from within the thought structure (e.g. relationship with alpha-individual) often depends on the level of thought understanding or nurturance provided to them. Certainly, without a thought structure within which they are understood, creative growth will be limited. They need to be able to find areas where they can positively reflect themselves, spaces where their creative effort can occur positively and for the benefit of everyone.

In summary, there are two forms of love occurring between individuals—

feeling love and thought love. Feeling love translates into quantitative effort, which is a function of both intensity and time. Thought love translates into qualitative understanding. The intent for both forms of love is growth of the other. Similarly, love for oneself channels expressively into growth oriented activities. Thought love for oneself occurs as a belief in one's potential for growth and positive purpose within the world.

The Cell Model of Consciousness

2

2.1

INTRO

The "I" of one's perceiving consciousness cannot know itself—for it is the observer, the processor. Life is the experience of thyself, and only through such experience does an individual ever come to know themselves. The observing self is individualized consciousness—the mind. An individual must reflect internally off of feeling or thought in order to think about themselves. The reflection forms within one's sensory awareness. In other words, people's experience of life is their individualized experience of themselves—the reflected form they create. This allows for self-reflection. Self-reflection gives the capability for internal change. Any internal change will be imbued into an individual's life-experiences. Thus, an individual's world can be changed, even dramatically depending on the significance of the internal change. However, to know themselves requires the experiencing of themselves, for no one may identify themselves as simply an isolated feeling or self reflective thought.

For the human mind to form a concept of itself, it must use analogy or metaphor—to be likened to something separate from itself. The cell membrane can metaphorically represent the ego consciousness. The cell membrane has the ability to attract or reject, take in or let out. Upon birth, the initial desire is to feel secure, and free of desire. Once the ego is imbued with the capacity to triangulate its judgment—or think—then the desire is for a sense of being loved and accepted. The ego seeks to depend on no-one, but independence itself does not lead to fulfillment, since being free of the tension of dependence does not produce happiness. Consciousness perceives outwardly and is unaware of the internal processes governing itself. Its role is to get what is sought, and avoid or repel what is foreign or threatening. Also, it aims to keep what it wants to retain, and get rid of what it doesn't. Metaphorically, the nucleus of a cell is symbolic of the self, as one is originally conceived. It contains the intelligence dictating function or purpose. The nucleus is the truth of being and is dynamic—it receives signals based on one's experience and is imbued with universal consciousness. The nucleus creates entities to imbue the cell's outward perception with intuitive awareness. The purpose of the nucleus is to express itself. To do so, it must infuse a higher level of consciousness into the cell membrane (as its being analogized to represent perceptive awareness or consciousness). To some degree, the nucleus acts as a receiver to the frequency of life energy from the sun, and thus, within each cell, the nucleus is the source of creation.

Having no ability to reflectively know oneself prior to the realization of oneself, life itself is the metaphorical experiencing of oneself. Therein lies the opportunity for corrective insight, acceptance of oneself, and a raising of awareness. Since life is a manifestation of oneself, realization of oneself is unavoidable. Whatever is consciously feared and guarded against, believed to be intolerable, denied within oneself—nevertheless, is magnetized into one's experience for one to undergo, to thus understand. Anything the membrane is conscious of but rejects, or seeks to avoid, is a shadow of itself. Until the necessary change of consciousness occurs, however, the membrane or ego cannot recognize the image of itself within the shadow.

The natural attachments formed by the developing ego will necessarily have to be broken in order for the individual to become independent. A fruition of one's individuality is genetically compelled. The first step is to achieve independence from one's parents. True freedom comes from a detachment from materials, including detachment from people. It is the conscious fear of loss which most often drives people's actions within their primary relationships. The process of loss, as it occurs consciously, is very painful, and the feeling/thought experience usually contains thoughts of death because of the emotional desire to escape the painful feelings. The process of breaking the attachments to others, to oneself, and to one's beliefs, should not be reacted to as if the symptoms are indicative of an underlying problem needing fixed. Rather, the sickness or symptom production is most often secondary to one's dynamic being or doing, rather than a condition. The orientation of one's ego relative to one's nucleus, and the relative alignment in time/space, has a significant causal role unto one's conscious experience. When the ego is having difficulty letting go or taking the necessary growth steps—and thus, with the passage of time becoming more out of sync with the directive energy from their nucleus—then symptoms manifest.

One's consciousness includes an inner awareness of—and belief system about—oneself, as well as an outer awareness and belief system about the world outside oneself. Levels of consciousness expand in a stepwise fashion, each having a unique orbital frequency. With each step, one's belief system must change, including a belief in one's dependencies or needs. Because childhood is purposed to culminate with independence, a letting go of needs is necessary for detachment. Thus, an increase in relational frustration and separation anxiety precede developmental steps toward independence. The child or adolescent, in first pushing away, will then alternate to a more clingy, dependent state. This back and forth continues until the necessary letting go occurs, enabling the step forward in conscious awareness, whereby their tension dramatically dissipates.

If one's conscious awareness could know itself, then there would not be the need for mirroring. Just as physical mirrors allow one to see themselves physically, psychological and emotional mirrors characterize the nature of one's experience. The human child must learn that they are looking at themselves in the physical mirror—otherwise, they will try to reach into the mirror to interact. An analogous process must occur psychologically and emotionally, where one's perspective comes to recognize oneself in those around them. In other words, within relationships individuals are provided a framework to reflectively come to know themselves. Each may see where problems arise because of them, even though they perceive the problem as being caused by the other.

Due to the nuclear direction occurring unconsciously, conflict necessarily comes about as conscious desires are frustrated and attachment is threatened. Because the signals and the creative work coming forth from the nucleus occur in a cyclical fashion, the membrane's desire for absolute control is always undermined. It must always face people and objects coming and going. To be in total control, one must be detached, for everyone's existence is rooted in the individuality of sensory experience provided for by the membrane. It is impossible to sacrifice one's sense of individuality to the extent so another's ego feels totally in control. The membrane's base conscious fulfillment is defense or protection, and so no human being—by entirely dissolving their membrane or conscious awareness of themselves as an individual entity—can truly merge with another.

The three elements of conscious desire existing naturally are—to feel loved, to feel secure, and to feel powerful or capable. They are preferred in said order, and if the preferred feeling or sense is unable to be gotten, then one's perspective will seek to fulfill the next desire in its place. This is significant within relationships, including the parent-child relationship. The parent-child relationship, from the child's conscious experience, is one which begins with them feeling secured through physical closeness. The positive feeling mom is able to provide to her baby and the delight in feeling their closeness enables the child to feel loved. However, with growth, the child encounters more negativity from parents in the form of anxiety or anger. If the amount of positive love energy is too little because of excessive negative emotion, then consciously the child will turn toward attaining a sense of control or security. They will seek to have things happen as they expect. To some degree, since it is externalized, such security requires reflecting control of the environment. In other words, if the child's external world is positive and as desired (i.e. in control), then they will feel good. If others are trying to make them do things they don't want to do—or if others are not doing what they want them to do—they will feel threatened and react negatively. As adults, being compulsive with one's environment and/or controlling of others stems from this childhood pattern of attaining a sense of conscious stability. If the child is unable to establish a sense of security through control, then they will consciously pursue power—the ability to influence the environment or interact with the environment in the fulfillment of want. If the child is unable to consciously influence their parent to fulfill their want, then they turn to their functional capability to do or get what they want themselves. If fulfillment of want is enabled though expression of upset, then the individual will never learn to channel their negative feelings into their effort to change things or make things better.

The ego consciousness seeks for things to go its way, as it expects. When things do not, upset results. The self-centered consciousness will perceive mistreatment in whatever was done, as if it was done to cause their upset. To the immature perceptive mind, everything done is related to oneself. Consciousness will see what it wants to see in order for one to then react in a way to get the outcome one seeks or to fulfill a desire. Consciously, a person will believe themselves having had no choice but to do (X) because of (Y) occurring. However, the truth of the matter is that (Y) was brought about by the conscious fear of (Y). Response (X) was thus planned for, without consciously realizing how planning to do (X) brought about (Y). If the response (X) has always been the defensive response to handling an occurrence such as (Y), then (Y) will continue happening until the individual consciously awakens to response (X) being out of alignment with the truth of their being. They must face (Y) and respond in the other direction (1/X) for the cycle to stop happening. For it is within the response (1/X) where they are then able to go forward with increasing awareness and alignment with the truth of their existence.

An individual can only know themselves based on beliefs from early reflections, experiences of themselves reacting to things which happened, and internal exploration of self (introspection). However, the progression of time (change) makes one's consciousness unable to know itself in the present. Everyone innately seeks to establish themselves, to form a fixed, stable world which revolves around them in an equilibrium of power, control, and feeling loved. However, the reality of universal connectedness (life stemming from a single source) prevents individual deviation from universal truth. Thus, stability must be found through an approximation of truth. The more an individual's belief system and direction of being is out of alignment with their nuclear truth, the more negative energy arises within them. The negative energy becomes conscious agitation, restlessness, or apprehension. Maintaining the negativity inside of oneself is detrimental to one's system, and so consciously people attach their negative feelings to others, or blame the environment for pressure they sense within. Doing so enables people to consciously feel as though they are able to alleviate the negativity. However, for an individual to believe the source of their negativity exists outside of themselves, they must continually maintain a source, or find cause for feeling the way they do.

Since the nature of consciousness is to realize oneself, unknowingly it will magnetize negative aspects of itself. One's experience will always entail interacting with various aspects of oneself through the perception of such elements in others. In other words, the human perception will preferentially see one's own problems in others in effort to control or relate to the problem(s). This allows the problem to be kept in front of oneself. The two-part human consciousness can represent itself as a feeling or a belief, and thus can always create itself. People will angrily try to change the mirrors reflecting negatively at them, seemingly unable to regard the other person as having a similar perspective, seemingly never seeing the true equal in the other. As a result, negativity in the form of rejection or judgmental disregard is actually a rejection of oneself. This strains the internal sense of bonded stability. An individual goes to great lengths to keep themselves isolated within their perspective—both of others and of themselves as they relate to others. Ultimately, realization of being rejected must occur, where the individual recognizes they were never entitled to believe themselves better or "right" relative to others being "wrong." When one's perspective steps out of its own representation and into a mode of giving to others, one gains significant insight based on the nature of interpersonal space. Specifically, since the space between is able to be filled with one's effort and intent, true control of the judgment from others is begotten through the giving of oneself —where there occurs a continual growth of understanding—both of oneself and of others.

To consciously feel happiness, one must be surrounded by happiness, for it cannot be manufactured autonomously. Individuals must develop the capacity to love in order create happiness. People bring of themselves and seek to reflect positivity. But unless one grows in their regard for others, whereby they seek to give of themselves to others, then happiness will always be elusive. The ego attracts itself. Like must face like. Each person must overcome certain beliefs or attachments—certain impediments to their growth. These will be experienced as painful situations where no answer exists, where one feels powerless to control the situation, and a loss of control is imminent. Since the ego itself is consciousness, times during development where an expansion of consciousness is required are frequently accompanied by internal anxiety which comes physically and seems to communicate a foreboding event. Classically, this is a panic attack—where from out of the blue comes a conscious awareness of nervousness and dread. This is a time of imminent change where, to continue forward properly, a letting go of attachment or support is necessary. If an individual understands the nature of such anxiety, and that it reflects a painful but positive process, then they will be able to respond appropriately rather than letting the symptoms guide their behavior. Naturally, the ego seeks to gain control over the anxious sensations by looking into the environment to see if one can attach blame to something, and then go about restoring control through correction of the environmental trigger. If nothing can be found to blame, then an individual will turn their conscious focus on their body, believing something is internally wrong. This leads to a hypochondriacal pursuit to find a cause to the panic which was experienced out of the blue. Ironically, it is consciousness itself which needs to change, to grow, to heal.

Shifts of consciousness occur dramatically, but signify a transition which must be made for continued growth forward. Whether it occurs from outside of a person's awareness—like a panic attack—or within a relationship struggle with another or the world in general—the person is subjectively overwhelmed by the experience. Everyone has times, throughout their life, where they can no longer stand how they are, where they wish to escape life, to give up. Recognizing these periods as preceding a growth step of consciousness provides the proper direction for which to deal with such symptoms.

Growth

If everything is contained within the whole, and an attraction naturally exists toward one's opposite, then through understanding and acceptance of one's opposite may one achieve an internal integration of oneself. The two-part consciousness (manifested as the two-sided brain) represents a separation state. The goal, within consciousness, is toward unification, which explains the human propensity toward relationships. Each seeks to get what they will come to learn, in the end, is what they must give. Despite each's perception of being a separate entity within an individualized existence, every individual is bound to experience themselves as though life is a virtual manifestation of their essence. Within the psycho-emotional domain, growth occurs in awareness of oneself and through an increasing depth of understanding of the nature of life. Quantum shifts of the individual consciousness are readily apparent, and each level of consciousness is distinct from the level preceding it. Thus, a fundamentally new perspective or "I" is formed.

If each is constituted by two poles, whereby each pole has two possible vectorial directions, then the alignment of each must occur relative to the other. One pole, through incessant magnetic activity, seeks to fulfill internal thought fantasy. The other pole, though electrification, seeks to structure a system which operates in a mechanized, predictable way, free from individualized impulse. The magnetic pole can be directed either toward itself or away from itself—to give of one's effort or to get for one's pleasure. The electric pole can either be oriented positively or negatively. A positive orientation of thought—open-mindedly—seeks to grow more understanding of the workings of nature. Negative orientation is judgmental and closed off relative to change. Through the use of these two polar forces, the "I" of consciousness grows into life. Through their relative alignment with each other, proper growth can occur. The growth eventuates in a mutual balance, where the innate tension of life is transcended.

People may have a representational memory of having struggled, but often, they can not truly relate to themselves as they were then. These growth steps are an integral part of the human maturational process, and psycho-emotional struggles are inherent in the experience. If the changes of consciousness, the quantum steps forward, are not taken, then one will remain embroiled in mental conflict, experiencing negative feelings (fear, anger, sadness, pain) as a result. Prior to a shift in a person's consciousness, they will sense themselves as falling apart, unable to psychologically sustain themselves. Usually, letting go of an attachment or a need for control is being called for, but "I" cannot see the relationship to "me" as the problem. "I" cannot perceive "I" as the problem, and thus, "I" will always take to *having* problems in effort to gain control. However, for "I" to have a problem means "I" sees a problem with "me." "I" then seeks to protect "me" or control "me." Yet, the curative path is for "I" to let go of "I's" attachment to "me," therein allowing for "me" to be channeled into the connected efforts of "I." The more steps forward in consciousness an individual takes, the closer they will come toward reaching an equilibrium within themselves, and a balanced relationship with the world outside of them.

Prior to achieving a unified alignment, an individual will fear their own desire. This manifests in their life as insecurity—either of others' rejection due to being unfulfilling, or of their own loss of control. Fearing their own potential causes them to interact internally in such a way where rejection occurs. Externally, they will experience the materialization of the metaphor from the first person perspective. For instance, an individual will be both rejective of others (e.g. coworkers) and sense being rejected (e.g. boss) within the same day. Most cannot perceive they are experiencing externally their internally occurring relationship with themselves. Anxiety indicates a lack of internal integration, whereby the third person "I" is rejecting part of themselves or beholding a misbelief about themselves. This is illustrated through the attachment to an outside cause for their anxiety, where threat exists outside of themselves. However, the sensory experience of impending threat arises from within their third person relationship to their first person experience. Therefore, attaching the cause of their anxiety externally simply externalizes the threatening aspect of themselves. If an individual seeks avoidance of themselves, then they will sense the world as their unconscious embodiment. For the perceptive life experience to be structured in such a way ensures each individual lives an experience of themselves.

Expressed another way, in terms of the third-person "I" and the first person "me," "I" goes toward the world and others, while life comes at "me." Invariably, "me" gets positioned between the world and "I." As a result, any protection of "me" or effort to control "me" involves "I" interacting with others as representative of a threat. Though doing so seems natural, and relatively innocuous, the experience by others of such behavior is negative. This is a result of the protective or controlling behavior having the goal of something else not happening. For example, Jack's goal is to not get angry at Jill. When he senses himself getting upset, he "shuts down." He believes he is being positive since he does not want to hurt Jill's feelings. However, Jill experiences Jack as being angry at her, and she experiences his "shut down" as a rejection of her. Thus, although Jack's goal was to not hurt Jill's feelings, his "shut down," as interpreted by Jill, causes exactly what Jack sought to avoid happening. When a behavior has a goal for something else not to happen, the likelihood of something of a similar character happening, increases. This is a result of the misbelief "I" has about "me" (e.g. needing to be controlled), or a misperception of others unto "me" (e.g. being rejected). People have an inherently difficult time seeing the manifestation of their thought. No one wants to realize the responsibility of their thought, or the determining power of their perspective in creating what is experienced. No one wants to let go the notion of being able to control their experience, or awaken to life being an experience of themselves. People do not want to recognize their actuality—the more threat they see outside of them, the more negative creative potential they are infusing into the environment.

The process of bringing one's identity into conscious fruition takes a lifetime. It is born out of the two-part consciousness with the attainment of a sustainable balance. To do so, each side needs to be accepting and supportive of the other. However, since the conscious "I" cannot know itself, it is dependent on the other part for reflection. Since there will be some degree of misalignment between what "I" believes and what is being reflected, there occurs tension. When a significant difference in character exists between the two parts, then by definition one part exists to reject or protect the other.

If an individual can seek to understand the experience others have of them, they will grow in understanding of both others and of themselves. Within the space they are accustomed to controlling, if they let go of control and seek to understand their effect on the world, they will find their value unto life. Having a goal toward internal fulfillment or protection of "me" causes separation from life—more distance between "I" and the world. Rather, to increase connectedness requires turning away from "me" and filling the space between the world and "I" with positive effort toward understanding others more. Bringing forth the effort of "me" positively within the environment is a relational approach whereby "me" is given rather than an approach centered around a getting for "me" or protecting the image of "me." The human consciousness can let go of the past quite freely and naturally, as illustrated by adolescents who expect their maturation to be reflected in the present, thereby being untethered to what they previously have done. One's present consciousness will carry with it the deeds done during its tenure. So the longer someone has maintained their present state of consciousness (i.e. not having taken a growth step), the more conscious memory will have built up, and the more potential energy or karmic tension which will exist.

2.2

PERCEPTIVE DEVELOPMENT

The process of nerves growing and making connections continues well into early adulthood. With such growth, an individual's understanding of the world around them deepens and becomes more complex. For a baby to recognize an object and give it a name (e.g. ball) takes a year's worth of growth in the brain, and it becomes growth upon growth for the next twenty years. The growth eventually enables the brain to conceptualize the world through abstract ideas. The rest of adulthood, then, is characterized by making deeper associations and refining one's perspective, experienced as increased clarity of view or awareness—wisdom in a cultural sense. Growth requires change and change produces conscious tension. However, this tension is simply potential energy interacting with uncertainty.

The human experience begins with a physical separation. The newborn, due to their dependence on having their physical needs met, must cope with physical separateness. Perceptively, once they grow the connections to be able to control their body, then they are able to perceive their physical separateness. Until puberty, however, they remain psychologically dependent and without a sense of psychological separateness. This perceptive state arises from a single-mindedness where the child is contained within a dependent dyad. The thought reality is controlled by the parent(s). The child forms their perceptive structure (their beliefs about themselves and the world) by reflecting a need-based cause of the world's reactions to them. Moreover, due to their direct, psychological dependence for reflections of "reality," the pre-thinking child cannot judge their parent(s) as being wrong in relation to them.

Sensory awareness produces physical feeling. Life itself is experiential awareness of discomfort. To be awake is to be in a state of change. A disturbance of equilibrium creates the negative awareness—seen in the newborn child's wakefulness as a cry out for a return to the unconscious equilibrium experienced in the womb. Growth leads to increased awareness of the environment, thus increasing their ability to form *wants* within the environment. Thus, there occurs an individualization of desire. Being consciously able to desire objects prior to having the function to obtain them, motivates the growing child to grow in capability. It also imbeds psychological frustration into the developmental period of childhood, to which the child will increasingly attribute to their state of dependence.

The ability to identify a want occurs during infancy. The ability to recognize judgment from others comes normally around age four to five. The ability to internalize this judgmental element comes with puberty in relation to what one wants or how one feels. Prior to this, a child can react to others based only on the child's reactive feeling or how the child is made to feel. Children sense themselves as directly susceptible to others making them feel a certain way. They perceive as if an emotional umbilical cord still exists between them and others. Because they exist from the feeling or self-perspective, and without an internalized 3rd-person, the alpha/judge element remains fused with the world outside of them. Their perceptive structure thus produces a two-dimensional existence.

Conscious awareness of what one wants and how one feels produces psychological emotion. The tension experienced with life drives the child to consciously organize their life into a system of being, by which they can have control and where their needs are met. Understanding comes from experience. Knowledge in the form of thought language occurs as the child grows, propelled by the need to communicate desire. Then, as puberty nears, consciousness begins to split, whereby the teenager begins internally reflecting themselves. In other words, they begin to think. This marks the beginning of the human being as a unique creature—transcending the single-mindedness of lower animals.

The Pre-thinking Mind

Initially, the child-mind operates from a single sensory consciousness, having not yet formed an independent thought element which they internally reflect upon. The thought part is contained within the parents, thus binding the child's mind to develop within the reflective experience with their parent(s). The early parent-child relationship thus comes to later characterize the thought relationship an individual has with their own feelings and thoughts.

The space between the two minds is the dynamic space of consciousness. It is within this space where the relationship occurs. The perceiving "I" of one's consciousness is initially a stream of sensory awareness. It forms ego boundaries, thus beginning to perceive separateness between self and environment. Children exist, however, in a singular consciousness. Until the child begins internally reflecting (pubescence), the experiencing "I" is dependent on others for reflections of themselves—for their reality. During the early period of childhood, the child's "I" perceives from the self position (feeling), and thus is bound to reflect off of parental thought (acceptance vs rejection) to form beliefs about themselves. Once consciousness takes on two-parts, the perceiving "I" will have to identify, or root itself, as one part or the other.

The experience of life begins as a sensory experience through one's physical senses. The physical senses are the bridge between one's nuclear "i" and the outside world. Being able to sense an environment outside oneself is the beginning of conscious awareness. It is this sensory experience which the child grows in effort to control. The effort to control one's sensory experience necessitates forming beliefs about oneself relative to others, and relative to the world which is seen as the source of satiation. The paradox is—in growing more capable, there comes an increased sense of knowing what one wants, and a desire to control the getting of what one wants—namely, a pure sense of loving acceptance. This occurs in the face of the parent(s) having to relinquish their sense of control. Like the mitotic or dividing cell which initially replicates its form internally, the child must undergo a difficult division. Thus, the love a child is able to reflect from their parent(s) steadily diminishes with the child's growth.

Awareness first comes as sensory awareness, and thus, children identify as these sensations. The child's initial self-conception is bound to how he or she feels. They regard themselves as physical capability toward fulfillment of want. The dependence on parents to fulfill their desires tethers young children psychologically to a dyadic relationship with their parent(s). Through a single-minded consciousness, based sheerly on sensory awareness, the child exists from within the relationship dependence on their parent(s). Through experiential learning, they grow a conception of themselves as they interact with and seek mirroring identification from others.

There exists a fundamental difference between the processing of sensory phenomenon which are consciously perceived as happening to oneself versus those experienced as happening within oneself. Hunger/thirst is the sentinel feeling which happens to oneself and represents a need outside of oneself (sensory tree). The difference is exemplified by the average person's sensory perception of hunger as opposed to their perception of internal gas. Hunger is consciously perceived as a phenomenon happening to oneself, and thus having a need outside of oneself (food). Internal gas, rather, is perceived as happening within oneself. Consciousness processes the sensory experience of gas in such a way where it is internalized or accepted, and thus, the gas feelings are handled through an internal management involving controlled or willed expression.

All negative sensory experiences, initially during infancy, are reacted to by crying out. This continues into toddlerhood, at which time anger, as a result of not getting what one wants, begins to manifest. If those in the environment (parents, siblings) respond to such outcries by trying to alleviate the toddler, then anger (as a sensory phenomenon) will continue to be processed as if it is happening to them. Not until the environment stops responding to their expressed upset will their sensory experience of upset become internalized. Then, they will be able to grow in the handling of their upset. No longer then does upset represent a need in and of itself, and being upset no longer derails them from their activities. Increasingly, they will incorporate their upset into their drive, whereby it gets channeled into the world as willful activity.

The first negative or noxious sensory experience of one's life is suffocation, followed by a heaviness in the chest as breathing commences. The sensory experience gets attached to the loss of connection with one's mother. In other words, within the newborn's chest, the negative pangs of life are first felt, and are imprinted as a loss of connection (later to be experienced as heartache). Not long after, an emptiness is experienced in the area of the stomach, compelling the newborn to cry out. Being fed then brings fulfillment and a return to sensory equilibrium. Feelings of disquietude thereafter will be responded to by crying out—necessarily following the template of emptiness/hunger in order to attain satisfaction from the outside. In doing so, if there is something truly needed (e.g. food, diaper change) then it will materialize. In being made to feel better, the infant attaches such feelings to needing whatever enabled them to feel better. If alleviation does not come from the environment then the infant will have to adapt their sensory perception of such feelings, whereby the sensory experience itself is no longer processed as representing a need. Put another way, the experience no longer encodes an outside need. As they grow more mobile within the environment, more self energy is directed toward intentional interaction with things. Purposed intent within the environment increases the risk of experiencing frustration, however, since limits will be experienced.

If a child's expressed upset either elicits upset in their parent or moves their parent to try and make them feel better, then the child remains attached to negative emotion needing to be either suppressed or made better respectively. When a child experiences their expressed emotion destabilizing their parent, then they affix a belief about the emotion (e.g. anger) being a problem. Then, experiences going forward—foreseen as potentially frustrating—are avoided. The more negativity an individual seeks to avoid (due to fear of themselves), the more they will try to control their experience. In doing so, however, they are not experiencing the experience, thus compromising the opportunity for growth. The more an individual characterizes the nature of something or someone based on their sensory experience, the less they will be able to understand the world outside of themselves. To judge the potential nourishment of a food based on how it tastes would lead to erroneous conclusions and eventually malnourishment. Similarly, to judge the world through the lens of one's feelings precipitates misbeliefs, especially as it pertains to the intentions of others relative to oneself. Most damaging, however, is the loss of the experience itself—where through avoidance, an individual misses out on the opportunity to travel further down the road toward knowing themselves.

Naturally, the desire to feel better or to experience better propels a young child's activity within the environment. When their perception is not solely on the sensory experience, a child's focal point can remain attached to the environment, forming autonomous intent. However, when the experiential feelings are encoded as representing a problem, thus signaling outside need, the child's focal point gets fixed on the sensory experience. Then, the motor system expresses the negative emotion until either alleviation comes or depletion occurs. When negative emotion is no longer processed as a problem in and of itself, then the child can begin to internalize or digest such feelings. Such experiences no longer will be rejected outright, nor will help be sought. Rather, the child interacts with the environment relative to themselves in order to generate an improved experience. Their focal point will not be on how they feel but rather maintained on what they are doing. Thus, despite having negative feelings, they remain attached to the present. In other words, they do not blame or entitle help because of the negative feelings.

If experiences are avoided because of fear, then throughout later development, there occurs a proportional narrowing of the individual's understanding of the world around them. Seen another way, their character will be more "shallow." Once the two-part consciousness is internally active (adolescence), being too guarded toward new experiences diminishes growth in understanding. Revolving their experience around one's feelings, rather than revolving feelings around their experience, underlies perceiving being made to feel. Perceiving as such, an individual is not growing in understanding or thought, but rather growing in the experience of their feelings at the expense of understanding. Growth can only come through the digestion of experience. Experience must be processed, whereby the necessary nutrients from the experience are absorbed and assimilated into their growing intelligence, and where waste is excreted, enabling further consumption of experience. An individual, once able to form a triangulated concept of themselves which they can reflect on relative to others, is able to generate increasing depth of both their character and their understanding of the world. Part of the character depth is being "in touch" with the complex subtleties of sensory perception and emotion. Thus, an avoidant relationship with their negative feelings leads to a distancing from certain experiential realities contained within the avoided experiences. The end result for such individuals is to remain blind to themselves, thereby having difficulty connecting with others at a deep level.

The experience of stomach emptiness during times of stress, for some individuals can be associated with a decreased ability to eat. An anorexic response to stress indicates the individual's tension is being experienced along the hunger pathway. In other words, the anorexic individual mentally perceives their stress being caused by outside circumstances, and seeks to exert excessive control over what they take in. However, in trying to reduce internal anxiety, consciousness tries to minimize taking in anything more to manage. This is because they perceive the inner chaos as being caused by outside factors, and in need of more control. In attempting to control themselves, they attach their anxious thought to food and then exert excessive control over food. What consciousness does is based on what is consciously perceived, and is actually the inverse of what is needed. This is because the uncomfortable feelings are not being processed properly as arising from within. If the sense of inner chaos is being inversely perceived, then the actual need is for more self-expressive outflow. Usually a misbelief about their anger and the need to exert inhibitory control of themselves causes the well up of tension, which then gets misperceived as coming from outside of themselves, and thus cycles on itself. The result is excessive tension trapped within their sensory system, near the hunger center, with an inability to channel it through the motor system into any purposed doing.

Once upset feelings are no longer positioned at the level of the stomach, then such feelings are able to be internalized and thus not mishandled, despite falsely being attached to the environment. An individual may thus forge a relationship with their feelings, where their feelings become less and less threatening. The line between feelings/emotions happening to someone and feelings/emotions occurring within them is fundamental to determining their experience of life and their concept of themselves. The former drives an individual to get help. The latter gets purposed through their activity. The former attaches to the world causing them. The latter takes responsibility for causing their world. The former causes them to escape from the world. The latter seeks expression unto the world. The former colors the world black and white. The latter gives color to everything.

The existence of intent is lacking in the infant since they cannot use their musculoskeletal arrangement for any purposeful movement. Once the growing nervous system makes the preliminary connections to enable the hand to grasp, then babies (no longer infants) can grab something from the environment and seek to experience it. For babies, the sensory modality is oral, and early intent is consumptive, which makes sense for the purpose of nourishing their explosive growth. Further growth leads to increased motor capability, and eventually the baby is able to walk and begin his or her toddle out into the world. With this comes a greater use of other sensory organs (touch, sight, hearing), and the next several years involve an interplay between a child's sensory system and motor system as the two develop in parallel.

The character of interaction with others—the child's personality—develops based on the nuclear or genetic potential interacting with sensory experience. Without the nuclear self, the membrane or ego would have nothing to protect, nothing for which to intervene between. As an adolescent, each is consciously compelled to detach from their parent and purpose themselves. Each conscious being has a specialized individual purpose within the greater organism (universe). The membrane, or ego, must thus respond appropriately to intuitive, directional impulses.

Children

The child uses the parent as a psychological mirror. An infant's initial sense of self comes through mirroring interaction with mom. Mom is essentially the world reflecting back unto the child what the child gives forth to the world. Thus, mom serves as a mirror of the child's being. Moreover, throughout early childhood, the parental reflections form who the child becomes in relation to their natural self. In other words, mom is the initial thought to a newborn individual's active feelings. The undifferentiated feelings become organized within the growing sensory system, thus organizing perception. Desire within the thought world gradually develops into conscious intent. The force of intent, in the child, manifests as externalized willpower. Early on, the willpower is directed toward fulfilling want through mom.

Children are unable to think about parental reactions in a way which makes sense of the reaction beyond the face of the reaction. For example, critical parents will produce adolescents who are similarly critical—whether the inherited criticism is primarily held as criticism of self or comes out as criticism toward others. Additionally, they will expect such criticism from others toward themselves. Parents should strive to reflect what the developing child needs to see. If the child is overly anxious, then the parent should react with confidence and lack of concern to the child's expressed doubt. Over-reactions from the child should be reacted to with calmness and a touch of ease. Often, children wish to get mirroring reactions which reflect how they feel, but doing so often escalates the situation. Providing enough mirroring to enable a sense of empathy is important, but once that level is reached, the parental reaction should always be centering or balancing.

Prior to the onset of the dual consciousness, the child's thoughts are directly determined by their sensory experience. Thus, there is no internal separation—no membranous bilayer (metaphorically)—where feeling and thought are independent of each other. Prior to a separation of feeling and thought, when the outcome to their action is negative or met with scorn, a child is able to express not intending to have happen what happened. Because they can represent not having intended the result, they take the conscious belief in it being the fault of another person or outside influence which caused the negative result. This is consciously reasonable prior to the onset of thinking. However, once an individual is able to have internal forethought, and thus, the ability to form an internal representation of another's perspective, then it is more difficult to legitimately blame others without compromising their reflective identity within social relationships.

The self-centeredness of the developing child's perception upon their environment is frequently overlooked. Everything they perceive tends to be related to themselves. For example, if a child's mother is worried in her interaction with the child, the child will believe they are the cause of the worry because of a personal deficiency. They will take causal ownership of people's treatment of them, believing they deserve it. The self-centeredness is further illustrated in how small they perceive the world to be. This causes adult news or news of bad things happening (e.g. natural disasters) to be anxiety producing for children. Their ears are very sensitive to bad things happening out in the world, and the younger they are, the less may be their contextual understanding. This is why children avoid speaking of their worry about losing their mother, for simply by uttering it, they believe it might come true. Children likely believe they are determining the behavior of their parents, which is an important realization for parents to have so to enable effective parenting.

Prior to puberty, a child is only operating mentally as a singular self, able to express feelings and intentions, but unable to internally consider themselves from a judgmental point of view. They are unable to reflect on their feelings apart from experiencing such feelings. Part and parcel to this is an inability to think about what others are thinking, and an inability to see a bigger picture behind individual and social behaviors. As such, they are unable to put much thought into what could have been or what shouldn't have been. Though a child can react angrily, they cannot form resentment. They are generally bound to the world in front of them, reacting to it in real time. Without yet the triangulated mind, their perception of time is skewed. They are more tethered to the moment, and thus bound to how they are at every moment, more so than adolescents and adults.

During the first decade of life, the child is unable to differentiate between the perspective of his/her parents unto the world and the actual world. Thus, the parental "take" on things—the picture they paint based on their level of optimism, confidence, and enthusiasm within the environment—literally creates their child's early representation of reality. As a child develops the ability to think ahead, or forecast, the color or tone of their projections gets shaped by the perspective and reactions they see from caregivers. This enables the young child to begin adapting to the world without directly experiencing the world—the world as it is perceived by adults.

Often, grade school aged children are erroneously perceived as manipulating. Being "sneaky" is expected, but the ability to manipulate has yet to develop. To manipulate, a child would have to be able to represent the other person's mind in their own mind—to where they can judge possible cause and effect scenarios, and then execute their chosen plan. To conceive of methods for manipulation requires the ability to internalize the judge and then separately judge the judge. What parents and teachers experience, mislabeled as manipulation, is a push-pull dynamic occurring with the child, where the struggle is for control.

In young children who have had an early activation of alpha-cognition, they demonstrate *valued judgment*. Their judgment is tethered directly to how they feel, and they expect outside effort to make them feel better. However, they are unable to create metaphorical representation of things due to a lack of abstraction ability, which is normally developed in adolescence. An early onset of alpha-cognition usually occurs because of a need to control what they are experiencing. In controlling judgment, they take representational control. The early onset may be due to relationship pressures from a self-personality mom, excessive environmental chaos relative to the child's sensitivity level, or instability of caregiving. Such children are notably more judgmental, controlling, and tend to power-struggle with parents. Self-personality mothers are much more likely to influence their child into having an early alpha-cognitive switch. The influence stems from the natural way in which self-personality individuals relate to others—by tethering their being to the other person's experience of them. Thus, the alpha-cognitive switch is more likely to happen during times where mom is emotionally struggling herself. A power struggle then arises as a result of the child's judgment being strictly based on their feelings within a two-dimensional world.

Once the shift occurs into the alpha-cognition, there is never a return to the self-cognition. This is an important phenomenon to recognize in children who have been through a period of unstable upbringing. Such children will be in a perpetual power struggle with any authority figure seeking to establish direct control of them. Thus, much of the problematic acting out, from the child's perspective, is to resist being controlled. Unfortunately, the more willpower which comes forth, the more destructive will be a power struggle. Children with the most willpower, although the most challenging for authority figures, have the most potential for creative productivity within their individual activity.

Pubescents

With the onset of pubescence, an activation occurs within the ego, where an added layer of awareness manifests. This dual-consciousness formalizes the ability to think or form judgment independent of their immediate conscious experience. In other words, the ego becomes compelled toward creation rather than reaction. The infusion of the sex drive into the ego is causally associated with the increased awareness, bringing the capacity to form an internal representation or judgment of oneself—in relation to the mindfulness perceived within others. Thus, they are able to engage in autonomous self-reflection without the reliance on sensory experience from the environment. Through the binary structure of the ego, a parent-child or judgment-feeling (alpha-self) relationship within every individual's own consciousness exists in conflict for most of life. This conflict exists between how an individual feels or what they desire and their beliefs about life and about themselves. A sacrifice of feeling and an adjustment of belief or thought is necessary in order to establish internal stability. A sense of harmony is produced through an equilibrium between the two aspects of an individual's consciousness. Imbalance or disequilibrium produces an internal sense of tension or negative potential.

As the ego grows in capability and maturity, the sense of self relative to others and the environment becomes more established. This imbues a sense of independence. Thus, a loss of self-control becomes more and more threatening to the pre-adolescent, and to do so feels less appropriate, and overall is more threatening to their relationships, as well as for the representation others have of them. By reflectively judging themselves, the thinking ego seeks to be reflected positively by others. However, if an individual is too guarded or shy, then they will have to reflect off of others feeling uncomfortable with them. The lamentable tragedy occurs in the self rejection, producing the expectation for rejection. The conscious perception from peers will be of the individual disliking them. Their peers will be equally sensitive to negative self-reflections, but usually have more self confidence in their interactive ability, and thus do not remain unexpressive.

It is a milestone of consciousness to recognize others are thinking the same way as oneself. They are not thinking the same thing, however. The perceptual error—where one's judgment is generalized—must be overcome. The thoughts beheld by others are not the thoughts which one is having about oneself. Others are engaged in a similar process and direction of thought. Since each's level of self-centeredness is extremely high, they are remarkably clueless about the other person. They experience others as they sense the other person relates to them. Their self-centered thinking, where the noun (person, place, or thing) being considered is only in relation to them, traps their consciousness in its own reflective bubble. A growth in understanding of others is thus not possible until they are able to open-mindedly think about another person, independent of themselves. The immaturity of an individual's consciousness is best assessed through the amount of reflective encapsulation of their perception. In other words, the more the individual sees people, places, and things only as they compare or reflect unto themselves, the less they are able to see others as true individuals. Furthermore, this reflective perception causes a quasi-psychotic phenomenon where they struggle with people's treatment of them without realizing the people are, for the most part, reacting to them. For example,

Jack's suspicious distrust, though born out of insecurity, leads to Jill feeling disbelieved and unaccepted, and will likely lead to fulfillment of Jack's fear. If the developing consciousness forms a belief in one's negative feelings requiring outside help or intervention, then one will seek to control the method of attaining such help as much as possible. However, such effort is the action which keeps them tethered to the negative feelings.

For triangulation of thought to occur, so to enable thinking as it is being defined, the brain has to grow to make the necessary interconnections. Likely, the connecting neuronal (involving nerves) growth is stimulated by pubescent sex hormones. In studying human consciousness across the life span, researchers have distinguished distinct stages or levels. The stages are presented in the accompanying table. Until reaching the conformist stage, the progression is part of the overall neocortical development. The pubescent capability to triangulate thoughts signals the transition from egocentric consciousness to the conformist consciousness stage. An important element to recognize within the egocentric stage, especially for parents and educators of younger children, is the level to which the child's perspective is self-centered—where the world revolves around them. For example, an egocentric child will believe themselves to be the cause of negative emotion around them, or that supernatural punishment will befall behavior they feel guilty about. They identify experience in such a way where they stand apart—for better or worse, they believe themselves to be special. Interestingly, their concept of others is such where the differences are only those visualized or demonstrated, through physical attributes or abilities. Without the recognition of others as uniquely minded, young children cannot conceive of life as being any different than they sense through experience. Once something is experienced, it literally comes into their existence. Thus, the possibility of an experience re-occurring necessarily comes into existence as well. Along the same lines, young children are unable to conceive of a higher level of consciousness, there is no way for them to imagine a mindedness beyond their own.

Stages of Consciousness
Reactive
Naive
Egocentric
Conformist
Affiliative or Achievement
Authentic
Transcendent
Unity

Adolescents

It is essential for an adolescent, in the formation of their identity, to establish relational bonds with peers out in the world. The bridge into independence necessarily requires such bonds to be created. Through these bonded relationships, a sense of connectedness and normality is instilled. This allows for the adolescent's consciousness to pursue independent development of themselves.

The frame of reference initially beheld by consciousness is from the creator position. In other words, conscious experience is processed as if awareness itself brought it about. This direct perception of causality results in the first reflective sense of oneself. The initial mirror is the birth mother, with whom the child experiences the warmth (love), influence (power), and stability (control), which become imprinted. Going forward, based on the initial imprinting from mom, the ego seeks to have an internal balance of those elements. However, because of the growth in scope of the child's conscious awareness, and the increasing ability to get for themselves, mom is unable to keep up with the child's desires, no longer able to fulfill them. The consciousness of the child sees his or her parents as entitlements for support. Once thinking commences, the child becomes able to judge the parent. Usually, the perspective onto their parent is the same as the perspective onto their body—where it is expected to work correctly in support of what they consciously want. When the parent does not do what the child wants, or intrudes upon the child, the child will reflect the parent not liking them or being mean to them. Not until the ego detaches from the dependence on parent(s) are parents able to be perceived as separate individuals.

It is non-sensical for someone to expect others to perceive their intentions. Such a perspective is ego-based. Ego-based perspectives necessarily objectify everything outside of oneself in the effort to create a balanced sense of power, control, and feeling loved. To consciously believe how one feels should determine what one gets from others is rooted in a retained connection between feeling and thought. As previously discussed, the splitting of feeling and thought which enables triangulated awareness begins at puberty. However, a full severance, for most individuals, never comes, and if it does, then it develops later into adulthood. If feeling is being attended to in order to generate a thought of the environment, then the perspective is consumptive, and others in the environment become objectified with one's thought in effort to quell the feeling. The greater an individual's level of feeling-thought connection, the greater their outward instability. This is because the reactive feelings are generating thoughts or beliefs which then determine the action taken.

In order to think clearly, it is necessary to live within the common lines of shared reality. To do so requires the ability to project and identify either one's self or one's alpha inside another person. Basically, for a person to establish a shared connection with someone else, one of their two personality parts has to be cast into the other person, enabling a complementary relationship (alpha-self). If unable to do so, then shared relationships are not formed. Such individuals have difficulty with communication, and their social mannerisms tend to make them appear odd. Their behavior often seems disorganized or bizarre. The ego-centricity in such individuals is extreme. Often, these individuals are diagnosed with schizophrenia. The disablement stems from the lack of relational depth combined with interpersonal difficulties and disorganized communication, creating a situation for the individual where existing in the common world (and being able to sustain themselves) is challenging. For such individuals, the world is a flat projector screen playing out the drama between their alpha-consciousness and their self-consciousness—between their thought-judgment and feeling-judgment. Because of their detachment from others, their thought-judgment has no tether to shared space. Interestingly, in some, their language semantics change rapidly as they cognitively alternate between an alpha and a self position of reference. Since there is an absence of connection with others, the reality experienced by such individuals is mostly a metaphorical representation of the conflict between their alpha and self aspects. The setting for the conflict is the outside world—but set like the stage of a play—in two dimensional representation, flat and without relational context. Nothing substantiates the props, and yet, they see no alternative to what they believe. For example, the occurrence, while driving, of a police car coming up behind them is believed to be intended to intimidate them into leaving town. The person will not see any plausibility in alternative reasons if presented to them. The extreme self-centeredness is very apparent. In tethering everything to themselves as if they are the causal force behind everything they perceive happening, then explanations must begin with themselves. This reflective perception supports the delusional thinking. Psychotic individuals are unable to form a shared reality within the environment, and thus cannot cognitively tether themselves to the world. Amongst the general population, episodic paranoia is common. It is seen mostly with individuals who feel vulnerable either when alone or in an unfamiliar environment. Trying to control what one believes to be negative potential within them is the base of such normally occurring paranoia.

Everyone is familiar with perceiving negativity in their experience. The natural progression of perceptive development has one, throughout adolescence, rooted in a reflective bubble, where they interact with the world based on how they feel relative to the world. Early adulthood is thus the formation of one's world outside the reflective bubble, while still perceiving reflectively—as if the world is shaping them. It is the world they will have to step into, to take responsibility for, and to recognize as an extension of themselves. The more a young adult builds their world based on their reflective feeling experience, the more difficulty they will have stepping into the thought world they create. Getting compelled out from their reflective bubble is usually because of relationship struggles stemming from the other person's point of view being disregarded. When an individual's consciousness grows out from its reflective captivity, they become more aware of themselves relative to the world and others. Unfortunately, to frame an image of themselves—as they are experienced by those they are closest with—requires a relatively mature level of consciousness. Thus, it should not be assumed to exist in an adult, but oppositely—it may be assumed to not exist in the adolescent.

The 3 Domains of Consciousness

The human consciousness arises from within the triangular interplay of *feeling*, *thought*, and *being*. Within the feeling dimension is the element of *love*. Within the thought dimension is the element of *control*, and within the being element is the element of *power*. Each of these longings are initially self-serving in their aims—to feel loved, to feel secure (control), and to feel powerful or capable. However, as an individual grows in understanding of themselves and life, they are increasingly called to love, to enable control, and to empower others.

Though consciously one-sided in the pursuit of control, power, and feeling loved, the ego is not naturally malicious or sadistic. Rather, when the outside sensory experience does not align with what one consciously wants or feels should happen, then the ego naturally reacts as if one is being mistreated. When one is consciously defensive, perceiving mistreatment is unavoidable. Children use anger to defend themselves, and later, once able to think, they will increasingly develop the ability to suppress the angry emotion or "shut down." Not losing control of one's emotions becomes more and more important to the adult ego, and therein a sense of control can be established by remaining stable despite frustration at the environment. Reactive emotion from the ego is originally purposed to protect one's individuality and fulfill one's desires, and thus is more likely to be seen arising from children or from those who are in a dependent position. Once the adult ego internalizes others within its frame of reference, one will seek to take responsibility for them. In other words, others will become relevant pieces in the person's perceptive life, and as such, the individual will consciously seek to represent each of them being stable, loyal, and still present in the same role or position relative to themselves.

The desire for control within the human consciousness has been the primary source of all human conflict. The two elements which make up the mind (thought & feeling) exist in a relationship, each formed in relation to the other. Feelings flow toward thought. Thought handles feelings. They are naturally drawn toward each other. However, neither will tolerate being controlled, since one cannot be in control of oneself while being controlled by another. The vulnerability associated with being controlled by another person is partly due to the loss of one's individuality. Since the fruition of one's individuality is an inseparable aspect of the life process, a forced de-individualization produces a sense of internal chaos.

The discordant, dramatically unstable relations seen amongst adolescents are illustrative of the ego-driven process where they are reflecting off each other and judging based on a sense of power, control, or feeling loved. The missing ability *to love* or to regard the needs of others in a genuine, heartfelt way inevitably produces discord, and yet, the discord is a necessary experience for identity formation. The detachment from parents enables also a letting go of certain beliefs or parts of their previous conception of themselves—parts of membrane problematic in their relations with others. This is usually experienced consciously as not liking how certain peers act or behave, and decidedly not wanting to be like them. Rather, the adolescent seeks to be more like other peers who are consciously liked, envied, or respected. While still attached to parents, there is greater fluidity of the ego to redefine themselves, and to let certain characteristics go. Once independent, and more and more as time elapses, the ego seeks to solidify and maintain a stable representation or self image.

Once independent, the young adult goes forward in effort to establish a balance of love, control, and power. Even though they are no longer bound to home, they frequently feel controlled by outside obligations or by what they "have to do." The battle between *should* and *want* typifies the young-adult consciousness. Fulfillment of thought versus fulfillment of feeling is the primary conflict within their consciousness. Everyone tries to fulfill both as much as possible, but doing so causes too much disturbance to an individual's sense of control. The desire to fulfill want at the expense of should will thus recede. Difficulty with the *shoulds versus the wants* typifies young adulthood. Sacrificing what they may want to do for what they believe they should do is often a daily struggle, and relationships often precipitate the conflict. A couple can exist through mirroring and reflecting positivity, but once a developing child comes into the system, then the call *to love* comes in earnest.

The following table shows the three elements of consciousness as they change through maturation. If a certain element remains fixed in an underdeveloped position, then the immaturity gets revealed within the individual's primary relationships. The maturational steps are consciously challenging because of the self-sacrificial nature of consciousness growth. Realizing one must become what they seek to feel—to be it—rather than seeking to feel it, is necessary in order for an individual to step forward into unfamiliar space, and to tolerate the vulnerability.

Child	Adolescent	Adult
To Feel Loved	To Be In Love	To Love
To Feel In Control	To Have Control	To Effect Control
To Feel Powerful	To Be Powerful	To Empower

The Ego

The ego is born out of the experience of internal emptiness, attaching to the potential for internal fulfillment through consumptive intake, and security through rejection of external threat. The ego is an individual's will directed for or into oneself. The hunger or longing felt internally is reflected by the ego to represent absence. A need for internal fulfillment is then attached to the world outside as beholding the source of such internal fulfillment. The ego's quest for the internal fulfillment thus occurs by trying to get from the world. Whatever attachments may form will perish. Yet, the ego is born out of need. The ego consciousness experiences a sense of death in the letting go of internal need. Whether an individual seeks to protect the internal sense of themselves by rejecting an externalized threat, or they believe there is something they lack, and thus strive to get from the world what they sense internally needing, neither method leads to fulfillment.

The internal space between mind and body is where the ego senses individualized potential. This reflected space is a triangulation from consciousness reflecting off the body—generating a sense of individuality or separateness. Within the internal triangle, eminent domain is maintained, imbuing the individual with a sense of creative potential and security. The creative potential is materialized in the body, which itself is an embodiment of time. Time is change, and thus, two aspects are inextricably bound to the life experience—growth and decay, gain and loss. If an individual is not willing themselves outwardly for growth, then they are willed inwardly to not decay, to not lose their sense of potential. The latter is a defensive positioning of an individual's relationship with life, which is simply an inversion of the will. Positioned as such, an individual can only perceive life through the lens of internal desire and incoming threat. Thus, life will be experienced as a back and forth or push-pull, which becomes more exhaustive as time progresses. This is because time depletes the materialized potential of the body, and so all erected defenses will invariably decay. Attachments are bodily in origin and, by nature, are based on incoming energy or substance. The more an individual prioritizes not losing themselves, the greater will be their sense of unbecoming. The internal sense of oneself is fundamentally different than the external experience of oneself. The ego is an inseparable part of each's perceptive life because life-energy drives toward full actualization of each's individualized potential. However, it is necessary to keep the ego's drive for internal fulfillment as motivation to grow forward, rather than seeking consumptive fulfillment. Thus, the mind must rule the body so the body doesn't rule the mind.

Each's internal space is sensed as the internal self, and is created from the mind's reflection off of the body. The only way the mind is able to internally reflect is by focusing on the afferent sensory system, therein enabling an internal sense of oneself. Thus, the data being processed as coming from the body is seen as happening to oneself, from outside. As such, the energy which produces the physical feelings is not integrated into the efferent sensory system, and thus is not available for willed effort forward. Rather, the energy is rejected or projected. When the energy is rejected, it is trapped in the afferent system. Perception is thus bound to interact with the feelings as if they are a threat or shouldn't be happening. From there, the rejective energy may stay contained in the body, wherein symptoms emerge. Otherwise, the energy gets expressed into the world as unwilled motor output (emotion, defensive action). Perception of the world will invariably be characterized by rejective or pessimistic thought. The world must thus absorb both the individual's negative thought and their negative energy. Moreover, the potential for positive efferent action is lost as a result of the disintegrated processing of the energy.

Efferent action which is willed requires a potentiation of energy within the body aligning with intent, which emerges as effort in connection to the present. Assuming everyone is positively intended, then an individual either wills themselves positively along their efferent or outgoing nervous system, or they are willed to not be negative. The latter effort requires an inhibitory or rejective position relative to the afferent or incoming nervous system. The structuring of the adult consciousness as an efferent entity means the mind is bound to either perceive something in the environment or an aspect of the body (outer appearance or internal sensations). The object of perception is thus always separate from the perceiving consciousness. When consciousness is willed to not experience something perceived in the environment, or is positioned to control or avoid a certain sensory experience, then perceptively reflecting off of the sensory system produces a separation of mind and body. Oppositely, when focused outwardly along the efferent system—with forward or outgoing intent—then consciousness is unable to perceive the afferent system separately. Thus, when connected fully with the present environment, there is not a mind-body separation. When an individual is positioned defensively, in effect, they are protecting the internal sense of themselves— their internal space. However, the internal space is made up of a mind-body separation, perceived from the positioning of consciousness relative to the internal afferent sensory system. Since consciousness perceives in an efferent fashion and intends with efferent effort, any perceptive interaction with the afferent system is a separation of mind and body. Thus, the relationship each's mind has with themselves relative to the world determines their sense of separateness from the world. The nature of the mind-body structure is such where life is experienced as a graduated awakening to existence as an experience of outgoing potential. Naturally then, as an individual matures, they increasingly are drawn to give of themselves outwardly.

Summary

The human child spends the first ten years or more bound perceptively to their parents who form the thought structure for the child. The child is driven to fulfill their own desire—to get what is wanted and not experience discomfort. Not until puberty does the child's consciousness develop the ability to reflect oneself—to parent oneself. This is when the singular consciousness of childhood develops the two-part consciousness which enables thinking. Most of one's life is then spent seeking an internal equilibrium. However, for this to occur, a full separation of feeling and thought has to happen. Otherwise, certain feeling—thought formations exist which prevent one's consciousness from realizing a sense of inner harmony. The goal is to return to a singular consciousness state, similar to the mindset before puberty, but with one fundamental difference—direction. Rather than being dependent on feelings an individual believes need fulfilled from the outside—where they are bound by a desire which cannot be fulfilled independently—in a state of independent self acceptance, they are free to give of themselves. To give freely and lovingly requires full separation of feeling and thought. The separation allows for their perceptive consciousness to fully detach focus from themselves, no longer in self-regard. Then, through a constant outflow of love, they are able to better the world around them and uplift those they come into contact with.

A notable feature of immaturity is the expectation for the world to relate to one's intention. To perceive oneself causing upset without having intended to do so is maddening and often taken as an offense. Similarly, positive intent is expected to be recognized by others and represented within outcomes. Thus, the immature frame of reference between themselves and the world is as the world relates to them. They reflect themselves off of the world, and their effort is either unto their own reflection or toward fulfillment of internal feeling. Thus, the perceptive process centers around the world as it relates to them. Unfortunately, they are unable to consider themselves as they relate to the world, and thus believe they are simply reacting to the world. However, in truth, each can only react to their experience of the world. Trying to force one's reality onto others will bring incessant frustration, for no two realities are created the same.

Prior to puberty, a child's behavior can be understood from within a two-dimension model, as in the laboratory rodent. In children, as in rodents, there is desire or want, and there is the environment which beholds what they want. Prior to puberty, when children are shown the Picasso sketching (pictured), they only see the lines (usually describing a tree or something). It astonishes parents that the "picture" is not seen. Even after pointing the image out for them, they have difficulty seeing it. It illuminates how the cognition of children is literal and concrete. Their experience of the world (people included) is based on what they see and feel—their direct sensorimotor experience. They do not fill in the space between. In contrast, adults read between the lines. Adults live in the space between. Adults draw conclusions and form judgments. The space is essentially a creation of the triangulated mind. The adult consciousness experiences life metaphorically. Feeling and judgment interact and produce a more indirect experience. It is a metaphor, and to perceive life metaphorically, one must first develop the ability to think. While the lines which are drawn to serve to structure human perception, the vast majority of life is spent toiling in the metaphor. Within the metaphor is where the meaning of experience is ascribed by the human perceptive apparatus—the conscious mind.

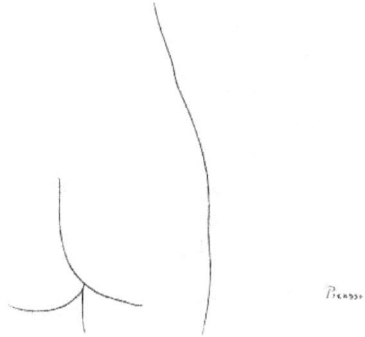

2.3

PERCEPTION

There exist two sides to every coin. If not, there would be no coin. The human mind can only perceive light and dark, where dark simply means a relative lack of light. The human mind has two sides, two poles, through which everything must be perceived, and between which occurs the experience of life. There are two sides of consciousness—the feeling side and the thought side. Thus, there are two types of people based on the two-sidedness of the mind, similar to the two-distinct genders which exist. Independent of which side an individual is on, each has two-aspects—the part which goes at the world and the part which receives the world. As a result, two modes of perception are possible—for the perceiver, the world is seen either as it affects them or for their effects within it. Along similar lines, two directions exist for which an individual's focus may point—internally or externally. Within the internal domain, there is memory and forethought. Externally, there is the living world, to which an individual may or may not connect. Being externally focused and connected is the operational perspective. In contrast, being externally focused yet disconnected is the defensive perspective. From the defensive perspective, the outside world is perceived for the potential threat it beholds.

When an individual consciously tries to determine *what* is happening to them, to form an answer requires reflecting off of their experiential "me" (the part which senses or receives experience). However, because connecting to the experiential world (including others) happens through the sensorimotor "me," answering *what* comes at the expense of connecting with the world in a way where true experiential understanding is formed. Thus, trying to form an understanding from a disconnected position is the human mind's pursuit to conclude *what*. The desire for certainty or control drives the attempts to know *what* is happening or *what* will happen. The uncertainty is innately uncomfortable for the mind which seeks to control itself. Thus, staying in a disconnected state keeps "me" protected from rejection or painful feelings. It is analogous to a person at the edge of a diving board who is considering jumping, trying to decide *what* to do—to jump or go back. Either decision involves a directional step—either into the pool or further away from the pool. If the pool represents experiential life, then, in standing at the edge of the diving board trying to decide whether or not to jump, they are not yet experiencing life, and thus have yet to connect. Truly, they cannot know *what* the experience will be like, and the more they try to answer *what* without the experience, the less will be truly known. To connect, to jump into the pool, they have to mentally let go of the need to know *what* will happen. They have to let go of the expectation to have a sense of confidence or a certain level of comfort in order to jump in, to connect.

Thus, every individual may either *be* or *not be*—for that is the question each must answer. Such is the crossroads everyone must face within their present life. In order *to be,* an individual cannot be thinking *what to be, what to do,* or *what will be.* Rather, they must simply *be.* In just *being,* an individual strives to relate to the present, to bring themselves as they are for the betterment of the environment and the growth of those around them.

What is given to the present moment to answer—where being themselves in connection with the present—enables a perspective of *whatever will be will be*. Pursuance of certainty or security within life is oxymoronic because, to most fully know, an individual must fully experience. However, trying to know without connecting comes via judgment—to conclude, to represent, to form a thought image. Doing so, unfortunately, ceases the growth of understanding. As time passes, and changes occur, maintaining the construct of belief—keeping the image intact—becomes increasingly difficult. Internal thought created—through reflective judgment between "I" and "me"—is thus beheld at the expense of experiential understanding or coming to know. True understanding is born between "I" and the world, via the connected experience of "me."

The Illusion of "not"

Life makes sense as an experience of two aspects which are not part of the governing principles of the universe. The first being—there is no such thing as nothing or *not*. The sense of nothingness occurs only in an individual's self-reflective human experience within their internal space. The second aspect is the experience of loss, which is an experience of detachment or losing part of oneself. Such loss is inseparable from an individual's growth toward fully becoming themselves. Thus, loss is a necessary constituent of gain, and most are familiar with losses (or letting go) having resulted in substantial growth. Furthermore, the universal principle of eternal becoming positions the human experience of loss, though painful, as an anti-truth—where growth to a greater degree is able to be found in the wake of loss.

Darkness has proven to be something—as science shows darkness has matter. Not being, not doing, not expressing one's potential—creates the internal effect of emptiness. The internal emptiness to which each may relate is made of each's potential positioned in opposition to their will. Put another way—the emptiness is formed from energetic potential which an individual has enacted so to *not* experience something foreseen—an occurrence the individual wishes not to come true. For example—if someone is trying to be likable because of a willed desire to not be rejected, their behavior is centered around an anti-truth about themselves. Thus, instead of willing themselves forward, they are willing themselves backward. Their effort for growth—to be better—is based on a *not to be* relationship with themselves. However, as will be explained, effort toward not experiencing something subjects an individual to such an experience.

Feelings are best regarded as the substance for doing—for action—thereby enabling change or growth. How one feels is always in relation to one's present period of consciousness, and thus may be understood as the gathering of potential for one's creative intent—to effect a cause or to cause an effect based on the laws of cause and effect. The cause is found in thought as one's thought forms the outline of the world one exists within, and the feeling element then integrates to effect one's potential therein. For instance, in response to a lion suddenly attacking, the surge of adrenaline in response is an energetic potentiation to act. It produces physiologic readiness in support of either fight or flight. When no materialized cause is evident, then people become much more uncomfortable with the adrenaline effects. If such feelings are perceived as a problem, then an individual will fight against the adrenaline-based feelings themselves rather than applying the feelings. The attempt to control it, as a result, is energetically depleting and undermines adaptive growth. The imagined lion is thus the individual themselves, though they are blind to such.

Rejecting oneself requires willpower to oppose output of oneself—thus trapping self-energy intended for growth. Such growth is enabled through a connected experience within the present, whereby a constructive application of willpower occurs within the environment. The more willpower aimed toward *not*, the more an individual's emptiness becomes characterized by a sense of numbness or absence of feeling. Thought then given in relation to the emptiness generates the experience of it. The thought also provides insight into an individual's dynamic handling of themselves. For example, the person who sees the emptiness as a lacking of love is themselves not adequately loving. If there is no such thing as nothing or *not*, then each's experience of their internal emptiness is an illusion. In other words, any thought formed from the emptiness is to rationalize the un-manifested potential—to find cause outside of them to explain why they are not.

Assigning internal thought to a feeling equates to turning the feeling into thought. Doing so, involves finding cause to explain the feeling separate from what one is doing or not doing, which equates to giving cause of one's doing or not doing to feelings. As such, consciousness gives cause to effect, and thus, must also effect the cause. In other words, the cause of the adrenaline surge is the perception of threat (e.g. the lion), where the adrenaline is to enable the individual to effect the lion—to fight the cause. The adrenaline itself cannot fight the cause, but comes to provide the capacity to do so. However, if the presence of adrenaline is sensed as something impending negatively, and where no immediate cause in the environment exists, then the adrenaline will be used to cause the effect—meaning, the presence of such feelings will induce finding a cause.

To illustrate, if Jack believes Jill is the cause of his worry because her rejective behavior is *what* he's worried about, then Jill's effect in him is negative despite no actual threat being beheld by her, and no intent to cause him worry. Jack thus perceives his sense of internal tension as the effect from *what* Jill is doing. From Jill's standpoint, Jack appears stressed, and so, in assuming he has too much already on his plate, she gives him some space. Jill cannot perceive herself as the cause of his tension, but she could say the cause of her distancing was the effect from his negativity. In such a scenario, Jack effected the cause of his effect (tension) by perceiving an outside source for his inner state—i.e. giving away responsibility. Then, the goal becomes *not to be* in such an internal state. This occurs through perceptive effort to control the relationship with the cause, and thus, secondarily, to not experience the effects. For Jack, this surfaced defensively in shared space—as negativity toward Jill—which then created the scenario in shared space which he was foreseeing (being rejected) based on his *not being* (defensive posture), which was actually the *being* which effected outside cause for itself. This perceptive reversal of cause and effect underlies the nature of the *self-fulfilling prophecy*.

The mind, in being composed of two components, each inextricably bound to answer for the other, is both a receiver of *why* and a creator of *what*. Through the perceptive apparatus of the binary mind, as one perceives the world outside oneself, reason forms *what* as communicable thought, while feeling is the *why*. Thus, the human mind seeks a balanced synchronicity where feeling/why aligns with thought/what. Attempts to control either are made by perceiving them as effects, therein seeking to identify cause. Using feeling to determine *what* creates a false reality, just as trying to determine *why* by materializing cause for *why* produces an inversion of cause and effect. For example, Jack suddenly experiences a feeling of dread, like something bad is impending. Naturally, he does not want to experience it, and thus tries to control it by finding a cause. He thinks *what is happening?* Then, *what is wrong?* And finally, *what do I need?* However, since Jack's pursuit is to *not* experience the feeling (a *why* phenomenon), his mind must rely on pre-configured reason—the structure of images and words—in the context of his materialized world. Thus, Jack's answer to explain his sensory phenomenon is restricted to the *what* or thought domain—e.g. he's dying. Unfortunately, there can never be truth in such thought, and truly—the thought is the cause (e.g. fear of death). The feeling experience, rather, if being related to as a *why*, would allow Jack to realize the feeling-thought experience provided him the experience of *what is not* (death as nothingness)—thereby leading him to a greater realization of *what is*.

Any willed effort toward *not* experiencing takes creative expression within an individual's internal space. Creation within the internal space is thus only true for what it is not. However, the more an individual believes such creations, the more their life will be experienced for what is not in accordance with the principles of outgoing existence. Within the internal space, the sensed effects are given material cause, but the cause then is a non-truth, as is the individual's reality. Nevertheless, each's reality is a necessary mirror of themselves, to which each is equally able to grow into, thereby gaining the same understanding once each gets past the mirror of non-reality—of that which is not. Until a full acceptance of life occurs, every individual tries to control and fulfill themselves by relating to life as the source for their internal fulfillment. From such a perspective, one's internal space is prioritized, and yet, in doing so, the opposite manifests externally. This is because life manifests as a mirror of each's willed input into the world. Naturally, individuals focus on what they are getting or wanting, or how they are feeling. However, this comes at the expense of perceiving their own willed input into life.

Each is born into existence without a conscious awareness of ever choosing to exist, and thus, life provides each the opportunity to come into willed existence. In doing so, the space of potentiated nothingness present within each is able to actualize into a singular, presently-minded consciousness. For a full actualization to occur, all the potential space must be integrated into the will flowing through the present *I am* or *I be* space. The proportion of internal space an individual can sense remaining unfulfilled within them, thus, is simply the inverse of the how fully they are integrated into their present being. Becoming fully willed into the present requires letting go of conscious rejection as a defensive tool, so one may step willfully into life— where then, the capacity to see threat wanes into non-existence.

Every individual has an eye which perceives what is threatening and an eye which perceives what is becoming. Following the growth impulse through life takes an individual more deeply into the nature of life itself—where principles of cause and effect enable each to come into a more harmonious state of being within the framework of existence. As an individual grows more internally synchronized, the eye which impends negative gets blinder, as the eye portending positive becomes more luminous and insightful.

First-Person & Third-Person (revisited)

The first person perspective is a subjective, sensory experience of someone or something. Because it is experiential, such a perspective can only occur within the present. Children are bound within a first person experiential perspective, which changes around the time of puberty as a result of an internal thought element activating separate from their first person perspective. This infuses their perspective with a third person awareness, and thus, thinking begins. The internal emergence of a third person perspective produces an awareness of oneself relative to the world/others as well as an awareness of others/world relative to oneself. The third person perspective assigns judgement or meaning, and forms beliefs. Having both a first person experiential awareness and a third person thought understanding within the same consciousness, however, is a double-edged sword. When a third person perspective is applied to judge the world/others relative to one's first person experiential perspective, then the formed judgment is an objectification based on personal sensory feelings or desires.

Third person judgment necessitates a consideration of two elements, and such judgment is expressed in the form of understanding or thought belief. When one of those elements is an individual's own first person experience, then the judgmental understanding, although expressed decidedly, is purely subjective. Such judgment is based on an individual's reflective experience, and thus involves no true understanding of the world or others. From the third person perspective, when the understanding is being formed of others relative to oneself, the perspective occurs from a defensive position. Oppositely, when someone seeks to understand more from the third person perspective, their perspective is open-minded, therein positioned for growth of awareness or to gather more knowledge. The resulting increase in understanding—whether of the world, elements within the environment, or others—is inherently growth promoting for an individual. In contrast, the defensive perspective is protective, and seeks to secure the individual's sense of self, but it does not enable growth in understanding.

When an individual's third person perspective is given to others in the form of a directive, the judgment is parental in nature. To demonstrate—the statement "You should perform the move you have been working on during tonight's game," is an example of a third person directive. If the directive relates back to the directing individual's first person perspective, however, then it will be experienced or heard differently. "You should bring me dinner when you come," is an example of a third person directive relative to the directing individual's first person perspective (desire). "You're being an untrustworthy friend," is another example of third person judgment being formed from internal insecurity. When an individual experiences others "using" them, they are experiencing being reflected unto the other person's wants or needs, without receiving the other's third person understanding which they expected to receive.

The inability of the human perspective to see itself—to perceive the perceiver of perception or hear the hearer of hearing, to know the knower of knowledge—underlies the potential pitfall from the third person perspective. For an individual's third person perspective to form belief based on their first person perspective produces a projective perception of others. In other words, others are seen as good or bad, liked or disliked—to be accepted or rejected. For someone to judge a person's treatment of them from a third person perspective equates to an objectification of the person being judged. Within relationships, each should be free to express their experience of the other, as it provides each with important information so to better understand themselves and the other person alike. For each to reflect an understanding from the other is integral to the security and stability of a relationship. Thus, in equal measure, each within a relationship must pursue a better understanding of the other.

The first step toward the promotion of better understanding within relationships is to undermine the use of the third person perspective based on first person experience in forming judgment of others. Such judgment perceives others as the cause of oneself. By externalizing the cause of themselves, however, individuals are bound to identify with how they feel. This forces them to make sense of how they feel from a source outside of themselves. Unfortunately, without forming an internally centered sense of themselves, their growth gets compromised. Without the necessary growth within themselves, an excessive amount of willpower will remain within their attachments. As a result, fears of loss or rejection permeate their life experience, which they perceive from a defensive perspective. As such, the individual's perception of life stays trapped behind the lens of their sensory experience.

Two Spaces

Two spaces exist for which thinking individuals may perceive—internally and externally. The external space occurs as the environment is sensed (affects) and impacted (effects). The internal space occurs between mind and body. For space internally to be palpable, there must be some degree of separation between mind and body. The separation is filled with energetic potential as the individual intends toward life occurring outside of them. The separation between mind and body may be conceived of as a disconnection, for potential exists which is not being willed outwardly—not being actualized. Directly willed effort to not have feelings requires a disconnection and division. This is a result of being primarily willed toward oneself—whereby focusing on one's body (feelings, image) separates the mind from the body, and thus occurs from a disconnected state. The result is a triangle which forms of mind—body—environment. The mind feels more secure from atop this pyramid since it enables a third-person separation from the body—environment. From the third-person position, a sense of control and security is sought. However, the focus on the body only reflects incoming sensory data from the environment. Because of the disconnection, there is no outflow of positively willed effort. From this position, the mind can only regard how one's body feels or how the environment is negatively impacting oneself. Expressions into the environment will thus be negative and rejecting. Although the intention is not to make others feel rejected, nevertheless, others experience such, and often distance themselves as a result.

It is important for individuals to mature to the point where the external space is prioritized rather than their internal space. Filling the space in front of them requires a giving of all their potential—a full actualization—whereby no internal space is kept separate. Prioritizing outward fulfillment is analogous to a seed becoming a flower. The flowering requires potential to be actualized, which occurs initially as the sprout comes forth, and then a continual push for outward growth leads to an eventual fulfillment of potential through becoming fully blossomed. If the seed prioritized the internal space, then growth would be conflicted and may not occur without excessive pressure. Since life energy within everyone presses for growth, attachments and forces opposing change precipitate the experience of internal fear and built up pressure. For an individual to prioritize growth, they cannot be focused on themselves. Growth requires a connected, outwardly willed effort forward. When the will is directed inwardly, unfortunately, growth becomes stymied.

Prioritizing external space keeps an individual's focal point ahead of themselves, affixed to what is in front of them. Primary effort then occurs through their efferent action unto the environment. Such behavior may be either willed or unwilled. If an individual's action is willed, then their effort must be positively constructed—meaning, they seek to directly bring growth or positivity. In contrast, when an individual is prioritizing their internal space, then positively intending themselves outwardly occurs through effort to not be negative. Doing things in order to prevent negative or to attenuate perceived negativity centers around the protection of the individual's internal feelings. When internal forethought is used to create potential negative, then an individual cannot be truly connected with their present environment. Rather, the environment becomes triangulated with the individual's internal space, and thus, their environment is perceived and sensed much differently than if actualizing themselves through connected, outgoing effort into the external space being prioritized.

Seeking to positively impact others may occur by seeking to either reflect afferent positivity from them or bring efferent positivity to them. Looking for others to be happy and approving is looking for afferent positivity. Rather, bringing efferent positivity requires effort outwardly, without reflecting back onto oneself. When the body and mind are aligned through efferent effort outwardly, no internal space is palpable. Thus, the space in which to reflect others as a sign of oneself does not exist. As a result, one is able to interact much more freely and expressively.

The 2 Modes of Perception

Every individual perceives either the world making the first move toward them or themselves making the first move toward the world. As a result, there are two modes of human perception: *defensive* and *operational*. *Defensive* perception is a triangulated perspective whereby one is judging the environment as it effects one's feelings or self-reflective thought. The *operational* mode of perception, on the other hand, is an outgoing perspective, whereby one, with an open mind, seeks to understand or experience what is outside of oneself. The defensive perspective reflects life occurring to oneself. The operational perspective experiences oneself as occurring to life. When assigning cause to an experienced effect, an individual may see themselves as the cause of the effect, or they may see the effect as causing themselves.

By turning the effect into an affect of oneself, the defensive consciousness determines its own perceptual experience. Also, in this way, one's consciousness is the threat despite perceiving the threat outside of oneself. One is the threat based on one's negative effects on the world. However, when one is perceiving through the lens of their affect, they are blind to their effects. Hence, within relationships with such individuals, others will sense being on the outside looking in. Forming a true connection with an individual perceiving defensively is not possible. Such an individual primarily connects with themselves, and their mode of perception relates the world to themselves. Thus, there is no real space for another except as a two-dimensional object for which to receive the defensive individual's projections. The two-dimensions are good versus bad—to accept or reject. The problem this causes for the defensively perceiving individual is from the lack of begotten understanding. Growth throughout life, especially as it may occur within relationships, is predicated on growth in understanding. The more an individual's understanding of others is underdeveloped, the more imbalanced they will be relative to themselves. An imbalanced individual cannot perceive the effect their defensiveness has on their surroundings. Rather, they tend to see reason for their defensiveness, finding supporting cause, without being able to see the cause as their effect.

From the operational perspective, an individual interacts in order to experience their effects on others, thus furthering their understanding of themselves and others. Through developing their understanding of themselves relative to others, individuals self-generate growth. The operational mode of perception is positioned at the interface between an individual's body and the environment. The perspective occurs at the level of the body, directed into the environment. In contrast, an individual's perspective, when occurring defensively, is positioned within the body. From there, an individual is interfacing with themselves (self-feelings or self-centered thought)—like a lens inserted between themselves and the environment. The defensive mode gravitates negativity, and depends on the use of rejection—either of themselves or others. An individual effectively rejects themselves through avoidance or self-destructive behavior.

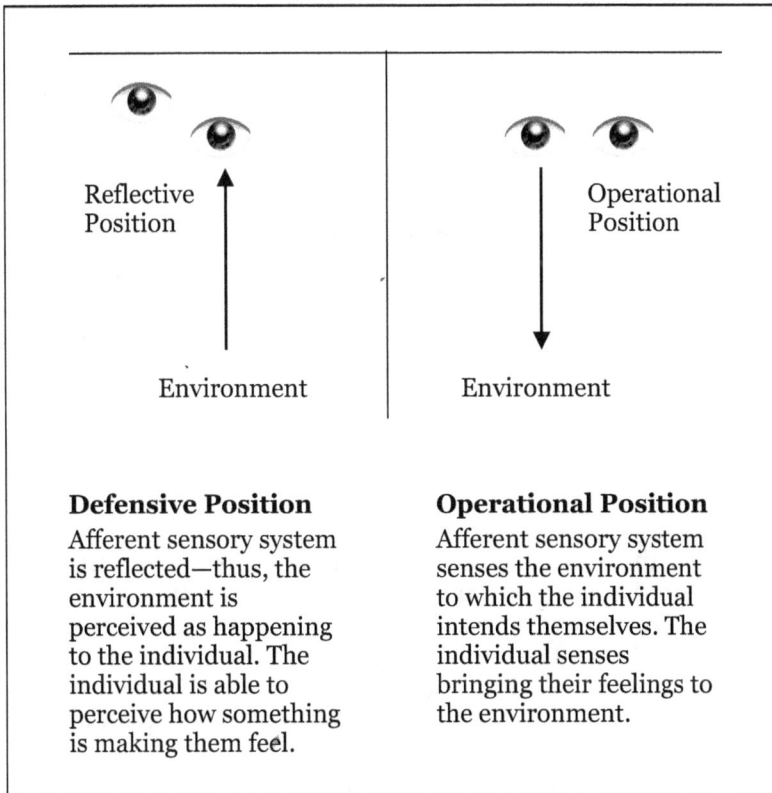

Reflective Position	Operational Position
Environment	Environment

Defensive Position	**Operational Position**
Afferent sensory system is reflected—thus, the environment is perceived as happening to the individual. The individual is able to perceive how something is making them feel.	Afferent sensory system senses the environment to which the individual intends themselves. The individual senses bringing their feelings to the environment.

For an individual in the defensive position to gain direct control or influence of others, they normally will employ expressions of anger and threats of rejection. When perceiving defensively, an individual's focus is on themselves, and thus they can only perceive "care" from those who seek to directly appease them or who seek to directly protect them. Individuals perceiving defensively are blind to those who regard them positively—whose thought regard of them is understanding and optimistic. Recognizing caring regard which does not come forth as direct effort requires an operational perspective. Only from the operational perspective can a true connection be established—one built from bricks of understanding. Therein, an individual, during times of internal negativity, can connect with others who reflect a positive, growth promoting image of them. Otherwise, such an individual, in their attempts to feel better, relies on the consumption of others' effort.

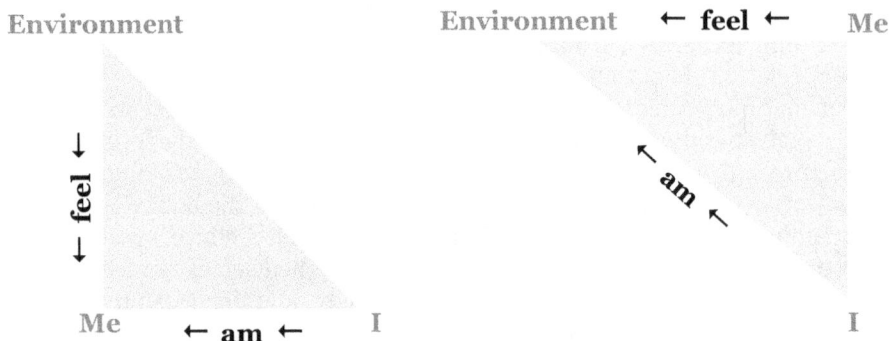

Environment   Environment   ← feel ←   Me

↓
↓ feel
↓

Me   ← am ←   I   I

"I" is focused on incoming sensory system—how one feels or in defense of perceived threat. The environment is perceived through the lens of the body, which mediates feelings and attachment (I feel).

"I" is focused on environment, aligned with the body/sensory system which is connected and being willed into efferent effort (I am) as directed by the "I" will.

Self-subject & Self-object

When perceiving or acting within the present environment, an individual's perception or action may be centered around something outside of themselves, maintaining themselves as the subject, and thus perceiving from the *self-subject* position. For example, Jack was trying to understand the topic being taught by the teacher. Perception through the self-subject lens generates an awareness of oneself going at whatever is being focused on. In other words, perception occurs as the subject "I" rather than as the object "me." An individual, as subject, sees life outside of themselves as the canvas wherein they will realize the positive potential within themselves, and thus, seek to grow more fully into it.

If perceiving or acting within the present environment based on protecting internal feelings or fulfilling desires, then the perception or action has oneself as the goal or the end, perceiving from the *self-object* position. For example, Jack felt Jill was being rude. The self-object lens causes the perceiver to focus on what is coming at them, what is happening to them, what is expected from them, or how they are feeling. Also, from the self-object position, an individual seeks to *know* rather than to *understand*.

The two-modes of perception are differentiated based on whether or not the individual's willed effort is being channeled into the space outside of them. The actively thinking individual will be either interacting with the outside world as a means or as an end. Perceiving as the self-subject is interacting with the world as an end. Perceiving as the self-object, rather, positions the world as a means. As a means, the interaction is for internal fulfillment of "me." If the individual is seeking to defend themselves, express feelings, or fulfill desires directly, then their willed effort is for themselves, and the space outside is perceived as either the means for fulfillment or the cause of un-fulfillment. Thus, when perceiving as such, the individual is not connecting their effort toward understanding or producing more. As an end, the relationship is for the external fulfillment of their internal potential. Through effort, feelings are transformed into kinetic activity of "me" within the world. The means by which an individual may grow more understanding and more capable occur through their "me" aspect (energy, power) being directed forward for growth.

The sense each has of themselves may occur either as the subject relative to the world as the object, or as the object relative to the world as the subject. As the object, the perception is of what is happening to them. Oppositely, as the subject, they perceive themselves happening to the environment, from within the game. Through the object lens, protection and consumption occur, and internal pressure grows. Through the subject lens, rather, an individual intends to effect cause and to grow in understanding. To have a sensory interaction with something or someone outside of oneself occurs from the subject position. In contrast, from the object position, an individual is sensing themselves—meaning, they are reflecting off of their body to determine how they feel. From the object position, an individual perceives being made to feel the way they reflect feeling, attaching cause to circumstances happening to them. Looking through the object lens produces want, need, and a sense of the world impending. In contrast, a sense of becoming characterizes the striving forward from the subject position, therein enabling growth of both understanding and capability.

Childhood is an experience of life from the object position, where the character of their eventual subject lens gets formed from the character with which their parents handle them. However, the game of life does not begin in earnest until around the time of pubescence—when thinking begins—where birth of the subject position is demonstrable by the third-person judgment which begins being applied. Since the third-person perspective is distinct from the first-person sensory experience, the capability to create, for the first time, becomes infused into an individual's perspective on life.

The two-part human consciousness perceives people as characters, represented in the thoughts of the observer. Stereotypes emerge from the natural thought patterning which occurs within the thinking consciousness. Early learning itself involves understanding patterns of sensory experiences in relation to the outside environment. As long as there exists a sense of outside threat, there will occur judgmental rejection of others. Consciousness will form a thought embodiment of the threat, to gain a sense of control through *knowing*, and therein naturally constructs an enemy. A false sense of security is constructed through representational labeling which stratifies others, and enables the observer to believe themselves differentiated from the threat. Culturally, *stranger danger* plants the thought seed which becomes the tree of negative judgment—the tree built from fear—which divides one's sense of security from people, as if security comes through protection from others. This conflicts with the natural sense of happiness being experienced through positive, loving relationships. Thus, the human individual is drawn toward others, and yet, the fear of rejection is infused into each's perception due to the capacity within each to themselves reject. The natural way of perceiving others is thus as they relate to oneself. Doing so, however, binds the human perception to see others as either objects to get something from, or as others regard oneself. However, the observation is a reflectively formed objectification. When in real time observation of another individual, the conscious perception of the individual can be as they (as a thought characterization) interact with their environment. Perceiving another individual as they relate with their environment is the proper position for the observer to truly regard another. From such a perceptive position, a connection is formed—a connection through which an individual grows in understanding of others and in lightness of themselves. Others will sense being more connected with, more attuned to—more understood—and thus, more accepted.

The implication beheld by an individual's mode of perception for their ability to learn is significant. To most effectively learn, students must perceive the material being taught from the self-subject point of view rather than from the self-object point of view. A true effort to understand material being presented requires approaching the material as an end in and of itself. Rather than seeing the material as a means to an end—the end being, for example, a good grade or not failing—approaching the material in order to better understand it, as an end in and of itself, enables students to develop a more extensive and sustainable understanding. When material is being learned as a means to an end, then much more emphasis is placed on what to know, thereby compromising the growth of understanding of the material. Synthetic understanding necessarily requires a self-subject approach to the topic or material. The effort put toward learning from the self-object perspective depends more on external pressures—such as the willed effort from teachers, or more commonly—the fear of failure or rejection.

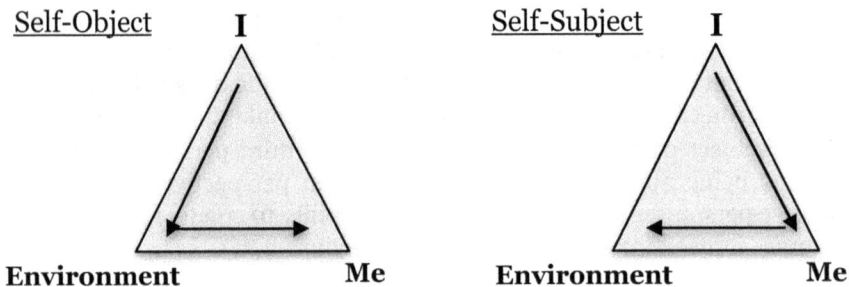

<u>Self-Object</u>   **I**   <u>Self-Subject</u>   **I**

Environment   **Me**   **Environment**   **Me**

Perceptive Effects of Fear

The human consciousness, when perceiving through the lens of fear, will see threat wherein lies fulfillment. For within what is feared is what an individual fears of themselves—aspects which are not yet accepted or integrated. What an individual does to protect themselves, to guard against the realization of their fear, actually magnetizes the experience of such. For instance, fear of rejection makes an individual more sensitive to rejection, which precipitates feeling rejected, leading to a distancing or avoidance which eventually creates a state of rejection. Individuals are attracted to a sense of positive likeness in another. However, with it comes negative likeness—whereby individuals see what they fear of themselves in the other. When aspects of themselves are avoided or rejected, then invariably the individual will fear themselves through the other. Doing so, interestingly, causes one to oppositely characterize the nature of what is or is not occurring outside of them. Fear gets attached in front of the person so it can be explained, so they can interact with it—to find reason, to get control.

Fear is a symptom of the disintegrated ego. A fully integrated ego requires full maturation, where no power is attached to the will of another. The last piece to be integrated is the scariest—the rejective sadism—which enables the use of outwardly directed rejection to escape life. Truly, during the process, an individual must turn and face themselves. Therein, they experience a freight train of impending destruction getting closer and closer to a frightened emptiness growing internally more painful. This force, as it exists before integration, gravitates toward the individual's consciousness. If the fear causes avoidance or self-protective behaviors, then the effect is in opposition to growth. Following integration, however, the same force pushes the individual's consciousness in the direction toward growth—propelling them forward. This energetic force, though it had been keeping them entrapped, is realized to be power when it integrates within them. It enlightens the individual's understanding, and their sense of themselves grows lighter. A conscious sense of freedom accompanies the internal completeness, whereby an individual senses themselves detached from outside threat.

Looking at it from another angle—from a more Buddhist-like perspective— the willpower of consciousness is attached to who and what an individual believes they need, and also is directed toward fulfillment of physically based desires. When need and want exist outside of the individual, which invariably is the case in life, then suffering is the rule. This is due to the lack of wholeness—from a disintegration of self within attachments—whereby integration is sought through being good enough for others or in protection from others. Both avenues, unfortunately, are misguided attempts to gain a sense of security. When someone seeks direct fulfillment of desire through use of their willpower, the fulfillment is unsustainable, and the desire grows more intense over time.

The ego may be thought of as the entity which perceives defensively and consumptively. The ego attaches fear and desire to elements outside itself. The sensory experience of being underpowered internally is equivalent to the sense of being overpowered from the outside. Both aspects produce anxiety from the lack of internal determination or sense of internal control. Whatever the ego does directly to gain a sense of empowerment and control, ultimately, will further the imbalance or prolong the suffering. This is because the ego itself is the problem—it is causing the imbalance through an avoidance or rejection of parts of oneself. Invariably, the ego, in sensing anxiety, will attach the cause to outside elements it cannot recognize within itself. Put another way, what an individual sees as the cause of their anxiety is simply an inversion of themselves. This explains the phenomenon of the ego-blinded individual (refer to chapter on efferent disorders) who experiences themselves as a victim of life, and yet who, as can be reported by those closest to them, is actually the victimizer. But the individual cannot see themselves as such. They perceive things being done to them—usually in the form of being "made" upset—and thus perceive themselves reacting to what was being done to them. The ego-blinded individual cannot conceive of being wrong in their perception of a situation. However, since their perception of life around them occurs as if life is revolving around them, they can only reflect how they feel about whatever is happening. This explains why the ego-blinded stage of adolescence is so frustrating for parents, since no true reason exists for adolescent accusations apart from how they feel. Reflecting everything back onto their own feelings makes it impossible for them to exist in shared space, where an understanding can be formed with their parent(s). The extent to which the ego-self can appreciate or understand another individual is contained within the mirroring of sameness or a reflection of likeness from the other individual. Differences will be seen as needing to be rejected or controlled. Staying encapsulated in the reflective cocoon is protective for the ego, but not for the individual as a whole since it prevents experience of themselves, thus impeding growth. The tragic irony in the situation is in the defensive ego only sensing itself, and thus, remaining trapped within the thought it constructs to account for its sensory experience.

Open-mindedness is required to gain an understanding. Thus, a judgmental perspective is inherently defensive, and thus egoistic. As such, the individual's perspective can never regard their effect on those around them. Forming an understanding of someone cannot occur through reflection. It requires connection, which occurs in shared space. The difference in perspective when trying to understand someone or something as compared to judging someone or something, is obvious, and indicative of two discreet modes of perception. What is so compelling to recognize is how one will experience others oppositely when reflecting negative feelings off of them. For the reflectively perceiving individual, excessive effort is spent trying to get others to understand them. However, meaningful growth in understanding requires effort be spent trying to understand others, which is unable to occur when the focus is on trying to get others to understand them. Moreover, reflecting on how others are treating them is similar to thinking about themselves in the minds of others, both of which are reflective in character, and thus do not generate meaningful understanding. Perceiving reflectively will only bring about a meaningful conflict with themselves, which manifests as outward conflict with others. Thus, meaningful peace and harmony must always be established internally with oneself before one can expect to experience it on the outside.

Reflecting Offense

It is very uncommon for an individual to take outward action intended to hurt or degrade another. Rather, in almost all cases, individuals lash out while in a state of defensiveness. In other words, actions which from the outside appear to be an attack are, in the perceiving mind of the offending individual, due to either anger in reaction to something they perceived as an offense, or from fear as they defensively attack a perceived threat. Both occur under the influence of emotion (anger or fear), which any individual who lashes out is experiencing as being unjustly experienced as a result of threatening circumstances. They relate to their upset as being inflicted, and thus defensively lash out. For someone to take offense from another's behavior toward them requires presumption of the offending individual's intent to offend. However, if such offensiveness is rare, then the person's "offensive" behavior must be assumed to be defensive in origin. The behavior then, if defensive, even though it was taken offensively, is best understood as having been an expression of negative emotion which, because of misunderstanding and misrepresentation, came forth in a rejecting manner. Since individuals attach their fear to outside rejection, rejection is internally offensive, and thus the occurrence of rejection is perceived as an attack. Rejection is also the primary method of human defense, serving a natural role in protection of the individual and their individuality. The dual nature of rejection leads to this *offense-defense dilemma* of perception, therein forming the shackles of the human mind's perceptive condition. Rejection forms the bridge, allowing the mind to perceive rejection from the outside as an offense despite the mind's own use of rejection as a defense. The more anxiety directed toward the avoidance of outside rejection, the more perceptively hyper-vigilant and emotionally sensitive the individual will be to rejection, and thus, the more likely they will take offense to signs of rejection from others.

If the human mind did not take offense to rejecting behavior from others, then the rejective behavior seen from others would be properly perceived as defensive. As such, outwardly occurring upset would be recognized as stemming from a misperception, recognized to be fear, though manifesting as anger—like a sheep, only in wolf's clothing. The perceptive pitfall from fear comes in the attachment of one's fear to others, thus seeing them through the lens of threat—either as an offensive threat, or as a passive threat (losing them). Thus, fear precipitates taking offense—because when fear is attached to being caused by others, then naturally others will be perceived as a threat. When the human mind is perceiving threat on the outside, then the mind is perceiving reflectively or from a defensive position. From such a reference point, judgment of others' behavior relative to oneself occurs, whereby others are seen as doing things to oneself, but there is no awareness of oneself unto others. Put more simply, when one is defensive, they will perceive others as offensive. If an individual could see others being defensive rather than offensive, they would naturally adapt their approach as part of their effort to grow better.

Growth in both understanding of others and awareness of themselves, which leads to a greater sense of connectedness, structures the path paved for individual growth. Therein lies the root of fear's evil—from the defensive position's propensity to take offense. The influence fear has on human perception precipitates not living, not experiencing, which is the opposite of living—like *live* spelled backwards. Thus, wherein wisdom is developed through life, invariably it is predicated on perceiving the threat within rather than without. The more threat perceived outside of oneself, the less understanding will exist. Those who are wise have centered the threat inside of them as fear itself, and thus they seek to oppose the threat by living fully within the present moment—by being in the now. In doing so, they focus themselves into the world rather than reflecting the world into them. Without perceiving the world's treatment of them, or how they feel from the world's effect on them, wise individuals step into the world—seeking to offend the world with the positivity of their being, and only seek defense against not doing so.

Physiologic Consciousness & Willed Consciousness

The mark of attaining grown up status psychologically is noted in the transition from a *physiologic consciousness* to a *willed consciousness*. To be considered a grown up, an individual must have a willed consciousness, where belief is the basis of perception. The preceding physiologic consciousness perceives through the lens of the body, conceiving thought and taking action based on protecting sensory feelings or fulfilling physical desires. Feelings are thus, for the physiologic consciousness, the basis of perception. Fulfillment for the physiologic consciousness is internal— metaphorically structured by hunger—where food is consumed for satiation. The physiologic consciousness takes a consumptive approach in perceiving life, alternating between consumption and rejection in effort to achieve a stable internal fulfillment. Since pleasure or positive feelings are prioritized, thought is formed to account for one's feelings or to entitle action based on feelings. In contrast, the willed consciousness is independent of the sensory attachment to one's body. From a willed consciousness, one seeks externalized fulfillment—like one would experience through sport or creative expression. Willed consciousness forms action to effect the environment. Thus, one is able to effect the world willfully through giving effort to either manifest a belief or to be aligned with one's principles.

In order for one's action or inaction to be principled, what one does must be willed. Reactive behavior is un-willed since such behavior is sensed as an effect from an outside cause. Feelings are the internal effects which are purposed to influence the cause. Thought or belief is the basis by which the willed consciousness perceives. The sensory experience gets incorporated into one's effort forward, and thus, one is primarily experienced in the connected context of interaction with someone or something outside of oneself. Having more sensory awareness of what one is putting forth to the world enables more realistic clarity of life. In contrast with the preceding physiologic consciousness, one's internal sensory experience is no longer triangulated with the outside world.

The awareness of one's internal state being a result of what one has or has not done in relation to what one sees, requires a willed consciousness. However, physiologic consciousness forms thought to explain the effects rather than forming action to effect the cause. From the physiologic consciousness, one's internal feelings are perceived as being from the world. Then, attempts to manage one's feelings can only follow the hunger—food—fulfillment metaphor, where a consumptive solution is conceived in both explaining internal feelings and dealing with their occurrence. The physiologic consciousness uses rejection of the world/others to secure oneself —perceiving the environment as the threat to one's bodily attachment—just as the physiologic consciousness consumes in effort to fulfill oneself, perceiving fulfillment through physical satiation or sensory pleasure. Consumption and rejection are thus the two modes by which physiologic consciousness perceives and conceives.

The temporal expiration of bodily life causes the relative impermanence of the physiologic consciousness. Maintaining a primary attachment to the physical senses, because of aging and the ever present threat of loss, infuses a ribbon of continuous threat running through life. To transition from the physiologic consciousness to the willed consciousness, there must occur a letting go of one's primary attachment to their feelings/physical state. Willfully, one must give up on prioritizing one's feeling experience, committing rather to the doing space—where one's self-identification shifts into prioritizing action unto the environment. A willed participation in life for the sake of experience and growth allows one to sense the fruition of oneself as occurring within the experience itself. Security is sensed in what one is able to bring to the world. When feelings are processed as a threat in and of themselves, then a primary, though rejective, attachment is maintained with the feelings—necessarily maintaining a physiologic consciousness. Then, there occurs added difficulty transitioning to a willed consciousness, due to the sense of chaos and loss of control which comes with letting go of one's rejective position relative to their feelings.

The substance of action—which enables the doing—is physical energy. Such energy, when non-integrated (not being channeled into action) often surfaces as emotion or bodily symptoms. Stress is an example of a perceived pressure felt by the physiologic consciousness, sensed as happening from the world, which compels action due to threat of inaction. However, from the willed consciousness perspective, the same pressure is experienced as motivation. The more an individual focuses on what has happened or is happening to them, the less they are able to regard themselves happening to their environment. Only from the willed consciousness perspective may an individual appreciate the ability to choose how they handle their feelings. Though certain negative feelings may be triggered by something which happens to them, the feelings themselves are experienced within the individual's integrated space from where willed effort emerges. Thus, feelings —being directed by a willed consciousness—are able to be willfully channeled into substantive action. As such, the willed consciousness does not process negative feelings as a threat. Thus, the willed consciousness does not perceive internal feelings as directly tethered to the outside world.

- **Positive behaviors** are those which are driven to accomplish a positive goal. A positive goal is sought through a direct cause & effect relationship between the behavior and the goal of the behavior. A direct accomplishment of something is envisioned. A positive goal cannot be to avoid something negative. In everyday life, the world affords reason to be optimistic (hopeful) as well as pessimistic (doubtful). Positive behaviors naturally involve an optimistic relationship with the world.

- **Negative behaviors** are those in which the goal is to not experience something. Behaviors which are positively intended to protect oneself are not positive behaviors since the goal is for something not to happen. Such behaviors are negative behaviors. Creating a "what if" scenario through forethought, and then behaving to prevent such from happening, is a negative behavior. For example, to dress like others for fear of standing out and being criticized. Negative behaviors relate to a world which is threatening. The sense of accomplishment an individual gets through negative behaviors is based on what they imagined could have happened. Thus, the accomplishment is false—for it is centered around an avoidance of what the individual imagined.

The Perception of Hunger

Hunger may be perceived two ways—as a lacking or as a drive. The feeling of hunger is a motor feeling. Although hunger may be experienced as representing a deficit, from a physiological standpoint, hunger is an activation of the sympathetic nervous system. In other words, hunger is an activation of energy (motor feelings) potentiated to forage for nourishment. As such, hunger is meant to trigger an individual to act relative to the environment—to effort themselves in connection with the world so to materialize nourishment. It is important to recognize that the feeling of hunger has substance. Although commonly reflected as representing an internal lacking, whereby it is experienced as an absence or deficit, truly, hunger is energy. The difference may be appreciated in the contrast between someone crying out to be fed versus someone working to grow food. The energy expenditure is the same, though to express the hunger emotionally depends on a rejective relationship with the feeling, where it is sensed as a need, and believed to entitle what is needed. Believing hunger is a problem misses the actuality of hunger as a drive to create. Thus, the more an individual sees hunger as a threat, the greater will be their sacrifice of hunger as a drive.

As potentiated energy, how one handles their hunger becomes an individualization of their consumptive intent. In response to hunger, an individual may will to eat or they may will to not be hungry. The more hunger is sensed as a lacking, the more threat gets imbued into the experience of hunger. Therein, hunger is rejected, where the willpower is directed to not eat. Those individuals who eat in excess experience hunger in such a way where the feeling is reflected into their internal sense of lacking. Thus, eating becomes emotionally fulfilling, but since the self fulfillment is occurring autonomously, without an equal giving of self, obesity results. The obesity is thus a product of the individual's creative potential being directed toward feeling internally fulfilled—in avoidance of the internal feeling of lacking with which they struggle. In other words, whenever an individual's creative potential is directed toward not experiencing their negative potential, a sense of lacking or hunger is created.

If permitted, every individual will entitle their motor feelings to get what they believe will gain internal satisfaction. Whether the satisfaction is experienced from the fulfillment of desire, or as an escape from the negative feelings themselves, every individual must relate their motor feelings to the world. Problems arise, however, when the feelings are perceived as being directly caused by the world. Being blind to the mind space, from which the world is conceived, binds the individual to the space between them and the world in dealing with their negative motor feelings. Rather than taking causal responsibility for their own feelings, wherein mind-based changes may be made as they relate to the world, the individual stays stuck trying to reject or control the perceived source of their negativity existing outside of them. Since the negative feelings are potentiated as part of the life experience, their predominance within an individual's consciousness will correlate with the extent of rejection of such feelings, which then determines the level of externalization—where cause for the negative feelings is assigned directly to the world. Doing so is possible based on the sensory nervous system, where sensory feelings are produced directly from the five physically imbedded senses. Motor feelings can thus be perceived as directly caused by outside elements or forces, where then the negative energy is expelled through the rejective defense of the perceived cause, without the individual ever taking responsibility for their negative feelings.

The approach to life whereby positive feelings are sought through rejection or avoidance of negativity, occurs from a misguided perception of life as being purposed for the feelings themselves. In other words, living life primarily to feel good misconceives the life experience. Similarly, living life in avoidance of negativity is a misconceived approach, for it results in an equal sacrifice of positivity. The cultural misbelief in life providing a happy experience causes negative feelings to be seen as the impediment to happiness. The individual pursuit of happiness is thus directed toward abolishing negativity. However, such an approach depends on perceiving something or someone outside of oneself as the source of one's negativity, and then rejecting the source, thereby enabling an escape into happiness.

Giving cause of one's action to outside elements gives power and control to the negative feelings one tethers to being caused by the elements. Whatever or whomever is seen as causing the negative feelings is thereby given power. When negative feelings determine what an individual does, the behavior is being compelled by the threat of rejection—thus, giving control to the threat. The individual's will to not suffer negative feelings generates their action in defense of themselves. However, since the action is a reaction, the individual experiences being caused, where their behavior is negatively willed— meaning, an action taken in order for something negative not to happen. Such behavior stands in contrast to positively willed action, which is willfully done with the goal of accomplishing something positive. Only positively willed behavior, through integrated channeling of the energy, retains the power contained within the negative feelings.

Even in the context of threat, an individual's effort may be positively willed if the experience of threat can be accepted. For example, in sport, an individual's effort to keep their opponent from scoring is positively willed. Willed effort to not experience what is feared prevents an individual from willing themselves to positively effect the situation they are perceiving. This accounts for the frustration in those seeking for more positive output from an individual who primarily is willed to not be negative. When an individual's will is primarily aimed at not experiencing what is feared, there occurs a lack of positively willed effort. Thus, others will experience a lack of engagement, with less overall productivity or output. As it may be applied to an individual's relationship with their hunger, the more they are seeking to not be hungry or to not eat, the less energetic output which will occur, thus trapping negative energy in the body. This occurs in contrast to a positively willed output in connection with the environment, whereby the potentiated energy of hunger is transformed into positive activity. The transformation of energy then enables weight loss if such is the goal, though it comes secondary to an increase in connected giving of their potentiated energy—part of which is experienced as hunger. When the relationship with hunger is negative, then the cognitive processing is rejective, thus trapping the energy in the body, where it forms weight. Rejection produces polarization, which keeps the energy condensed internally as fat. When energy is intentionally used to get stronger or more capable, proteins are created, which lead to increased muscle mass. In contrast, energy which is consumed but not purposed becomes stored as fat. Most weight loss programs do not incorporate the use of hunger as energy into the approach, and thus do not properly orient the mind's relationship with hunger. As a result, the success rates seen with weight loss programs are less than expected, where most become fads rather than prescribed regimens. Only a weight loss regimen which is able to transform the experience of hunger from an experiential phenomenon to a purposed phenomenon has the potential to be of widespread and lasting benefit.

The Two Illusions

Two perceptive illusions exist among human beings—where every individual is bound to overcome one or the other. The first illusion is in relation to an internal sense of something lacking. Such individuals have an internally palpable sense of being incomplete, not good enough, or missing something. This feeling gets reflected along the hunger metaphor, whereby these individuals perceive needing to consume what they lack. Usually, such an individual attaches to getting what they internally seek from another person, therein longing to be regarded in such a way where internal fulfillment is achieved. These individuals, if they internally reflect on their internal space, will be able to identify what they sense to be lacking. Most will describe a sense of not being loved, accepted, or understood. However, in truth, what is sensed as lacking is potential not being fully given. For example, if an individual feels internally unloved, then in actuality they are not fully loving. The sense of lacking is thus born out of the individual's internal potential. Reflecting the sense of lacking as an emptiness—caused by what they have not gotten—is thus an illusion, for it stems from what they have not yet given of themselves.

The other illusion which binds human perception relates to a sense of internal security being gained through outward rejection. Attributing feelings of internal unrest to outside cause, and then rejecting or distancing from the perceived cause, generates a false sense of security. Pulling away or giving up in an effort to secure internal feelings is illusory. By ascribing their upset to others, who are then perceived as a threat, the perceiving individual feels trapped by their upset, which they can only sense as being inflicted. However, the rejective impulse which arises within the individual is truly the threat, but since it gets projected, the individual expresses the rejection and escapes the perceived threat all at once. The resultant sense of security is an illusion however, because the internal unrest was potentiated energy for the purpose of dealing with the threat the individual was perceiving from the environment. The opportunity being afforded by the upset energy is through empowerment of the individual's will. Yet, when the will is in opposition to the upset—to where being upset is threatening to the individual, then rejection is the only method they know, though the security sensed therein is an illusion. The internal relief from the rejective potential (energy) which gets expelled is falsely believed to indicate security. Generally speaking, individuals are unable to appreciate the effect of their rejective expression into the environment since it occurs from a defensive perspective, and thus the release of energy was unwilled. Rather, the individual's will was to not experience the upset. Thus, rejection of the energy propels them in the opposite direction than if the energy was integrated within their willpower. If willed, then movement or action is sensed as heading forward or toward growth. Otherwise, the individual's effort is to negate whatever is perceived to be a threat to their stability.

When the illusory consciousness is grown past, the subsequent consciousness has more energy available to the individual's will. A greater degree of willpower represents increased unification, begotten through a letting go of the willed effort to not experience what is feared. In other words, by letting go of the rejection or avoidance of efforts relative to certain aspects or feelings contained within the life experience, an individual becomes proportionally more actualized. As such, they sense themselves more capable and more secure, and naturally channel more energy into their efferent or outgoing effort. This is a direct result of efferent willpower detaching from the afferent sensory system, thereby enabling afferent energy to integrate into the efferent system.

The pairing of couples, in order to be truly complementary, requires the pairing of illusions in a complementary way. For this to occur, one individual must be a *lacking-type* and the other must be a *rejective-type*. When paired as such, each's effort in relation to the other compels growth from the other in order to keep the relationship intact. Moreover, the growth is due to what each is forced to do in relating to the other. The individual who pushes for more because of a sense of internal lacking must adapt to limits and believe fulfillment will come through growing good enough for the other. From the other side, the individual who finds security through rejection is compelled to focus on the other, thereby setting limits and creating structure. Doing so positions them to grow in understanding and to let go of direct control, which further enables growth. The relationship will grow in equal measure, if not exponentially, as long as each is able to prioritize the space between. For either individual to prioritize their internal space comes at the expense of the relationship as a whole, and growth occurs one-sidedly. The relationship thus, over time, will grow lopsided.

Through a complementary relationship, the goal for each individual is to overcome their illusory consciousness. For the lacking-type individual, letting go of the internal space means letting go of getting more internally—in favor of being more externally. For example, letting go of the space wherein they seek to feel loved so to be more fully loving enables a full fruition of themselves. The problems brought about through an individual's pursuance are due to projecting the lacking onto others, and therein feeling internally rejected. From there, efforts to compensate for the lacking will be detrimental to the relationship. The rejective-type individual, on the other hand, is faced with overcoming the impulse to reject when their occurs internal discomfort. Letting go of self-control being prioritized enables them to prioritize outgoing nurturance. Those who prioritize control of their own feelings will naturally be rejecting of visible upset from their partners. The internal triangulation with themselves involves a self-rejection of negativity, wherein they prioritize the need for self-control. For these individuals, a belief in the loss of self-control being potentially destructive to others is a self-fulfilling prophecy. While their effort is positively intended, their misbelief about the nature of negative feelings precipitates relational struggles. The internal rejection of their own negativity causes the negativity to be expressed into the environment, where it is experienced by others as rejection. Defensiveness from others then leads to the discord which eventuates in separation. The internal rejection, purposed to keep part of themselves controlled, thus precipitates external division.

2.4

NUCLEAR SELF

The "I" which everyone consciously has awareness of themselves to be—whether arising from the alpha or self position—is the ego, born of sensory experience and bound to the desire to be fulfilled and protected. The "i" is the nuclear self or the potential self—imbedded as genetic code and imbued with divine purpose, and only can be known consciously when it manifests as conscious illumination, transcending the barriers of previous awareness. The greater the alignment of I & i, the more there will be a conscious sense of internal security and a synchronicity within one's outward purposing of oneself. The higher power within—the aspect which fuels growth and imbues a sense of purpose within life—is the "i." It is both part of the whole and individualized. The "i" carries the sixth sense—the warehouse of intuition—wherein the phenomenon of inspiration or conscious illumination is produced.

In the atmosphere, the static of electromagnetic tension, in reaching a threshold of intensity, explodes, producing a separation of electricity and magnetism. The electricity is seen in the form of lightening. The magnetism is felt and heard as pressure waves of thunder. What had been unified in a stable electromagnetic bond, existing as an equilibrium of potential, and thus, not actively being perceived by human senses, divides into expressions of the two elements. Electromagnetic bonds of a similar nature hold together base pairs of DNA, enabling cellular creation and synchronicity between elements. The electromagnetic bonding between base pairs of DNA is characterized by a mutual, electrostatic bond. The bond is more akin to an equilibrium, a balance—each being directed toward the other but also away from the other. The power available for creative activity exists as electromagnetic potential. The more balanced the bond, the more stable, and the greater will be the harmonized resonance between the two constituents. The synergistic effect of the bond necessitates each element gives complementary support to the other. For one of the elements to disregard the other except as the other is or is not unto itself, produces a one-sidedness which compromises adaptability.

Creation requires a pairing, a coming together of the two forces. In order for an individual to control their experience, they have to polarize life outside of them. Every individual must sense their own threat, but each will see it existing outside of themselves. Thus, the human consciousness divides itself in order to gain a sense of control. Since individualized control requires dividing perception into good and bad, finding bad outside of oneself and rejecting it, or seeking to control it, is the natural method of the ego consciousness. In fact, finding problems outside of oneself provides the ego with a sense of security. The phenomenon whereby the ego perceptively polarizes the outside world in order to sense control, is rooted in creationism. The ego puts itself at the top of the triangle and divides the world into good and bad, naturally identifying with the good. Perceiving two sides instills a creator position into the ego consciousness. Thus, control is sensed. However, it is illusory, for the perceived elements are only a triangulation of oneself. In other words, the human awareness is trapped in an experience of itself. Thus, any rejection of another actualizes as a rejection of oneself. When stability is sought by any means other than sacrifice and growth, the opposite is realized.

Within human consciousness, electromagnetic existence is generated through the interaction between feeling and thought. The mind is where discrimination occurs, but also, the mind makes integration possible. When an imbalance exists, more energy is expended in maintaining stability, imbuing a sense of chaos or potential loss of control. A greater proportion of behavior is thus applied to "create" a reflection of control or stability within the environment. To a certain degree, individuals attach to the world in order to stabilize themselves. However, doing so prioritizes their internal state rather than their outwardness. Moreover, an individual's expression of negative tension gets absorbed by the world, and the individual's connection with the world weakens as a result. Bridges of understanding must be built in pursuit of integration, whereby what is separate to the senses becomes unified in understanding.

As a visual metaphor, consider the three subatomic particles which form the atom—protons, electrons, and neutrons. The protons are positively charged and are contained within the nucleus of an atom. Within the nucleus is the genetic code or the information—the thought. The negatively charged electron is outside the nucleus, and is like a wave of potential fulfillment—it is the energy, the feeling. The neutron is neutral and located within the nucleus, buffering the attraction between the electron and proton. If the neutron did not exist in an intervening position, the electron would collide into the proton. The electromagnetic bond could not exist, because the collision would produce an explosive separation. If the proton represents the thought side of the mind and the electron represents the feeling side of the mind, then the neutron represents the world, wherein the process of life occurs. The goal, no matter which side an individual is identified with, is to unify with their opposite side. This occurs through the process of coming to understand and accept the opposite side of themselves. Each senses their opposite as a threat within life, for each's fear will naturally form the outline of the threat. Individuals can only fear elements within themselves which get projected into the neutron—into life—and then perceived as threatening. Living in such a way where the goal is to keep the sense of threat outside of oneself invariably produces a sense of disconnect, whereby one's only accomplishment comes in not succumbing to oneself.

In assessment of an individual, therefore, much insight is gained by understanding how the individual relates to their negative pole. What entity (person, authority, general sense of judgment) does the individual see as potentially rejecting? Is their potential source of fulfillment perceived as positive accomplishment, or is fulfillment seen as not experiencing what is feared? Is the threat within them or projected onto others? Is the individual striving toward something or away from something? To be or not to be, is the question which is most relevant for every individual. The relationship someone has with the threat they imbue into life gives metaphorical illustration to the relationship they are pursuing internally—either toward unification or in growing separation.

For the electromagnetism of one's existence to align means the feeling side and thought side are aligned. Proper alignment equates to a directional heading toward unification. Energy within one's sensory system gets channeled into effortful activity, into a connected *doing* with life. The motor system executes intent and communicates understanding. Expression of oneself through motor activity or verbalization of thought is thus necessary for proper expression of one's self-energies. In concert with the sensory system, one is thereby able to experience oneself. Such experience, for every individual, is necessary for the never ending process of self-realization. The depth of awareness outside of oneself must be mirrored within oneself. What one gives to the world will be similarly begotten from the world. Thus, a proper alignment of one's perspective requires one to make the first move in life—to take the creative step. If one's move is toward one's own internal feelings or self-reflective thoughts, then one is not properly aligned. As such, one remains trapped in their bubble, unable to connect with the world. By establishing connectedness with the world, one is able to have the proper expression and experience of oneself, thereby equilibrating their sense of internal balance. For one's focus to remain openly connected to the environment, an open-minded, outwardly directed interest must occur.

If scientists are in agreement that "life" (as far as can be physically and intellectually perceived) emerged from the Big Bang, reason supports everyone being derived from a single source. Yet, each is divided and naturally imbued with a longing to be internally complete—with themselves and for themselves. Life will always reflect an individual's internal state, not cause it. But each is born blind to such. Paradoxically, each believes their intent should be reflected by others and their desire fulfilled. Each therefore is bound within a web of their own wants and beliefs. Fruition however requires the input of one's energy and willpower—both which increase the more an individual's belief system and intent align with the universal truth of existence or the laws of nature. Rejection or denigration of others is reflective of an internal conflict just as much as fearful avoidance and insecurity. Once an internal equilibrium has been reached, a sense of internal unity is achieved, thus opening up an awareness of the invisible other. It may be conceptualized as a genetic activation of an individual's nuclear self in interaction with the love frequency. Or it may be thought of as God. Either way, the sense of loving purpose getting infused into a person's life fundamentally changes the individual's relationship with life—in both its meaning and their meaning to it.

Self Activation | Independence

Until independence is achieved, one's nuclear self will be aimed at becoming independent. An independent self-conception is fundamentally different than the self-conception one has during the effort to become independent. The concept of self activation relies on an independent self. Prior to becoming independent, one is self activated to become independent. Thus, becoming independent is the first step.

The Binary Psychology model illuminates the importance of becoming an individual first, and most fully, prior to establishing a long term (binary) relationship. The process of achieving independence should be understood as the primary developmental effort from the time of pubescence, spanning and characterizing the period of adolescence. Once the child gains the capability to think about self in relation to self and others, then he or she can begin the process toward emotional and psychological independence. The ability to triangulate their perspective gives an individual the capacity of choice. Thus, once this cognitive milestone is achieved, the pubescent child is able to pursue an independent perspective and identity. However, to complete the process—to achieve independence—a severance of their psycho-emotional dependence is required. This does not mean they are to stop caring for their parents, or the bond must weaken. Rather, the psychological and emotional dependence which exists in the adolescent relative to his or her parents must cease for young adulthood to commence without the strain of excessive vulnerability and fears related to loss. Only after reaching a state of independence may an individual seek to love and unify with another person, and have the necessary security to make it a lasting relationship. Moreover, a moderate amount of security is required to make for a lasting and growth promoting relationship. Otherwise, the relationship will be dominated by possessiveness and clinging, or destabilizing push-pull relations.

Becoming an independent individual is fully completed when an individual has left home and is functioning independently. Dependencies frequently persist into adulthood and precipitate rising anxiety the longer they are maintained. Normally, independence is accomplished during adolescence—finalized (and therein accomplished) by leaving home and living on one's own. The process of becoming independent is painful (at a minimum = frustrating and exhausting) for both the adolescent and their parents. When it is complete, the adolescent should feel liberated and full of revel as they go forward into their bright future. The parent(s) usually feel as if they have been run over by a car and somehow robbed at the same time. Fortunately, they are consoled by the momentum and optimism their child seems to behold while stepping forth independently.

The process begins with physical independence, or detaching from physical dependence on mom. Toddlers best illustrate the self-determination to physically fend for themselves. They demonstrate the importance of what they want, but being able to get it themselves is mostly what they seek. In doing so, they realize their physical independence from mom, and can thus become "quite the handful." Achieving cognitive independence—where they form their own thoughts and ideas separate from the present environment—occurs around the time of pubescence. Many children have taken on an alpha cognition by seven years of age, but not until the activation of the two-part consciousness during puberty can the cognitive independence truly occur. The last milestone—emotional independence—is the most challenging. It usually occurs near the end of high-school and is completed once the adolescent leaves home. Having difficulty with the emotional severance, however, can impair the process, leading to mood symptoms and worsening anxiety. The process toward emotional independence begins at birth, just as with physical and cognitive independence.

The first momentous separation milestone (not including childbirth) comes at the time of toddlerhood, ushered in by the child's newfound ability to walk away from mom. The separation anxiety can be dramatic, and it illustrates the vulnerability felt by children of this age. As noted in previous chapters, mom's comfort level with the diminished physical control, and her sensitivity to loss, are heavily influential in shaping the child's level of security in life. While some separation anxiety is normal (none would be abnormal), a memorable amount is often predictive of later issues during adolescence. The difficulty a child has during toddlerhood with separation anxiety—the clinginess and fit throwing and overall resistance to being dropped off places or having to stay with others—becomes forgotten as the child grows into a more secure period. The peak of vulnerability with physical apartness occurs in first-grade, followed by the secure years *(latency period)*. Then, as puberty nears, before even the onset of any physical changes, subtle psychological changes are noted. It is analogous to a seed having been planted which begins to grow as an impulse to separate. The impulse upsets the relatively calm waters of the early grade-school age years. The child senses it as being outside their control, as an aspect of their growth. Children are confined to an existence of inexorable change. Reaching out for parental support, which had been customary and dependable, with the onset of puberty, however, becomes antithetical to the purpose of the separation.

The importance of achieving complete independence cannot be overstated for its impact on someone's mental and emotional well being. Individuals who are emotionally bound to parents or siblings become more emotionally unstable and anxious the longer they remain in a dependent state. This is especially true if a person remains living at home with parents. Anxiety, specifically fears of loss and social anxiety, grow in intensity. Partial-independence is a frequently observed phenomenon, represented by lingering attachment anxiety or over-reliance on parental support. The support can be psychological (decision making), emotional (comfort), or material (financial). The ties which bind are usually woven with guilt and fear. Certain mothers, in effort to stay needed and provide "help," can become too functionally supportive to their growing child, where the child grows up feeling excessively insecure about their independent function. During the adolescent period, the teen is less likely to engage in the necessary pushing away or rebellion. An adolescent will continue to entitle maternal support for aspects of their life until doing so begins to get in their way. Normally, the longer their need for support continues, the more it weakens their self-esteem toward becoming independent. Anxiety, in one form or another, usually grows worse the older an individual gets if they remain dependent. This is due, in part, to a pressure wave toward independence being resisted within themselves.

Living at home after high-school (even if working a job or going to school full-time) is the most common state of partial-independence. Logical excuses (most often economic) provide conscious justification, but the underlying motive is usually found in their fear of becoming independent. For them, it makes sense to take more time to lay the bricks necessary to build a sense of independence. However, if a parent is laying the mortar, then the process continues as more of the same. Then, in effect, the attachment is walling them in. Without letting go of the attachment-related needs, full independence is rarely realized. If the swell of anxious energy is not turned into functional strivings, but rather empowered through avoidance and worried thinking, then the risk of getting stuck in the partially independent state becomes real. Individuals existing in such a state will often develop physical symptoms highlighted by physical lethargy, mental cloudiness, and dull pain symptoms. Depression is common in such individuals, as well, which makes it even more difficult to have the necessary self-activated function.

Living away from home while still keeping an emotional attachment to home often generates relationship ambivalence. Also, it tends to correlate with a weakened self-esteem. With the tether in place, it is difficult for there to be much strengthening, since an increase in confidence necessarily would lessen the attachment need. Such individuals, because of their emotional connectedness with or dependence on their parent(s), resist breaking their attachment to home. They seek to develop themselves to where they feel secure enough to let go. In other words, they seek to feel good enough to let go—to no longer feel like they need parental support. However, believing in the need to feel well enough first—before they are able to be as they will to be—disables their potential.

When fully independent, an individual believes they could deal on their own with any emotion or scenario which potentially could occur. This enables their consciousness to step past feelings or self-reflected thought, and thus focus on purposing themselves forward. The period of young adulthood extending into middle adulthood is where an individual's functional identity comes into fruition—where their grown-up identity manifests. An individual's identity will have an internal arm and an external arm. The internal arm is within one's internal, private consciousness. The external arm is as one is able to be represented by others. Both arms have relationships reflecting them. The more compensatory a person's personality, the more dualistic will be their personality. In other words, the more the individual seeks to have a compensatory external arm, the more "split" the personality. However, for the nuclear self to activate, there has to be an integration of arms, a unification of one's "I."

Self activation is a purposing of oneself toward fulfillment of one's potential within the environment, or striving for growth of such capability. Self activation is an energetic fruition of one's capability. For everyone, self activation forms a unique relationship where each interacts willfully, purposefully with the environment. Self activation occurs through one's motor system, where one takes their attention off of their own sensory system (feelings) and utilizes feelings for motor energy directed outwardly. Independence must first be accomplished or else self activation will occur within the context of one's primary attachment. If it occurs within a relational dependency, the self activation will be directed toward fulfilling the other person's expectations (parent, partner, spouse), and thus is not a true self activation. Basing one's identity on the reflective approval or sense of security from someone else does not allow for the individualized self to fully activate. Self reflection stands opposite to self activation. In trying to be good enough for another, activation occurs. Yet, it is only reflective activation since the goal is to feel good enough about oneself. Self activation is goal directed to be good enough, not to feel good enough. Thus, one's conscious attention must be directed outside of oneself, where both the motor effort and the mental focal point are directed outwardly. Thus, self activation occurs as an experiencing of oneself, thereby allowing one to come to know oneself as one is rather than as one feels.

To say "I want to be seen as" characteristic (x) is not equivalent to being (x) since there must be conflict over a belief that one is not (x) in order for there to exist the drive to be seen a certain way. In other words, a person who consciously tries to be seen as (x) can be presumed to be just the opposite. Therein lies the underpinnings for the defensive accusation of others being what the accuser seeks not to be themselves. Others experience such a person being hypocritical with a characterologic double standard approach to life.

The Game of Life

Everyone has to experience life as if born into a game without ever making the choice to play. Yet, meaning and purpose occur in the relationship each takes with the challenges in life. It is natural to resent the experience when it involves suffering and loss, since such are never willed and rarely intended. Within the life experience itself, an internal emptiness occurs—like a psycho-emotional hunger—which each relates either to themselves or to life—meaning, the emptiness is attributed to either life's treatment of them (rejected) or their treatment of life (rejecting). For everyone, recollecting the past to account for the emptiness creates a belief of having been mistreated.

Then, an entitlement to express negativity in effort to get reparation becomes incensed. However, each's present effects (feelings) are tethered to their present perception (thought), which is experienced as the cause. The handling is then where adaptation is expected and where growth is possible. Unfortunately, growth is undermined by self-reflecting present or previous mistreatment. Also, discord is precipitated since others invariably react poorly to being treated as the cause of another's negativity. Being responsible for negative effects which were not willfully intended is a common source of conflict and an inescapable part of the life experience.

Everyone attaches their feelings to life, and the same internal effects occur within each as part of the life experience. Individual differences occur in the handling or application of these effects—both within themselves, and as they are perceived emanating from others. The adrenaline surge—enabling a fight or flight in response to a tiger attack—is to help. Yet, if the focus is on the internal discomfort, then such gets expressed with the expectation of such negative effects gaining influence in and of themselves. Telling the saber tooth tiger about the fear or agitation being triggered is not adaptive—meaning, there occurs no application of the energy potentiated by the tiger attack. True action produces a change in position or fights to sustain one's position, in the face of pressure to change.

Expressing how one feels often occurs in effort to get relief through the expression itself—where no action is taken—which, at times, is necessary for homeostasis. However, to express feelings with the intent on effecting change is misguided since it depends on outside action or change relative to oneself. The substance which enables an individual to effect the world in order to manifest their will is the energy of doing, which is the same substance, when misaligned or trapped, which forms feelings or emotion. Thus, a will toward not experiencing the effects of negative thought positions an individual perceptively in a rejective position, as if the world outside is the threat. Creating a sense of security through rejection, then, is undertaken. The sense is falsely imbued, however, as it is an illusion based on the expressive flight away from the perceived cause. In other words, the act of rejection itself—whether emotion was expressed or action was taken—enables an individual's system to return to an equilibrium, within which they are able to sense having secured themselves. Doing so amounts to running away from the perceived threat. However, any forward progress is sacrificed and the individual must restart where they began, though remaining on the same level or plane. Falling back to a previous level does not occur since doing so would regress consciousness, which is antithetical to growth.

Due to the nature of how the thinking consciousness perceives, life may be likened to sport—wherein effort occurs unto life for the experience of living, and to most fully realize oneself therein, rather than as a resource to consume for internal fulfillment. Approaching the game of life for consumptive purposes is analogous to playing sport for the trophy. In other words, expecting a materialized payout—just as it would be in sport—is antithetical to the nature of life. This is because the game requires overcoming fear to get further along. Growth necessitates change. Thus, painful sacrifice and loss are an inseparable part of gain forward. To live for secondary purposes misrepresents the experience of life. Any secondary purpose is in effort to take something away from life or keep something safe from it—both of which detract from outgoing effort emerging from the *self-subject* position. Such is the forward effort within the present, while fully connected, which is experienced when playing sport. Also like a sporting match, there is a sense of an existence outside the match itself, and yet during the match, as one is giving oneself fully to the effort, no such awareness is maintained, nor does one's play conflict with one's generalized existence.

To fully realize one's potential in life, one cannot fear for their life. Doing so has life conflicting with one's existence—meaning, life is perceived as a threat. In actuality, life is an opportunity. All threats encountered in life are manifestations of oneself—as though the opposition is always the mirror, thereby requiring continuous change. Each individual experiences only a mirage of self progression when they do not let go to grow, thereby producing a cyclical experience of themselves. Adaptation by way of individual growth is the only way forward. The further someone gets, the more subtle and undetectable becomes the threat. Eventually, stepping through the mirror, though frightful, enables an individual to step into willed existence.

Individuals are not grown through the mirror, nor is anyone pulled past it. Though the mirrored experience makes each individual face the mirror, life is an opportunity to choose existence—to willfully step into eternity. To take such a step, an individual must be "all in." They must give all of themselves to life, and thus must give up the power of rejection. Letting go of any defense toward life is the final, necessary step in order to be fully in the subject position. Then, through the subject lens, the individual is able to begin their eternal becoming—where life, lived as a game, stands as the portal into eternity.

Love Frequency

Modern physicists have demonstrated all matter—everything, both living and inanimate—exists in a state of vibration. The earth itself is vibrating, its frequency having been realized in the middle of last century. Interestingly, the electrical waves of the human brain, when in a relaxed, reflective state—termed alpha-waves—have the same frequency as the earth. With active work or attention, the brain frequency increases (beta-waves), peaking with active thought (gamma-waves). In addition, scientists have been able to detect the frequency of emotion. Just like the color spectrum, there is a spectrum of emotional frequencies. In other words, emotion creates a vibrational wave which travels throughout one's body. The frequencies are received at the cellular level and resonate with one's DNA. Signals of certain wavelengths will activate certain genes, causing *expression* or the creation of proteins. The emotional vibrations are in reaction to the outside world, and thus, one's response to the environment has a determining effect on the genetic response. For human genes to thus respond to one's experience of the outside world illuminates the existence of space between what happens to an individual and how the individual is effected. Considering it is within such space where one's perception upon an occurrence becomes one's experience of the occurrence, the capability to shape one's experience of life is profoundly self-prophetic. Seemingly, life truly is what one makes of it.

The vibrational frequency flowing from individuals into the environment—termed *neurofrequency*—can be thought of as the vibrational resonance of one's nerves as they are outwardly sensed by measurement devices (or other people). In other words, having devices which could detect the frequency being emitted by a person's nerves would enable scientists to measure *neurofrequency*. A person's nervous energy as it combines with cortical arousal (brain wave frequency) will form the person's *neurofrequency*. Ideally, one manages their energy so it is channeled in a balanced fashion. Energy imbalance is a common problem where individuals experience anxious exhaustion. When the energy is not flowing smoothly into purposeful thought or action, a damning effect takes place within the afferent nervous system, and excess anxious energy is experienced. This anxious energy is often visible to others, and readily felt by others. Anxious energy is uncomfortable, and staying busy by doing tasks is a natural response. The energy of life (life-force) feels purposeful, and thus, being in a state where one cannot give intention to the energy, causes problems in the form of physical deterioration or adaptive vegetation (lethargy, obesity). Within the mind, energy is required to deal with energy not being purposed. Thus, energy is needed to inhibit oneself or fight against unacceptable desires. For thought or feeling to battle within one's mind—in the form of conflicting desires or anxieties—requires a significant consumption of one's energy. Similarly, energy purposed for protection of oneself is draining. Energy which is in excess will often get channeled physically (e.g. tic). This channeling into one's peripheral nervous system increases one's *neurofrequency*.

The emotion of fear lies at one end of the emotional spectrum, emitting a low frequency wave. At the other end of the emotional spectrum is the emotion of love, which has a higher frequency. A higher frequency wave is more penetrable than a low frequency wave, meaning it more readily passes through barriers or membranes. People emitting love are sensed differently than those emitting fear. Those who are in a loving state will appear brighter, more sunny and alive—overall, more attractive. Moreover, the higher frequency of love is impenetrable by any of the lower frequency emotions, thus being protective. A life of love would theoretically be a healthier life, improving the expected longevity of an individual's life. The *miracle frequency* or the *love frequency* is 528mhz. Remarkably, 528mhz is the frequency scientists serendipitously found as the frequency which causes DNA to spontaneously repair itself. This intersection has galvanized modern interest in the power of sound. Furthermore, activism to change the standard tuning so that it includes 528mhz is gaining mainstream interest. Sound can also be toxic or dissonant—for certain frequencies can trigger a fear sensation internally. Noxious sound, including the sound of anger, as well as the industrial metropolis, undeniably, has an unsettling impact on those who live within the smog of such dissonance. White noise, because of the static hum of electrical power, has become increasingly omnipresent. More and more people are seeking "peace and quiet" due to the unnerving nature of obnoxious sound and its cumulative strain on the nervous system.

At some point in one's human life span (usually mid 30's), there has occurred enough degradation of one's outer membrane (ego) for the nucleus to activate toward an externalized fulfillment or outward fruition, like a flower. It is analogous to a seed under the soil. A breaking or loss of intactness (conscious death) is necessary for growth to take place. Prior, the individual (seed) is in a state of protected dormancy where it readies itself. Once the internal tension is too great to sustain the balance or containment, the shell breaks and a green stalk of growth comes forth. It grows the structural supports based on its eventual bloom size or purpose, as well as through adaptation within the environment. The flower cannot know itself until it blooms, for knowing itself is realizing itself, not regarding itself. The individual human being must go through a similar process. The activation of the nucleus in response to received frequency induces an "awakening" or a heightening of conscious awareness, thereby enabling the individual to receive conscious understanding of the true nature of life. At the DNA level, there occurs an activation of certain genes, previously dormant. The observation of DNA spontaneously repairing itself in response to the 528 mHz frequency illustrates the nature of this effect. Creation of proteins or structural elements then occurs, eventually altering the membrane so to accommodate the new intelligence or understanding.

If the life force or truth of existence (universal intelligence, divine consciousness) radiates from the sun, and each is born with a receiver within the nucleus of every cell, then it must be presumed the double helix (existing in a state of vibration) responds to a certain wave frequency (e.g. 528 mHz). The cell membrane or ego consciousness thus absorbs it and seeks to utilize the life force and creative potential to control one's own experience. Using such energy or creative potential to fulfill ego desire or protect oneself, however, becomes toxic from the resultant imbalance. The imbalance comes about naturally because of the ego's difficulty with self sacrifice. When an individual senses being asked to give more than they perceive getting, it is common to become defensive and for a power struggle to result. In such a situation, each is trying to represent having a secure level of control over the other. However, for each to receive such security, the other person must make self-sacrifices, thus feeling more controlled or dependent, and potentially more vulnerable. The cycle will continue indefinitely until each's ego or membrane gives up their own feelings or expectations as being paramount to what is given out of love. Once the membrane has thinned to the point where the certain frequency is no longer getting absorbed, then the frequency is able to pass through and into the interior of the cell where it makes contact with the nuclear membrane.

If the connection with one's anxious belief system and need-based attachments is not overcome, then one's consciousness will remain at a lower frequency. The person will resent the world, feeling it has mistreated them. If they have a belief in God, they usually will also believe in eventually being rewarded for what they haven't done. For such individuals, the older they get, the more they trend toward seeing potential threats all around them. They will see what could go wrong and how it may go wrong. They will see their fears staring back at them from the distance, seemingly coming closer minute by minute. "Bad" is seen everywhere, positioning them as "good." The same goes for "wrong" and "right."

When an individual is seeking to feel loved, then they are unable to put forth as much love energy. In other words, someone seeking to feel loved will have a frequency which compels others to help. Wanting to feel loved is from the child mindset, and thus is conceived within one's internal space. Help is a positive, growth promoting energy. Recognizing how much the effort to feel better consumes one's attention and energy brings into sight the lack of positive fruition from such activity. It is important to recognize the effort to be helped casts negative energy into the environment. Often, the realization makes one shameful for not being further along in the ability to give of oneself.

Nuclear Symptoms

The misalignment between one's construct of reality and the truth of one's existence produces symptoms of anxious restlessness. The feeling of skating on thin ice is imbued into one's consciousness to the degree one is misaligned. The more one tries to alleviate their anxiety through giving the anxiety meaning or significance, the worse it becomes. Since one's consciousness ("I") believes in getting what one wants and maintaining what one has, there will always be some degree of conflict with one's nuclear self ("i"). The source of creation must be respected as emitting a directional pressure onto oneself, and yet, consciousness cannot know it—for it is *unconscious*. However, if an individual can interpret symptoms of misalignment correctly, then they can make corrective changes, thereby reducing symptom intensity. When there is a significant misalignment between one's "I" and one's "i" then the compromise of one's functional ability becomes manifest. A prolonged, severe misalignment will show itself physically through decreased vitality and increased pain. A proper clinical assessment, therefore, should take into account the individual's level of self-activation versus self-suppression or inhibition. In doing so, an individual's state of being is regarded. Continued disregard of the body's expressive nature, clinicians within the mental health field are missing the opportunity for a corrective change.

The dynamic nature of every cell's nucleus is demonstrated by the creative activity emerging from it. Outside forces stimulate a messaging cascade which then triggers either an activation or a deactivation—either creation is activated or inhibited. When activated, the necessary creation of proteins occurs in adaptation to one's conscious efforts. Furthermore, since growth is coded for, and thus determined at the nuclear level, a nuclear purpose has to be assumed, even if the purpose is evolutionary advancement. The nucleus may thus be properly conceptualized as bringing the current evolution of what has been.

Life requires a balancing of opposing forces, and thus, the nucleus is likely balancing to one's system. One's body adapts to enable one's being, and thus, will always be illustrative of one's conscious activity. A nuclear adaptation to one's activity is clear throughout the first three decades of life. The transition into middle adulthood however requires one to develop a relationship with one's body—to care for one's body instead of using one's body. The aging process causes a decline in physical function, thus triggering consciousness to de-identify with one's body as one's source of power. Interestingly, as the physical decline occurs, a growth in conscious awareness takes place. As it is impending, one consciously will feel unsettled, possibly to the point of panic. If such feelings are externalized—therefore blamed on others or outside circumstances—then one may react to the anxiousness by dissolving relationships or held positions. Then, a significant change in life circumstances occurs in conjunction with the change in consciousness. To the outside observer, it would be a *midlife crisis*.

Life, generally, can be divided into two stages: childhood and adulthood. However, for no definition of *grown-up* to exist beyond the legally defined age of eighteen, misses out on psycho-emotional definition to apply as a yard stick or mile marker. The achievement of independence should not be used to define *grown-up* since a tremendous amount of personality growth occurs after one becomes independent. The experiences as a young adult, while living independently, shape their sense of who they are and what they want out of life. Each must make their way in the world and find self-acceptance before a sense of being *grown-up* comes into their consciousness. When an individual's own feelings are consciously the most prominent focus, then they have yet to grow up. For feelings to determine how one interacts with the world is characteristic of the childhood mindset. The grown-up mindset, on the other hand, primarily regards their effect on the world. Put another way, childhood is characterized by a conscious effort for internal fulfillment, while adulthood is characterized by the conscious aim toward externalized fulfillment. For the latter to be one's conscious goal, the nuclear self must activate, enabling the ego to sacrifice itself for the betterment of others. To be grown up is, thus, to no longer be driven by fulfillment of internal feeling—where feelings are not themselves the goal. For such to occur, an individual's sensory experience can no longer be prioritized.

The growth necessary to develop the capability to function independently requires a net consumption of energy. Prior to becoming grown-up, an individual's perspective will be self-centered. Behaviors are driven to get something, to feel something, or to reinforce an internal thought. The world is perceived relative to themselves. Once an acceptable amount of development takes place, an internal sense of becoming grown-up occurs. A shift in perspective then takes place—whereby the individual begins perceiving themselves relative to the world. In other words, they begin regarding themselves for what they can bring to the world. Increasingly, their conscious outlook detaches from their internal sense of themselves, attaching rather to their sense of others and how to bring themselves meaningfully to others. This outward purposing of themselves is the blossoming of their nuclear self.

Nature & The Nuclear Self

When individuals are told how they should live or what should be important to them, they usually become defensive—either by making excuses or feeling criticized. There is something within each human which propels them to make their own decisions, to depend on themselves. Studies of the human character have been numerous, where various personality traits have been looked at as they pertain to adaptability for life. Though character traits enabling a more fulfilling life have been elucidated through research efforts over the past century, it has not had much impact on the human individual. This is because the human consciousness cannot recognize itself—one cannot really understand their own personality as it occurs within interpersonal space. An individual's sense of their own personality is a reflective concept which does not develop until formal thinking begins, where they begin reflecting on themselves relative to others. Plus, the more disordered or problematic a personality, the more self-centered will be the person's perspective. This means the more an individual's personality is problematic, the more blind they are to their effect on those outside of them. In other words, individuals with problematic personalities are less able to have a concept of themselves which aligns with others' perspective of them.

Since the "I" of consciousness is drawn naturally to focus on the world relative to oneself, a description of the personality of the world—or life as a personified other—would be much more beneficial for people. The world is alive and relates to each living being as each relates to the world. In other words, each individual is in a relationship with life. The world relates in a consistent way and can be used to chart one's course. The universe, within which one lives, can be related to as a partner reflecting oneself. Again, nobody can be told how to be, for each is purposed to grow in experience and understanding of themselves. Thus, it can be reliably said the universe, as the other, wants all of oneself—for each to come into a full, individualized fruition of themselves—and yet, the fruition must fulfill the world. The fully actualized individual has a loving purpose within the universe. Each may come out of childhood imagining their potential greatness for the world, but the experience of one's greatness will not be simply an imagined thought, nor a feeling experience. Rather, one will become great through a realization of their capability as a loving force within the world, growing in magnitude and magnificence along the way. With each growth step in consciousness, with each quantum step of growth, an individual's awareness increases—both of themselves and of the world. Thus, an individual's awareness of their importance within the universe, and their sense of connectedness to the universe, will intensify. As an individual properly grows, the gravity of their life lightens, and their sense of themselves becomes more diffuse and universal. Inseparable from such expanded awareness is the purpose they have for the growth of others within their world. Advances in consciousness, thus, are always de-centering. Maturation requires perceptively becoming less self-centered. This amounts to having less gravitational weight sensed within oneself, which equates to having less need or less attachment to the world for the sustenance of oneself. Naturally, an individual grows lighter the more they are properly giving of themselves within the world.

As a personified partner, the universe never rewards what one does not do. Rather, the universe is bound to respond to what one does. When one avoids experience of oneself within the world, one senses the universe as rejecting or unfulfilling. For reasons unknown, the world gives each individual the first move. But until they can grow into realizing their creative determination of their experience, they will be bound to perceive themselves reacting to the world. So if an individual is consuming from the world based on self-perceived needs, and reacting to what they perceive being done or not done to them, then their relationship with the world is going to be contentious and unfulfilling. When an individual is running from themselves —where they are trying to escape or avoid themselves through the world— then they cannot truly connect with the world.

Since time moves forward, not doing something is actually doing something—it creates a vacuum of space or a pocket of negative potential. Seeking not to be (x) means the individual believes they are (x). Thus, seeking not to be (x) is a rejection of themselves. For then, they interact with the world as if the world is potentially (x). The individual is bound to see the potential for (x) in everyone, and thus they feel controlled to some degree by everyone's potential to be the (x) which they seek to reject within themselves. The world, however, either does not believe in the individual being (x) or does not understand the nature of being (x), and thus expects the individual to grow past themselves as (x). Life will delightfully manifest how one is not (x), but cannot do so if one is locked in either being (x) or trying not to be (x).

In further characterization of the world as a reactive partner to each, life compels each into a full blossoming of their individuality. The term *individuation* is best thought of as the process of becoming one's own individual—a process which takes a lifetime. As previously noted, the world wants each to fully realize themselves. However, this can only occur when no longer bound to certain internal/external attachments, and also within the framework of the purpose each has within the whole. The world has a positive judgment of each based on their potential, and thus, when an individual is not oriented properly, or not having the necessary experiences within the world, then they will feel subjectively unwell. Similarly, when not sufficiently expressing themselves into the world, individuals feel chaotic and pressured. The degree to which an individual fears themselves within the world will be the degree to which they feel disconnected from the world. The universe expects each to take responsibility for their feelings by transforming them into effort. An individual will then be able to learn from the world as they relate their intent with what actually occurs. Therein, through growth of understanding and self-awareness, an individual gains a better alignment between intent and outcome.

The defensive position, where a person is focused on being wronged (whether based on a thought or a feeling), induces blindness to their effect on the world around them. The perspective is purely in reaction to what they perceive being done to them. However, usually this is a manifestation of what they have done to the world, and thus is a karmic experiencing of their effect. However, when the individual is blind to this, then they cannot see anything but themselves being mistreated or improperly regarded by the world. Judging the world in such a rejective way causes a severance of connection. While defensively it may feel stabilizing for some, the effect is to perpetuate the cycle they are trying to escape.

Through an individual's every experience, by deciphering the purpose within the experience for their growth, they gain further information about themselves. Each individual's nuclear self recognizes the importance of painful and challenging experiences for inducing change, for growing past fears. The letting go of internal elements being held onto for security is exceedingly difficult, and yet growth promoting, Keeping themselves confined internally for a sense of security exacerbates insecurity, and lessens the light each brings forth. However, only through experiencing themselves positively in the context of stepping forth past their limits of conscious comfortability does an individual grow into the positive realization of themselves. However, this requires them to change, to believe in themselves enough to be wrong, to accept an awareness of themselves needing correction, of needing to get better. Because life is purposed for growth, an individual should always seek growth through experience and understanding —both of the world and of themselves. Effort to not change necessitates rejecting growth, to be closed-minded and defensive. In truth, going after the goal of internal security, rather than growth within the world, opposes the actualization of the nuclear self. Doing so is narrow in scope and precipitates leading a life of "quiet desperation."

Two Paths of Growth

There are two ways in which the human mind conceives of psychological growth. The most natural method occurs from a singular sense of self, whereby the individual's effort is to grow better—where capability is acquired and a greater understanding of the world develops. The other approach to growth commonly encountered in individuals—though less adaptive—occurs by way of an effort to not be a certain part of themselves. The aspect which they seek not to be is usually tethered to being hurtful to others or hurt by others. Their effort away from this part of their personality is sensed as a positive pursuit, and usually centers around maintaining control of their anger or avoidance of rejection. A sense of having to be "nice" or pleasing to others puts an undue pressure on their interactions. Thus, in relating to others, they get a sense of being controlled. This is a result of the ongoing effort to not be a part of themselves, where the threat of being perceived for who they seek not to be drives their behavior. Thus, their growth most often equates with keeping control of themselves, as well as maintaining within the mind's of others a positive image of themselves. In contrast, for those who singularly grow themselves better, their growth involves becoming more self-willed and self-assured in the context of being more outwardly purposed.

For those who seek to not be a part of themselves, threat will be perceived as being on the outside and pointed toward the person's insides. Oppositely, those who perceive through the lens of a singular self who is able to grow better perceive threat on the inside in the form of fears of not being. When the threat is sensed internally, the individual naturally strives to grow outwardly better. For the individual seeking not to be, the primary effort is toward internal security or control. Thus, they perceive the outside world for the threat it brings to their sense of internal security. In other words, they must always sense themselves in others, and thus, they are bound see others as beholding a similarly rejective perspective. Those who primarily utilize rejection are naturally compelled toward outside division, and gravitate toward sidedness. The rejective position in relation to others—based on certain identifiable differences—creates a false sense of security through an expressive reaffirmation of the position they are keeping relative to themselves. The security is illusory and only conceived based on the feeling of relief following the expression associated with their rejective behavior.

As a metaphor—each individual, as they initially were conceived, may be likened to a seed. The seed contains all potential, but no fruition, and thus must be regarded as purely evil—where "evil" is the backwards spelling of "live"—meaning, evil opposes life. In other words, evil is the resistance to growth—the force which compels an individual to not change, to not potentiate themselves, to stay contained. Even when growth is occurring, there is a natural resistance which balances the forward growth, enabling controlled growth. Thus, every individual is able to have simultaneous awareness of the forward pressure compelling growth as well as the vacuous uncertainty contained therein. A seed which grows into a flower begins as potential, and ends by fully flowering. Life energy infuses the pressure to grow, which materializes within the encasement until the shell breaks, and the stalk emerges. Growing toward an outside source of life provides direction, where the stalk eventually breaks through the earth, emerging out of the soil and into the light. The stalk uses the density of the soil as a foundation for growth, and the force to not live becomes the root system formed to not die. Such effort is utilized for structural support and for continued growth of the stalk. There occur times where the resistive pressure becomes too great, where a node is reached and division is required for continued growth. As growth continues, and the force of gravity intensifies, a greater proportion of the growth becomes radial. The eventual blossoming is induced by the diminishing life force, whereby the flowering is a full giving of potential in effort to sustain the relationship—to sustain the inflow of life energy.

During the process of growth, of change, two spaces exist for which an individual's focus may fall upon—outside themselves or inside—whereby the internal space is the space which amounts to their remaining potential. Since the potential is not yet manifested, the internal space can only be experienced for what is not, or for what is feared to be. In contrast, an individual may focus on what may be positive in the context of what is, thus becoming blind to what is not. As such, growth will always predominate the person's awareness. When being positive is framed as not being negative, then the individual is taking a double-negative approach to life. Unfortunately, doing so does not prioritize being positive, and so the potential for negative must always be created in forethought. As a result, the amount of positivity which comes forth into the environment is lessened.

Problems

3

3.1

CREATING PROBLEMS

The most essential aspect for any culture to understand about life is how to raise children to go forth into it. Children are naturally full of light and optimism in their approach to the world, believing the horizon will materialize their positive potential. Each enters life growing forward, scripted toward an individualization of purpose, where capability and understanding develop in tandem with the child's growing independence. In order for each to grow into an independent young adult, they must believe in being able to meet their own needs. They have to experience not needing parental help. Independence equates to parenting themselves as they make their way through the life experience. The essential importance of becoming independent is appreciated within an individual's level of potentiated capability. For anyone, of any age, the greater the needed input from others, the less self-actualized output. When the human will is pointed toward self-fulfillment, control, or protection, then the willed effort is not oriented toward achievement or in pursuance of growth. Parenting in a way where the goal is to either fulfill, control, or protect the child, engenders the belief in needing such. They will then grow to see the world and others through the lens of need—to the degree such was provided by their parent(s).

Parental methods which center around control or protection infuse fear into a growing child's perception of life—especially, the child's perception of others relative to themselves. This comes into conflict during the child's pubescence, where they begin relating to an internal self-image. When actively rejecting a part of themselves (the dependent child), an adolescent will have a self-image they seek not to be. This rejected self-image may be aggressive, where control is sought, or it may be fearful, where a sense of security si falsely found in avoidance of what is feared. Such avoidance, generally speaking, is the primary potential pitfall within child and adolescent development. Proper parenting is thus positioned as a framework reflecting optimism for a child, and thereby infusing them with fortitude as they grow into life. Enabling such strength cannot be done, however, through a parent-child relationship which is primarily protective or restrictive. Nor should a parent try to fulfill their child—to make them happy. Doing so, unfortunately, structures the child's expectation for others to make them happy—to do things for them. The more influence a child gets through their expression of negativity (fear, anger, sadness, sickness), the more readily they will express such negativity in hopes of eliciting positivity from others in the form of "care." Putting forth negativity always occurs as a rejection of such negativity—where such feelings are expressed into the world through perceiving the world as the cause, and thus entitling some positive regard in return. Inevitably, come adolescence, doing so will induce "drama" as others become defensive at being perceived as the cause of the expressed negativity. Proper parenting enables a child to develop a sense of being the cause of their own negativity, thereby giving them the ability to put their energies into positively willed activity. Otherwise, their willed effort, to some degree, gets directed toward not feeling negative, which is, in effect, a division or rejection of themselves. Such effort to separate from their own negativity necessitates either perceiving an outside cause for the negativity or believing in a need for something to alleviate the negativity. The paid expense therein is a proportional weakening of willed effort forward, for the willed opposition of negativity is an opposition of their energetic potential.

Finding cause outside of themselves to explain their negativity is an inexorable aspect of every child and adolescent. For adolescents, a natural distancing from the perceived cause, when parents are seen as the cause, facilitates increasing independence. However, if peers or school are perceived as the cause, then the distancing occurs in the wrong direction—where an adolescent becomes more isolated within their dependence at home. Thus, a parental culture which seeks to be accommodating to children and adolescents actually impedes the process of becoming independent. For adolescents, a natural distancing from the perceived cause, when parents are seen as the cause, facilitates increasing independence. However, if peers are perceived as the cause, then the distancing occurs in the wrong direction—where an adolescent becomes more isolated within their dependence at home. Thus, a parental culture which seeks to be accommodating to children and adolescents actually impedes the process of becoming independent. Increasing in scarcity is the adolescent who senses their dependence as a threat—who sees separating from their parents as a positive despite the feelings of vulnerability in doing so. Adolescents are increasingly showing signs of excessive dependence through their perception of the world in front of them as being the source of their negativity, rather than seeking to distance themselves from their attachments. Believing they need emotional support traps them in an experience of the world as the source for their sense of impending negative, where they reflect needing something or someone for which to cope. Keeping their sense of themselves on the outside prevents the formation of an internal center from which their individuality may grow into fruition. Thus, not only is the current approach to parenting promoting dependence, it is stymying individuality. Until a change in perspective materializes, the manifest result will continue to be underachievement and a dimming of creative output.

Diagnosing Problems

The modern ability to study the physical nature of humans down to the atomic level has biased the current cultural consciousness toward blaming an individual's physiochemical makeup for mind-based symptoms. It is hard to imagine one's body determining one's consciousness rather than consciousness becoming aware of one's body. Furthermore, there exists a relationship each must take on with their body—wherein to experience life an individual depends on the conscious ability to control a functioning body. Each is naturally compelled toward a consumptive approach to managing their experiences. The individual consciousness seeks to keep disintegrated feelings or thoughts outside of oneself. Consciousness, in order to reject or avoid what is feared, must attach the problem to something which can be perceived. Since consciousness can perceive the body (and interact with it), an individual's negative internal experience can be perceived as arising from their body. Methods or treatments advertising alleviation without consciousness having to take responsibility are commonplace. This is because people want to feel better without having to change or to let go, without having to be better. Consciousness prefers to be changed rather than to change. The more an individual is accustomed to their negative feelings doing the work for them (through direct influence or entitlement), the more ill-prepared they will be for life—to undergo the necessary struggles and challenges which ultimately are inseparable from growth.

Physicians are educated about the nature of the body and bodily diseases. They are trained to identify and treat diseases. In the doctor's mind, the approach to each patient occurs as an interaction with the body in order to determine *what*, to make a diagnosis. A medical diagnosis confers an understanding of *why*, and thus determines *what* to do. For physical diseases, the nature of the derangement is understood, including the precipitant factors, as well as the available treatment interventions. Thus, patients can assume their doctor, in answering *what*, has an understanding of *why*. In fact, with no physiologic understanding of *why*, then intervening with physiological treatment is reckless and potentially harmful. Physical conditions where no underlying cause is identified, nevertheless, can be understood by the character of physical symptoms produced, and thus, physicians can intervene with treatment at the level of symptom production. Over the counter treatments, as an example, target common symptoms (e.g. sinus congestion), rather than treating the underlying disease (e.g. infection). For medical diagnoses which are not physically rooted, the diagnoses themselves are based on a deviation from the norm. In other words, a certain level of maladaptation serves as the foundation of non-physical diagnoses.

The mental health diagnoses are based on functional, behavioral, and perceptual factors. A physician—in approaching the patient as a *what*—approaches the patient's symptoms as representing a problem existing separate from the patient themselves. However, mental symptoms are imbedded in an individual's sense of themselves and the world around them. Except as they are represented objectively, people do not sense themselves as a *what*. The search for *what* necessarily involves an individual's focal point positioned to explain themselves. Thus, the patient's belief in having a problem gets reinforced through an encounter with a physician pursuing them as a diagnosis. Naturally, when experiencing mental discomfort, human consciousness seeks to identify *what* is the problem or *what* is needed. Such a perceptive position is defensive because it is reflecting threat and seeking to identify need as a result. Doing so enables a sense of control, but gives up the potential for corrective growth found through believing oneself to be the problem, and making changes through insight and understanding. There is a fundamental difference between a person saying "I have problem" versus "I am the problem"—as the two statements cannot come from the same perceptive position. If the belief in having a problem leads to being the problem, then logically an individual may correct themselves only through letting go of the belief in having a problem.

Since the psycho-emotional goal of development is independence, there must occur a breaking of the adolescent's original dependencies. Often, the severance occurs in the context of a relationship, and thus, necessarily will involve mood and behavioral problems as experienced from within the relationship. Normally, the parent will see the adolescent as being the problem. However, from the adolescent's perspective, the parental handling of them is the problem. Enabling the parent to bring their child in for treatment as the identified patient, where the child/adolescent will likely receive a diagnostic label, further solidifies within their identity the idea of having a problem. The more an adolescent identifies with having problems, the more they will be a problem. Usually, they will conceptualize the problem as involving their feelings, believing their feelings are disabling and unchangeable, and thus seek to not take responsibility for their feelings, but rather to have them and entitle their expression for help.

Because parents, in dealing with a problematic child, feel helpless and consciously chaotic, they seek to gain control. However, in doing so, they usually go about it in a way which exacerbates the problem. Often, they will turn to the medical system for help. Naturally, the parent is concerned something is wrong with their child or teenager. However, it is the parental concern or worry about there being a problem which the child/teenager is rebelling against. Invariably, the child/teenager feels they need more positive feeling inside, which they seek to get from their parent. So for the medical system to individualize the problem by diagnosing the child or adolescent with a psychiatric disorder which is currently conceptualized by the lay public as genetic and carried through life, causes problems in two different ways. First, it forces the child or adolescent to regard themselves as having a problem at a time in their life where they most need to feel similar to others or connected with others. This further degrades their sense of capability and likelihood for success, as well as increasing their social nervousness due to feeling comparatively less like the general peer populace. Secondly, the primary parent will often become more controlling or protective as a result of the diagnosis, seeing the problem as a condition within their child. This further imbalances the focal point of treatment away from the relationship dynamic. As a result of these two effects, the child/adolescent becomes more imbedded with the problem. While acutely with treatment things can get better, in the long run of the child's development, the effect is an increased likelihood of psycho-emotional impairments extending into adulthood.

An internal source of the problem ascribes the issue as existing within the individual's consciousness, within the interplay of feeling and thought. The capacity to correct the problem through growth is inherently a potential of the human spirit. If one believes in a mind-based source to their symptoms, then by looking inside of oneself to determine *why*, insight is generated. Changes in how one relates to oneself lead to the internal corrections which then outwardly manifest in one's environment. On the other hand, if the symptoms are believed to have a bodily source, then naturally one will seek to identify *what* the problem is and *what* the problem needs. The fundamental error in doing so, as it pertains to psycho-emotional symptoms, comes in the symptomatic individual's separation of their symptoms from themselves. Truly, an individual cannot "have" something unless they can conceive of it separate from their perceptual experience of it. For this to occur, an individual must see their feelings as a problem rather than as an aspect of themselves, as they are being. Then, if a feeling or emotion cannot in and of itself be a problem, mental struggles or mental disorders must be due to an error in the cognitive processing of feelings. For a patient to conceive of themselves as having a mental disorder equates to a belief in needing help— either in the form of medication or interpersonal care. Such attachments to outside help are used to manage an individual's sense of themselves, but cause a triangulation of their consciousness. Thus, their perceptive interaction with the world is defensive—they see the world as it effects them rather than being able to regard themselves for how they effect the world. Such a protective approach, unfortunately, causes an individual's world to narrow, and they become more and more dominated by how they feel.

There exists an inherent flaw within this country's current approach to mental health and substance abuse. As it currently stands, most attempts to help are having a precipitating effect amongst the nation's youth. Strategies to identify *at risk* youth are based on an assumption that, in doing so, those identified as having mental health or substance abuse problems, subsequently, will receive help. However, with the current treatment approach to mental health and substance abuse problems, the medical model is creating problems, not curing them.

Children who are considered mentally ill, when frustrated, act like babies. Adolescents who are diagnosed with mental disorders, when not getting their way, act like children. Adults who believe they have a mental disorder, like teenagers, make the world in front of them responsible for their negativity. Thus, it is no wonder adults with issues fight against such issues when they manifest in their children. Doing so creates an erroneous belief in the child's mind about themselves, thereby leading to an avoidant or rejective relationship with part of themselves. The part, or issue, stays attached to outside needs, creating dependencies and compromising growth. The more an individual keeps part of themselves separate from integrative growth, the more energy they have to spend opposing themselves. A depletion of energy available for conscious activity then develops. Therein, the purposing of their effort revolves around keeping things the same and minimizing discomfort. However, in doing so, they are striving against growth.

A problem-based approach to mental health is providing support for a growing proportion of the teenage population in their perceptive experience of life itself being a problem. By seeing mental health and substance abuse through the lens of the medical disease model, an adult population was formed which, generally, did not take responsibility for their feelings, thoughts, and behaviors. The population, as a whole, lost sight of maturational factors—of the essential importance of growth. Thus, emotional identification with children was inevitable. Especially in relating to the emotional volatility and insecurity of adolescents, adults began overly identifying with their teenagers. However, what is normal for an adolescent is not normal for an adult. Yet, the adult population has grown increasingly blind to the difference. Being unable to see the immaturity in themselves, the adult population (including the mental health system) began to regard adolescents as having mental health problems, attaching pathology to normality. Thus, at present, a relatively normal adolescent, during the period of *identity crisis,* is readily seen by the adult population as having a mental health problem. However, at the same time, they are being given mirroring support from adults for how they are feeling and for reaching out for help.

The systematic approach to children and adolescents has been to minimize insult and provide help by identifying those in need of help. Seeking to protect them from each other has created the sense of needing protection from themselves. Therein, adolescents are being lead astray. In search for help with their emotional struggles, they are being taught to reach out. Yet, in doing so, they are being labeled with problems and treated as if they have a mental disease. Most will identify as such, and thus, the belief in a part of themselves being a problem becomes solidified. Most of their adult life will then be spent coping with how they feel relative to life, blind to the potential growth which is possible through integration with themselves. Instead, they identify as having needs outside of themselves, for which they depend on people or substances. Yet, in actuality, believing they have such needs, and the fears of loss contained therein, is their greatest impediment to growth. Because of an erroneous conception of themselves (their problematic potential), they seek to not be—to not feel, to not experience. Thus, most symptoms they struggle against are a result of what they seek to avoid— themselves.

The Belief in a Problem

Negative sensory data enters consciousness through the afferent sensory system. The data is initially processed by a reflective thought filter—the ego consciousness—where it undergoes *problem/no problem* determination. If the experienced feeling is processed as a *problem*, then it becomes associated with an outside need. The analogous *feeling-thought-need-alleviation* paradigm existing naturally is: *hunger —> problem —> food —> alleviation*. All negative feelings are initially processed as being analogous to hunger, and thus, the young child will express upset outwardly. But when a *no problem* response is provided, then the child cannot keep processing the sensory data as a *problem*. If processed as *no problem*, then it gets naturally diffused into one's purposeful intent. During early childhood, when upset feeling is expressed, having it regarded as *no problem* allows the child to accept it and deal with it. In doing so, the feelings get integrated into their developing will and manifest through their functional efforts. In effect, the feelings get channeled into their activity.

When a negative feeling is believed to be a problem, the child will direct their effort toward getting help for the feeling through *acting out*. This enables them to be the feeling and experience the parental reaction. The impressionable years are the pre-thinking years, where the child's feelings are tethered to parental beliefs about the feelings. Before thinking begins, the human mind is unable to independently interject a belief atop their feeling. Thus, the developing mind is bound to believe as their parent reflects them to be. The parental reaction comes to form the child's perspective in dealing with such feelings internally. Thus, the *how* to handle it is experienced from within the relationship rather than learned through being told how they should handle it. The *acting out* of the negative feeling believed to be a problem will continue into adolescence, therein getting fuel added to the already existing fire. The parent usually reacts to the behavior itself rather than seeing it as an attempt to display the emotion their child is struggling to handle. Once the child experiences being reacted to as if they don't need anything, then they can step past the acting out and grow in understanding and acceptance of themselves. However, as long as the parental reaction reinforces feelings being a problem, then the child will continue to act out the feelings in hopes of being helped.

When a parent perceives a threat in something their child does or expresses, then getting defensive is automatic. For the child, being reflected as a problem and needing such a reaction is believed. Thus, for parents, the aspect of themselves which they relate to as a problem will be seen and reacted to as a problem in their child. This gives experiential reality for the child of having a particular problem. However, if the parental reaction is defensive, then they are giving the child a problem without a solution. Therein, the problem is passed on.

The child attributes causality to the way in which they are treated. Everything which is done for them they must believe is needed or desired. They form beliefs about themselves based on how their feelings (wants, fears, anger) or behaviors are responded to by their parents. The parental response determines the meaningfulness of how the child is feeling or what the child is experiencing. For the child, the significance of their emotion or their behavior is encoded through the parent's defensive or emotional response. Seeking to make the child feel better confers to the child their negative feelings are a problem requiring parental support. It also roots the child in the dynamic where they bring negative feelings to their parent to see how much the parent attaches to such feelings or thoughts. In other words, the more a parent has a negative or fearful response to their child's emotional expressions or acting out behaviors, the more the child must regard themselves sensitively. This is because they are sensitized to negative feelings requiring outside help to be made better. When a child experiences parental worry for them, they must regard themselves as causing the worry or needing to be worried about. They will thus believe the cause is a deficiency about them or an incapability with what they are doing. In effort to get their parent to stop worrying, a child will try to prove themselves through risky, rambunctious behavior. In other words, a child will act in ways to try and counterbalance the thought belief they are reflecting from their parent based on their parent's relational treatment of them.

Once puberty initiates the ability for internal self-reflection, causing upset to the parent triggers the adolescent to feel insecure and unaccepted. The adolescent continues to perceive everything their parent says or does to them as being caused by them or reflecting their level of need. As a result, they are quick to get defensive when they perceive parental criticism. Furthermore, the more their parent, in raising them, strove to make them happy or to alleviate negative feelings, the greater will be the teenager's perceived need for outside help in order to feel better. They are then more likely to form a belief in having a problem, thus entitling a remedy.

When their feelings do not receive help from peers, they are quick to believe no one likes them. In order to achieve some sense of separateness from home, they will begin to seek autonomous ways to make themselves feel better, for they intuitively know they cannot achieve independence while depending on their parent for emotional support. Most frequently, drugs and relationships are used by adolescents who are having excessive difficulty managing their negative feelings. Whatever becomes their emotional bridge into social integration, they will attach to as a need going forward. Therein, the initial "use" can quickly become "abuse" as it solidifies into something they believe they need. Psychologically, it is a re-creation of the emotionally supportive parent, for which they may depend on to help them feel better.

Increasingly, young adults are believing they need functional support from their parents. As a cohort, they are very sensitive to their feelings, and yet also expect their expressed negativity (criticisms, complaints) to gain influence over those around them. They readily identify problems outside of them without regarding how they are coming off in doing so. Not being held accountable for how one feels undermines taking responsibility for managing such feelings—noticeable at the cultural level for at least a decade. Increasingly, young adults are emerging with a hypersensitivity to negative feelings and hypercritical thoughts of the world in front of them, producing a lukewarm engagement with life and their potential therein.

The child learns to deal with negative feelings because they have to—believing such feelings are not problem enough to warrant outside help, they take to dealing with them through their growth and development. The physiologic tracks which determine one's *neurofrequency* are laid during early childhood. How one relates internally to their own feelings is patterned during early childhood as well. Thus, the early relationship experience with mom is foundational for establishing a sensory connectedness with one's own feelings. How mom reacts to the feelings of the child will be how the child, when older, comes to react to their own feelings.

When a toddler hurts themselves and comes running to mom, she empathizes with their pain but reacts with calm conviction in telling them they are going to be "okay." Then suddenly they are—usually back playing within seconds. Normally, mothers do not take responsibility for keeping their child protected from physical pain, and since mom's body is separate she does not actually feel her child's pain. However, when the pain is emotional or psychological, then it becomes more difficult to react with certainty that things are going to be okay. Reacting to the child's upset feelings (anger, crying) the same way as when reacting to the child's physical "boo-boo" is hard because, unlike with physical pain, there is no clear separation between mom's feelings and her child's feelings. This sets the stage for mom to see concerning aspects of herself in the child, thereby externalizing her own issues onto the child. By identifying problems in one's child, a parent will treat them as if they are a problem—illustrating the primary way psycho-emotional problems or disorders are passed on. It is fruitful to recognize the toddler running to mom because of their "boo-boo" is not coming to be made better—they are simply coming for a *problem* or *no problem* designation—in order to give thought structure to the experience. Thus, once they get a *no problem* reflection, almost magically, they are able to return to play as if nothing happened.

An analogy in this case is helpful. Imagine a parent reacting to a child passing gas by getting upset. Naturally, because children identify with their feelings, the child will have to believe gas is a problem, believing their passing gas needed the reaction from their parent. The need is assumed based on the occurrence of a problem, and therein the belief is formed. Going forward, the child will be hypersensitive to feelings of gas inside them, thus becoming more "gassy" in character. They will be quick to express stomach upset. Also, their anxious reactions to the feeling of gas exacerbate the gaseous milieu of their bowel, thus perpetuating itself. If a time comes where the discomfort is too great or defenses overwhelmed, the flatulence would most certainly explode inappropriately, problematically, and therein fulfilling their belief. Acutely, they will regard themselves as a failure for having lost control. Similarly, when negative feelings from the child are reacted to by their parent(s) as if the expression of those feelings is a problem, then the child believes such feelings should not be happening. Thus, they form the perspective of such feelings, when being experienced, representing a problem. Thoughts related to the problematic feeling become more anxious, just as the anxiety related to feelings of gas worsen because of the belief in the gas being a problem. Once the child reaches puberty and starts to think, and thus begins internally relating to their feelings, believing uncomfortable feelings (fear, anger, anxiety) are a problem will precipitate the problem. Adding to the difficulty—the more an individual believes certain feelings within them are a problem, the more dependent they will feel on whatever they believe they need to handle themselves, to be able to feel better.

A praiseful response to a child is appropriate in reaction to something positive the child has done. However, praise for the purposes of motivation or display (bragging) should be avoided since the effect becomes to create a need for such external input. Children entitle (x) within a belief system which ascribes a need for (x) simply by having gotten (x) from their parent in the context of the sensory experience (y). Thus, preparing children for a fulfilling life requires not doing things for them. Support for the child's function comes through providing them optimistic regard when they are doubting themselves, as well as through functional modeling. If the parent is doing it for the child, then the child must adapt to needing it done for them rather than developing the independent function to do it themselves.

False beliefs are created from reflecting themselves as causing the response from their parent as if the response was needed. However, the child can also form false beliefs by associating discomfort or pain with the context in which it occurred. For example, a toddler who experiences pain while having a bowel movement on the toilet will associate toileting with being painful. This will precipitate avoidance of going "number two," thus worsening the potential pain through a growing constipation. If the child continues to consciously associate having a bowel movement with pain, they will begin to develop gastrointestinal issues, and physical symptoms may generalize. Finally having a bowel movement will cause significant pain, thus reinforcing the belief. Once a child is old enough to conceptualize what is happening anatomically, and understand the reason for the pain, they are more readily able to deal with it as part of the natural working of things, rather than representing it as a problem.

The more an individual has the sense of needing to feel better or be better (thought), the greater the likelihood of dependence on something or someone. The internal relationship one has with oneself can either be in relation to how one feels in their present context, or in relation to the judgment of one's being. If reflecting off of feeling, then two aspects become crucial to understand—in reflecting off of feelings, is it primarily one's internal feelings which are reflected off of, or the external feelings from others? And secondly, how does one go about alleviating negative feelings? Avoidance and blame are maladaptive methods of handling negative feelings —meaning, they do not promote growth of understanding, nor foster interpersonal intimacy. The more an individual can believe negative feelings within themselves are non-threatening, and when observed in others are likely based on misunderstanding or misperception, the more naturally an individual will react to negative feelings by seeking to understand more deeply the situation at hand.

Growing Problems

The culture has been steadily progressing toward a more child-centered approach to raising children. Adults have become more sensitive to the needs of children. During times of affluence, few will oppose energy/resources going toward meeting the needs of children. However, who is identifying need? The nature of a child's psychological development, up until the present, has not been understood enough to accurately meet the needs of children. During times when survival must be prioritized, children will be adapted toward survival rather than having their experience prioritized. The relative peace and affluence for the past fifty years afforded an increasingly child-centered culture. However, doing so has exposed the character of the child mind and how their mind integrates what is done for them. Moreover, the process of development as preparation for life has been reaffirmed though the current wave of maladapted youth—who are demonstrating difficulty with life's challenges and believing their needs are going unmet. More and more children are struggling with their emotions in the school setting, being unable to channel their negative feelings into effort. Such children are becoming adolescents who seek to self-medicate through drugs, excessive gaming, and other various addictions. Adolescents, in increasing numbers, are having difficulty moving on—the step forth from home, whether into college or into independent living, isn't being accomplished. The cultural response, in attempt to identify the problems, has focused on finding something tangible (e.g. drugs), while increasingly trying to meet the needs of children. But since the psycho-emotional needs of children have not been outlined, children have been determining their own needs through their expression of need. In doing so, however, they are being taught to form thought out of feeling. In other words, children are being taught to see the world and themselves through a lens of how they feel. But since feeling is meant for energetic effort, turning feeling into thought comes at the expense of experience. The more a child turns their emotion into thought, the more they will be reliant on others regarding how they feel, and the less the child will then channel their feelings into action, into experience.

Presently, for adolescents, their surge in hormonal activation is having difficulty finding expression through mindful movement forward. Thus, they sense pressure from the outside, or *stress* as they term it. Like adolescents of any era, they are bound to blame parents/authority. Within the cloud of their stress, adolescents perceive an endless amount of need. Accordingly, as the culture increasingly moves toward meeting the needs of children and adolescents, without knowing what they need, supports are having to be put in place to meet the demand—to meet the "need." Without psychological separation being attained between their feelings and their thoughts, adolescents are unable to transition into independence without excessive psycho-emotional instability (anxiety, depression, anger). Increasing numbers are being diagnosed with a mental illness when they ask for help from the medical system. As a result, the proportion of the population believing they have a mental health disorder or illness, especially among the younger generations, is growing. More and more individuals, in believing they have a problem, are not growing. Exponentially more individuals are simply having trouble "adulting."

As previously noted, within one's internal interaction with oneself, a belief in having a problem can only be supported by believing feelings themselves can be a problem. The source of the feelings, then, must be identified—which must either be oneself ("me") or elements effecting oneself. The latter may include the environment, people, or one's personal circumstances. Assigning the problem to elements separate from oneself creates a sense of control through the perceptive handling of the problem element. Through one's relational interaction with such elements, one establishes physical separateness, and then, if need be, a sense of being able to escape or dominate the element. However, in doing so, one interacts problematically toward the outside elements, where then problems manifest. For example, Jack sees Jill as the element responsible for his jealous insecurity, and tries to restrict her behavior, causing Jill a sense of being rejected. A great deal of relationship strain comes from individuals being unable to perceive space between how they feel and how they are. On the other hand, if the source of negative feelings is within oneself, then one must focus on how one is being, whereby corrections occur as one approaches others and the world. The difficulty in doing so is from the sacrificial nature of the process—the letting go of what one believes one needs, as well as the facing off against what one fears losing. For those who believe they have a problem with their feelings or thoughts (or both), they will attach to needing something or someone to manage themselves, thus consciously centering their stability around such needed attachments.

When the problem is a belief in oneself having a problem, necessarily then, one perceives the world through a lens of having a problem. Beliefs crystalize and manifest, and so to change one's belief structure as one relates to oneself requires a change in consciousness. A new structuring of one's perspective is born from destruction of the old one. This requires a conscious giving up or letting go of oneself. Letting go of what one believes they need is scary. However, the belief in needing emotional support traps an individual in depending on something or someone outside themselves. As a result, life becomes riddled with anxiety the more someone believes what they need is outside their control.

The vast majority of adolescent mood problems occur in the context of the teen's emotional dependency on a parent. Adolescents are developmentally directed toward independence from their parents—who often reflect them being a problem and in need of parental control. The adolescent fights to reflect not being a problem, desperate to be treated as if they are not a problem—as if they do not have to be controlled, monitored, or restricted. They cannot become independent without a belief in their ability to do so. When their functional capability has been tied to help from the parent, then becoming independent threatens to undermine their function. In a patient who is not yet emotionally and/or psychologically independent from their primary attachment figure, treating them for individualized psycho-emotional problems is non-sensical. By the very definition of what an adolescent is trying to achieve—independence—problematic moods and/or behaviors have to be approached with an understanding of the context in which they are occurring. Often, the goal of an adolescent attaining independence is not prioritized by the parent(s). If safety or protection is the primary goal, then there will occur a directional conflict. The adolescent will reflect the safety driven parenting as if the parent is judging them to be incompetent. This causes a reflective conflict, since the adolescent wants to reflect confidence and a lack of concern from the parent. An adolescent will thus rebel against being treated, in their eyes, as if they have a problem. Furthermore, for the system (representing society) to attach a label or diagnosis traps an adolescent in a belief of having a problem and an entitlement to be made better.

Part and parcel to becoming independent is a letting go of dependencies. This requires a fundamental shift or step forward in consciousness, which occurs in a quantum or step-wise fashion. Preceding this event is an intensification of anxiety and mood lability, and necessarily the adolescent expresses feelings of being stuck, unfairly regarded, and wanting to escape life. The latter conscious desire brings about the thoughts of death, dying, and possibly thoughts of killing themselves. Truly, this is a death of consciousness (as it feels), and is inherently tied to the process of adolescent detachment. Seeing it as representing a problem rather than a developmental process, however, triggers teens to try and reject part of themselves rather than grow themselves.

From middle childhood onward, there is an aversion to consciously believing one has a problem. Thus, adolescents will often react angrily to parents when they feel treated *as if*—as if they are being mistreated, unaccepted, or misunderstood. The extreme self-centeredness of their perceptive sense of causality makes it so they truly see the world as relating or revolving around them. This creates discord between the parent and the independently judging adolescent. In the historically normal situation, such discord motivated the adolescent to leave home. However, with increasing parental anxiety and a generalized breakdown of male-female relations, male children are becoming more and more unmotivated, passive, and fearful about separating from home. Female children are generally demonstrating increasing anxiety and an anxious need to feel in control. Increased anxiety invariably degrades self-esteem and infuses more threat into the world which they forecast facing. There is a strong correlation between the level of continued emotional or psychological dependence on one's parents and the intensity of anxiety and/or mood symptoms. This correlation is strongest and most visible during adolescence and into an individual's early twenties.

To believe one's negative feelings or negative thoughts are a problem binds one's consciousness to perceive such feelings or thoughts as a threat. Thus, one becomes fearful of oneself. Countering negativity with fear causes further imbalance, thereby further worsening the negative feelings or thoughts. When in relative fear of one's ability to tolerate a feared scenario (death, abandonment) or of one's potential behavior when upset, then one has yet to come into an internal acceptance. Such an individual will be primarily focused on their own feelings or thoughts, thus perceiving the world and others therein as two-dimensional or only in relation to themselves. Often, such problems are only appreciated within one's relationships wherein the expectation is for one's attention to be in regard of the other person's feelings.

Too much negative feeling is blinding to one's consciousness, essentially trapping it within itself. The ego consciousness cannot perceive suffering as justified when none was intended or desired, and thus, will search to identify the source of the negative feeling outside oneself, so to alleviate the suffering. However, when consciousness itself is operating under a belief system about a sensory feeling (e.g. anger) which is erroneous, symptoms of consciousness occur. Symptoms of consciousness are sensory feelings triggered by a critical misalignment between one's ego and one's nuclear self. Usually, a conscious attachment one believes they need is incompatible with one's nuclear direction. Consciousness must attach to the feelings as indicative of an underlying problem threatening one's stability, which is half true since the ego consciousness is threatened by the impending doom of itself. Since the ego cannot conceptualize the death of itself as a rebirth of oneself, it naturally fights to sustain itself through a pursuit to uncover something it can identify as causing the feelings.

From the perceptive experience of an individual who believes a negative feeling (x) (x = fear, anger, sadness) is a problem, they perceive (x) as happening to them. Consciousness cannot perceive it happening from within themselves. Feeling (x) is automatically attached to an outside cause. Put another way, feeling (x) is the basis for explaining the world unto themselves rather than perceiving feeling (x) as representing themselves unto the world. Thus, in management of feeling (x), they will either avoid certain elements of the world or will be overly controlling of the environment (the individual's world). The adaptive approach is to recognize feeling (x) as an indicator of how they are or are not engaging with the world.

From the analogous standpoint of the mind, hunger happens to an individual. Nobody blames themselves for feelings of hunger. Hunger is seen as happening to oneself and signaling a need outside of one's body. When negative feelings are kept similarly outside of oneself, then consciousness must perceive them as happening to oneself. For instance, the individual who believes anger is a problem will always perceive themselves being made angry. The feeling of anger then necessitates a distancing or suppressive action, thus separating themselves from the situation. However, once such negative feelings are internalized or accepted, then a processing or digestion can take place, whereby the negative feelings get expressed appropriately, systemically, and are a part of the individual's energetic effort.

The Marriage and Family Problem

The children born to the *Baby Boomers* were late to grow up. Their young adulthood was prolonged, likely as a result of more privileged lifestyles. Romance had been idealized through movies and television. Most got married seeking to be made happy, while still developing their identity. Mirroring relationships—where each reflects the other's positivity unto themselves—have always been full of promise. Thus, the getting married process should be relatively free of discord or push-pull dynamics. Two individuals getting married who are not internally accepting of themselves—who are not *grown up*—is now commonplace. However, once a child is brought between them, the relationship becomes a triangulated system. A child requires a significant input of positive energy. This necessitates a shift in the flow of energies, where both parents are called on to give more than they get. However, prior to being grown up, an individual will consume more of the world around them than they put in. Thus, to continue growing up while raising a child is a recipe for conflict.

When a parent has not yet grown up, they will seek, to some degree, emotional fulfillment through their child. If a parent still has a conscious desire to feel loved or approved of, then the parent will seek to feel needed by their child. When feeling rejected, such a parent will often act out emotionally. For the child, an unnatural fear becomes induced, eventually producing a hypersensitivity to causing upset. Later, come adolescence, the child will excessively try to shut-down when upset, or else have emotional eruptions. As they relate internally to their emotions, they do so with intense suppression and minimal processing. They grow to regard emotion as a threat, and thus, they have a limited understanding of their feelings.

More commonly, a parent will pursue a sense of control through their children. Parents who crave feelings of security often seek excessive closeness or compliance from their child. An infant's complete dependence allows the parent to feel in total control. However, the level of control begotten of the baby soon becomes lost with the emergence of a pushing and pulling toddler. Parenting is then a gradual letting go of control. For the parent, pulling at the rope rather than giving more slack produces the opposite results they intend.

Pursuing a sense of control through one's child will either involve *mirroring control* or *complementary control*. *Mirroring control* tries for positive emotional reflections from the child, where the parent seeks to feel liked and impressive to the child. *Complementary control*, on the other hand, seeks agreeability and compliance from the child so to enable the parent a sense of control. Mirroring control is driven by self desires while complementary control is from the alpha perspective. The need created in the child, when the parent is seeking mirroring control, involves needing what they want based on the desire itself. When complementary control is sought by the parent, it instills in the child a sense of needing to be approved of by the parent/authority. When a parent seeks emotional fulfillment or security through their child, it forces the child into the other relational role position (self or alpha), therein shaping the child's character.

A child is meant to identify partly with both parents—ideally, being able to do so while having stability and security from the environment, and through the experience of a balanced relationship between parents. A balanced parental relationship allows the child to consciously experience how each regards the other positively, and how each is able to accept the other's faults. This then allows the child a greater internal balance between their two parts.

When their is extensive instability between parents, where the threat of relationship fracture is actualized in the child's consciousness, then the child will have more difficulty developing self integration or self acceptance. Thus, despite aging into adulthood, becoming psycho-emotionally grown-up is delayed, and for some, meaningful maturation never occurs.

The dissolution of marriages is producing a growing percentage of children who are the primary partner for their parent. This is forcing an increasing number of children into the complementary role within a binary relationship with their parent. This naturally imbalances the child, though not until the onset of thinking does it become individually evident. For within the two-part consciousness the imbalance occurs. The imbalance will occur as an underdevelopment of whichever position is occupied by the primary parent (usually mom)—either their self aspect or their alpha aspect.

When a child grows up without a stable family unit, then, as an adult, they do not know how to form a stable system themselves. To be raised in an environment where one feels secured through their membership in a nuclear family is priceless. Otherwise, being a dependent within a family which is unstable or fractured is a source of insecurity. The source of insecurity will also behold, at times, illusory feelings of security. Thus, unstable families have the most attachment related discord. Interestingly, families and extended families having the most members with emotional problems, generally, demonstrate the greatest level of relational entitlement conferred to each from each. Thus, when an individual is struggling, they tend to entitle support. Reflective judgments ping-pong back and forth, and sibling rivalry like relationships can permeate an extended family network. In such scenarios, each is judging the other based on themselves feeling negatively judged or mistreated. When the family is believed to be a safety net, and yet the net comes with strings attached, then the supportiveness usually necessitates frequent contact. This keeps dysfunctional families clumped in close proximity with each other. Mood problems are thus able to stay somewhat contained, though each must attach to the other's subjectivity of them.

Parents are no longer able to rely on the village in raising their child (*It takes a village to raise a child*). Prior to the media induced paranoia about "what could happen" children would play throughout the neighborhood—they were all over the place like little explorers of their own world. Parents knew very little, but each child knew when they needed to be home, and they complied. It was usually by dark. Parents did not judge other parents through a standard of hyper-control over their children. This allowed for much less parental stress about what others may or may not be thinking about their parenting. The media explosion toward the turn of the millennium fed into the parental desire to stay informed, and yet, it also lead to parents questioning themselves. The *what if* worry within the parental instinct faced a barrage of bad news, seeding their consciousness with troubling thoughts. Taking measures to protect children was en vogue, but soon became over sterilizing to where children increasingly are dependent on parents to provide them entertainment. No longer are children expected to use their curiosity and creativity to play amongst themselves, and increasingly, children are getting their entertainment at home through video games. When adolescence arrives, however, and they become conscious of the need for social integration, doing so feels too foreign. They run into a social discomfort which impedes their maturation and lessens their likelihood of being able to become independent from home.

Scenarios where a young adult is living with their parent who is still living with their parent are becoming more common. The parent-child relationship, in such situations, is frequently typified by power-struggles which can resemble sibling rivalry. The more the parent's parent (grandparent) tries to parent their parenting (tongue-twister unintended), the more it will precipitate a power struggle between them and their child. The grandparent tends to identify with the child, and thus, the child is compelled into mirroring the grandparent, thereby seeking to be like the grandparent in the relationship with their parent. Frequently, when the child's parent is still growing-up, the grandparent will be controlling of the parent. Thus, the child will seek controlling interaction with their parent. Often, in these situations, the parent flees from their parenting responsibilities into unstable relationships, essentially leaving the child to be raised primarily by the grandparent. This then forces the child into the role their parent vacated, and a similar dynamic will eventually result—the same dynamic which kept their parent overly dependent on their grandparent.

The Relationship Problem

The character of relationship with one's feelings is patterned according to the relationship between the young child and their primary caregiver (usually mom). For instance, if mom is a worrier, then the child will perceive causing mom to worry based on a need to be worried about. They do not want to internalize the belief of being worrisome to others. Yet, they are bound to perceive the worry coming at them as reflecting their lack of capability or fragility. Thus, they will get more and more wild or daring to prove their capability and resilience, to get mom to stop worrying. However, in doing so, from mom's perspective, they fulfill being a problem in need of worry. Eventually, they will get themselves in trouble to the point where they acquiesce to the belief in needing to be worried about. Anxiety then begins to manifest as they take to worrying about themselves.

A personal relationship (including an intimate or love relationship) involves 2 components: emotion and judgment. When one seeks to bring positive feeling to another or alleviate negative feeling, and each gives relevance to the other person's judgment of them, then a relationship exists. An acquaintance-type relationship involves surface regard, but does not maintain the personal component. The parent-child relationship is uniquely authoritarian. Its purpose is to provide stability, nurturance, and guidance, with the goal of enabling independent function, where they step forth in pursuit of their own potential. In an authoritarian parent-child relationship, the parent must be in the alpha position relative to the child who should be in the self-role. Thus, the parent's sense of themselves is not tethered to the child's happiness toward them. The more the character of the parent-child relationship is appropriately authoritarian, the less there will be elements of a personal relationship within the parent-child dynamic.

The authoritarian parent is able to provide reflections of confidence for the child which are very significant to the child's belief in themselves. Despite a child's nervousness or lack of self-assurance at times (in attempting something new or challenging), being able to reflect positivity from the parent enables the trying and succeeding process. The parental anxiety sensed by the child is usually based on personal issues in the parent, meaning fears of loss, fears of not being good enough, or fears of something bad happening. These issues stem from insecurities within the parent. The more a parent identifies themselves through their child, the more the relationship takes on the character of a personal relationship. The personal relationship dynamic drives the parental effort to reflect happiness from their child or reflect "success" in their child. This latter effort usually revolves around the child's academic performance at school or athletic performance in a sport. The problem comes in the child's reflection of needing to be pushed or helped because they are not capable enough. Once thinking begins, and they begin internally relating with themselves, they will have to internally relate with the belief in needing help or pressure to get things done well enough. A child or adolescent's ability to do something they do not want to do is based on the internal relationship with their feelings. The more they are accustomed to their negative feelings influencing their parent, the more difficulty they will have doing something in the face of not feeling the want to do it.

The child is bound to represent their parent and the outside world as thought. Thus, parenting with emotion gets misrepresented by the child. Children do not naturally regard the feelings of others since they are perceiving thought outside of them. They are thinking about outlets for their desires, focused on objects around them, seeking to understand something or someone, or seeking to demonstrate their ability. Prior to being able to internally think about their feelings, they will not be able to conceptualize others' feelings as relevant. So when a parent expresses upset or anxiousness, the child will perceive it as a negative thought about them. Not until reflective thinking begins around puberty does the child begin to see the worry as "care." However, by then, excessive insecurity has been imbedded into their perception of themselves relative to the world.

When the parent-child relationship is personal in nature, then the child's personality will form in a way which is suited to make the relationship most stable. For the developing child, an individualization of being and purpose is thus compromised. The more a parent emotionally or psychologically relies on the relationship with their child, the more the parent will seek to feel approved of or needed. Because consciousness forms from a dependent perspective, such parenting perpetuates neediness in the developing child. To the extent a parent seeks to feel loved or secure through their child, the child will require outside help to deal with their negative feelings. As an adolescent, they perceive things through a lens of what they feel they need and tend to be outwardly expressive of such needs. Others experience such an individual as "high-maintenance" or "spoiled." However, if such individuals are able to sustain themselves in such a way, they will never develop security by independently fulfilling their own needs.

The experience of happiness, when it occurs within the context of a relationship, produces a sense of emotional dependence on the other person. This brings about insecurities related to fears of loss, since the positive feelings are consciously tethered to the other individual—where the thought of losing the person threatens loss of the positive feelings as well. When a mom takes a personal relationship approach to her child, she seeks to protect the child from negative feelings. She takes reflective positivity in her own mothering when she is able to reflect her child being happy. However, within the perception of the child, he or she needs to be made happy. The reflective belief will be of their unhappy feelings being a threat and needing external intervention. As a result, the child develops more sensitivity to negative feelings, and thus, will consciously feel and express negative feelings more frequently. This is the *spoiling effect*.

The developmental goal of growing up is to first achieve physical independence, then psychological independence, and finally emotional independence. To become independent, an adolescent is compelled to relate to themselves emotionally as mom related to them (internally), and psychologically as dad related to them (externally). Furthermore, the nature of the child's perception of causality makes them reflect needing the parental responses or reactions they experience. They are bound to reflect themselves as causing the fear or negativity they experience from their parent(s). They believe they are not adequate. They believe their deficiencies are causing the parental worry. They don't want to think of themselves as needing to be controlled, needing to be worried about, needing to be protected, needing to be reminded or told what to do, etc. Thus, they will eventually rebel against parental worry or negativity. In effect, they do not want to believe something is wrong with them which merits rejection. They will angrily try to control their parent's emotional reactions to them. Once the child begins internally thinking and thus independently judging (puberty time period), they become further critical of the parent(s). The pubescent will judge their parent on a personal level for upsetting their wants—for not attending to their feelings. Accusations toward the parent for not loving them are commonplace at this age. Until they let go of the belief in their parent being positioned to enable their happiness, their adolescence will be marked by mood volatility at home. The anger and explosive moods are driven by insecurity within the relationship, where usually they will lash out at feeling criticized or disregarded to the proportional degree in which they are psycho-emotionally attached. The degree of attachment can be measured based on the level of reactive feeling—meaning how much feeling is induced in the child/adolescent when the parent gets upset with them. The child/adolescent will internally have a proportional amount of fear regarding separating from the parent as the amount of anger which gets externalized onto the parent, essentially pushing away with the same force. As a result, a *back and forth* or *push-pull* dynamic characterizes their relationship with parents. Recall, the child/adolescent will always reflect the parent as representing the thought judgment of themselves. Thus, they perceive their own self goodness or acceptability within their parent's treatment or interaction with them. As a result, when the parent is upset with them, they cannot see it as their parent having emotion in response to their behavior. Rather, they will automatically take it as personal judgment of their effort or intent. This phenomenon underlies the majority of discord between parents and their adolescents.

When a parent is having excessive difficulty letting go of control, and thus trouble giving ample autonomy and space, they will often jump on a diagnosis for their teenager. This enables the parent to further restrict the adolescent's behavior in the name of keeping them safe. Rarely is this done with negative intent. Rather, the aim for the parent is to reduce their own anxiety, which is usually regarding their adolescent's potential for recklessness. Also, there is often a moderate amount of fear unto the possible perils the outside world may present. Thus, keeping one's teenage child on a tighter, more controlled "leash" feels more secure to parents. The opposite experience, however, comes for the adolescent—where the restrictive tethering to home feels like a noose. The tension which gets backlogged and builds up can be disorganizing and destabilizing for the teenager. The arguments can be intense, usually peppered by explosions of frustration occurring volcanically. The parents see maniacal anger and reactions to feeling wronged or unfairly treated which are over-the-top. The arguments, though they manifest variably, have a commonality underlying their occurrence. If the screaming matches are analyzed, it becomes clear the arguments, though they are seemingly about a certain thing (a restriction, permission, autonomous privilege, etc.), each side is arguing about something different. This makes the possibility of a resolution nearly impossible, and usually contributes to the overall frustration both sides feel, sensing a wall in between their efforts unto the other. Each wants to get through to the other side so they can be understood and respected. Banging repeatedly against this wall helps both sides eventually give up on trying to fight through the wall, hopefully then facilitating independence.

The further adolescence goes, the more psychologically conflictual it will be to need help or input from one's parent(s). Needing help increases conscious anxiety in regards to what they have to do, what's coming up, and what they worry could happen. Internally, the adolescent then relates to those things as *stress* and, to some degree, expects supportive understanding. Once they have sought to manage themselves independently, they will be quick to react indignantly when they sense their parent adding pressure or not being supportive. They will continue to expect their parent to regard how they are feeling or thinking, and they will also maintain a hope for their parent to make them better. This makes it difficult to let go of needing the relationship, since there is a consciously perceived need for parental reassurance. The adolescent increasingly will see outside, personal relationships as beholding more potential positivity. Taking this direction, then, enables a gradual, psycho-emotional giving up on their parent as beholding what they feel they need.

Invariably, because of their psycho-emotional "needs," such adolescents will maintain an attachment (usually with mom) they believe they need. Then, the step into psycho-emotional independence is not taken. The consequences of not attaining psychological and emotional independence involve severe anxiety and mood instability. The belief in having a problem and the sense of being cared about are inextricably bound within their consciousness. In effect, the individual is entrapped in having a problem in order to be feel loved or understood. To regard oneself as having a problem with how one feels or what one thinks is a rejection of oneself. Having a problem then forms certain attachments to what is "needed" to alleviate the problem. Parents must therefore oppose their own personal desire to feel needed through their children, especially when their children are perceiving the need to feel better.

When a psychological and/or emotional dependency on one's parents remains active, the relationship with one's spouse will often triangulate— meaning, the spouse will experience rivalrous feelings. While spousal expressions of such insecurity may outwardly be juvenile, nevertheless, there is validity in the threat they perceive. The tethering of consciousness to one's parent makes it impossible to grow forward in the area of dependency. Whether the dependency is primarily emotional or psychological, the conscious anxiety related to separation opposes the drive toward independence. Since the structure of the adolescent consciousness remains built upon the emotional and psychological needs of childhood, taking a growth step in consciousness requires independence from one's parents. Otherwise, the emotional goal to feel loved or the psychological necessity for reassurance remains tethered to the parent. If the attachment remains intact into young adulthood, the level of conscious anxiety will usually become excessive and at least mildly debilitating. This is due to the outside attachment for internal fulfillment which necessarily comes at the expense of an external actualization of potential.

When a parent is in the self-position, it causes the child to make an erroneous reflection about themselves. Since such a parent is seeking to please their child or protect them from negative feelings, the child must reflect needing such external care. The ability to internally process their negative feelings, as a result, never develops much. Rather, they will focus their attention on identifying things to get upset about, expecting others will recognize the legitimacy of their upset and subsequent entitlement to be pleased. When thinking begins, they will expect others to be as sensitive to them as they are unto themselves. When the parent is relating to the child from the self-position, the child's sense of themselves is outwardly tethered to feeling loved by the parent. They are unable to internalize the feeling, however, if the parent themselves is seeking to feel loved. The more the parent reacts emotionally or defensively to the child's fearful or angry expressions, the more the child must regard their feelings (and thus themselves) negatively. Doing so eventuates in an individual who seeks to suppress negative emotion, and characterologically tends toward being excessively rigid and potentially too controlling of their environment.

When parenting from the alpha-position, the parent does not emotionally depend on the child. They do not seek to please the child. Rather, they care for the child but are not threatened by the child's feelings. Moreover, they do not seek to adapt to the child's judgment of them. Excessive insecurity from the alpha-position results in an anxious need for transparency and control, thus producing the *helicopter parent*. The children of such parents tend to experience themselves as causing concern and needing to be controlled, therein diminishing the child's self-development. The need to feel better within themselves drives adolescents to try drugs. In those who have helicopter parent(s), escapist behaviors (e.g. drug and alcohol abuse) are more prevalent, demonstrating the rejective relationship with themselves.

From the alpha-position relative to one's child, if their feelings are entirely cut off, and thus unavailable for their child to mirror, then the child's emotional development will be compromised in favor of thought or representational development. In other words, the child's sense of goodness and esteem will be tethered to their outward performance and/or how well they are outwardly regarded or judged. As grown-ups, such individuals are very confident in their system of thought, their perspective, and do not internally feel empathic feelings. Others, at a personal level, experience them as emotionally cold. Care from such individuals is not "felt" but rather is represented through their actions. From their standpoint, their care is normally provided by including the other person in the benefits of their efforts.

The less an individual's developing consciousness is tethered to their relationships with others, the more potentially odd others will seem. However, gradually such an individual will have to recognize themselves as being in the estranged position, and thus, they are odd. The person who is generally regarded as odd will themselves perceive people generally as odd, and is a good illustration of how consciousness cannot see itself, but sees itself in others. Thus, children who are very "normal" often have more difficulty with becoming independent since their sense of self is tied to familial approval. In other words, their sense of being akin to those around them provides them structural support for their identity.

Relationships inevitably are compromised by the natural imbalance produced by both people seeking to feel a balance of the following—being in control, having power or influence, and feeling loved. When young, there is no natural desire to sacrifice self for the betterment of the other. The ability to love must grow throughout life. To do so relies first on recognizing the importance of a purposeful giving of oneself during the course of one's life. Also, to love requires a deep understanding of the other, and thus, an individual must grow past the self-reflections of their own feelings and/or ideas. They must open their mind rather than seeking to close it around someone.

The stability of any relationship is determined by what each puts into the space between. An individual's intentions are invariably positive, and yet, how they bring themselves to the relationship—to the space between—will most directly determine the character and sustainability of the relationship. There is nothing positive which comes about through criticisms, complaints, threats, or attempts to have more control. Even though such negativity may be intended to bring about a positive change, by seeing what is disliked or disapproved of, the other person feels degraded and cannot appreciate any positive potential for change. For someone to perceive the world such where they express their negativity, and then believe those who seek to help are those who "care," is misguided. Since life always comes to reflect what one has given to it, the individual will gradually face isolation. Sadly, such an individual sees themselves mistreated by the world, lamenting their feeling state which they blame on the world's handling of them. Yet, it is the individual themselves who is rejecting what they see within the world. Instead of using life as an opportunity, they are using life to try and fulfill themselves. In trying to control their feeling experience, however, they form judgmental thoughts of the environment relative to themselves—relative to their lack of internal fulfillment.

Self-Medicating The Problem

The propensity for certain adolescents to develop a drug problem is best understood through the psychological and emotional factors driving their perceived need. In adolescents, the relationship with their internal feelings is such where they sense needing outside enablement to feel better. In other words, negative feelings (fear, anger, sadness) require an outside influence to calm them. Their ability to internally feel good enough requires getting something to make them feel better or enable them to be better. This pattern of relating to themselves is able to be seen with their primary emotional attachment (usually mom), who is relating to them with protective worry and a desire to be pleasing. Invariably, the maternal reaction, as it occurred toward their upset feelings when they were a younger child, was one of discomfort, and where she made willed attempts to alleviate their negative feelings.

When maternal anxiety is dominated by *what if* worries, a protective approach to parenting is usually employed, where she looks ahead of the child in effort to anticipate problem or peril. The child must believe themselves needing to be worried about and needing to be controlled. Usually, they will fulfill such expectations as a teenager, from not feeling good enough internally. In effort to feel better independently, they will be attracted to anything on the outside which beholds the promise of making them feel calmer or be able to function more confidently. Thus, experimentation with substances is highly likely. The normality of experimentation cannot be overlooked, and blaming the drug itself for causing the problem in those who develop a drug problem misses the bigger picture. Specifically, the adolescent is seeking to establish an internal sense of security and confidence so they can establish the necessary relationships to enable a tolerable step away from home attachments. The more they experienced being controlled as a child (as they perceived it), the more, as an adolescent, they will try to independently control themselves. However, the control is often directed toward their negative feelings, wherein their attempts to control their negative feelings often occur through taking drugs. In effect, the substance ingests alleviation— enabling an escape or avoidance.

The abuse of benzodiazepines (e.g. alprazolam) and opiates (e.g. oxycodone), especially the latter, have been a growing problem among adolescents. The benzodiazepines have an *alcohol-effect* upon one's consciousness, and thus, the inebriating effect can be readily noticed by parents. Since alcohol itself is more readily obtainable, drinking behaviors and episodes of excessive alcohol consumption would be expected in conjunction with benzodiazepine abuse. Those who have a high level of generalized worry or thought-based worry are most attracted to benzodiazepines. This is due to the chemical effect of benzodiazepines producing a slowing or settling effect on one's anxious thinking. The abuse of benzodiazepines tends to be more common amongst young adults than adolescents, as young adults are dealing with more generalized anxiety than attachment anxiety. Generally speaking, benzodiazepines and alcohol appeal more to those who are seeking a sense of security through control of their feelings.

The opiates, comparatively, cause less conscious sedation, and thus are harder to notice by an outside observer. For those individuals who are susceptible to developing a problem with opiates, the chemical effect produces emotional reassurance. The *opiate-effect* is heart-warming in character. Usually, problematic abuse occurs in those adolescents who are used to having maternal support for their negative feelings. In other words, they have been accustomed to being made to feel better when upset. Moreover, they usually have deep-seated anxiety—sensed physically— imbuing a sense of vulnerability in being away from their emotional supports at home. The opiate use is thus employed as a transitional blanket, to produce their own internal reassurance, as they seek to integrate socially and step away from the dependent position. As a general rule, the opiate-effect is more appealing to those who fight an internal sense of lacking.

The psychological need to internally feel better than they normally do is a base belief in individuals who become drug or alcohol dependent. This belief forms during childhood, initially patterned by the maternal response to the child's negative feelings, as well as the overall protectiveness toward the child. Since a child identifies themselves based on how they feel, and the relevance of how they feel is determined by the parental responsiveness to their feelings, parents should position themselves in a way where they are not influenced by their child's negative feelings. When a mom seeks to please her child and protect them from experiencing negativity, then a hypersensitivity to negativity will result. This entitles the feelings to be externalized to receive help, and also retards the development of internal affective regulation. Needing such emotional support from their mother creates anxiety in adolescents since internally they are being driven toward independence, and so they seek to establish a replacement. Most often, a romantic relationship serves to bridge their step into independence. Externalizing negative feelings within the relationship jeopardizes its intactness, however. Thus, the individual will seek to manage their feelings themselves, though psychologically still believing they need something from the outside to help them feel better. Drugs, alcohol, and materialism constitute the primary ways such individuals emotionally support themselves.

Thus, when seeking to understand an individual's substance abuse problem, if the substance itself is understood as being subjectively needed, then significant insight can be gained. Within those who develop a drug problem, there is a false belief in their negative feelings being a threat, and so they seek to regulate them through substances. The particular substance is determined by the particular feeling the individual believes they need to oppose. For example, a belief in one's anger being a problem and needing to be made better often precipitates alcohol abuse. Depressive struggles gravitate toward amphetamine abuse. Attachment fears or dependence, on the other hand, have an affinity for opiates.

Power/Control

Power—based on early relationships and gender role identification—is perceived as either individual capability or influence of others. An individual's power source will be based on how they best were able to fulfill their desires as a child. The more an individual's parent(s) sought to make them happy, the more sensitive and likely intolerant they will be of not being happy. This often entraps individuals in unhappiness or chronic discontent and a longing for others to demonstrate care about them. Seeking love from others comes in the form of expressions of negativity—whether communicating a negative physical state or a criticism of something (or someone) in the environment. Those who care are believed to be those who are influenced to provide help—those who allow themselves to be controlled. An individual will feel powerful in having such influence. The care, however, is in effort to bring about reflections of happiness, thus creating reflections of functional self-value. The key for both is in feeling effectively able to meet self perceived needs through the other. The problem arises when one begins to feel ineffective because they are not getting the desired reflections off the other. Increasingly, feeling ineffective will bring about thoughts of worthlessness and helplessness. Insecurity regarding the stability of the bond will ensue, and behaviors driven to feel more secure through the other will necessarily bring about further negativity. This is because, through the reflections from the person's insecurely driven behavior, the other individual is made to think worse about themselves.

In essence, a relational struggle between a parent and their child is driven by the child's effort to get the sought after reflections from their parent. When the child cannot reflect positivity, they will fight for control of themselves. In other words, if they cannot reflect being loved emotionally (parent: smiling, pleasant, not upset), they will fight against being controlled. To allow themselves to be controlled by someone who is upset equates to believing they need to be controlled through emotional negativity. They will thus have to angrily control themselves going forward. Prior to thinking, and forming an internal relationship with themselves, their interactions with others (siblings, peers) will be characterized by this emotional style of control. If the child submits to being controlled, then consciously they can only pursue power or influence, for they have already let go of the conscious pursuit to feel loved. Instead, they strive to develop more functional capacity so to be loved for their achievements. To be able to get others to do things for them feels good and becomes represented as love. This will then open up the world of victim entitlements where, by representing themselves as incapable or not feeling able, they get a sense of closeness and care from others trying to help them. The development of functional capability or emotional wellness is thus paradoxically threatening. Put another way, the more such a child is able to do for themselves, the less help they will receive, and thus, the less "care" they will experience from others. Such children usually do not surface as having problems until middle-school brings the expectation for autonomous doing of their schoolwork. They are able to keep up only through parental support. Naturally then, they are quick in attaching to a label which reinforces having such needs. By the time they are in late adolescence, they are likely to believe they have emotional or psychological problems creating limitations which entitle assistance.

If self individuals are asked whether they have problematic feelings or thoughts, they will be easily able to identify their thoughts typically being the problem. Self individuals usually balk at the idea of their feelings being a problem. This is why children, naturally in the self position, cannot see their feeling expression as the problem. Rather, they regard whatever thought reflection they are experiencing in response to them as being the problem. They experience negative feelings arising internally in the context of the environment. The environment, including the parent, is perceived as the thought or the inciting stimulus, and thus, is what the child must see as being the problem. Parents will experience their child blaming the world around them and being unable to take responsibility for the effect their behavior has on the environment. Individuals in the self position will manifest problems if they believe in their negative or unwanted thoughts. An important point to emphasize regarding the self individual is their feelings arise from their internal thoughts, and therefore, negative thoughts will cause a change in how they feel. Therefore, self individuals who manifest symptoms must learn to not believe in their negative thoughts.

On the other hand, if an individual was raised in an environment which led them to believe their feelings were problematic, once *thinking consciousness* is attained, they will "flip" into the thought (alpha) position with the belief they will feel better through the control of their feelings. If you ask an alpha-individual whether they primarily experience problematic feelings or thoughts, they will almost always answer how they feel, and are dismissive of the idea of having problematic thoughts. Unlike the self personality, the alpha forms thought based on their initial feelings in response to the environment. Typically, mental health symptoms arise in individuals within the thought position if they have mistaken beliefs (thoughts) about how they feel, causing them to exist in a state of rejection. Thus, symptoms typically manifest depending on the the extent of their internal rejection of their feelings. Although the initial "flip" into the thought position was to control how they feel, the individual can move past their feelings if an acceptance of their feelings occurs. The individual, then, will truly become the thought, where they are able to accept feelings regardless of whether they occur within oneself or in others. Only the alpha element can truly regard feelings themselves as a problem. Thus, an individual's cognitive style is relevant to identify when seeking to understand them, in assessment of how active and conflictual is their non-dominant side.

The Perceptive Error

The "I" of consciousness is the *processor*. It assigns cause to sensory perceptions, where the line of demarcation between something happening to oneself versus within oneself is drawn. Hunger provides the template for feelings happening to oneself—*disintegrated* feelings. Bowel gas provides the other template, representing sensory occurrences which are processed as happening within oneself—*integrated* feelings. Control of hunger is begotten through food. Control of gas is achieved through expression. Hunger is not handled internally, and thus is disintegrated. Conversely, gas is handled within the internal relationship one has with it, and thus is integrated. When negative emotions are processed along the hunger pathway, then such emotions get attached to an individual's circumstances, where they perceive such feelings as happening to them. There then occurs entitlement to be made to feel better. In effect, they are avoiding the integration of their own feelings. In doing so, they are perceiving the cause as originating outside of themselves, thus seeing themselves as being victimized or mistreated to some degree. Unfortunately, what they do in response to this misperception is to behave in ways where others feel unfairly blamed or mistreated. This accounts for the phenomenon whereby those who victimize others believe themselves victimized. In their experience, they were made to feel upset, and thus, they were only reacting to how they were treated.

One's processing of hunger as a feeling, and the relationship with food as a needed source of alleviation of the hunger feeling, is of fundamental importance. It serves as the foundational template for one's psycho-emotional relationship with the world. For all negative sensory experiences, when initially experienced (not yet integrated), in order to structure the perception of them, the child will cry out. Whatever is needed will be provided. If nothing is done then nothing from the outside is needed, and such a sensory experience will be integrated and handled internally. When anger, experienced as a feeling, gets outside support to make the child feel better, then anger feelings will be processed analogous to hunger, remaining disintegrated. As such, there occurs no internal digestion of the angry feelings, but rather one must try to control or alleviate the feelings in the space outside of themselves. Since anger has no analogous need like hunger has food, the human consciousness attaches it to people, places, or things within their environment, then tries to control or alleviate the angry feelings through consumption, control, or avoidance. When there occurs a welling up of angry tension in the mind because it is disintegrated, it will be sensed as emptiness within one's stomach. However, such an individual will have difficulty eating because they feel full when they try to eat. Often, the thought worry will be a fear of vomiting since the base worry is a loss of control of their angry feelings. Vomiting is a good example of a disintegrated event, and so it is often what an individual will fear in order to materialize the fear of their own rejective impulse.

Anorexia can be understood as a mis-processing of angry feelings within an individual's motor system, triggering an anxious sense of needing to keep strict control of themselves. The outside object controlled is food since the anger is positioned perceptively along the hunger template but without a tenable object on the outside (like food). The anorexic individual will seek to avoid causing outer upset, and thus is prone to perfectionism in the context of being judged (e.g. schoolwork, hypersensitivity to criticism). Outflow of angry feelings, when they do occur, will occur usually at home and toward family members. But since they believe they need the emotional support from their family, they become more insecure and feel more guilt ridden following externalization of the angry feelings. This then reinforces their sense of needing to control themselves, thus continuing the anorexic behavior with cyclical mood symptoms based on the disintegrated processing of their angry feelings. The fullness caused by the negative tension in the hunger area of the brain makes eating very difficult. Within the brain, excessive self-energy gets trapped, thus pressing for outflow. There is thus a mindful aversion to consuming energy despite the bodily hunger. The amount of energy expenditure required to suppress feeling/emotion which has not been integrated (and thus digested) is significant. In part, this is from a lack of naturally occurring expressiveness through their activity. In fact, their activity will be outwardly very controlling of their environment and suppressive of others—symbolizing the internal effort to control disintegrated feelings.

Having anger positioned alongside hunger is in order to keep the feeling separate from themselves. Also, like hunger, the anger empowers them to get support or alleviation from the environment. Put another way, it keeps them from having to take responsibility for what they do or do not do within the world. The occurrence of anger triggers an entitlement to get what they feel is needed. However, since not getting what is wanted triggers anger, the anger will be an important element in getting what they want. In effect, the more they can find something to get upset about, the more they will be able to get what is wanted. Similarly, when feelings of emptiness occur, what they believe is needed will be contained within the world. The emptiness itself belies the fullness of tension existing within and the need for either expression into the world or integrative digestion within themselves. Normally, children and adolescents will offload negative feeling/energy onto their parents so to both get it out of themselves and to experience a way of handling it. However, when such expressions cause parental destabilization (e.g. the parent having hurt feelings), then the child will feel trapped by the feelings—unable to express them. Yet, when still representing anger as a problem, they cannot integrate it. Trapped in *no-man's land* with the anger, they try to be perfect enough to avoid triggering upset. This usually involves avoidance of potential conflict through a significant amount of *what if* forethought. At home, they seek to control their own needs, leading to their hyper-controlling approach to food. Attaching the issue to food allows, also, for something outside of themselves to absorb the worry—both their own and the worry of their parent(s). This deflects the focal point from other's anxiety off of themselves. Doing so enables a mild increase in their sense of environmental control and control of those they depend on.

By recognizing the mind's preference to analogize one's sensory experience to hunger, the relationship one has with food provides insight into their early relationship with parent(s). Needing help from one's parent(s) for feelings which, when expressed, cause hurt to one's parent(s) is clearly conflictual. Needing food for sustenance should not generate conflict since food is readily available and not subject to one's abandonment/rejection fears. However, when one's relationship with food is analogously expressing one's relationship with their parent(s), in the context of anger/anxiety feelings, disordered eating patterns are able to be understood much more clearly.

In an effort to control negative feelings which one's consciousness is processing as a problem, such feelings are either attached to the environment or to the "me" element. When attached to the environment, the negative feelings are perceived as happening to oneself. Therein, control may be found through a mixture of avoidance and controlling dominance. When the negative feelings are attached to "me," then one believes something about their body (e.g. external appearance, internal chemistry) is causing the negative feelings or thoughts. Consciousness then tries to compensate by rejecting certain aspects of oneself. However, the belief is not true. Thus, to reject part of oneself is misguided, for integration and growth come through acceptance, never through not being oneself. For instance, the person who believes anger is a problem attaches it to an inner meanness they try to compensate for by outwardly being hyper-considerate and avoidant of conflict. However, neither part is true, not unless being within an integrated whole. Tension arises as a result of the internal effort consciousness must put forth to keep the two aspects unnaturally separated.

Summation

A feeling cannot itself be a problem. A broken leg is the problem, not the pain. The pain is the feeling, the signal. Equally, a thought occurring within one's mind cannot be a problem. It is simply a thought. Consciously, if an individual processes a negative feeling as a problem, then they perceive being *made to feel*. To believe upset feelings should not be happening forces one to find an outside source. For example, increasingly "stress" is being blamed for causing individual upset. Unfortunately, an individual will then seek to control their negative feelings through controlling their environment or their experiences, and thus, their world becomes clouded by the negative feelings. Such an individual does not develop the consciousness space between feeling a feeling and being a feeling. For them, feeling a feeling and being a feeling are the same. They cannot perceive an inner source, and thus, control is sought within the environment, usually through a mix of avoidance and compulsivity. When a problematic thought is given focus, then it will tend to blur the thought reality outside of oneself. For example, a thought about one's partner being with someone else can take on its own obsessive reality, thereby obfuscating the actual thought reality emanating from one's partner.

For fear or anger to determine one's thinking is a tragic reality. To consider humans forming their beliefs to account for their feelings—to manage them—provides insight into the process of belief formation. When the feeling is deemed to be a problem, then it serves as the foundation for which all thought in relation to the feeling occurs. Children and adolescents identify as their feelings, and thus, their thoughts will revolve around how they are feeling about themselves or their related efforts to feel better. When children and adolescents do not feel well, they tend to externalize blame, as if such feelings are being implanted from the outside. This perceptive error then leads to misbeliefs about themselves relative to others—not being liked, being mistreated, etc.

If a parent can avoid letting the upset of their child influence them, and thus not react to make their child feel better, it allows for the child to integrate the negative sensory experience. Doing so provides the foundational mirroring needs for the child to develop a stable emotional center. Negative feelings are disempowered when their expression lacks influence over the parent. The developing child will attach within themselves what they see reflected from the parental mirror in reaction to them. Thus, when there occurs an accomplishment, they will demonstrate their excitement to the parent. In effect, by seeing their excitement reflected in the parent's facial response, the child is able to integrate it into their identity.

Beliefs related to oneself which are formed during early childhood (pre-thinking period) are related to one's feelings. The meaning ascribed to negative feelings determines the amount of subsequent *integration* versus *disintegration* of the feeling. Put another way, the more an individual believes negative feelings are a problem, and thus in need of external help, the more they will be unable to take responsibility for how they feel. Therein, they perceive their negative feelings as being caused by others or by circumstances. Thus, they will express their negativity in the form of blame or criticism, believing themselves entirely justified in doing so. It is consciously impossible for an individual to perceive their negative feelings (fear/anger) arising from a false belief within themselves—a belief about their own negative feelings being a threat—and thus, the negative feelings get falsely attached to being caused by others/environment. So when consciously feeling disliked or rejected, a conscious defense will emerge to avoid internalizing such reflections. The entrapment which results is because the ego consciousness has sought to preserve or protect the internal sense of themselves. When the internal concept of oneself in relation to the world (and the world in relation to oneself), as well as one's internal relationship with oneself, is based on a misappropriated fear, then preserving one's internal sense of identity or stability will not help as one hopes. In fact, help comes necessarily from letting go of oneself. Doing so allows for a significant change in perspective. But most importantly, it leads to an increase in conscious awareness or a leveling up of one's consciousness. The result is an increased integration of oneself and subsequent actualization within the world.

3.2

PARENTING FOR GROWTH

Most parents, when asked of the goal in raising their child, believe in providing love, support, security, and guidance. Such answers illustrate how parents conceptualize their value occurring within the parent-child relationship. However, such answers do not state the goal of raising one's child—for the child to become independent. At the most fundamental level, the purpose of a parent is to raise their child to become emotionally and psychologically independent, thereby as prepared as possible to integrate into society and adapt to the unavoidable challenges life will present. The importance of complete independence cannot be overstated for its impact on someone's mental and emotional well being and resultant adaptation to life. Individuals who are emotionally bound to their parents become more emotionally unstable and anxious the longer they remain in the dependent state. This is especially true if a person remains living at home with parents. Fears of loss and social anxiety grow in intensity, disabling them further from becoming independent.

An effective methodological approach to parenting may occur only in the context of independence being the goal. If independence is not the recognized goal, then any parental method will lose its structure. Such is the case when parents take a relationship based approach with their teenage children. In such scenarios, the parent is burdening the child with their own emotions and desires for closeness. The effect is negative in the context of the teenager's development being purposed toward independence. The teenager will believe in their emotional need to feel cared about, and thus, from their standpoint, guilt feelings and fears of loss predominate. The teenager—rather than getting positive, stable thought of themselves from their parent—in receiving parental worry or emotional negativity, their sense of self-assuredness going forward is weakened. Thus, their ability to step into independence becomes compromised by their feelings of inadequacy and excessive self-doubt. Providing positivity for their child to reflect upon allows the child to build self-esteem. Optimism for their capability, especially when they are unsure of themselves, builds the proper perspective toward life. Every parent has predetermined beliefs about what success looks like and what it means to be a "good person." The more a parent interacts with their child's burgeoning individuality with understanding rather than criticism, the more harmonious will be the parent-child relationship. A similar harmony will then exist for them as they relate to themselves and others. Thus, others will regard them as a "good person."

The more energetic effort a parent provides in direct support of their teenager, the more daunting the prospect of independence will be for the teen. During the teenage years, a parent's desire to be needed is a pitfall for their teen's development of self-reliance. Likewise, a parental desire for closeness is invariably threatening to their teen who is driving toward detachment. Following puberty, parental effort must recede to allow for space into which their teenager can grow a personal center or internalized sense of self. When the time comes for the teenager to separate from home, the goal is for them to traverse the emotional difficulties which are inherently part of becoming independent. The goal is for them to believe they can handle whatever comes their way—whether it comes from outside of them or from within—rather than believing in needing help from others. For this to occur, they must be able to manage their feelings independently. In other words, they cannot believe in needing help to feel better. Such a belief causes emotions to be cobwebs in which they may get stuck, instead of creative energy to be purposed.

The most influential relationship in life occurs between a mother and her child. The maternal instinct is protective, and thus, the child's pursuit of autonomy necessarily strains mom's sense of control and security. The child cannot know her perspective of them. From the beholding viewpoint of the child, mom provides what they need. Since the child perceives themselves the cause of whatever they experience from her, they will internalize mom's negative feelings (worry, anger, sadness) as thought of themselves. Naturally, moms who are self-personalities will be drawn toward making their child feel loved. Also, they tend to be more sensitive to the emotions of their child.

The importance of providing a stable environment for the developing child cannot be overstated. For within this environment, their relationship with themselves and the world is patterned. Giving them one world which remains stable under their developing feet fosters intimacy and mastery (confidence) in later adulthood. Routine gives the day a rhythm and minimizes uncertainty. The environment includes the emotional state of the parent(s), which color a child's world like weather to a golfer. Thus, the emotional stability of the parent(s) is a primary determinant of a child's sense of stability within their environment. Efforts by the child to compensate for instability generate behaviors aimed at reducing tension and establishing control. This will largely determine the personality of the child as experienced by authority figures. Moreover, for a child in need of more environmental stability, their back and forth struggle for control underscores their relatedness with the environment, and most likely will continue forth into adulthood, manifesting as compulsivity and "control-issues."

Part of a child's development involves learning to manage his or her emotions. It is expected, by puberty, the child can control his or her emotions outside the home environment. At home, on the other hand, most early teenagers have frequent outpourings of emotion. A transition occurs for some, however, where they seek to maintain emotional control in all settings. They feel uncomfortable losing control of their emotion, where doing so causes them more insecurity in their relationships. The expressive child who is destined to be a suppressor, upon entering puberty, begins experiencing an increase in relational insecurity when they get outwardly emotional. They come to experience more of a sense of control and internal stability with the retention of negative emotions. Through the process of enacting control of their feelings, they gain a sense of security. The transition by which they begin holding emotion in is often signaled by episodes of stomping off or isolating in reaction to negative emotion. Initial attempts at self-soothing are often characterized by immature coping behaviors, such as breaking things, passive-aggressive threats, and self-injurious cutting. Such behaviors must be appreciated as early attempts to self-soothe, with the expectation of more mature coping mechanisms developing as they mature.

For each adolescent, their character formation requires reflecting on their relativity to peers and pleasingness to authority, mixed in with autonomous values. Of course, the judgment of their parents is meaningful, but is often difficult to internalize for the adolescent seeking to no longer depend on them. The effort of the average teenager is toward being good enough for independence to be granted. However, what makes for a sense of being good enough changes as they mature. The growing child fantasizes of not needing anyone, and yet, they also long to be wanted or needed. Normally, such is sought through growth of capability and knowledge.

Advisement on how to parent equates to telling someone how to relate. There has never been a formula for how to parent, and parenthood is a learning process which occurs in parallel with the child's development. Adaptability within the parent-child relationship is a priceless character trait. For a parent to see where their own relational struggles are manifesting in the child empowers a corrective step. Though taking such steps is very difficult (because it usually requires character maturation), the benefit is significant and pays itself forward. Ironically, children believe they cause the frustration they see in their parent(s), but cannot accurately perceive how the parent is frustrated with them. Often, children develop the same character style in dealing with frustration as they experience with their parent(s). In other words, children will react to a parent upsetting them in the same way they see the parent reacting to worldly or relational frustrations. In truth, parents cannot expect their thought judgment to mean much, for children truly behave as they see, not as they are told.

Attachment

The foundational importance of attachment comes from its formative effect on the relationship between the two parts of the human consciousness. The drive to internally unify or to achieve stable harmony necessitates a balanced relationship between the two parts. The security of an individual's attachment outwardly represents the security existing between their two parts. Moreover, a lack of acceptance between the two elements generates more conflict and thus more negative energy.

One's childhood attachment pattern is extremely relevant for later relationships as an adult. For a relationship to grow into a stable family system depends on many variables, but none greater than interpersonal security. The pattern and security of a child's attachment anxiety (fear of loss) is primarily determined between 18-36 months of age, but becomes most visible during adolescence. Positive experiences within the context of adolescent love relationships and friendships are important for getting over the inevitable hump of insecurity. Thus, these relationships open the portal for the adolescent to become independent from home. Once separated from home, attachment issues continue to play out. Adult attachment is not fundamentally distinct from childhood attachment, though losing control of one's independence becomes a more prominent issue. Attachment can be understood as a key issue throughout one's life, and is at the base of the human experience.

Consciousness cannot conceive of oneself independent of parents until thinking begins. With the ability to triangulate one's perspective, an individualized concept of oneself begins to form. This is why people's memories of themselves begin during pubescence. Memories of the years prior to puberty exist as flashes of experience, but they are not three-dimensional. They lack volume, they lack an identity. The identity growth is occurring unconsciously through mirroring interaction with parents. A sense of being the same as one's parent is common. Thus, the onset of thinking is marked by perceiving separateness from the parent, where one's newly formed sense of oneself is fragile and insecure.

Increasingly, neuroscientists are recognizing how the developing brain depends on mirroring experiences from mom and dad. Mom's effect on the child is predominately through the child's sensory system. A mother's reactions to her child significantly effect the child's sensory reactions to the world. Eventually (pubescence and beyond), the level of maternal sensitivity to the child forms the child's sensitivity level unto themselves. In other words, the manner in which a person internally reacts to their own sensations (whether originating internally or from the outside) is formed from one's interactions with their mother during development. For example, a child who is hyper-aroused or over-reactive either has an impairment in bonding (thus unable to be soothed as naturally by maternal interaction), or they are mirroring mom's level of tension.

Most research into attachment has been focused on children. The psycho-emotional importance of attachment between a mother and her child received a great deal of attention in the early to middle part of the last century. Object-relations theorists sought to elucidate the relevance childhood attachment has on a person's mental and emotional struggles later in adulthood. Subtypes of insecure attachment were described. However, not much meaningful information as to the nature and recommended nurture of childhood attachment difficulties made it into the modern, biological conception of childhood. Nevertheless, over the past decade, brain research has begun to show signs of coming full circle, beginning with the recognition of *neuroplasticity* or the ability for adult neurons to change, to adapt. Historically, the central nervous system (brain and spinal cord) was seen as unable to change—that the wiring was a "hardwiring." As such, it was difficult to imagine how the environment could interact with the nervous system in a way where the nervous system was dynamic, where it could adapt or be shaped by experiences. Moreover, if the wiring was genetically encoded, and thus determined, then it was hard to see how the environment, apart from an insult, could significantly impact the developing nervous system of a child. If such a perspective were true, the goal of raising a child would be to provide them with the purest, most unimpeded environment possible for their genetically scripted period of neuronal growth. However, this has proven not to be the case. As science has gotten a more detailed understanding of the brain, the more the brain appears to be an adaptive organism, inseparable from its relations with the environment (people, places, things). For example, in the ongoing research into *mirroring neurons*, scientists are capturing the neurologic reception of maternal signals which relate to the attachment behavior. In other words, increasingly being understood at the basic neuroscience level is the significance of early interaction with parents on the neurologic make-up of their children.

In general, the development of the child depends on—and is significantly influenced by—the mirroring experiences the child has with mom. Imagine a toddler, newly having gained a wide based gait so to amble about, gets wide-eyed and expectantly seeks to fetch something. The toddler is very sensitive to the mirroring feedback from mom—the look upon mom's face, the tension displayed through her body language, her overall anxiety—as she watches them go intently after something (e.g. a ball in the grass). The toddler cannot perceive the context (the ball being near the street) and goes forth to get it with a sense of adventure and excitement. Mom's reaction, experienced by the child, could range from excitement to trepidation. If it is trepidation, then the child can only perceive having caused mom's fright through their autonomous pursuit, through the exertion of their independent will. The child cannot see the context to which mom is responding (street, car), and thus, will misinterpret her reaction—sensing their autonomous, willful behavior as having caused her alarm. If it becomes a pattern, the child may start anxiously relating to their own intentions. The child's behavior is then likely to take on ambivalence or excessive inhibition/avoidance.

Object constancy must develop for a toddler to separate from mom without being impaired by separation anxiety. Object constancy is the ability, when not physically with mom, for the toddler to hold onto mom's image. In other words, to picture mom's face when apart from her. The purpose is to derive internal feelings of reassurance from this maternal *object*. Such is necessary for a healthy experience of being apart from mom, and for integration into new, strange environments (e.g. daycare). Otherwise, the separation anxiety would be excessive. The *transitional object* a toddler uses (e.g. blanket) serves as an outward representation of mom, and the child seeks to have it at all times when apart from mom. Transitional objects behold mom's smell, and the feeling upon the child's skin is associated with maternal nurturance, and thus serve to soothe the child during the expected times of separation anxiety. Such an object was labeled transitional because it was noted to serve as the bridge between infancy and childhood. It allows the baby to take on toddlerhood, where they seek to enact intent and follow their impulse to do things autonomously. Without a firm sense of people (and things) remaining real, present, and intact during times of separateness, the anxiety experienced by the child would be deleterious upon their development. Since this internally reassuring presence or object is derived from a toddler's relationship with mom, a mother's emotional stability and availability were noted, in the mid-century research, to significantly impact the ability for the child to develop a stable, soothing internal presence. The more maternal instability or maternal anxiety with separation or loss, the more likely the child demonstrated an impaired ability to regulate his or her own emotions and anxieties. In other words, the less calm a toddler's mom, the less calming will be the internal sense of mom's reassurance.

The shaping influence of attachment on the outward personality of developing children remains significantly under-recognized. If the goal of childhood (from the standpoint of the child) is to detach, then attachment (as a theme) must always be the area to consider first when attempting to understand the behavior of children. Fear of loss is imbedded in the human existence, inescapably. The greater a child's level of dependence (sensed internally), the more anxiety they will have regarding loss or separation. The child perceives independence as a portal of escape from the anxiety. Similarly, though under-appreciated, is the plight of the parents, especially mothers, in having to gradually relinquish control—to tolerate the waning closeness and eventually let go. To raise their child to leave them is, arguably, the most emotionally painstaking duty within nature.

For parents, being able to control the mirroring experience of their child by first empathizing, and then responding in a more adaptive way, is very powerful. In relation to their parents, children frequently say and do things in order to learn how to respond to such things. They learn about themselves based on their parents' reactions to them. In other words, the child's two-part consciousness forms as they relate outwardly with their parents who represent the thought element. This is especially true during the pre-thinking years when the child is operating from a single consciousness point of view. From the pre-thinking perspective, individualism or the ability to conceive of themselves separate from their parent(s) does not yet exist. Without the internal thought element active, the child must perceive the parent as a mirror of themselves. Once they do develop thinking awareness, then they begin fighting for different reflections. Eventually the mirror breaks and the adolescent escapes into independence, where the process of individualization —life—truly begins.

In summary, attachment is relevant across the life span. The human condition—the state of being alive—has attachment anxiety inextricably bound to the experience. A sense of being detached comes with the separation at birth, and thus, the threat of detachment or loss is imbedded into the human's experiential memory. The vulnerability of early childhood propels efforts to become more capable, but then most of life is spent trying to hold on while being forced to let go. To see issues of attachment as relating only to children misses the continued relevance attachment anxiety has throughout the average person's life. In adults, attachment anxiety usually manifests as being hyper-controlling and having difficulty letting go. The necessity of letting go of attachments (people, objects, ideas, aspirations) is because the more people do not, the more fearful and stagnant they become. Moreover, letting go of fear within attachments enables the realization of a universal connectedness. The illumination of this oneness within an individual's sensory perception is an important part of the maturation process later in life, attenuating the fears related to aloneness and death.

Parental Types

Broadly, there are two types of parents—*self-first* and *child-first*. Self-first parents see children as growing in value the older and more autonomous they became, and the more like the parent they become. This provides the child a sense of growing in dignity with age and increasing capability. Child-first parents, on the other hand, put the interests and needs of the child before their own. Such parents tend to go down to the child's level to provide mirroring experiences, and thus interact with more overt empathy. Each of the two styles has merit and potential pitfalls. The most difficulty comes when a parent puts the child first so to placate the child. In other words, the parenting is child-first ostensibly, but being done by a parent who is self-serving, and thus, has to mirror their own expectation to have their own needs/wants met first and foremost. Thus, they have to treat the child as though they seek to be treated, but are unable to do so from a position of actually putting the child's needs before their own. Seeking such mirroring necessarily becomes discordant once the child hits puberty and is able to think—thus, being able to recognize the parent's self-serving treatment of them.

If a child-first parent is psychologically able to put the needs of the child first, then the primary challenge will be an emotional one. Letting go of one's child is extremely important and inexorably difficult. The job of a mother especially—being to raise the child to leave them—is likely unrivaled in its difficulty. Allowing autonomy and not imbibing in the child's worry comes forth as a show of optimism for the child. The reflection given to one's child should not be characterized by worry, nor an anxious desire to keep the child close. The child must see love and positivity in their parent's reflection of them in order to develop a positive regard for themselves. Worried expressions or worry-filled interaction is not love. Rather, externalizing anxiety unto one's child is how anxiety is "passed on" or engendered. Recall, for the child to eventually become independent requires they take the parental worry unto themselves. Loving parenting thus necessitates holding the unavoidable anxiety inside, seeking to limit its visibility to the child. Also, child-first parents must guard against empathy induced difficulty with setting limits, as well as being inconsistent with their limit setting. Setting limits in the face of a child's emotional meltdown and literal agony is a challenge to any parent's fortitude. Yet, if they give in, it endorses the intolerability of the suffering. Suffering then brings power, as with anything which moves a parent off of their line. Whenever a child efforts to get their way, it is important to recognize the employed tactic, if it is successful, will become imbedded into their character. Since parents often determine how the child most influences them, it is important for parents to be aware of the personality getting created.

Children of a self-first parent are rewarded by their sense of growing closer to being like their parent. As long as the child is able to feel, through their growth and increasing capability, a gradual increase in mirroring likeness, then their confidence will blossom accordingly. If the self-first parent has insecurities to where they feel threatened by the child's growth and attempts to be like them, then they may rival the child or be overly critical. If the other parent takes pity on the child, then it may precipitate a greater divide due to a further increase in rivalrous resentment for the sympathetic treatment from the other parent. In general, when one parent believes the treatment of their child by the other parent is too harsh or derogatory, then efforts to compensate will occur naturally. The downside, however, is for the child who, in feeling the pity, identifies as being treated too negatively. In effect, the compensatory concern shown will heighten the child's sense of being mistreated. Also, receiving extra sensitivity and comfort empowers a victim entitlement dynamic. Children should never be treated with pity. Doing so forces them to reflect being a victim. When parents speak angrily of the other parent, or demonstrate fear of the other parent, children will feel ashamed and victimized. Often, parents who are divorced will each speak poorly of the other parent, usually in the form of criticizing the other's parenting or level of involvement. Such parents will often perceive their child being victimized by the other parent. It is not uncommon for children to keep positive feelings for the other parent muted. The more victim entitlements are reinforced, the more a child will report on the negative aspects of their experiences. In effect, the more negative will be the child's experience of life, generally.

The present generation of parents seek to be pleasing to their children, or to minimize frustration. Prior to the 1990's, children grew up in a culture which sought to toughen their feelings. Boys believed power was achieved through bravery and overcoming negative feelings. Boys believed men were in control because girls were more sensitive. The gender inequality still existing socio-culturally at that time was built around the suppressive ability men demonstrated emotionally. In the 1990's, political correctness standards and publicized lawsuits gave momentum to an era of entitlement. A competition of sorts for victim-based spoils became a slippery slope. The social hypersensitivity which developed gradually morphed into the current climate of judgment. The judgment is reflective in its character, meaning people are increasingly judging what they are being subjected to or how they are being *made to feel*. The judgment is not coming from evolved intelligence or from experience, and thus, it does not manifest wisdom. Rather, it is defensive—thus, occurring in effort to protect feelings. Ironically, fearing potential consequences of conflict, and a hypersensitivity to conflict in general, gives willpower to others' potential upset.

Just as gradual has been the build up of paranoia. Tethered to the extent of media exposure, a social awareness of potential bad things which could happen has gotten increasingly infused into the collective consciousness. Social support to better protect one's child fostered the overly protective approach to raising children which has now become the standard. Based on a reactive consciousness to media reports of tragic occurrences, public policy has increasingly been driven to protect children. However, by doing so, the children are forced to believe in such a need to be protected. Thus, there must be a threat. The formation of a child's belief system requires binary structure, and thus, to be protected makes rational sense only if a threat exists from which the child is being protected. Hence, threats are popularized and passed on.

The first incident of media induced fear which got implanted in children came in the early 1980's. Specifically, a Halloween epidemic of paranoia about apples with needles being passed out to children took ahold of the public consciousness. Parents insisted on inspecting the bags of candy brought home by their child. At that time, children would trick or treat with each other in a relatively unsupervised manner. However, once they returned home, the bags would be inspected. If anything was not sealed/wrapped, then it was discarded due to potential tampering. Parents believed they were doing the responsible thing based on the information they received from the news broadcasts.

The current generation of adolescents and young adults have been brought up within a culture which sought to protect their self-esteem. Phenomenon felt to be wounding to the self-esteem of a child (bullying, losing) were vilified and seen as harmful. In doing so, children believe their self-esteem must need protection, and so they believe themselves to be fragile. With such a belief structured in their consciousness, hypersensitivity to feeling mistreated or not adequately regarded then imbues fear and resentment within their perception of life. Naturally then, interpersonal discord has risen. This is reflected in the increasing inability for individuals to stay married. The proportion of individuals expecting their self-appointed needs to be met—relative to the number of individuals seeking to be needed or pleasing—is imbalanced, and growing more so as the parental culture continues to support a pleasing approach to raising children.

Two Modes of Parenting

Parenting is a natural aspect of life. Whenever help or guidance is being provided, parenting is occurring. From the parental position, there are two different relational approaches (or perspectives) an individual may take in helping another. The *soldier position* is one, and the *coaching position* is the other. The differences, as will be illustrated, occur at a fundamental level. Moreover, the impact on those who are being helped differs based on which position the helping individual is coming from, and demonstrates the importance of the approach taken in helping people.

From the soldier position, movement occurs toward a perceived problem or threat. The goal is to eliminate the problem or lessen the threat. Effort is thus centered around the problem and is rejective in character. In contrast, from the coaching, there is no movement toward a perceived problem. The coach sees growth as the solution to problems which require correction. From the coaching perspective, there is no aspect of the player which is targeted for elimination—rather, the coach sees the growth potential within the player. The coaching position is thus dependent on each player's willed effort forward—to improve, to build strength and skill in the context of a greater understanding of the game. Because each player has growth potential within them, the coaching position perceives each as beholding their own solution. Within such a context, then, to enable a player's potential, the coach reflects a belief in the player's potential—especially when the player is focused on their own limitations or outside obstacles which seem insurmountable.

Any help in the form of action from the coaching position must occur as mirroring. Otherwise, the coach is doing for the player, which means the player must then believe they need such help. In other words, the player has to believe in their helplessness. Mirroring action is demonstrative—where the player is shown how to do something. The mirroring action shows them how it is done, but with the expectation for the player to then be able to do such themselves. Such action from the coaching position maintains the belief in the player's potential. In contrast, from the soldiering perspective, action occurs with the intent to remove or neutralize obstacles. However, if the obstacle is internally experienced (e.g. panic attack), then effort to neutralize it, in effect, is a negation or rejection of potential. Similarly, to be the motivation for another, pressure must be applied, which will come at the developmental expense of an internally centered source of motivation.

To illustrate, imagine the scenario in which an individual is startled by a lion coming forth from the woods. Rightly, the person's fight or flight response is activated within their body. Action is potentiated—the energy for which is contained within the state of fight or flight. However, decisive action requires a willed acceptance of the activated energies—otherwise, inaction or unwilled action occurs. The greater the sate of inaction, the more consumed an individual will be by their activated energies of fight or flight. Trapped fight or flight then becomes the object of suffering—experienced as either anger or anxiety and often expressed as "stress." Naturally, an individual in such a state will reach out for help—either to escape the perceived cause of their unrest or else to alleviate the unrest itself.

Direct action which is taken to enable a sense of alleviation from the feelings of fight or flight occurs naturally through consumption. Intake of food or substance (including medication) or an acquisition of materials (e.g. money, objects) are the natural methods of such pursuit. The expectation, to a certain degree, is for the world to materialize alleviation. Unfortunately, this positions the world in the parental position, when an individual's effort depends on getting something from the world. Increasingly, in modern individuals, such effort entails expressing the negative feelings of trapped fight or flight—bringing such forth as a problem, and thus depending on a parental structure to soldier their problems. As an individual matures through life, the natural course is for them to take an increasingly parental role unto the world. Doing so is an essential part of life, where the less an individual seeks from life, the more fully they can parent life. Being mindful of the parental approach taken should thus be an imbedded aspect of the adult culture, where the goal of parenting for growth is prioritized. Unfortunately, this runs counter to the current culture's protective approach to parenting. However, the culture is increasingly becoming witness to the problems being precipitated with the protective approach, and thus the parental culture is beginning to reformulate the approach to parenting.

Creation

For parents, each time a child reflects off of them is an opportunity for creation. In interacting with their parent, a child perceives themselves determining the parental emanation. Whether it is negative (anger, fear, sadness) or positive (joy, wonder), the parental expression provides the reflective impression for the child's mirroring neurons. Then, since the pre-thinking child believes themselves to be the direct cause, their personality forms between their sense of themselves and their image of others. Each reflective interaction presents parents the chance to either *create* or *engender*. For the parent, to create means to give what they wish for the child to believe. The parent has the ability to respond to the child in a way which forms how the child will internally react to themselves. Recall—the internal dialogue characterizing the adult mind arises from within the two-part consciousness. The parental reflections become the voice. If a parent is not creating, then the reflections are directly based on how the parent is feeling. This is engendering since it passes on the feelings, and is contextual. For example, eight year-old Susie is crying to her mother about having an upset stomach before school. Mom can reflect either concern or understanding without concern. The former reaction engenders, the latter creates. A reaction which lacks concern does not infer coldness, but rather provides acknowledgment to legitimize the feeling and confer understanding, followed by a reflection for the child of them being strong and without need. Hypersensitivity to a child's complaints will necessarily sensitize them— meaning, the child will become sensitive to themselves in such a way. Ultimately, the goal for most parents is to give their children a better life than they had. However, to do so requires preparing them to experience life better. This requires creation. Otherwise, it becomes engendering of the parent's experience of the child directly and only mirrors the child's efforts in relating to the world. Creating a better life involves the parent having to hold negative, potentially engendering feelings inside, while outwardly reflecting the wellness they wish to give to their child.

Parents can either seek to give their children the experiences they had as a child or provide the child what they perceived lacking from their childhood. Being aware of such areas of deficit thus provides the opportunity to fill the space by creating it. If a parent is not conscious of issues stemming from their childhood relationships with their own parents, then they are more likely to parent the way they were parented. Insecure parents often seek to please their child, thus reacting to and identifying with the child's emotions. Essentially, they are empowering their child's experience of want. Eventually, this produces an adolescent who expects others to subserve their judgment. For parents, by the time their child has become an adolescent, the years of appeasement have run them ragged. The willpower then needed in order to impose limits is in short supply.

If mom is apathetic and unable to support ambition, then the child will feel more rewarded as they are regarded outwardly for their accomplishments, usually at school. They will apply more of their developing self to such areas, attaching their ambition to the positive regard they get. During times of illness, when the child is listless and passive, they will necessarily feel closer to mom since mom is able to provide mirroring empathy to the helpless victim child. Also, they experience more closeness from not being outwardly ambitious while sick, thus existing in a more dependent state, which adds to the closeness the child senses with mom. Likely, the child will experience ambivalence while in the state of dependent closeness—finding both reassurance and potential entrapment in mom's empathic mirror.

The expressive language used by parents is taken literally by their pre-thinking children, and thus, caution must be maintained to avoid seeding fear. Common expressions of exaggeration, not to be taken literally, would include hyperbolic statements such as "I'm going to kill you," or "I'm dying," in the context of being emotionally disintegrated. However, a child under the age of ten is likely to take such expressions literally, unless he or she is familiar with the saying and its lack of meaningful intent. The more the language used by parents is clear, concise, and literal, the less uncertainty and confusion it presents for the child. Language requiring an abstract understanding of duality will not be understandable. Moreover, children learn language initially by having words paired with materialized objects. Facial expressions and the labeling of the child's experience bring language into more subjective territory, so if a parent has a dry or "poker-faced" way of expressing themselves, there occurs added comprehension difficulty for the child.

Children expect their parents to enable them increased capability and achievement, just as they expect their bodies to enable them to move according to their will. Similar to the difficulty individuals have in respecting their body rather than feeling entitled for it to function as expected, so to do children have difficulty respecting their parents. True respect can only develop once the child becomes independent, usually associated with moving out of the home following adolescence. Even then, respect should not be expected since the self-centeredness of the average young adult masks their ability to reflect upon their parent's perspective. Normally, it is when an individual becomes a parent themselves, and through the parenting process, whereby respect for one's own parents develops in earnest.

The greatest gift given to parents for the raising of their child is the ability to create the reflective experiences for their child. To be interested in their child, to like their child, to reflect faith in the child's capabilities, to paint the world as beholding positive for them—is a sewing of love. Parents must use caution in filling the future with *what if* worries, where all the possible things which could go wrong are brought to their child's attention. Since children believe themselves to be the cause of the worry, they will feel deserving of being worried about, and thus, will internalize a sense of deficiency and fear. To not reflect worry about their child, though difficult, ultimately is more fruitful for both the parent and the child. In effort to parent through a perspective which is properly oriented, it is helpful for parents to remain mindful of reacting to life as they would want their child to react. In other words, parental understanding *through the eyes of the child* will enable a more effective resonance with their child.

The Parental Relationship

An established value system for the family provides some buffering against a child's tendency to be individualistic and self-serving. By definition, a family value is something structurally and commonly sought by the family—held as an expectation which supersedes individual want. If a family value can involve compassionate treatment of others, then being angered is never allowed to justify mistreatment of others. A family, by default, will inherit the sociocultural values which accompany modern times. Furthermore, advancements in technology have brought the outside world into the home, and thus, people are more bound than ever to the collective system of values. Capitalism, for instance, underscores commercialism, which in turn imbues materialism into an individual's value system. When the predominating value system within a family is rooted in personal success or individual materialism, then its members are bound to battle for themselves. Such an environment will be competitive, antagonistic, and judgmental.

The importance of parents standing "united" has little to do with each's perspective on the parenting approach to their child. Of significance, rather, is the support or backing each provides to the other when dealing with issues related to their child. If both parents support the parenting of the other, where the other's parenting behavior is not judged negatively, then the child will have less internal conflict. A child is likely to fill any fissure between parents with guilt and victimization. In contrast, the more positive each parent is with their representation of the other parent, the more positive the child will feel internally, and the less anxiety they will experience.

The amount of parenting done by the parental relationship itself is significantly under-recognized. In other words, the relationship existing between parents sets the standard for how the children relate with each other and with each parent. Children are attuned to the relationship between parents like an antenna. The greater the discord, the more tension generated within each child. Since the developing child takes on character elements from both parents, the importance of those two primary figures—as they relate and regard each other—cannot be overstated. A secure, mutually loving relationship between parents provides a secure base for the child's foundation of development. Moreover, the interactions between parents will be modeled by children, especially if there are siblings, since then acting out is facilitated. A more harmonious house is a natural byproduct of a loving relationship between parents, where mutual support is demonstrated.

More than anything else, the power of love between parents, when palpable to children, makes the act of parenting flow more naturally. Without love between parents, the two parts which form the child, and eventually characterize the two-part consciousness, are more likely to have conflict. Relational struggles will then be more frequent and more volatile. A loving relationship demonstrates the synergy between opposites. The output sum from a binary pair can potentially exceed any total from each functioning individually. Part of the frustration existing between parents stems from each at times feeling unsupported by the other, where one's efforts with a child are undermined by the other's perspective. Frequently, when one parent is feeling frustrated with the other, the frustration will be expressed vicariously through the child. When such exists, the frustrated parent perceives the children as being victimized by the other parent, often producing a situation where the child is being used to assail the other parent's treatment of them, thereby being turned into sacrificial pawns.

In families where both parents are alpha-personalities, the children tend to manifest an exaggerated duality between feeling and thought. In other words, the feeling aspect of their personality takes on an intense suppression. As young children, they will have eruptive outbursts at times, but the frequency fades with age. Once they enter pubescence, the ability to express emotion is very limited, and the logical thought side of their brain tends to dominate. This makes such individuals seem less emotionally available or accessible, which can compromise their ability to integrate socially due to the expressive nature of teenagers. Moreover, there is often a high level of self criticism in the form of thinking they are likely not good enough for others. However, a high level of academic ability and achievement in extracurricular activities usually enables them to establish adequate levels of self-esteem. Nevertheless, they tend to have a sense of judgment occurring both outside the home and inside the home. Through adolescence, they tend to grow intolerant of feeling controlled at home. In effort to control themselves, a power struggle at home with parents develops. The psychological and emotional investment in outward achievement, often doubly motivated, may come at the expense of self-driven efforts to please within the home. Adolescents from double-alpha families will often have trouble generating motivation at home (despite pleasing compliance outside of home), and yet are resistant to parents pushing them.

When an expressive individual is in the alpha-role, their feelings are usually the basis for their judgment of others, environments, and scenarios. How a situation makes them feel will then determine their judgment of the situation. A child experiences an alpha-expresser parent empowering the emotion itself. The child learns to be sensitive to the parent's emotions, and during grade school, the child tends to be very pleasing to others, including having found peace by keeping the alpha-expresser parent pleased. In doing so, the child feels internally secure and positive within themselves. With pubescence, however, their newfound ability to judge (doing so self-centeredly) brings forth thoughts of being manipulated. For they are able to compare their thoughts about a certain matter with the alpha-parent's expressed thoughts about the matter, and see their parent's judgment is in subservience of selfish feelings. This triggers anger and distancing. Also, the pubescent will frequently seek to get in-between parents, rivaling the same-sex parent. Doing so often precipitates discord between parents, thereby inducing guilt and an increase in mood symptoms (irritability, depression) in the young teen. Parents maintaining the strength of their bond in the face of this strain, though angering to the pubescent, provides them a stable foundation for which to develop toward independence.

Single parents are becoming commonplace, though the term *single parent* has taken on recent division, for the term was established in description of the abandoned mom—whether having been widowed or divorced by her husband. With the recent surge in female-initiated divorce and shared custody arrangements, the co-parenting set-ups are not adequately represented by the term *single parent*. Having to parent without the other person precipitates a binary relationship between parent and their child. This parent-child relationship feels stabilizing and comfortable for the single parent when they have a complementary other in their child, and it functions more smoothly as such. Less mirroring is received by the child, and they identify more based on their relational role unto the parent. The parental dependence on the complementary support puts more pressure on the child. The arrival of adolescence tends to bring forth anxiety symptoms related to detachment from the parent, where the adolescent will worry about the parent's wellbeing. If the necessary steps toward independence trigger their parent to destabilize, then the teenager's guilt and anxiety can be disabling. Furthermore, the parent's anxiety associated with their teen becoming independent is tethered to their sense of potential loss and aloneness (if there are no other children). Thus, for the single parent, there will be an increase in anxiety when their adolescent begins the normal distancing behaviors (increased isolation, seeking to be gone from home more). During this period, it is possibly advantageous for the single parent to get into a love relationship. Doing so buffers the pain for both the parent and the child, and tends to make for a smoother transition into independence—without as much guilt, worry, and conflictual feelings in general. The more the parent has established a personal relationship with their child, the more likely the adolescent will have difficulty attaining independence. To prepare them for independence is not to give them relational control by striving for their positive judgment. A parent cannot seek to have a relationship with their child and prepare them for life at the same time, as these aims cannot align.

Fathers

A father's role becomes increasingly important once puberty nears. While reflective thought of oneself comes from the mother, reflective thought of the world comes from one's father. Thus, the child is given a microcosmic metaphor for either *self unto world* or *world unto self*. Does one subserve the world or does the world subserve oneself? While it can be said of mothers, in general, having more impact on a developing child's sensitivity to the world, fathers have a determining role in forming their child's cognitive perspective of the outside world. Fathers usually represent the outside world, and thus, they shape the child's sense of potential efficacy within the world. Also, the child's sense of how receptive the world will be of them is greatly influenced by their father's level of acceptance of them. Analogous to the two sides of a football team—offense and defense—fathers tend to be the offensive coordinators and mothers the defensive coordinators. The offense represents the motor system, the drive to produce, to achieve, to possess. The defense represents how one reacts, senses, and feels. Being able to identify with one's father enables the pubescent child to generate self-esteem and functional confidence, as long as one's father is able to model such. Father's with excessive negativity or anxiety will paint a picture for the child of a world which is unfair or threatening. If the world can affect dad to such a degree, then it must be a difficult, nearly unbearable place. How dad represents the outside world shapes the child's sense of what they are heading for, and excessive paternal anxiety or negativity makes achieving independence more difficult. The outside world must get the adolescent's hope and invested potential, and ultimately be where they build their framework to serve as their foundation of independence. Dad is thus the bridge between a child's internal sense of themselves and the world, into which they step forth in search of fulfillment.

A parental relationship can be imbalanced but stable. In fact, the growing child will always perceive an imbalance based on their myopic, self-centered perception. The *oedipal rivalry* is an example of identification with one parent who the child perceives as not being treated fairly by the other parent. However, if the relationship is stable, then the child will grow to better understand both sides, not latching onto one as "good" and the other as "bad." Instability precipitates the formation of judgment or the closing of open-mindedness. Thus, the more unstable a child's environment, the more it will precipitate a controlling child who seeks to gain control through expressed judgment and domination.

If dad is not present (divorce, gone frequently), then a female child may fill the complementary role. This creates problems (false-alpha, see bipolar section in chapter on afferent conditions), especially in her efforts to establish balanced, stable relationships later as an adult. In a scenario of an absent father—where the son is filling the complementary role—the son experiences significant thought anxiety in reaction to mom's negative emotions. As an adolescent and young adult, his ability to be "in touch" with his own emotions is underdeveloped. Such male individuals tend to experience emotion internally like a deer in the headlights. Thus, single moms who are emotionally unstable tend to raise male children who are suppressive, but who, at home, tend to have volatile eruptions of anger in reaction to feeling out of control.

As mentioned previously, fathers serve as a bridge away from home. The manner in which the child brings themselves to the world—their sense of purpose and the way in which they effort themselves—is developed through modeling of their father. Is the father stepping out into the world to fulfill his purpose, following feelings, or protecting the home? Early patterning of a child's belief structure involves sensory feelings crossing over and becoming outwardly directed motor potential. The channeling of energy into expressive motor function within the environment is a fundamental aspect of being alive. Fathers serve as a character model for the bridging of the child's sensory system with their motor system, and therein influencing how their child's motor system interacts with the outside world. A child's bonding with their father creates a sense of potential acceptance from the world. However, for the the acceptance to occur, a child's father cannot be rejecting of the world or representing himself as victimized by the world. The more a father's behavior is inhibited or controlling, the greater will be the developing child's sense of the outside world being a threat. Doing so precipitates an increase in anxiety, thus creating more ambivalence about becoming independent.

If a father is in the alpha position at home, then the *alpha justification* should be related to his work. A sense of value in the father's effort within the world is instilled through respect and gratitude shown to him. This creates a culture where children foresee power being obtained through outward accomplishment, through their functional productivity. If the father's work is devalued or nonexistent, or if he uses too much emotional expressivity to gain control, then the *alpha justification* will appear to be based on angry dominance rather than intelligence or ability. Thus, the children will put too much emphasis on externalizing their negative feelings to get what they want rather than toward developing functional or intellectual capabilities.

A brilliant piece of advice for fathers is—*In seeking to love your child, do so by showing them how much you love their mother*. This accomplishes two important things for the child—it provides the child the experience of a loving relationship outside of how they feel, and it provides an inflow of positive energy in support of mom's continual outflow toward the children. Replenishing mom's tank through a positive giving of themselves benefits the entire system. Similarly, taking care not to externalize negativity or put their feelings first fosters a positive living environment for the family.

Point of View

An infant's interaction with their mom—before they become a toddler—is primarily a sensory experience for the child. Their physical dependence on mom and soothed response to physical affection leads to much time spent in close physical contact. In such a state, and with ego boundaries (sense of individual separateness) just developing, the baby freely absorbs the parent's resting level of tension as well as the parental responses to their discomfort. The sensory experience is a mirroring one, and its formative influence on early neurological development, through ongoing research, has increasingly demonstrated significance. The disparity between a parent's positional viewpoint and their child's viewpoint is significant, but normally does not cause interpersonal discord until adolescence. A parent necessarily views their child as a separate individual, and thus interacts with them as such. However, for the child, the parent is a connected part of them. A child has never been psychologically or emotionally separate from their parents, and thus, their positional perspective is fundamentally different than the positional perspective of their parents unto them.

Recall, there exists, from the time of birth, a psycho-emotional attachment to their parent(s). Since the child has never known detachment (under normal circumstances), it is impossible for them to have the necessary level of gratitude to demonstrate legitimate respect for parental efforts toward them. This issue usually comes to a head during adolescence because the adolescent's capabilities have matured, and so they feel entitled to the autonomy which comes with growing up—to do what they feel they are able to do. In running into a parental retaining wall, they reflect being unjustly devalued. The arguments which ensue usually get down to a stalemate, where the adolescent believes they can and thus should be able to do (x), and the parent(s) trying to defend the parental position which is usually based on caution/worry/normal standards. The adolescent believes their parents are misrepresenting them, thus triggering their self-righteous indignation. Since the conflict has no common ground or shared reality to fight over, the arguments do not normally find resolution as much as they find exhaustion.

A struggle to get compliance from their child is experienced by every parent. Hopefully, it is not a constant battle. Parents need not feel compelled to defend their decisions, for it is not the rightness or wrongness of the parental decision which is relevant. Rather, parents should focus on how their child responds to being forced to comply with something the child disagrees with or wishes not to do. Parents, when trying to convince their child through the use of logic and reason, are shooting for the stars. Expecting rational thought to influence a child (even an adolescent) will cause parents unnecessary frustration. Simply arguing with the child in a defensive way weakens the parental position, for children readily take to fighting emotion with emotion, and usually win. Parents are privileged in no right being truly beheld by their child to object to a rule or command. Once children hit puberty and begin thinking, then they will begin internally questioning the parental judgment of them, and thus, the dynamic with parents becomes fundamentally different. However, prior to pubescence, the more a parent can hold their line—calmly and resolute with their word—the more secure the child will be in their relationship with the parent. Conversely, the more a parent is inconsistent with their temperament or has an inability to walk a dependable line, the more uncomfortable becomes the child in being dependent. As a result, children are more likely to oppose feeling controlled, precipitating a power struggle at an earlier age than is normal (adolescence).

The push-pull behaviors of pre-thinking children are two-dimensional—occurring within the dependent dyad, and can be mimicked by the lab rat. The behaviors are pleasure seeking and based on previous experiences of reward. Not until the development of the three-dimensional thought structure do children transcend the two-dimensional model of a rodent. Before the onset of thinking, a push-pull relationship occurring with one of the parents is indicative of ambivalence about separation. Push-pull behaviors from a child may be assumed to represent attachment anxiety. Such children seek excessive control on the outside, with alternating signs of internal insecurity through clinging behaviors. Though parents often feel manipulated by the behaviors, the push-pull behaviors should not be equated to manipulation. Rather, the child is having conflicting wants centered around separation. They are not thinking about what the parent is thinking, and thus cannot seek to manipulate the parental perception. Manipulative ability requires thinking capability which, in general, does not develop until around the time of puberty.

A parent's perspective is based on the consideration of their child, the world, and the perspective of other parents (societal standard), mixed together in a broth of parental protectiveness. On the flip-side, the teenager has been a child, and all along believed their growing capability determined increased opportunity and privilege. The child sees the parent as the judge of their capability, standing between them and complete autonomy in the world. So when they come into their adolescent perspective, they can reflect upon themselves relative to other peers, and thus triangulate their perspective. Their view of parental restrictions is driven by their relative position and their feelings. They cannot see why they are being restricted since they firmly believe in their capacity to handle themselves. They want to be allowed, and will plea to be given the chance, so they can prove everything will be okay. "Nothing bad is going to happen, give me the chance and you'll see" tends to be a common line. When the parent does not concede to their plea bargaining, the adolescent often turns to accusations of not being loved. In their minds, parental love (as they are able to conceive of it) means they are entitled to the help and support they deem they need or deserve. They do not understand why their parent would not want them to be happy. In the adolescent's non-independent, self-centered perspective, the ability to see themselves through the eyes of the parent is minimal. They are bound to believe the parent is making them feel upset, and thus precipitating their mood or behavioral problems. They expect their positive potential to determine how they are treated. They expect parents to support their intent and disregard negative effects which they did not intend. The parental perspective, however, is determined by who their child has been, and the parental sense of what is reasonable to expect from the adolescent. The less understanding pursued by a parent, the less their child, later as an adult, will be accepting of their upset feelings. In other words, the more the parent responds to their child with negative feelings, the more the child must reflect negative thought of themselves. Then, it is this negative thought they vociferously rebel against during adolescence, seeking to keep it from becoming a belief.

If the discordant scene between an average parent and their adolescent is seen objectively, it is clear the parent is imposing restrictions in order to maintain a structure for the adolescent to live within, in effort to keep the adolescent safe from their own impulsivity and lack of experience-based forethought, enable a decision which is best for the family/system, and retain some relational control of their underage teenager. Each of these parental goals does not involve direct consideration, and thus, is not judgment. Yet, the adolescent cannot see it as representing anything other than direct judgment of them. This is important, for it keeps the adolescent feeling misunderstood and under-appreciated. Both of these thoughts are essential for an adolescent to develop in relation to his or her parents since it propels them further into the peer world where they are able to sense commonality. The shared experience among adolescents in relation to each's unfair entrapment within a parental system is liberating in itself, and provides a significant amount of confidence toward being independent. They need optimism toward eventual freedom from the tether to home/parents being the direction for which to become the person they are supposed to become. A growing sense of self-actualization (or the blossoming of self) should develop hand-in-hand with socialization success outside of home. The more successful and securely they integrate socially, the less tension which will exist in relation to parental restrictions or the experience of being controlled at home. Crossing into independence necessitates a detachment of an adolescent's consciousness from perceptively depending on their parent(s). This enables the necessary growth step in conscious awareness to occur, wherein a separation between feeling and thought is realized. This imbues them with the conscious awareness that differences between people represent diversity rather than a threat, and provides the space to grow into their individualism.

The ideal belief system for the young adult stepping into the real world is one which supports excitement about the challenge, believing it is through the challenge they will grow in confidence and ability. The belief system should support a lack of worry about themselves, and an awareness of being able to meet their own needs. To regard their feelings or thoughts as normal, non-threatening, and the world as generally receptive, enables them to step into the unfamiliarity of independent living without anxious impairment. No matter the experiences had while growing up, each will primarily be conscious of what their parents did not do. Ironically, parents are bound to remember what they did do, and are relatively blind to what they did not do.

The more an individual seeks positive regard from others, the greater they sacrifice their individualized fruition. In other words, to give themselves a sense of being accepted or liked outwardly, they have to be pleasing and helpful. Thus, as they effort to be liked, their perception of what others want or need produces their outward identity. The self-belief in being good and having good to offer spurs the development of themselves as they seek to bring themselves forth. However, when the individual, as a child, attaches their value to the judgment of others, then they base themselves on how they think others feel about them. A negative judgment of the themselves eventually occurs because experiencing themselves as good enough (being loved, accepted) is unable to be achieved through the pleasing of others. Giving up on such self-effort enables stability through independent control of their self-image and what they do. This is usually associated with a transition into alpha-consciousness or a rebirth of self identity.

As a general rule, the more clearly someone can understand themselves, the more clearly they will be able to perceive others. The more an individual's own issues are unrecognized, the more they will see such issues in those they depend on. In other words, problematic or conflictual elements within them which are not consciously acknowledged are perceived in others or within the environment. Such individuals, because of their externalized negativity, are difficult for others to get close to. Others grow tired of the double standards, since never is their negativity directed toward themselves. No matter what, it is the fault of another—which is true, as they perceive. However, the misperception is because no perceptible space exists between their feelings and thoughts, and thus, they do not see the space where they can control their reaction to the way they are feeling or to the thoughts they are having. Thus, they are unable to recognize the extent to which their experiences are being determined by their internal feelings and thoughts.

Outside Influence

Children are being educated by the school system about potential dangers before they have developed the natural awareness of such dangers. In effect, the existence of certain threats are being introduced to children artificially— meaning, not from the threat itself. For example, teaching children about the dangers associated with strangers is, in effect, teaching children they should not trust someone they do not know. Naturally, this causes a sense of confusion laced with mild panic, and the children develop intense curiosities about the bad things which could happen. The belief in strangers possibly wanting to kidnap them or hurt them is frightening and casts a shadow on people prior to the age where thinking takes place. As with early exposure to sexual material, a child's mind will usually process it obsessively for a few weeks to months. Often, the education about strangers being potentially dangerous to children includes teaching about inappropriate touching and "private parts." This adds to the overall perplexity for children and potentially brings about early sexual curiosity. Similarly, subjecting grade school children to intruder drills (shooter scenarios) introduces a reality which emblazons into children's minds a haunting possibility. It is impossible for children to understand the context of the education they are receiving, nor can they sense the improbability of the bad things happening to them.

The younger the child, the more they will sense the likelihood of whatever it is happening to them. The schools feel less safe to the children because the safety measures signal to children things are potentially unsafe. Who feels safer then? The parents, whose children are away from them while at school, are less afraid when they know safeguards are in place. However, the institution of the safety measures increases the overall anxiety in the children, and thus, the anxiety gets reduced in the parents but increased in the kids. In effect, the fear gets passed on. By taking the expressions of children literally (guns, kill statements), the school system is reacting in a way which reflects the child's upset to be both problematic and powerful. In other words, rather than seeking to understand the child's frustration, they react as if they are frightened of the child's potential. Then, come middle school and high school, having police officers in the school gives kids the impression the threat is amongst them. Unfortunately, the more such fear is present in the school culture, the more potential power gained by someone willing to exploit the fear.

Interestingly, the term *safe place* is being used to denote certain environments, especially schools. The conception of the *safe place* is a place where an individual may be free of interpersonal victimization, where their feelings are safe. Ironically, the school educates about societal dangers, including the danger of an intruder coming in and shooting them, and yet, the child is supposed to feel safe at school. It is paradoxical for the developing mind of the child, and precipitates more social and school-related anxiety disorders. Moreover, since school is the bridge for most kids into the world, increasing numbers are not making it across due to the pitfall of anxiety.

Studies done in the mid 1940's of children exposed to bombings (WWII, London) produced interesting results, surprising many at the time. The young children showed no signs of being traumatized despite exposure to a bombing raid (even if multiple episodes were experienced), as long as the child was with their mother. Heightened anxiety was seen in those children who were separated from their mother or primary caregiver. In those children who were not separated, their anxiety correlated with the anxiety level of the mother. It demonstrated the power of the maternal shield to protect the child from the environment. On the flip side, the study also demonstrated the significant influence of a mom's anxiety state on her child. Essentially, a child's mother is the environment (mother nature comes to mind).

An important aspect of parenting in the current culture occurs in the buffering of a child's anxious reaction to something exposed to them at school. Parents should help the child, as much as possible, to form a reasonable perspective on the subject matter, and to internally de-escalate the sense of threat. Generally, a child's experiences at school, or exposures to certain subject matter, can be effectively balanced by parents. This is especially true for the incidences of interpersonal difficulty. As the child goes through the pubescent period, parents must seek to offset the negativity their child is perceiving in the minds or actions of peers. A pubescent is quick to project rejection into the minds of peers. Then, when combined with their intense self-centeredness, they create the experience of being negatively judged or mistreated. Reacting negatively to social relations, especially if handled through avoidance, can become cancerous for the child's self esteem and overall identity development, and thus, parents must reflect a more adaptive perspective. Parental caution must be exerted so as to not endorse their child's belief in peers disliking them or having mistreated them. The school system's effort to decrease *bullying* kindles the potential within the child to report being bullied. Most instances, however, involve the child reacting to interactions poorly because they are interpreting the peer behavior toward them through the lens of how it made them feel. Usually, children and adolescents will perceive the person as intentionally trying to upset them. Truly, such negative judgment of others' treatment of them is bullying, thereby, casting light on the situation—namely, where the bully is the individual sensing themselves bullied.

The onrush of video gaming into popular culture came very quickly. The pure stimulation of modern gaming systems is very entertaining for kids, and seemingly addictive for some. Parents are having to confront an excessive amount of video gaming, and thus, an imbalance in their child's recreational activity. The imbalance can impair social skills development since experiences with co-operative play (friends playing together) are not supported by video game playing. Parents are thus having to impose time-limits. The threat of taking a child's video gaming time away for misbehavior is often employed by parents seeking to gain a controlling influence over their children. For parents to leverage taking away an addictive activity, however, is too inflammatory and will likely backfire. The incessant threat of it being taken away causes excessive tension, and a child is likely to resent the control wielded by their parent(s). What follows is an intensification of the power struggle which exists normally to a mild degree, potentiating excessive discord within the home.

Another issue with video games which parents must consider is their child's brain is actively growing, and thus adapting. The adaptation occurs to suit the child's experiences in the context of the child's environment. Anything a child pursues with motor planning, intentional effort, and positive regard, will be adapted to more readily by their growing nervous system as compared to passive activities (e.g. watching television). Due to the stimulating, fast-paced nature of video games, the neurological adaptation can cause slower paced, less stimulating environments to be excessively boring. Certainly, school is a slower paced setting. Thus, the child's ability to sustain attention on less stimulating and more auditory based information is compromised as a result of excessive video-gaming. Furthermore, video games have lessened the use of imaginative play, and children are engaging in less creative activity within their environment. As a result, they have a relative blindness to their creative potential within the world. The world is thus more boring for them.

Parents cannot make the necessary friendships for their child without compromising what adolescence is meant to accomplish—independence. Negative judgment of a peer or peer group ("bad influence") is usually detrimental to an adolescent's development, and degrading to their self-esteem. Parents must enable relationships to blossom by providing the necessary utility (permission, transportation, coordination) when needed. But as much as possible, parents should refrain from judgment of what their teenager is doing and whom they are doing it with. An important phenomenon for parents to appreciate when considering the quality of friend influence upon their child is, for a friendship to take hold, certain things have to overlap. There must be a relative similarity in position between two adolescents relative to the center—meaning, distance out from the absolute center point of the pack. If every peer group (e.g. high school boys) takes the form of a pack of sheep, each trying to get closer inward toward the middle and coming from all sides, then it can be represented like orbital layers, each layer out being further from the nucleus of the group. Friendships almost always form between those circling along the same layer, or in other words, between those at a similar distance from the center. Since the distance is partly determined by each adolescent's subjective sense of the center relative to themselves, those with anxiety and/or undervalued esteem (excessive self criticism) will tend to align themselves with others with similar issues, or they may seek more confident individuals. The attraction to the latter is to compensate for their lack of confidence, but the peers will nonetheless have a similar position relative to the center. Such individuals are often rebellious, counter-culture personality types—who tend to be seen by adults as the "bad kid." Moreover, within each friend group there is usually a teen who takes the most rebellious, anti-rules approach, and another who tends to be the most trepidatious. Within another friend group, the same trepidatious adolescent could take the rebellious role.

The relative position within their primary friend group does more to influence the personality development of an adolescent than the characteristics of his or her friends. This is a crucial point for parents to understand in approaching peer-related issues with their teenager. The meat and potatoes of peer influence comes in the role, so a kid who feels somewhat bad but wants to be more good will get with friends who are bad and take more the good role within the relationship/group. If the binary principle of either *being it* or *being with it* characterize the relationship, then having a friend who parents feel is a bad influence may represent an expression of bad in their child (like a tattoo). This would mean their child is seeking to be inwardly good relative to the outwardly bad, which then changes the perspective for parents. Bad friends being a wet paint phenomenon—rubbing off on their child like wet paint—is the inverse of what happens in actuality. Their child needs experience with good interacting with bad, where their child is in the good role (relative to the friend). Thus, time spent together allows for identification within that role—in perception of bad and identifying as good. The same dynamic is at play when an adolescent rebels against feeling criticized at home, perceiving the parents as only seeing the bad, and whining about their good being unrecognized. Feeling misunderstood pushes the adolescent into the peer driven world, where they find commonality amongst peers—who they perceive as understanding them. Ultimately, within the peer world, they establish the foundational relationships to enable their step into independence.

Nourishment

Just as a well balanced diet is sought for children, so must parents realize the importance of a well balanced *neuro-diet*. Simply put, various sensory and motor experiences are essential for the developing brain. The ease at which the developing brain can mold itself to enable the acquisition of skills (e.g. riding a bike) should be capitalized on during childhood. Children's lack of awareness of things outside their experience requires parents to facilitate new experiences for them. Often, because of nervousness, children resist new experiences, and thus, parents must apply the necessary pressure to balance the experiences for their child. Taking breaks from activities which are becoming too consuming enables a rebalancing, and also forces children to let go. The experience of letting go of things, though painful, helps the child develop the ability to let go, which is the most difficult psycho-emotional task imbedded in life. The more a child can grow in their ability to make sacrifices, the less threatening will be the perishable nature of life. Thus, part of proper parenting is to provide guidance during adversity or challenge. Tribulations are a part of life. Ideally, the difficulty of life is also its reward. The more a child can experience their parent responding to challenges positively, if not excitedly, the more potentially fulfilling will be their experience of life.

Challenges are a necessary constituent of a balanced experiential diet. Ideally, the parent does not have to force such difficulties on the child, but rather is able to guide the child into properly dealing with challenges on their own. For example, rather than having to pull the plug on the video game console to get the child to stop playing, the child (based on parental suggestion) stops the playing themselves. To an approximate degree, the amount of pressure a parent puts on a child equals the stress the child when grown will have to sense in order to fulfill an internal "should." The older a child becomes, the more they will bring challenges home from their socio-cultural experiences, allowing parents to be more reflective and less directive. Being directive to a post-pubescent child will normally cause a power-struggle which parents cannot win. The adolescent becomes consciously conflicted about needing parental help—expecting positive support for their activities despite an attitudinal intolerance of doing things in support of the parent/family.

There normally occurs a *social dead period* which begins following 8th grade and ends sometime during sophomore year. Normally, when grown-ups recall their "high-school days," the memories, and certainly the tone of the experience, stem from the period following the social dead period. The demarcation is tied to the acquisition of driving ability—not necessarily marked by the individual's ability to drive, but by the general prevalence of peers driving. This enables more autonomy to be with friends without having to rely on parental transportation. Spending free, aimless time with friends outside a pre-arranged context or at one or another's house is an important nutrient for identity formation. Positive, lasting memories from adolescence should be from moments with friends, out in the world. To have a few years of recess, involving unstructured free-time with peers out in the "real world," amounts to a scrimmage prior to doing it all the way (leaving home). It is hard to fabricate the experience, and thus, the time period where it is rampantly happening (high school) must be recognized and supported.

Energy Dynamics

Children function as receptacles of parental energy. Even more-so, parents should be receptacles for their child's negative tension. To offload tension in the form of anger or aggression is necessary for the developing child. Moreover, the process of taking out their tension on the parent provides them with an opportunity to learn how to respond to their own tension. Put another way, once the two-part consciousness forms (thinking age, puberty) an internal dialogue becomes possible. The ability to internally speak to themselves drives the expectation for managing their own emotion in the face of triggers. Outpourings of angst provide them a sense for how bearable or tolerable they are, and produces a sense of limits. Ideally, a child would not experience being emotionally overwhelming to their parent. If it happens frequently, the child will be more insecure and imbued with a sense of being intolerable. Later relationship security as an adult then becomes compromised.

For parents, being the target of negative emotion is a thankless position. Children develop in a manner where their attachment gradually thins and finally pinches off. Until it severs completely, they retain the ability to rid themselves of negative emotion straight into the parent, as if there exists an emotional umbilical cord. It enables the child to develop psycho- emotionally without excessive tension from the negative emotions. It's a tough gig to raise children, especially the feisty, negative ones. Care should be taken by parents to not get defensive. Getting defensive is being fearful or angered, and perceptively binds their attention onto the negative aspects of the child. Doing so mirrors the child or adolescent rather than absorbing the emotion, and thus gives it back to them without demonstrable help in dealing with the emotion. The child knows how their upset feels and does not need to see what it looks like being mirrored back at them. They seek to experience how to effectively deal with the feelings they are still struggling with internally. The parent should calmly reflect the parental thought (judgment), which is held firm, but without mirroring the emotion back at the child.

How worrisome can the child be if they cannot worry their parents? Parents should strive to put forth positive energy unto their child—characterized by encouragement and appreciation—and minimize taking negativity out on them. Parental fear or anxiety must be recognized as negative energy for their child. Due to their level of self-centered perception, a child will believe themselves the cause of parental negativity. Then, they will take a negative view of their own potential or draw conclusions about having a negative effect on others. The more parents can fill the child with positive thought, the more such positivity will grow as a part of the child. Often, the flowering comes outside of the home, and thus, parents do not get to witness the fruition. Nevertheless, parents can assure themselves of their positive thought toward the child having a positive effect for their child's character development.

Being mindful of the type of energy—positive or negative—one is emitting into the environment is essential for societal stability. Awareness of one's consumption of energy, as well as the positive energy from others being expended in effort to balance out one's negativity, is essential for an appreciative life. If everyone was able to recognize the return on their energy —where their expressed negativity unto the environment brings forth negativity from the environment—then each would be inclined to stop the cycle of negativity. Negative energy in the form of negative feelings can be turned into positive activity within the environment. If someone cannot regard negative feelings in this way, then they will experience such feelings as a threat. Thus, they will not be able to accept the negativity within themselves. Rather, they will seek an avoidance of such emotion. Not accepting negative energy within themselves prevents them from transforming it into positive activity, thereby creating a web of such negativity around themselves.

Due to the alarming epidemic of anxiety beginning to grip the culture, a revolution of consciousness must occur where anxiety is recognized as negative energy. Thus, when outwardly expressed (as it occurs in a myriad of ways), anxiety has a degrading or depleting effect on others. Fear has grown beyond containment, overflowing into the culture itself. However, the anxiety epidemic remains unrecognized because, currently, anxiety is the culture. Only through public recognition and education about the deleterious effects of anxiety will there be a significant change in public consciousness. Doing so without spreading alarmist, negative energy, however, is the primary challenge.

Significant change in one's conscious relationship with their anxiety can only come about through one's primary love relationships. In being aware of the detriment it causes to those one seeks to nurture, one can let go of aspects of oneself being protected. A woman can sacrifice for the betterment of her kids, as a man can sacrifice for the betterment of his spouse. Grown children make sacrifices to love their parents. Within each of these primary relationships is the opportunity to sew positive seeds of oneself. Others should not be seen as resources for oneself, nor saddled with one's negativity. To do so is not loving. In the perceiving mind of an adult, individuality is imbued into their perspective of others. It creates a sense of separateness which is believed, a space into which the child is created, where becoming apparent to themselves literally occurs through becoming a parent. However, to remain blind to oneself, as a parent, misses the opportunity for personal growth and the potential to create a better life for one's child. For those who cannot recognize problems in their child as problems within themselves—who, instead, see issues in their child and then try to fix themselves through their child—pass their problems on as result.

ADHD

Over the past decade, no diagnosis has been on the rise more than *attention deficit-hyperactivity disorder*. What was once a diagnosis limited to children and adolescents is increasingly being applied to adults. A large majority of the adults are simply having difficulty keeping up with the accelerating pace of modern life. Complaints about attentional difficulties are common across all ages. Increasingly, teachers are dealing with short attention spans, restless bodies, and stimulation seeking behavior. The latter feature provides the most insight into the neuropsychology of the disorder— the hallmark hypo-arousal* underlying ADHD in its *classic* form. Furthermore, the hypo-arousal underscores the large benefit seen with stimulant medication in reducing ADHD symptoms.

Every child has a set point of wakefulness, where their brain waves demonstrate alertness. This set-point is established in relation to stimulation from the child's early environment. Each child's sensory system will experience a certain level of stimulation from any given environment. If the environment a child is born into is chaotic or volatile, then their set-point will calibrate in order to adapt. Children who are obsessive or anxious tend to have a hypersensitivity to stimuli, and overall demonstrate a tendency toward hyper-alertness and excessive sensitivity to environmental stimulation. The brain waves of hypo-aroused children, during normal activity, are closer to sleep than the average child. Thus, hypo-aroused children find environments low in stimulation excessively boring, therein compelling their physical restlessness. They gravitate toward thrill-seeking activities and tend to go from thing to thing looking for excitement. The hyperactivity produces more stimulation for their brains which crave the arousal provided by the stimulation. Stimulation wakes them up and they feel calmer as a result. If they are having to inhibit their impulses so to focus on something non-stimulating, their bodies will remain fidgety and restless—in effect, generating physiologic stimulation.

The heightened stimulation children get through digital entertainment, especially video games, affects the child's sensory nervous system. Throughout a child's development, the brain and nervous system adapt to the experiences of the child. In other words, what a child pursues with ambition, effort, and thought, the brain will necessarily adapt so to become more skilled or adept toward what they intend. Because video games involve mental effort, vigilance, and acquired skill, the brain acclimates to the high stimulation, reflexive, and fast paced world of playing video games. The sensory nervous system forms a stimulation set point in accordance. The problem presents itself when the child is expected to function in a significantly less stimulating environment, like school. There then arises neurologic tension from the disparity in environments to which the child's nervous system is adapting.

Low wakefulness in children generates restless anxiety, usually verbalized as boredom. When it occurs in certain contexts only, like school or work, then the hypo-arousal is tied to the child's interest in the environment. This contextual hypo-arousal can be seen in gifted, obsessive children who, when doing what they are primarily interested in (even if the activity has a low level of neuro-stimulation, e.g. Legos) their arousal gets stimulated. Thus, they engage fixedly and calmly. However, when they are in an environment which does not compel their interest, hypo-arousal behaviors are demonstrated. In such scenarios, they will be restless and inattentive. Their thoughts often drift obsessively toward their primary interest. For this reason, they are often noted in school to have attentional difficulties and usually a certain level of psycho-motor restlessness. The disparity in experienced arousal will increase the likelihood of such children growing up and applying their giftedness toward that which they are most naturally inclined. Society advances because gifted people do what they love—a necessary combination for creative brilliance to become innovation.

Conceiving of gifted or obsessive children as having ADHD creates a heterogeneous group. ADHD and anxiety have similar manifestations in children in the school setting, or any setting for that matter requiring calmness of mind and body. Anxiety in younger children will produce physical restlessness. Intrusive worry will appear as inattentiveness and seemingly not catching on to what is being presented. Young children cannot account for their restlessness, nor their attentional difficulties. Thus, observations by teachers and parents provide the diagnostic testimony. Unfortunately, the diagnosis does not shed much light on what to do, other than pointing toward certain medication. At the medication level, the diagnosis of ADHD does not predict response to medication. This is partly a result of the zebra-like grouping of two fairly opposite types of young children under the ADHD umbrella. In obsessive, anxious kids who are put on stimulants, the response is more unpredictable, with increased risk of agitation.

If ADHD is sub-typed based on arousal level, then helpful information is provided. Importantly, in hypo-aroused children, stimulant medications can

---

* Hypo-arousal: The electrical activity of the brain is characterized by slower waves during normal awake time. The slower brain waves are those normally seen during stage 1 sleep.

be very beneficial. By normalizing the brain's arousal level, the child no longer has to generate stimulation through physical movement, making noise, thrill seeking, or novel stimuli. With stimulants normalizing their level of wakefulness, they are able to sustain attention on schoolwork or other less compelling stimuli. Looking at ADHD treatment through the lens of neurological arousal, a hypo-aroused (classic) ADHD child needs an increase in arousal. However, with hyper-aroused (obsessive, anxious) ADHD children, non-stimulant medication may be more helpful than a stimulant. Also in obsessive children, enabling a release of their physical energy is worthwhile, since the level of bottled up tension drives the surface symptoms and behaviors which underscore the ADHD label. In contrast, the hyperactivity of the hypo-aroused child does not represent excessive energy, but rather is stimulation seeking. The adrenaline which lingers after recess can increase a child's arousal level and thus reduce the classic ADHD symptoms for a short period of time, but it is not due to an expulsion of excess energy. This is a common misperception involving classic ADHD as being a problem of too much energy, too much "boy."

In early grade school, the development of boys normally positions them as less verbal and more mechanical relative to girls of the same age. The auditory based curriculum has visual elements, but those elements are described verbally rather than interacted with mechanically. Boys are thus going to be more physically restless and have more difficulty paying attention. This occurs in addition to the general stereotype which holds true of young boys being more rambunctious. When combined with modern boys' need for more intense stimulation, teachers at the early grade school level are having increased difficulty capturing boys' attention with what is being taught. Around 30-40% of those diagnosed with hyperactive ADHD in early grade school will grow out of the diagnosis by high school. Another 30-40% will no longer need treatment once they reach adulthood. The latter percentage illustrates how gravitation into one's area of interest, finding one's niche, and having more control over the stimulation level of one's environment, lessens the need for medication treatment.

Most adults who have ADHD are self-personalities, which makes intuitive sense based on their cognitive relationship with the environment and relational style with others. Individuals who externalize or reflect on thought will naturally be experienced by others within a shared environment as more distractible and more likely to express aberrant thoughts which pop into their head. Such individuals seek to relate to the environment and have difficulty making decisions beyond the response to what's in front of them. Thus, they are prone to things popping up which "need" their attention or causes distraction. At present, their distractibility is likely being exacerbated by the numerous lines of communication coming at them in the form of texts, calls, emails, letters, posts, etc. Adults, in general, are having to adapt to the socio-cultural shift being driven by technology and the transformation into the digital age. In seeking to keep up, many adults are now turning to stimulant medications to increase their cognitive processing speed and attention span, and also, to help with energy. Thus, for many adults, stimulants are helping them adapt rather then treating a condition.

3.3

UNDERSTANDING & ACCEPTANCE

There exists an important distinction between *understanding* and *acceptance*. *Understanding* occurs in the space between the perceiving individual and the world, while *acceptance* happens within an individual's internal space. The potential to understand another's words or actions is always possible if understanding is sought. However, such understanding must be pursued in connection with the person, whereby the understanding is begotten in the space between. An understanding forms in a way which grows. Understanding has no bounds, and thus, may always be sought to a greater degree. Acceptance, on the other hand, is an internally represented binary phenomenon (yes or no, off or on). Acceptance has the character of *taking in,* and centers around the potential to reject. Protection of one's internal space occurs via rejection. Thus, for a large proportion of individuals, acceptance is experienced as a letting go of their defensive position. When the goal is control of oneself, then rejection is being applied to an aspect of oneself, and thus, letting go of such control is necessary in order to accept. Seeking for fulfillment within the internal space necessitates self-consumption, or an inflow of effort from others—to which one may reject or accept. Without the internal space for which one seeks to fulfill or control, rejection and acceptance diminish as modes of relating to the world.

The only method which achieves internal acceptance comes through one's willed effort in conjunction with a de-centering of oneself as the object of such effort. Put another way, the more an individual's effort to achieve internal acceptance occurs through getting external acceptance, the less likely either will be experienced. Acceptance, as an internal state of psycho-emotional wellbeing, cannot be attained through external attempts to get it. Along the same line, understanding, which is generated externally, cannot be gotten through internal attempts to know. Such internal processing only occurs when the first-person element is disconnected and being reflected off of internally—i.e. *what is happening to me?* Rather, the pursuit to more fully understand requires a connected position, whereby one's first-person aspect is connecting to what one is seeking to better understand.

The ability for individuals to be understanding of each other but not accepting is very important. This is due to the growth which is facilitated in doing so. Nobody should be accepted for where they are, at present, if the potential for growth still exists, though each can be understood for why they are presently being the way they are. Being understood provides a sense of capability and commonality, thus promoting a continuation of the forward facing effort to grow. For these reasons, the ideal position for which to parent is one in which understanding is given but not acceptance. The more the child's effort to feel accepted can be nurtured into the *doing* space, the more they naturally will channel their feelings into activity. The result is improved capability and experience, both of which are foundational for forward growth. For example, imagine coaching a young children's soccer team, where enabling them to be better depends on a lack of acceptance for their current skill level.

If acceptance is defined as not being rejective of something or someone, then such a baseline lack of acceptance is defensive and comes at the expense of understanding. As a general rule—individuals reject what they don't understand and fear what they have rejected. This illustrates the cyclical process whereby a lack of understanding compels rejection, which then increases fear, where increased fear then inhibits the pursuit of understanding. The lamentable tragedy which lies therein occurs between individuals—where a lack of understanding drives the discord which eventuates in division. Since the cornerstone of the division is fear, proper parenting of one's own fear involves an understanding of the fear, but not accepting of its direction or the thoughts which may form from its substance. Any acceptance of fear's push toward securing oneself, or any attachment to thoughts born out of fear, will result in more fear.

The proper way to internally parent the occurrence of fear within oneself necessitates an understanding but not acceptance of the fear. Externally, parenting children is a mirrored process—as is, generally, the character of care each provides when they are being "caring." Put another way, every thinking individual will care for others in a way which mirrors the way they care for themselves. For example, someone who expects those who care about them to make efforts toward their upset—to try and make them feel better— will be quick to try and make someone feel better who they see as being upset. Others who are caring for themselves by keeping control of themselves are centered around not being upset. Such individuals will generally take a pleasing approach to others—the goal being to not cause upset.

Communication

To understand behavior requires an understanding of the two components of the behaving individual. Every individual must be regarded for having an internal "I" which intends toward the environment and forms thought about others. The perceiving "I" is outgoing and connects with or acts unto the environment via the efferent/motor pathway. Also, each must be understood for their "me" component—the part which senses themselves and receives the world. When consciousness is focused on the afferent or incoming sensory data, the perceived aspect is the "me." When an individual acts based on their "me" experience, then they are blind to the experience others have of them. Yet, at the same time, they are expecting to be understood. Others experience an individual's outgoing "I" component, but often, the individual expects their sensory "me" to be understood. Instead, others often experience the individual or interpret their behavior based on how the individual is or is not in consideration of the "me" within them. Thus, without the behaving individual being understanding of those expected to understand them, their behavior is more likely to cause unintentional conflict. When an individual intends upon the world or others on behalf of their "me," then they will be thinking about other's treatment of them. Their goal will be to feel understood/accepted or loved. However, in doing so, no regard for the "me" of others is given. Rather, their judgment of others occurs based on their "me" experience of other's regard of them. Again, the judgment is of the other person (as an "I" entity) based on the sensory experience of the "me" aspect, without "I" forming an understanding of the "me" within the other. Such a reflective interaction is an objectification of the other person. Whenever someone only regards another for what they can bring to "me" then they are relating one-sidedly. A true understanding of another cannot be developed through such reflective judgment, however. Furthermore, the less understood others feel within their interactions with an individual, the more there exists potential for conflict.

Communication is necessary for the growth of understanding. However, when an individual seeks to be understood, they will often experience barriers to communication. Interpersonal communication depends on expression and understanding. Errors in communication underlie most every failed relationship. The errors occur primarily in understanding the other's expressions. When another's expression is understood for what it expresses about oneself, then what is driving the expression gets centered around oneself and taken personally. In doing so, however, the expressing individual is misunderstood. What had been their attempt to be understood turns into a sense of being rejected. The misinterpretation of the expression drove one's defensive reaction, which was the basis for the expressing individual to experience rejection. However, their perception of one's defensiveness occurred reflectively, thereby the individual perceived a rejection which was never actually expressed. Rather, the rejection was committed by the individual reflecting themselves being rejected. Whether it happens as a self-fulfilling prophecy or the projection of themselves, the result is the same—rejection.

Effective communication is unable to occur when individuals are perceiving reflectively or defensively. Trying to understand the expression of another cannot be accomplished if the explanation or understanding revolves around the effect. Tethering an internal effect to external cause, and then interpreting the cause as if the effect was directly intended, equates to entrapment of the expressing individual. This phenomenon, because of the level of influence gained, is the most pressing sociocultural issue at present, for it has free speech under threat. To believe understanding of another can be formed through judgment of them relative to oneself is foolish. When an individual expresses themselves, whether their expression involves emotions or not, has a strong impact on how the individual is perceived. The presence of negative emotion in the countenance of the expressing individual triggers the other to react defensively. People automatically sense another's anger as if it is being directed toward them. Thus, understanding is less likely to be gotten when an individual's expression is angered. The more fear someone has of another's rejection, the more they will encounter difficulties when responding to expressions infused with anger. The triggered anxiety closes off their mind. Thus, whenever anxiety is attached to someone, the development of understanding is impeded.

When people seek to be around those who make them feel best, it obscures the significance of relationships for character growth. Often, individuals are most intensely magnetized to those who behold the most growth for them. To grow in understanding of oneself and acceptance of another is painstaking at times, and yet doing so is an inseparable aspect of relationships and the inherent challenges they present. One's weakness should be the other's strength. To occur properly, each has to recognize their own weakness or deficiency and the corresponding strength in the other person. This is essential, for otherwise the other person's strength, when perceived defensively, will appear as a threat. In other words, when one is perceiving through their defensive lens, the other person's strength will appear as a threat to one's security.

Relational understanding cannot be built from a triangulated position. Trying to know another's feelings or thoughts based on their behavior toward oneself causes most of the problems in human relationships. Such judgment occurs from a triangulated position because, despite being part of the relationship, one's judgment is coming from a third-person perspective. The human capability for third-person judgment causes problems when the judgment is applied to others as they relate to oneself. For one to judge another based on how the other person is affecting oneself, then a third-person judgment is made without being able to see one's effect from a first-person perspective. Only through the first-person, experiential perspective—in connecting to others as they experience oneself—can one develop the proper understanding of oneself.

Expressed thought, too often, is being hijacked by reactive feeling. The reactive feeling of consciousness is defensive and should not be entitled to form thought judgment about what was said. When listening to thoughts being communicated, a defensive cognition will cause erroneous conclusions. The purpose of the defense is self-preservation. However, when the problem is rooted in consciousness itself (rejective, reflective), the behavior for self-preservation occurs as an acting out of the problem. It can be thought of as a staging of the problem. The individual cannot see it themselves, and thus, it will occur repeatedly until they become aware. Doing so occurs through conscious recognition of their pattern in the midst of a situation where they are unable to follow their impulse toward self-preservation.

Judgment

It is normal for people to have 20/20 vision of other people's faults and relative blindness to their own. One's level of outward criticism—whether of others or the environment—is a "passing it on" of sorts. People are very sensitive to someone expressing disintegrated negativity (negative emotion not being channeled), and naturally it is seen as threatening. The defensiveness which arises in others will populate the person's life, trapping them in their expressed negativity. If this occurs in the home (or any other closed system), then expressed negativity tends to get passed from family member to family member or person to person.

The process of the ego conscious turning a negative sensation into a negative thought about an outside element for causing the negative feeling—is a break from the reality of the individual being blamed. When one's subjective feeling experience of another generates a judgment of them, then it can be passed around to other individuals who can take it and possess it internally as an internal belief about the person. Usually, the situation involves an erroneous reflection off of another's defensive surface. For instance, when someone feels insecure about themselves due to negative self regard, they often hide the belief behind an outer layer of either arrogance or stoicism. The latter style is more common, where the individual appears serious and lacking in expression. Though purposed to hide the fear, the lack of expressive outflow increases the likelihood others will reflect the individual not liking them. This may then stoke other's insecurity and trigger their defensiveness, precipitating a situation where the individual perceives themselves disliked or degraded.

The empowerment which stems from being internally balanced is significant. Relationship success requires each to balance themselves, where in doing so, positive growth occurs. Thus, for a couple to be stuck in a battle of who is right and who is wrong means they are both wrong. Simply by each regarding themselves right and the other wrong, neither is relating properly with the other. On the flip side, pursuing a better understanding of how it is the other person perceives themselves right would be fruitful for both sides.

Since both are experiencing themselves equally correct in their judgment, each must be equally wrong about themselves. Moreover, only through understanding the other person's perceptive experience may someone transcend the confinement imposed by their own belief system and self-image.

The style in which one judges their primary partner or spouse has a fundamental impact on the couple's ability to form a balanced union. When judging people, there are two types of judgment—*outcome based* and *method based*. This is not to be confused with the cognitive processes of forming internal judgment (*valued judgment* and *associative judgment*). Rather, the judgment being discussed occurs between two individuals in a primary relationship and is an important aspect of the space between. *Outcome based judgment* is representational—meaning, it is able to be used to create an impression—and can be sub-typed into *subjective* and *objective*. For example, the claim *Joe is a jerk* is a subjective outcome judgment based on self-feelings. On the other hand, if Joe won a trophy for being "The Biggest Jerk," then it would be an objective outcome judgment because it can be objectively represented through facts or symbols. Using facts to generate one's judgment does not make it objective unless the facts are externally maintained (e.g. points scored in a game). *Method based judgment*, in contrast, is based on a person's effort, intent, or manner of pursuit toward achieving a goal or desired outcome. To judge someone based on those factors requires, for both, a clear comprehension or agreement as to the desired outcome. Then, the interpersonal judgment expressed will be in reference to the other person's goal seeking method. The most relatable example of this type of judgment is in a parent's judgment of their child. The judgment is directed at the child's behavior and is not for the child to label themselves. It is the difference between "he is bad" and "he is being bad"—the former being outcome based and the latter being method based. When an individual feels judged within their relationship, seeing it as the other's attempt to correct or refine their behavior, rather than feeling characterized or typified by the judgment, is much more realistic and adaptive.

Partly, the danger presented by one person judging another is in the basis for the judgment being the person's internal concepts and ideas, which are solely based on the character of impressions. Memories are character impressions of experience. Life, however, is a process of growth, while a judgment is a snapshot. Snapshot impressions risk ignoring directional growth and frequently lead to judgments made of faulty assumptions which assign misdirection to another's behavior. When one is judging one's feelings, then one's conscious attention is on one's afferent or incoming sensory system. As such, the motor system is only being used to form judgment off of one's negative feelings. Perceptively putting feelings between one's motor system and the outside world is effectively revolving the world around one's feelings. To understand is to experience what something is rather than simply how something feels. Thus, to judge the nature of something based on how something feels increasingly traps one behind the experience of discomfort. Blaming others will eventually cause isolation, and then one's body will increasingly have to be blamed for one's negativity (how one is feeling).

When drawing a conclusion about another's behavior as if their intent centered around oneself, then the conclusion is almost always wrong. Everyone has the tendency to interpret the offensive behavior of others as if the other person revolved themselves around them—as if the behavior was purposed to cause them the negative feeling they experienced. People rarely do things with the intention of making another person feel a certain way. Even behaviors which clearly cause others to be concerned (e.g. threatening to kill oneself), involve an individual expressing disintegrated feelings in effort to be helped or regarded. Thus, even the most offensive behaviors are defensive in origin.

Within a primary relationship, having a common goal or an outside system of reference allows mutual use of method judgment. This makes each feel supported and respected. To provide method judgment, one has to attend to the other's effort, intent, or manner. Improved understanding of the other person thus gets generated naturally. Moreover, receipt of help can promote a sense of mutual nurturance. Feelings of degradation are thus less likely to occur. In outcome based judgment, however, one must attend to the outcome. If it is objective, then outside facts or symbols are focused on or cited. If subjective, then one's own feelings and reflective thoughts must be paid attention to in order to provide subjective judgment. Put another way, the other person is judged based on how they make the one feel. If the goal of the relationship is to make the one person feel good, then that person's focus must remain centered around how they feel, for it is how they feel in reaction to something which drives their expressed judgment. As a result, the other person may sense relative invisibility as it pertains to their efforts and intent.

In limiting each other to method-based judgment, a triangle is formed which replicates the triangulation of the thinking brain. This enables the relationship itself to be framed around a shared goal. If the purpose of their relationship can exist in effort to achieve a future point in common, through mutual efforts toward one another, then each can trust the other is striving for something above and beyond individual wants or desires. Otherwise, the relationship is relying on mirroring satisfaction. It is necessary for each to recognize the relationship's potential synergism, including the depleting effect of self-centeredness, before method-based judgment can be implemented. The goal is for both to recognize the transcendent power of the relationship—where through their synergistic bond, each experiences empowerment through the entity. In contrast, when each seeks to power themselves, difficulty arises once sacrifice and selflessness are required (usually triggered by having children).

The importance of one's feelings or thoughts in a method-based structure are only as they relate to the shared effort. One's feelings or insecure thoughts cannot constitute the end-goal. When the goal exists within either person's internal space, no common direction or point of pursuit can exist in the space between. Feelings are relevant for action, for connection, and should not be held in determination of judgment or action. In cases where an alpha-individual forms their judgment based on internal self-feelings, as discussed in previous chapters, a one-sidedness develops, and the power imbalance widens. The more an individual subserves their feelings, the more energy and attention the feelings are given and the hungrier become the feelings. Gradually, from the excessive consumption of the other person's efforts, and the basic empowerment given to their own feelings, the individual becomes more anxious and irritable. This is a result of the rejective relationship with their disintegrated feelings, where they are unable to channel the feelings into activity. Thus, they depend on other's effort in response to them. In other words, if an individual's feelings serve to get care, then the feelings get intensified. The feelings get rewarded, and thus become increasingly dominant, in the end—controlling the individual's take on life in general. Similarly, the more energy or focus given to internal thoughts, the more such thoughts will bloom into the individual's experiential reality.

In relationships, one person normally will be the personified problem. The individual personified as the problem identifies as needing the care provided by the other. The other person, *the caregiver*, is stabilized through the externalization of problems. This allows them to focus on the other person as the threat, and thus, consciously believe themselves to be needed. Also, it allows them to reflect being "better" by comparison. Being competitive versus others and reflecting judgment from others is indicative of the individual consciously reassuring themselves through a belief in separateness, thus allowing for stratification. They personify a figure with supreme judgment on the outside who they believe is judging them. They then relate to this judgment as if it is always understanding of them, in alignment with them, and beholding preferential judgment of them. Judgments of right and wrong, good and bad, thus occur continuously in their thoughts. However, such judgments are based on feelings of like versus dislike or comfort versus discomfort. By forming judgments in this manner, the effort is toward upholding the truth as they have constructed it to be rather than toward building a greater understanding.

Others cannot center themselves around the sun of an individual's expressed feeling. For a relationship to be healthy enough where growth takes place, any judgment must be understood to be occurring within interpersonal space. As such, the judgment may pertain to the shared goal. The shared goal, necessarily, must exist outside the subjective feelings of each. Thus, the relationship becomes a mutual, binary support system unto a shared goal. Too commonly, people's relationship goals lie within the domain of internal feelings. If an individual is in a relationship to feel better about themselves or to attain a feeling of security, then by definition they are objectifying the other person. Trying to find satiation through another person is a consumptive effort, where stability is thus dependent on the other person's giving of themselves. Consider it emotional or psychological cannibalism.

The importance of balance, when recognized, diminishes the validity of judging another's behavior as right or wrong or labeling someone as good or bad. If an individual does something which improves their balance, then it was right for the individual. For another person, the same action could be wrong if it adds to an imbalance. Since the balance is maintained internally, it is individualized, and thus, cannot be known by others. Casting judgment based on another's behavior does so from the reference point of an individual seeking to represent the other as being like them. They seek to apply rules of engagement. However, the behavior being judged as bad could actually be balancing, and thus good. Hearing right or wrong, black or white, creates a sense of truth being beheld by the human intellect. The reality in humans judging other humans, however, is an improper reference point by which the judgment is centered does not promote the wellness intended. It does not help. Nobody can be right about another if they are judging the other relative to themselves.

Fear or anxious uncertainty induces one's mind to form a judgment. In judging an experience, there becomes a conclusion. Thus, the open-minded, experiential manner of existing in the present is interrupted. From the point of view of others, a person forming internal judgments appears less engaged and more presumptive—less present. They give off arrogance and skepticism, and tend to be more difficult to get along with. In contrast, someone who is open-minded and *in the moment* comes off as more accepting and without pretense. In general, such individuals are more fun to be around.

To form thought judgment outside of oneself is to assign quality to a person, place, or thing—to qualify a noun. To reject without first having either personal experience or a thought understanding of the positive and negative elements constituting the noun, amounts to a rejection of oneself. When an individual rejects the world, they are avoiding life because of fear of their own feelings or thoughts. Their goal will be to not cause upset in others and to avoid upset within themselves. However, just as time goes forward, feeling goes forward. In effect, any rejection of feeling is a rejection of creative potential, a rejection of growth, of change. Within the uncertainty of life, the more someone seeks to not have something occur or to not be perceived a certain way, the more they are believing in negative potential. Leading with fear as one's source of guidance (i.e. doing things to prevent or avoid) will trap one in a very limited space, depleting the creative potential for which to impact one's life. In other words, when an individual forms negative thoughts about the world relative to themselves, then their goal will be to minimize the negativity of their experience. Unfortunately, doing so is giving their creative willpower to the world—thereby experiencing their state of existence as determined by pressures and obstacles from the world.

Defensiveness

For every thinking human, the defensive position roots their consciousness in perceiving incoming threat. The world or others are perceived as if their internal sense of threat or agitation is directly caused by what's coming at them. In such a perceptive state, an individual is reflecting their negative feelings (anger, fear, sadness) off of the world, whereby the world is the victimizer. However, such beliefs are based on reflections of an individual's negative feelings, and thus, cannot be represented independent of their subjective experience. In other words, an individual may feel victimized, but such does not equate with the circumstance being innately victimizing. People rarely intend to victimize another, especially within a close relationship. Despite the lack of conscious intent, however, when someone blames another for their negative feelings or hurtful behavior, they frequently act out in ways which are victimizing. Ironically, the individual will do so while perceiving themselves being victimized. This evidences how blind individuals can be to their own precipitating influence on a situation, and explains why such individuals have so much difficulty taking responsibility for what they have done. It also explains why the bully is an individual fighting against being bullied.

The inability to know oneself—as one is experienced by another—causes the vulnerability with being "open." When expressing oneself to someone, the other person's judgment becomes meaningful, and thus, one will feel more anxious. Within interpersonal relations, articulations of judgment can incite emotional reactions in those being negatively judged. When perceiving someone whose judgment is threatening, the natural response is to get defensive. Normally, this involves confrontation or avoidance. The tragedy occurs for those who, because of excessive internal criticism or insecurity, falsely read negative judgment coming at them. The more someone compensates for internal weakness by having a tough shell, however, the more likely others with similar issues will feel threatened and react defensively. Others usually don't perceive the shell as defensive, but rather will see it as offensive. Thus, they will get defensive. So then two people are fighting, each feeling wronged and each feeling justified in their behavior toward the other.

When in a state of conscious defense, one can only perceive through a lens of being rejected. When defensive, individuals only see what is happening to them. Often, this induces judging another for how the other is making them feel (as they are perceiving it). The error in consciousness which occurs when defensive, or in seeking to make oneself feel more secure, is due to the effect which the attempt has on the other person. The insecure individual cannot see what they say or do as having the effect it does—namely, to precipitate the other person feeling not good enough or not acceptable (distrusted, disbelieved). The insecurity is thus passed on, and the insecure thoughts and behaviors triggered in the other then precipitate a vicious cycle. The viciousness is the synergy of defense versus defense, where each gets worse with every worsening from the other being reflected onto themselves. In such a situation, neither is seeking to better understand the other, nor bring themselves to the space between. Rather, each is trying to get the other to understand them, and thus each perceives being blamed and misrepresented. In a defensive state, however, neither individual is able to see themselves or understand themselves through the other. Rather, each is rooted in the negativity of their own feelings or thoughts and perceiving the other person as the cause. When an individual feels mischaracterized or criticized (reflected negatively), defensive efforts to get the other person to reflect them differently are triggered automatically. However, doing so, triggers the other person to get defensive. Then, each's focus is in judgment about the other's treatment of them, and in defense of themselves. The capability to reflect on one's effect of another is lost when defensive. Thus, a cycle of wrongly perceived rejection pings back and forth. Interestingly, when the relationship is binary (composed of an alpha-personality and a self-personality) the self-individual will be fighting against the perceived thought or belief in the alpha-individual, and the alpha-individual will be fighting against the perceived feeling in the self-individual. Thus, the arguments, from both points of view, run into frustrating stalemates. The defensive consciousness cannot see oneself as wrong when one intended (either by thought or by feeling) to be right. This self-centered, defensive operation of consciousness both misperceives and is misperceived, and thus is toxic within relationships, for it precipitates threat being seen from the other.

Since the ability to receive criticism constructively is absent during a state of defensiveness, each's efforts toward the other are futile. Until each has calmed and is no longer postured defensively, neither can meaningfully hear what the other is trying to say. Because of this gap in self-perceptive ability when defensive, guarding against getting defensive within a relationship must always be each individual's conscious commitment to both themselves and to the other person. When relationship problems exist, usually the reactive defensiveness of each causes them to do the exact opposite of what they should do in order to make things better. If one can consciously reflect on what they do when defensive, and realize their defensive behavior is the problem, then stopping such reactions and responding in the opposite direction will produce visible changes almost immediately. Experiencing improvements in others by simply not letting oneself react defensively will, thereafter, generate its own momentum.

Reality testing is judgmental and must be graded by whomever is judging. It occurs from a center point frame of reference which necessarily must center around the observer. As far as being truly objective, the best an observer can do is to represent the perspective from the middle of the bell curve. When judging the thought processes of another individual, if the individual has impaired reality testing, an interactive dialogue will expose difficulties with communicating along a linear, logical train of thought. To communicate to another human being in a way where one is able to establish a sense of being understood, establishes sanity. Crossing the line into someone's belief system and casting judgment, morphs into a judgment of right versus wrong. Since an individual's belief system structures their conscious perspective, feeling judged as wrong precipitates conscious defensiveness. Everyone seeks to avoid rejection, and sensing a lack of acceptance of one's beliefs triggers the insecurity leading to the defensive reaction.

Within binary relationships, a perceptive error is invariably at play when discord has arisen—namely, in each perceiving the other as making the first move. The *first move dilemma* is a common perceptive error which occurs between individuals. If each individual is reacting to how they perceive the other is feeling or thinking about them, then they are forcing the other into having made the first move. In other words, reading the other to determine oneself gives the other person's attitude or behavior the first relational move. However, the other is unaware of this, and thus feels unfairly blamed. The adult consciousness does not tolerate being held responsible for doing something or being something without accompanying awareness or intention. If each believes they are reacting to the other, then they are making the other person the starting point for their subsequent judgment. However, if each is focused on the other's affect on themselves, then neither can focus on how they are effecting the other. A binary relationship, in order to function correctly, must be in phase. In other words, there has to be a starting point to avoid a mirroring interaction which loses complementary balance. The alpha-individual must take responsibility for creating the thought for which the self-individual takes effort to fulfill. Otherwise, each is reacting to the other, and without a clear structural starting point. If the self-individual makes the first move, then it will be a move born out of desire, and the desire will be to reflect being good enough, accepted—loved. Thus, the self-personality will naturally seek to adapt to the alpha thought structure. Otherwise, the relationship becomes characterized by self effort based on self desire with varying levels of rejection from the alpha-individual in order to maintain structure. In total, each must sacrifice their non-dominant side so they can focus properly on the other.

The phenomenological occurrence of passing on fear through defensive perception evidences the interconnectedness of humans. What an individual defends within themselves will be imbued into others through the defense itself. This allows someone to conceive of how they must be "coming off" to others when defensive. Though unable to see oneself, one can recognize how they are being mis-perceived, and thus, why they are running into relational frustrations. When consciousness makes a negative feeling one's sentinel problem, then one will construct the world in order to explain the feeling. The feeling will be attached to people, places, or things so to give consciousness a way to organize the feeling and thus consciously control it. Doing so, however, externalizes the negative feeling, thus giving it to the world. In doing so, an individual consciously believes elements within the world are making them feel negatively. Forming thoughts about themselves or the world in order to explain the negative feelings is an inversion of perception— causing them to perceive the negative feelings being inflicted. If an individual believes others have a conscious intent to cause their upset, then through such a portal of paranoia, a significant break from shared reality can occur. Ascribing intent to others for causing their feelings makes others into two-dimensional props set relative to the scenario constructed of the individual's own thoughts.

Change

Consciousness is not wired to change itself. If anything, it is wired to not change. However, the developmental or growth driven nature of the human lifespan brings inexorable impasses, where consciousness is forced to bifurcate. At such junctures, to grow forward, individuals must let go of themselves as they have been. They must undergo a change of consciousness to keep going forward, or else they will cycle back around. People will continue to encounter the same type of dilemma or unintended outcome until they expand in awareness of themselves and others. The bifurcation point will be characterized by a significant amount of consciousness anxiety and a sense of chaotic loss of control. The longer someone seeks to hold their position, however, in effect straddling both sides, the greater will be the anxious tension.

When anxiety occurs and consciousness cannot find the source, then likely consciousness itself is the source. Individuals who struggle with conscious tension which builds throughout the day naturally seek conscious relief. The tension is a buildup of negative energy as a result of suppression of themselves because of a misbelief about their potential for outwardly expressed negativity. In other words, the conscious tension is a symptom of consciousness, and thus, may be avoided through a lowering of consciousness (alcohol), an alteration of consciousness (drugs), or an escape from consciousness (sleep). Since consciousness is constructed of feeling and thought, changing belief about feelings or detaching from internal thoughts is required for a change in perspective. The change occurs as a quantum step, where the individual is unable to remember how they used to think. Following a step forward in conscious awareness, what normally remains in their consciousness are vague recollections of a change having occurred. The nature of the change and the experience of it happening are unable to be accessed by the newly formed consciousness.

The expiration of time makes it impossible to ever consciously experience sustained stability, since everything attached to inevitably dissolves. Moreover, beliefs which are inconsistent with the truth of one's life become threatened through growth. The more one seeks to keep themselves intact, the greater will be their tension. More energy will have to be spent seeking to oppose the growing sense of instability, thereby producing conscious exhaustion. Rather than trying to oppose life or control life, individuals should strive to go with it and, as they flow along, give of themselves the best they can.

A magnetic attraction occurs which draws into experience the fruition of one's beliefs. An individual cannot consciously control the fruition since it depends on nuclear creation and an alignment from others. Each individual's experiences are purposeful if the experiences enable them to grow past themselves, reconnect, and grow in understanding. However, if an individual continues to behold the same conscious perspective, rooted in a non-truth, then the same experiences will manifest in the person's life until they break the pattern. If a person continues their previous pattern of behavior in reaction to a similar type of experience, then it will not resolve—they will not grow past the experience. The electromagnetism generated by the reflective-creative process of the mind is able to attract positive or negative based on what one puts out. Put another way, the human mind attaches to what it thinks about. Thoughts magnetically attract the experience of what one fears, though the fruition cannot be truly envisioned since it has not yet happened. Only the pattern has happened before. By letting go of thoughts imbued with hurt, fear, or anger stemming from previous experiences, one is able to integrate the experience. In other words, one is able to stop keeping separate what happened to oneself as if it should not have happened, as if one did not determine its occurrence. To think or reflect about (x) is an effort to relate to (x) as if (x) is separate from oneself. However, since all of life derives from a single source, separateness is illusory—it is only perceived. Thus, if one has negative feelings toward (x) or about (x) then one has yet to integrate (x) through an experiential understanding of it.

The ability to change a belief is part of being human, and adjusting one's belief system through experience is significantly adaptive. A belief is simply a crystalized judgment or thought. But since beliefs lead to beliefs, a belief tree forms, where one belief will produce associated beliefs and so on. Certain beliefs thus can be foundational, where they serve as the tree trunk for which other beliefs are based. Such beliefs are thus consciously much more difficult to change. Need-based beliefs are determined during early-childhood. These beliefs lay the foundation of how an individual experiences and conceives of themselves. Believing in the human as born perfect and then disturbed by experiences is just as short-sighted as believing a human is born with genetically imbedded problems with their feelings. Life is a process which is inherently challenging. Born with conscious desires each human seeks to feel loved, secure, and powerful. However, life demands for fulfillment to be realized through the process of being human. Only by learning to bring forth the strived for element may an individual possess it within themselves, thereby no longer perceiving its absence.

For nearly any adult mood or anxiety disturbance, if the suffering person can let go of their effort to feel a certain way, turn outward and, through a giving of positive energy, focus primarily on engendering growth in others, then their own suffering will diminish. For example, an individual who wants to be liked by others can stop focusing on getting others to like them, and focus, rather, on liking others. In doing so, the individual must focus on others and appreciate things about them. The more people who experience the individual as liking them, the more the individual will, in turn, be liked. Seems simple, however, to do so requires a certain amount of faith in order to neglect reflecting on themselves, and tolerate the vulnerability in being wide-open. Some find it helpful to realize they will attract what they willfully put out. The tendency for people to look for mirroring experiences dictates a continual confrontation of themselves throughout life. By experiencing what's being reflected back, people are able to understand themselves more fully. In doing so, each is provided the opportunity to get past their own suffering.

The onset of thinking marks the beginning of the internal relationship between one's feelings (and desires) and one's thoughts (and beliefs). Only after an internal acceptance of oneself does the unification occur which allows for a transcendence of oneself. The transcendence produces an awareness of oneself as an expression of a greater force, purposed outwardly. Within the transcendent plane of consciousness, one experiences love for one's being and truths of existence. The internal relationship, to reach unification, cannot behold fear for oneself or fear of oneself. Nor can there be an avoidance of thought or idea one believes is true or potentially true.

Control of thoughts and acceptance of feelings is established through the necessary corrective and learning experiences. Certain experiences are challenging, frustrating, and painful, but essential to undergo. For within the experience comes truth. However, if an individual seeks to uphold the truth of their belief system, then they will have to continuously judge their experiences as wrong or not what they deserve or want. But when someone seeks change through changing their beliefs, then they are able to experience life more truly, and therein learn where they are wrong, and thus, where they can become more right.

Since the nature of consciousness is to realize oneself, unknowingly consciousness will magnetize negative aspects of oneself. One's experience will always entail interacting with various aspects of oneself through the perception of such elements in others. As a result, negativity in the form of rejection or judgmental disregard is actually a rejection of oneself. This strains the internal sense of bonded stability. An individual will go to great lengths to keep themselves isolated within their perspective—both of others and of themselves as they relate to others. Ultimately, realization of being rejecting must occur, where the individual recognizes they were never entitled to believe themselves better or right relative to others being wrong. When one's perspective steps out of its own representation and into a mode of giving to others, one gains significant insight based on the nature of interpersonal space. Specifically, since the space between is able to be filled with one's effort and intent, true control of the judgment from others is only begotten through the giving of oneself into shared interpersonal space—wherein, there occurs the continual growth of understanding and awareness.

There exists a quagmire with consciousness being unable to know itself. The operating "I" of consciousness can only see outside itself. It cannot relate to itself. Misbeliefs, through which consciousness is experiencing life, must be let go. However, one cannot see any other way of being beyond what is believed. Thus, consciousness cannot consciously fix itself. Rather, one must consciously let go of oneself. However, the process of consciousness growth can only occur during sleep. Thus, during times where one is having difficulty with the letting go process, it is daunting to go to sleep, and waking with panic in the middle of the night may occur. However, it is in sleep where the necessary changes of consciousness occur. More scientific investigation is needed into changes of consciousness during sleep and how certain sleep interventions may facilitate the growth process.

Consciousness may be likened to a computer operating system. The operating system is bound to the hardware of the computer just as sensory consciousness is bound to the physical brain. Additional data is gathered from various methods of input. The data is organized and processed based on beliefs about the data. Although learning can take place through pattern identification and optimization of the data handling method, a growth in capability requires an update to the operating system. The operating system can recognize needing an update based on performance analytics. However, it cannot know what the update needs to be. Similarly, consciousness operates knowing something must change but without an understanding of what needs changing. When a change of consciousness occurs, there is a quantum shift into a more integrated perspective. More of the individual's will is directed into the efferent connection outwardly. In effect, more potential becomes actualized externally.

Consciousness is able to misbelieve negative feelings signal a problem about oneself as far as one can conceive of oneself. However, feelings are related to one's being, one's directional alignment, one's un-manifested potential, and one's conscious uncertainty. One's level of conscious uncertainty inversely correlates with one's awareness of universal love. The more one feels who they are on the inside is different than who they are on the outside, the more one will consciously be tethered to the judgment of others. Only a negative judgment about oneself will manifest outwardly as concern for others' judgment of oneself. The path leading to an internal sense of acceptance is through experiencing oneself, not rejecting oneself or creating oneself falsely in the minds of others. For it is within the experience of oneself where the necessary growth becomes possible, both of oneself and in one's understanding of life.

Binary Choice

The hypothetical scenario of a lion jumping out illustrates the nature of the mind-body relationship, and where within the life experience occurs each's free will to choose one way or another. If an individual experiences a lion suddenly jumping out, invariably, they will feel frightened. The reason for the fright is in perceiving the threat (the lion). The third-person "I" perceives the lion as a threat. The first-person "me" experiences the fear feelings, which are caused by the physiochemical impact of adrenaline producing the sudden potentiation of energy. The feelings are not to communicate a threat. The purpose is to activate the sensorimotor system to act—to do something—to fight or flight. Whether the energy is used to run away fearfully or fight forward angrily, the feelings are purposed for action—action in relation to the perceived threat, which is adaptive. However, the feelings themselves do not tell the individual what to do. The third-person "I" stands both in perception of the threat and to decide whether to run or fight. Deciding to run away cannot be legitimately done by reacting to the fear feelings themselves, for the feelings are simply the substance for which to act. Running away from the lion because of the fear is wrong. Rather, running away for self-preservation is right. The former, where the first-person sensory experience determines what is done, is unwilled. The latter, in contrast, where the third-person "I" forms a positive intent, is willed. Furthermore, if an individual, instead of taking flight, takes to fighting forward, doing so must be willed, for such would require an intention of their energy. When unwilled, an individual senses the environment causing them, where they are fleeing from the experience rather than willing within it. The less an individual utilizes the potentiated energy willfully, the more their experience will be negative— framed traumatically—and without the strengthening of character which results from willed action in the face of threat.

Efforts taken to feel better internally—less threatened, less anxious—when sought to be had directly for oneself, often lead to purchases in order to make oneself feel better. Unfortunately, the opposite outcome eventuates. As the human condition is structured, in order to get, one must first give. For example, if one is struggling with worry about bad things happening and feels desperate for a sense of security, instead of doing things to secure oneself or protect oneself, one could seek to give reassurance and create relational security for someone. To do so, one has to pursue an understanding of the person's situation—their perspective on the situation and where they are struggling to see positivity. In doing so, one brings oneself to the other individual in a positive way, therein giving effort and attention to someone other than oneself.

To think about life through the lens of how life is reflecting oneself necessitates judgment of oneself. Such judgment must occur based on one's sensory system, thus requiring one to focus on how they feel. To judge life or others in such a way is simply making life responsible for oneself. This does not produce a positive experience. The task for consciousness, is to make oneself responsible for life. Rejection of experience, especially sensory experience, should thus not occur. Interacting with life by judging it relative to how one internally feels or desires traps one's consciousness behind a reflection of oneself. Having one's feelings or desires at the forefront of consciousness means one's self efforts will be toward feeling good enough about oneself. The world will thus be a reflection of one's own feelings relative to oneself—either approving or disapproving.

Individuals are bound to treat others as they are treating themselves, not as they wish to be treated. Thus, as long as an individual is striving primarily to feel better than they are experiencing the need to be better, but cannot see past the feelings. When an individual believes they need someone, their own feelings related to the person become dominant. Often, insecurity feelings related to loss of the needed person opacify the effect such expressed feelings have on the person. Invariably, expressed insecurity will degrade the relationship since the other person begins to reflect not being good enough to enable security. Either way, the insecurity is passed on to the other person.

Individuals who have difficulty controlling their thoughts normally also have difficulty making choices. Either, they are wrestling with uncertainty and anxious thoughts or they are embattled with problematic doubt. Intrusive doubt is the thought manifestation of a fearful feeling attached outwardly to potential rejection. By internally transforming the feelings into thought, the feelings are given meaning, and then the individual consciously experiences doubt. The more the conflicting, fear-based thought is disregarded in their decision making, the less powerful it will become to their consciousness. The more often an individual is able to will themselves forward positively in the face of a negative pull in the opposite direction, the more empowered the positive becomes relative to the negative. Thus, challenging experiences are important, as are being in situations where choices must be made. No matter whether willed or unwilled, each decision is a directional step.

The groundswell of support for positive psychology has stemmed from the creative efficacy of the human consciousness. For the environment to materialize an individual's will—to bring into form what was envisioned in thought and pursued with unwavering conviction—is a powerful realization of each individual's capacity to determine their experience in life. It also illuminates the perils of negative thought—those based on fear and aggression. Worrying about what is coming up, though consciously imbuing a sense of control, in truth, magnetizes the realization of such fears. The problem with positive psychology is in the approach being rooted toward the fulfillment of want. However, this ignores the imbalance produced by self-centeredness—both of perception and self-desire—which necessarily comes at the expense of others who must sacrificially give of themselves. Individuals who find themselves in control of getting what they want often face the most difficult time finding happiness. Invariably, they are seeking happiness primarily within their internal space. Internal happiness, however, is never realized if primarily sought. This is because of the stunting of consciousness which occurs when individuals are not being driven to be better and are not facing challenges. The human consciousness, when simply in pursuit of want, tends to become addicted to either substances or materialism. Since such a pursuit is not toward growth, an individual has to work harder and harder to make themselves feel good enough. Further pursuance of want—to manifest in a sustainable form—must occur along the path of growth. Otherwise, the want is simply a feeling desire, and no amount of positive thinking will create the elements needed to fulfill the creative process.

The current generation of adolescents and young adults have been raised with the belief in life being intended to be a happy experience. The concept of happiness is often used in reference to an elusive internal fulfillment, often articulated as how the individual seeks not to feel. Often, the effort materializes as effort to get what is perceived lacking. For most, the concept of happiness is synonymous with internal fulfillment. Thus, the pursuit of happiness is usually a consumptive or possessive effort—to get what is believed to be lacking or to not lose what is believed to be needed, respectively. Materialism does not lend to happiness, however. Due to the strain in sustaining the materialistic lifestyle, materialism has forced a bolus of tension into society at large. Happiness sought through another person's affection leads to frustration and disappointment unless one matures and becomes more balanced, since getting it requires an equal giving of it. Plus, the fears associated with loss or betrayal make relationships challenging. Naturally then, individuals turn to medications, drugs, or alcohol in order to try and self-fulfill happiness. However, no ingested substance, despite inducing pleasure, can make someone happy in the way such happiness is sought. Materialism advertises happiness through pleasure. However, without love, life is just sadomasochism. When one is bound to a life of pleasure and pain, gradually, the pleasures grow stale and the pain becomes the everyday strain of life. The deep sense of being loved or having fulfilled one's destiny is nearer to the state of universal oneness characterizing the state of nirvana. The path to nirvana is marked by a transcendence or overcoming of self, which is directionally opposite to the current western culture's pursuit of individualized happiness.

The current culture is increasingly manifesting the conflict between feeling and thought. Historically, thought or belief held dominance and feelings were branded as a sign of weakness. Strength held strong feelings inside. Feelings were not accepted or nurtured. They were not grown. Rather, feelings were rejected. At present, however, the pendulum has swung toward the opposite direction. The expression of thought is gagged by fear of the thought causing upset. Increasingly, how grown adults feel is determining what they do or do not do. Acceptance and understanding for individual feelings has been, at a societal level, rightfully sought. However, what has been wrongfully capitalized on has been an entitlement to not feel upset. Allowing for expression does not equate to believing in the feelings. Acceptance of the feelings has nothing to do with the feelings entitling help or positive input. To understand one's feelings does not mean to endorse them. Rather, feelings need to be purposed—they need to be transformed and given as purposeful activity.

The River of Life Metaphor

The river of life flows for growth. Life energy forms the current. As it brings life, it infuses creative potential into each. The current compels experiences which further understanding and precipitate self-awareness. The river leads to a unification of oneself, eventuating in an integrated experience of love and understanding. However, each comes into life standing in the river, facing upstream, attached to a tree extending from the bank. As such, each perceives life coming at them. In facing upstream, the current is a threat and presses uncomfortably at times. An individual—in pursuing control and security—has a damning effect, and thus experiences the current as threatening pressure. There within, the individual's life—experienced as waxing and waning chaos—is an exhaustive effort to remain in control. Standing against the current, over time, wears down an individual's resistance. The natural human resistance is two-fold—fear of rejection and fear of loss. Such fear keeps people holding onto the tree, where their creative energy, in part, flows into the attachment. Similar energies must go into staying grounded or stable in the face of the current—the current they perceive as seeking to uproot them and carry them forth.

To the degree which an individual is not flowing along with the current, will be the degree to which they perceive life happening to them. The actuality of each happening to life is underscored by the nature of human perception—which emanates from subject to object, and thus is truly going at life. The more an individual can go in the direction of the flow, the more they are able to recognize themselves going at life. The consciousness frequency of the perceiving mind may reach the speed of the current if the individual is in total alignment with the purposed life energy flowing through them. In such a state, there is no reality apart from the individual's willed doing. A sense of security therein comes by way of one's being toward life. Individuals who are still attached to their family tree are unable to perceive themselves independently going at life in front of them. From the very nature of the attached position relative to the current's directional pressure, an individual still attached cannot sense themselves flowing toward experience. The desire to not experience the loss of attachment fuels the maladaptive efforts to secure the bond. However, such energetic effort is in conflict with the purpose of the energy which is growth via going forward. Any energy utilized for the individual's effort to not experience what they fear—is fighting the current—and thus, will produce electromagnetic tension within the individual.

Misbeliefs supporting an individual's attached position will be perpetuated from within the attachment itself, and thus require the input of outside willpower from the other person. The pursuance of fulfillment is inherently sensed as existing downstream, but cannot be achieved through *not* being something or *not* experiencing something, as if "holding on" leads to fulfillment. When the goal of living becomes to *not* experience something externally or to fulfill oneself internally, then a consumptive purposing of life energy occurs. Intake then exceeds output and the opposite of growth ensues. All experience promotes a realization within the space between "I" as perceiving subject and outside world/others as object—much like the painter's perception of painting. The process thus flows toward a growth in understanding as to the nature of oneself relative to life. Thus, the further downstream one travels, the less one is able to perceive life happening to them. The further downstream, the higher must be one's frequency of consciousness, thus enabling the perception of oneself going at life.

The nature of attachment involves a belief in needing the attachment. Thus, letting go of an attachment requires detaching from knowing what one needs. Since the attachment occurs at the moment each is born suffocating, it is founded physically in the chest. The heartache experienced within the process of detachment is painfully frightening, and thus so often avoided. Yet, doing so opposes the direction of the current and occurs at the expense of growth. An awakened life is in a state of becoming always, since it occurs as growth in understanding and awareness.

Only in facing upstream do individuals sense—and therefore perceive—a need for control. The task in letting go of one's pursuit to control their feelings requires letting go of the belief in being able to control how one feels. The belief in such control necessarily requires one to believe their negative feelings are caused by outside factors. From such a perspective position, an individual is unable to perceive themselves as the problem, and thus, they see life or others as their problem. They attempt to explain the negativity which they behold within them by subjecting the world as the cause. They direct their negativity outward toward tangible objects in a rejective way, thus temporarily feeling better or more secure. However, such is only an internally generated illusion based on having expressed negative emotion into the environment, thereby lessening the amount inside them. The illusion clouds them to the reality of their effect—namely, creating turbulence. Part of the illusion involves a belief in others being understanding, which unfortunately is founded on the misperception of oneself being caused or victimized by life in a way others would find realistic and extraordinary.

The less one seeks to understand, the more intense will be one's compulsion to know. However, seeking certainty requires pre-construction of what one seeks not to happen and then effort toward ensuring it doesn't happen. Such an approach is centered around staying secure or safe. The tragedy occurs in assigning threat to the world and then living in relation to such threat, because then internal fear is in control of one's behavior and perceptive relationship with life. As such, one will experience everything they are not. A void is thus created and life is experienced for what it is not. In contrast, the river of life seeks to take each into an understanding of life as life truly is, and with it, a realization of all which is purposed positively within oneself. The more an individual is not being themselves, the more an emptiness or a dead space will occur within them. The emptiness is a vacuum which fills with agitation, where expression occurs destructively. However, as along as, in an individual's perception, causality remains reversed—namely, they are primarily focused on what is happening to them—then they will remain shackled to their position, unable to grow forward. The resultant lack of growth retards awareness of themselves relative to life and necessitates an avoidance of any effort to understand. Normally, avoidance occurs through the use of rejective judgmentalism. To not become aware, as a goal in relating to life, partly manifests as a pursuit of sleep or to not feel. Again, to *not* experience the life they believe in traps an individual behind the wall of the belief. Fortunately, to "not what is not" eventuates in a state of what is—a transcendent, nirvana-like state. However, such a state is a de-individualized awareness of the potential energy which makes up the universe. In the transcendent state of consciousness, freedom from the current is experienced rather than the individualized fruition of purpose which occurs through the current.

The river of life metaphor is to provide individuals an illustrative template to imagine the human condition—to conceive of life as purposed toward awareness and understanding. The approach to life—the metaphor for which to live—is contained within. The nature of perception and subjective experience is demonstrated as well as the tasks required for proper growth. The metaphor enables a healthy view on the nature of suffering and the maladaptation of attachment, thus illuminating the challenges within the process of becoming better through change. Most importantly, the two-step process required for meaningful change is captured in the analogy of the river

—illustrative of the necessity to both let go of needing outside attachment, and accept what is and the experience therein. Admittedly difficult, the letting go and acceptance process requires a relationship with purpose, where the individual goes continuously toward the horizon unfolding before them. The scariest aspect of the letting go process occurs within the acceptance of oneself relative to life and life relative to oneself. In other words, letting go involves stepping into life fully, thereby giving up the potential to reject what one perceives happening to them.

Symptoms & Disorders

4

INTRODUCTION ON DIAGNOSES

The medical system deals with physical abnormalities or bodily problems. Medical doctors are experts in understanding and identifying disease or structural derangements. Doctors have learned how the human body works from a foundation of anatomy and biochemistry, as well as the workings of disease within the body. They have seen what disease looks like under a microscope. They know how disease acts at the microscopical level, and thus understand the underlying cause of the signs and symptoms. Physicians focus on the body, on the disease. They are not trained to think about the patient as a whole. How people treat their bodies and the character of their consumptive habits produce the majority of conditions doctors treat. Yet, for doctors, intervening in the relationship an individual has with their body and what they take into their body is rarely fruitful. Thus, most doctors avoid doing so—instead, they focus on treating the condition itself. However, if no physical condition exists—nothing the doctor can focus on separate from the patient themselves—then the structure of their approach goes away and their ability to "help" becomes debatable. When a patient seeks help for psycho-sensory symptoms (anxiety, depression, anger), there is nothing physical for a physician to approach. A patient's subjective experience takes the place of the body. The doctor is forced to focus on the patient's subjectivity, having nothing separate from the patient's report in which to objectively base their assessment. The patient's subjective experience becomes the problem itself—their life, their sensory experience of themselves. The doctor, thus, is unable to have true authority of the condition. In other words, the doctor cannot know more about the condition than the patient. Rather, the patient is the consumer, the customer. They do not come to get better—most present wanting to feel better, not be better. However, their will is to feel better, and their belief in needing outside help to do so is the underlying problem.

Remaining a child emotionally—within the physiologic consciousness—causes psycho-emotional problems from the impedance of maturation. Also, it conflicts with life's increasing call, as one ages, to give of oneself. Yet, the medical system is unable to provide the necessary promotion of growth. The medical model either treats a problem or finds no problem. However, in patients presenting with mental health concerns, a physician, without any way of objectively establishing a problem, cannot objectively tell a patient they do not have a problem. They are thus compelled to try and help, which normally comes in the form of a diagnosis and medication treatment. Unwittingly, in doing so, the doctor perpetuates the patient's divide between themselves and their feelings. By attaching to the patient's thought of having a problem and needing help, no true help is given. In underage patients, who are toiling toward independence, being diagnosed with a mental health problem darkens their sense of self-potential and increases their sense of needing help. Attaching a diagnosis to a child or adolescent runs the risk of solidifying them in a debased belief of themselves. Many will believe their diagnosis is a lifelong condition. At the very least, they will attach to needing outside help in dealing with their sensory experience of life.

Each patient brings themselves to the doctor believing they have a problem. Invariably, each has been experiencing the inability to control their feeling or thought experience. The manifestation will be individualized, but the core belief is the same—they have a problem. By the time they walk into the doctor's office, they have experienced their attempts to not experience the problem making things worse. Attempts to gain control have been fruitless, and outside help through substances or people (often both) has been disappointing. They believe they have a problem. But to understand the nature of the problem, to fix the problem, an individual must have an understanding of how it is they are perceiving having a problem, how they have created a problem in the handling of themselves, the misbelief about their feelings, and finally, the path they must travel in pursuance of correction.

The first sensory-thought experience in life is chest discomfort, compelling one to begin breathing on one's own. The suffocation experience gets associated with the loss of connectedness from mom, which later becomes conceptualized as heartache. Therein, the experience of being born structures the human condition such where each seeks to be fulfilled through a reunification. This creates the space outside of each for one's feeling effort to pursue growth, hopeful to re-unify, to be loved. For everyone, this is the carrot in life. The next sensory-thought experience is stomach emptiness, where crying brought about being fed and alleviation of the emptiness. This then lays the tracks for the the perceptive handling of new, negative sensory experiences—where what's needed will manifest, forming the associative object-need related to the sensory experience. In the hunger schema, hunger is the feeling, crying out is the handling, and food is the object-need. The hunger feeling and need for food is the foundational sensory-thought paradigm which forces one to be dependent on the outside world for food/water. It serves as the cognitive schema for one's feeling interaction with life, and enables one to structure the perception of other sensory experiences as such. However, hunger/thirst is the only sensory experience which truly happens to oneself which entitles a need from outside of oneself. Thus, if feelings of anger or agitation (emotions) are kept perceptively outside of oneself, similar to hunger, when feeling internally upset, one will perceive either being in need of something (deprived) or being caused to feel something (mistreatment, stress). Then, attempts to alleviate the discomfort occur by increasing control of one's environment or ingesting something from the world. The first perceptive step, however, is attaching one's upset to something or someone outside of oneself. Thus, there is minimal ability to process and diffuse the feeling internally beyond a nausea-like holding it in—trying not to lose control of it. Rather, the effort occurs in relation to the perceived source—which is simply effort in relation to oneself.

Prior to puberty and the activation of internal awareness, the child must believe they need what the world gives them. Thus, when expressing their upset outwardly, if responded to by parents/teachers with attempts to alleviate the upset, then the child must believe they need to be made to feel better. Because of the base fear of loss/separation, every child is uncomfortable with their dependence, and come adolescence, they will try to develop ways to self-manage such upset feelings. However, trying to do so as if the feeling is happening to them (like hunger) and needs something outside of themselves (like food), traps them in a conscious battle with the feeling and their immediate environment. The immediate environment (home, school) is seen as both being the cause and beholding the need. As a child grows, they will see more cause and less need within their home environment. This enables them, as adolescents, to pursue independence from home as a solution to their unrest.

When a patient presents with mental health concerns, most of the time, they are seeking help either for anxious symptoms or symptoms related to anger (depression, relationship loss). Anger being expressed externally causes guilt and relationship instability, and yet, the same negative tension being expressed internally causes depression and bodily symptoms. Thus, if presenting for help with anxiety, the patient will feel inflicted with the anxious feelings or the need to worry. If presenting because of symptoms related to anger, invariably the patient is experiencing the symptoms as entrapping. In both scenarios, the patient presents believing they have a problem. The medical system, as it is currently structured, is unable to disagree. For if someone believes they have a problem, then they are experiencing a problem, and thus, a provider in the position of making thought judgment will naturally approach the patient as having a problem. The very act of presenting for help determines them to have a problem, even if it is limited to the person's belief about themselves. Since psychiatric symptoms cannot be objectively represented as they are experienced by the patient, the medical provider is unable to cast independent judgment of the problem. The provider cannot take responsibility for the problem separate from the patient's experience of having the problem. However, it is the belief in their feelings being a problem, and there subsequent misperception and mishandling, which is problematic.

The subjective problems come from an individual's rejection of experience, effectively rejecting themselves. Thus, in experiencing themselves as having a problem, the patient is being the problem. In other words, the patient may be told they do not *have a problem*, rather, they *are the problem*. The difference is characterized by the orientation of their perspective—whether the problem is seen as external to themselves or internally sourced. An external problem needs to be fixed. An internal problem needs correction. An internal correction occurs in the space where control exists—where choice is faced. Individuals want to know what they can do to fix the problem or how to make the necessary correction. The ego consciousness wants to do what is necessary to feel better. However, usually the needed correction requires a letting go of themselves—of the fear, of the control, of what they seek from the world, or of what they believe they need. Unfortunately, doing so is an ego death process, and thus, by its very nature, ego death takes an individual to the brink of what they consciously believe they can bear. Thoughts of escaping into death or feelings of wanting to die may mark the culmination of the struggle, and thus precede a positive step forward—a shift of consciousness.

The consciousness growth process is frequently undermined by the medical system, however. In conferring a diagnostic label and providing treatment with medication, the patient further attaches to having a problem and being in need of a fix from the outside. As long as they remain focused outside of themselves in trying to identify and control the problem they are experiencing, becoming better is limited to feeling better. Unfortunately, feeling better usually comes at the expense of the world outside of themselves —for life is always compelling an individual to be better. Yet, to be better requires a growth step in consciousness.

When approaching a mood, anxiety, or behavioral disorder in a child or adolescent, the clinician must avoid conceptualizing them as an individual. Since children and adolescents have not yet emotionally separated from their parent(s), focusing on them in a vacuum misses the relationship context from within which the symptoms or behaviors are emerging. Generally, approaching how someone feels and thinks in effort to diagnose them loses the individual in the process. An individualized understanding of the person is sacrificed. Diseases have tissue damage, and thus, to some degree, structurally undermine normal function. Mental disorders, in contrast, have been named based on symptom and/or behavioral groupings. The lines demarcating one group from another are blurred. This includes the line between normal and abnormal. Patients thus get put into subcategories within the primary category of *non-organic*—meaning, not secondary to physiologic damage or malformation. The problem is not with the physical parts themselves. Rather, mental disorders are labeled *functional* because of a disordered function of the parts. If someone does not feel emotionally well or is not thinking properly, or is not behaving appropriately, then the person is disordered. Since not feeling well depends on how the person is internally relating to how they feel—specifically, their expectations and entitlements to feel otherwise and their comfort in expressing how they feel and reaching out for help—establishing truly objective criteria for mood and anxiety disorders cannot be done. In children, disorders are usually based on behaviors and outsider observation, and thus, children are wholly dependent on the judgment of those they are impacting negatively.

Receiving a mental health diagnosis can be fool's gold for individuals or parents who equate it with other medical diagnoses. In doing so, they believe the diagnosis will enable correct treatment. Unfortunately, most mental health diagnoses do not have an identifiable *disease maker* (evidence of tissue/structural derangement), and thus, they do not stand as true diseases. Furthermore, the medication treatments are not aimed at correcting or balancing an underlying disease process. Rather, psychiatric medication is prescribed to mediate symptoms. In other words, medication is used to make the person feel or think better, and thus be better. However, if consciousness attaches to needing the medicine to manage problem feelings or thoughts, then the base misbelief of consciousness is perpetuated. Having a disease tends to be viewed as life-long, and adolescents and young adults are resistant to believing anything is wrong with them, let alone acquiescing to a disease or functional disorder for life. Ironically, such efforts fuel the problem behaviors for which they are being diagnosed and treated.

What comes first, akin to the chicken or the egg, applies to the perspective on mental health disorders. If the disorder comes first, then it becomes necessary to fit people into a disorder in order to make sense of the person's struggles. However, if the person comes first, then the assessment and understanding must be an individualized one. If such an approach is taken, then the identified problems would be those which get in the way of an individual being well. For example, an overly self-centered perspective or excessive self criticism can be roadblocks, and thus, those elements get focused on as part of the individualized portrait of the person. Such elements would increasingly be recognized and understood if the individual comes first rather than the disorder.

The Binary Psychology model reveals disorder as an imbalance within the triad of thought, feeling, and being. Since these three components or elements exist relative to each other, an imbalance of one often comes at the compensatory expense of another. Rather than any structural or chemical imbalance, an imbalance within the triad of thought, feeling, and being arises from rejection and lack of integration. For growth and a subjective sense of wellness, a dynamic harmonization or synchronicity of the three components is required. Consciousness is created from within this triangulation, and thus is always subject to the interplay of the three components. Each element is bidirectional. The element of feeling pursues love or security. The element of thought pursues understanding or control, and the element of being pursues approval or actualization. Love, understanding, and actualization are externalized fulfillments. Oppositely, security, control, and acceptance are internally conceived fulfillments.

Every psychology created over the past one-hundred years has been created from the perceptive position of thought onto feeling (alpha). From the alpha side of the two-part consciousness, one's perspective is rooted in thought and thus interacts with the feeling side of consciousness. This causes feeling to be seen outside of oneself, where one primarily interacts with feeling. The goal, from the thought side, is for control of feelings and to feel stable. However, the thought-based perspective is just one side of consciousness. To understand human psychology as human adults actually occur, both sides of consciousness must be looked at. In doing so, what comes into view is how erroneous thoughts about negative feelings (alpha), or erroneous thoughts given to feelings (self), underlie the problematic processing of feelings. Within this mishandling arise the behaviors and attitudes others experience as a problem. Also, a person's subjective suffering is greater, and their perception of life is much more dominated by negative feelings or thoughts they attribute to the outside world. Therein lies the discordant relationship which forms with life when the two sides of consciousness cannot co-exist. The lamentable tragedy in the situation, however, is each side wishes to get along with the other, but a lack of understanding of the other makes them a threat. Thus, through education about the nature of feeling awareness and belief formation, people become able to recognize the way in which they create their own negative reality—therein, enabling an experiential improvement of their life. Education provides the stepping stones for individuals to see through their perceptive misbeliefs, especially of others relative to themselves. Therein, relationships stabilize as each better appreciates the other person's perspective. Experiences of being misunderstood or misjudged—which are frustrating and alienating for individuals—diminish as a result.

A large proportion of "mentally ill" individuals have not yet become emotionally independent. In believing certain negative feelings can be problematic—anger, anxiety, sadness—the patient maintains an attachment they believe they need—either to their parent or to alcohol/drugs/people. In those who have not yet become emotionally independent, problems usually manifest within the context of their primary relationship. "Mentally ill" individuals who have established independence generally demonstrate an erroneous belief in needing to remain in control of certain feelings—usually anger. The belief in needing to exert control of their emotion drives excessive forethought, stress, and relationship distancing. However, the effect is a welling up of negative tension which increasingly threatens expression. Any expression will be consciously overwhelming, often coming forth explosively or dramatically, and thus, further solidifying the belief in such feelings or emotion being a problem. Then, attempts to control or avoid the feelings are undertaken, perpetuating the cycle. Mental illness from the feeling (self) position will be experienced by the suffering individual as a thought problem. A problematic, erroneous thought (loss, rejection, abandonment), when given attention internally, grows into a subjective problem. In other words, a negative, erroneous thought is "cared" about. When a negative thought is attached to, and thus given feeling (self), experiential reality is generated. Since the thought is normally based on fear of losing an attachment, mental problems from the self (feeling) position most often occur within the self-individual's primary relationship(s). From the thought position (alpha) mental problems are rooted within the thought handling of one's feelings. Misbelief about the nature of a feeling occurs on the thought or motor side of consciousness. In an attempt to avoid or control the problem, alpha-individuals take a rejecting approach to their negative feelings.

The present impediment to understanding the cause of mental illness is also perpetuating it—an erroneous belief in negative feelings being themselves a problem. While uncomfortable, the pain from a broken leg is a necessary part of the healing process. The broken leg is the problem, not the feelings surrounding it. The mind will attach thought to negative feeling in order to organize perception. Attaching feelings to certain environments or experiences structures a conscious sense of control. However, when an individual's thought consciousness is centered around not feeling a certain way (fear, anger, sadness), when they do feel upset, they perceive the cause (or a need) to be outside of themselves. There exists a binary division between feelings processed as representing an outside need and those processed as part of willed existence. Attaching thought to negative feelings occurs in effort to control or separate from them. Within this interaction creation occurs, thus generating experience. However, since the experience was generated internally, a shared reality cannot truly exist. The more an individual's focus is on negative feelings (thus generating negative thoughts), the more negative will be their experience. The direct attachment of thought to feeling or feeling to thought gives meaning to the feeling and relevance to the thought. However, a feeling is not a thought and a thought has no feeling. Yet, perceiving feelings as representing thought gives thought reality to such feelings. Therein lies the sentinel misbelief—a feeling-thought formation where the negative feeling is framed like hunger. The feeling is thus perceived as indicating a need and where alleviation is found through an outside source (parent, partner, substances). Eventually, the dependence on the outside, in combination with the erroneous feeling-thought formation, causes problems. The maladaptive processing of the feeling usually becomes an impasse within relationships. The hunt for the problem is an effort to find the source of the feelings an individual believes are a problem. Yet, feelings cannot be a problem unless believed to be a problem. A thought cannot be a problem unless acted upon through injection of feelings (energy).

The healthcare system is the thought which seeks to cure problems in patients. Generally, individuals positioned on the thought side of consciousness who reject their negative feelings are seeking to confirm how they feel is a problem. Thus, the healthcare system is perpetuating the problem by believing the negative feelings are a problem. The mental health system's use of judgmental diagnostics based on the medical disease model is perpetuating the problematic perspective of feelings being the problem element. If the mental health system corrected itself, then it would gradually be eliminated. The concept of mental illness would fade from public consciousness. However, the current conflict within the two-part consciousness—between feeling and thought—has brought increasing numbers of people forth who find the feelings associated with life intolerable. Up to this point, the mental health system has been trying to make sense of mental illness as if sourced within the body—like hunger. Naturally, "foods" in the form of medications have been increasingly sought to manage feelings. Such an approach, however, roots the patient in having an illness—an affliction. Yet, if the symptoms stem from a conflict between feeling and thought secondary to misbeliefs about feeling, then it cannot be sourced from the body. Moreover, focusing on a patient's bothersome feelings—where medication treatment is in effort to make them feel better—affixes the focal point wrongly. Therein, rather than focusing on the actual problem point, providers unknowingly participate in the problematic approach to feelings.

Since the transition from reflective thinking to independent thinking necessitates a detachment from (or acceptance of) internal feelings, a belief in feelings indicating a threat makes it more difficult to transition to independent thinking. When an arrest of perceptive development occurs, an individual remains embattled within their reflective bubble. Therein, they are always reacting to something they see outside of themselves in explanation for how they feel. However, since the world did not actually inflict such feelings, the individual is facing the wrong direction in their fight to feel better. To battle the world is counterproductive and perpetuates entrapment within feeling-thought formations. Such is the path of the black-hole. The transition to independent thinking necessitates an individual to first give outside of themselves, independent of internal feelings or internal thoughts, where their focal point is on outside feeling or outside thought. As such, their perceptive position is properly on the path of the sun, where striving for growth outside of themselves—within the world—is the royal road to becoming lighter and more universally connected.

Symptoms are subjectively experienced—meaning, consciousness perceives a sensorimotor state which is aberrant and bothersome. Thus, symptoms are in the eye of the beholder. Since the perceiving consciousness can only relate to the first person experience, symptoms are considered affective phenomenon. Although the presence of symptoms often precede times of change or growth, certain conditions are more inherently a manifestation of an impending shift of consciousness (e.g. panic), or related to potentiated shifts (e.g. bipolar). Such conditions are grouped as being manifestations of a transitional consciousness. With a positive intention to not be negative, individuals perceive the world so to separate themselves from negativity. Through the use of their rejective willpower, individuals distance themselves from what they see as the threat. When an individual primarily seeks internal fulfillment or stability, then threat will be wrongly sensed outside of themselves. Negative thought and rejective action will thus occur outwardly. Such negativity is thereby injected into the individual's environment, which necessarily has negative effects. When an individual puts forth more negativity than they absorb, an effective disorder is present.

AFFECTIVE SYMPTOMS

Anxiety (fear)

In life, there is nothing an individual should fight against except fear itself. A natural sadism occurs within the human being—it forms the fight and enables rejection. Its projection gives rise to fright. Historically, humanity imbued the sadism into an outside god (or gods), into authority, or into an outside entity, from which individuals sought protection or acceptance. However, in keeping the threat—and the salvation—outside of themselves, individuals were blind to themselves as the threat and saw no source of salvation from within. As a result, the innate sense of uncertainty got attached outside of each individual, where it drove formation of groups and eventually countries—where seeing other countries as a threat caused wars. The culmination came in the form of two world wars. The human condition had boiled down to two sides divided, each believing the other side was the problem and needed to be eliminated. Neither could see themselves as the primary threat. In tragic irony, each believed their aggression was necessary so to control the threat.

The sensory experience of fear triggers the human mind to re-establish control through "fight or flight." Seeing the threat outside of oneself is a property of the human mind's desire for control of itself. Whenever a threat exists internally (from a non-integrated or denied aspect of the individual) consciousness finds a reason for the threat outside of itself. Whether the threat is seen in a separate entity, another person, or the individual's body, human consciousness has never been able to see the threat as itself. In seeing either the cause or the need as existing outside themselves, an individual either pushes away or reaches out for help. Necessarily, both induce conflict —either from rejection of others (outside) or rejection of themselves (inside).

Sir Francis Bacon wrote in the early 1600's—"nothing is terrible except fear itself." Franklin D. Roosevelt, three-hundred years later, addressed the country by saying—"the only thing we have to fear is fear itself." Though true, the paradoxical nature of the expression has kept its full meaning veiled. Fear is the only evil. It comes forth as rejection of others and avoidance of oneself. It comes forth as fight or flight. Fear and hate are inseparable, as anger seeks to control or eliminate the source of fear. Fearing fear does not neutralize the fear. Turning fear into fight enables one to push past the fear. Thus, there is nothing to fight against except fear itself. Fighting fear outside of oneself would be nonsensical, for people, generally, do not take offense when others are fearful of them. In fact, a fearful demeanor outwardly has historically been equated with respectfulness. The fight against fear must ultimately occur internally. Therein lies the crossroads between fear and anger. When nothing remains between fear and anger—no relationship or intervening substance through which to escape the fight—then one must turn and face oneself for the inevitable standoff. After it is done, once the smoke has cleared, one's consciousness will be more integrated.

The psycho-emotional separation at birth begins the life experience— within which each seeks independent unification. The process requires a detachment of one's needs from others and from the world so one can most fully be oneself and most fully give of oneself to the world. The fear which accompanies the letting go process is frightening, and the anger which protects the scorned heart is raw and blind. However, through the process, the *internal center* is born. An individual's *center* is the source of psycho-emotional nutrition and stability—the soil from which an individual grows into the world. Until such a unified center forms within an individual, their perception will be divided—both as they see the world and as they sense themselves. Their life experience will thus be marked by conflict, where they fight for themselves rather than properly fighting as themselves.

How one relates with their anxiety is much more relevant than the feeling itself. As previously noted, anxiety as a feeling is from an activation of energy. The sense of anxiety compels change and thus imbues one with the sense of losing control of one's position in space/time. Anxiety is an experiential feeling as one perceives it. However, the consciousness belief about anxiety, and the resultant handling of the feelings, determines it's impact on an individual. The older an individual, the more likely anxious feelings are being primarily channeled into their forethought, thus producing a greater proportion of generalized worry.

Broadly defined, anxiety is the feeling or manifestation of tension. Life itself is a tense experience. Tension is necessary for the human nervous system to maintain a state of potential readiness, for function. Salt-ions, rich in charge, surround nerves in an electrochemical bath. Within the nerve itself is an opposing charge generated by pumps which use energy. This creates a pull from the inside, as if a pressure wave is pushing against the outside wall of the nerve, analogous to someone being under water. When stimulated, a nerve will open the flood gate, triggering an inflow of electricity or ions. This creates a wave of energy within the nerve. The wave travels to the nerve ending where it propagates the wave of energy to an adjoining nerve via release of a chemical (neurotransmitter). Trillions of nerves lie in a state of potential or charge, in a state of pressure from the outside. This is tension.

When tension is in excess, a state of anxiety is formed. Nervousness is an appropriate term when the cause of the excess tension is related to something directly impending. The term anxiety is normally reserved for conditions or states of excessive tension without a reasonable environmental influence or cause. However, there are a myriad of ways in which anxiety can manifest— from a purely physical manifestation like tics or certain pain syndromes, to entirely mental worry-based processes such as social anxiety or obsessive-compulsiveness. It is helpful to see tension as potentiated energy which seeks willed expression. How this tension or energetic potential flows, and its various directions and surface manifestations, largely forms one's personality.

Exploring various anxiety disorders does not promote an understanding of anxiety. Furthermore, anxiety, because of its omnipresence and variable ways of surfacing, accounts for a number of different disorders. If one takes a step back from the labels—from the names of the different disorders—looking at the nature of anxiety as it surfaces across a lifespan, it is evident that anxiety, at any age, is associated with periods of growth or change. A much better appreciation for the truncal essence of anxiety is seen in its early lack of differentiation. Put more succinctly, anxiety in babies is separation anxiety (fear of loss). At approximately 18 months-of-age, anxiety related to control (of self and environment) can manifest as obsessive-compulsive anxiety. This latter form of anxiety is built on the foundation of the original loss-based anxiety in the context of a misbelief about anger. Although the loss anxiety necessarily precedes obsessive-compulsive anxiety, it may not have been in excess and thus not appreciated in the toddler's behavior. Thus, a child's anxiety, as it is noted and deemed problematic by others, requires a spillover into being excessive. To be excessive, the child is unable, through their activity, to channel enough of their potentiated energy into the environment.

Trapped tension within one's brain and body causes internal restlessness, producing increased psychomotor activity, which results in noticeable hyperkinesis or physical hyperactivity, especially in children and younger adults. Such individuals frequently go about their environment with mild agitation and increased neurofrequency. Increased neurofrequency can be thought of as nervous hyperactivity. Tension produces vibration. Vibration only ceases when there is no tension, no neurologic arousal—when one is dead. For anxious individuals, if the rate of vibration or frequency of their nerves is measured, it will be above average. The nervous energy is a result of a lack of energetic flow into the environment and thus represents energetic entrapment. Unfortunately, the conscious symptoms of the trapped energy often become one's focus, thereby exacerbating the problem.

Anxiety (adult)
Adult anxiety manifests along the mind-body spectrum—not at a single point, but throughout the entire spectrum in different degrees. To worry about everyday life is a mindful anxiety, a nervous stomach is a physical anxiety, while restlessness exemplifies a midpoint between the two. Individuals manifest various proportions along the spectrum, and these variations partly define their outward personality. There are individuals who have almost no worried thoughts, but whose anxiety manifests as a physical sensation only. Tension, when palpable, may be focused within a circumscribed area (e.g. headache) or may permeate the musculature— whereby the person feels tight and restless. It is difficult for an individual to do much internal reasoning in order to quell physically bottled-up tension. However, activities requiring physical exertion sublimate some of the tension into productive outflow within an individual's environment, illustrating the relevance of physical activity for people's sense of wellbeing.

A person's thought-based worry normally involves anxiety related to control. Most such thought will be geared toward preparedness and thus will be tethered ahead of time. Nothing actually gets done, but a sense of preparedness, readiness, or security is gathered, essentially creating a feeling of being more in control. Since feeling is subjected internally, it is illusory and thus unable to be truly realized. A lack of synchronization with the present moment can make it difficult to ever feel calm or experience stillness of mind. Usually, staying busy is the tonic by which such people self-medicate— keeping their focus tethered to what they are doing in the environment, in real time. This prioritizes most of their conscious energy onto what they are doing rather than getting entangled in a web of their own *what ifs*. Only in the present moment can there be an actual outflow of energy, whereby change in the environment occurs.

Stress existing in someone's life is normally felt rather than experienced. A stressful experience speaks for itself, and others will take interest in such situations (e.g. car breaking down on highway). Otherwise, stress is felt and derived from an internal sense of uncertainty in relation to the environment (people, places, things). Expectations individuals place upon themselves to accomplish something which is negatively willed (e.g. to avoid rejection), underlie most of the stress people experience. Within a competitive environment, self-reflection or each comparing themselves to others precipitates a pandemic of inferiority. While this is normal following the onset of puberty and extending into adolescence, it should not extend much into adulthood. However, in compensating for inferiorities, facades of assuredness and happiness are commonplace. This then creates an impression of others generally being happier and better off. An individual can devote decades to making the grass of their life greener before the quest grows stale. When the sense of a hollow core becomes palpable, the idea of their pursuits having been purposeless often precipitates depression and a desire to change. Sadly, in such scenarios, the individual's binary partner gets associated with the construct of life they are seeking to dismantle, often getting disproportionately blamed. Therein, divorce or separation is a lamentable reality which often occurs. Rather than taking responsibility and seeking to change within the context of the relationship, negative feelings about their life are blamed on others. The more someone blames those closest to them, the more likely they are setting their mind up to flee or have an adulterous relationship. The fracturing of families is tragic for the attachment security of children involved—whose wounded acting out often peppers the parents with guilt for years thereafter.

Anticipatory anxiety—or worrying about what is coming up—requires identifying a scenario, whether actual or imagined, and then thinking preparedly about it. The conscious effort is to reassure oneself about either the unlikelihood of it happening or one's ability to handle it. The conscious imaginings are creations of thought being sewed into the not yet manifested future. Ironically, doing so increases the likelihood of the negative occurrences, and produces a sense of stress or impending pressure. The more one's consciousness is thinking ahead of time, the less one is able to attend to the present. Thinking about what is coming up or what could go wrong—for adults—is an attempt to control their life experience. Since one's expectations have magnetic or creative influence on what actually happens, the more one expects things to go wrong, the more things will go wrong. The conscious belief in having to worry is reinforced by what has happened, without awareness of their expectations having potentiated the reality they ended up enduring and are likely to continue to encounter.

Through the perceptive lens of desire, one regards the outside environment based on what one has known and whether it beholds what one wants. The perspective is from a consumptive point of view. Thus, things will quickly spoil and seem boring or displeasing. A "spoiled" ego will exude the attitude of an addict, where the restlessness for the next pleasurable experience drives a constant looking ahead, wherein they wrestle internally with desirous cravings and an inability to be settled. The energetic feeling of desire when attached to a substance produces craving. When attached to doing something, it produces compulsion. Compulsive behavior is almost universal. Nearly everyone will have habits which serve to compensate for the internal anxiety related to a lack of control or certainty. These habits usually pertain to organization or cleanliness of the environment. Behaviors imbedded in one's daily life become part of the scaffolding for one's security and thus become habits. Most are taken for granted and get minimal conscious attention. Those habits, however, which require effort to satisfy are more noteworthy and potentially bothersome. Similarly conflictual are compulsive habits which are detrimental to one's physical wellbeing and yet reduce psychological tension (e.g. smoking). Ideally, compulsive habits are part of one's daily flow and thus cause minimal dysfunction.

Anxiety (child)

Due to the developmental pressure away from dependence, anxiety in children may be assumed to be attachment or separation anxiety. To appreciate how attachment anxiety plays out in a grade-school aged child the following phenomenon must be understood—children will push away with an intensity proportionally equivalent to the intensity of the separation anxiety or desire to stay attached. Thus, children with intense attachment anxiety have frequent outbursts which involve aggressive distancing from parents or authority figures. Recall, in allowing themselves to feel controlled, children are ascribing to their state of need or dependence. Where there is excessive attachment anxiety, feeling needy or dependent becomes an aversion. Often in such children—at their surface—is an interpersonal attitude characterized by oppositional-defiance. This character of attachment anxiety is most commonly seen in the first grader.

Invariably, attachment anxiety is initially seen at bedtime. To fall asleep requires a separation, for the child has to let go of conscious awareness or control. Behaviors to avoid sleeping alone, resistance to settling down, or middle awakenings are common signs of separation anxiety. Also, emotional meltdowns at bedtime are a frequent occurrence. The comfort level for sleepovers is well indicative of a child's level of anxiety regarding separation. If the attachment anxiety is more than mild-moderate, it may spill over into the child's going to school. Such children usually give up resisting going to school, but being at school is a stressful experience filled with intrusive worry. Normally, children who are anxious at school because of separation anxiety will be more episodically oppositional with the teacher. During such times, they are less tolerant of feeling controlled, more sensitive to being corrected, and quick to believe they are being unfairly scorned. Meltdowns or throwing fits at school begin with the child trying to shut down or run off. The behaviors are attempts not to lose control, but once the child's attempt to push away or distance themselves is impeded, and they feel trapped by authority, a significant amount of aggression can come forth. During such times, their minds are stuck in a nightmare where they are being smothered. It becomes wild self-defense. The intensity of the fear causes a significant distortion in their perception of the intentions of the authority figures trying to get them under control. Thus, during such instances, despite efforts otherwise, the actions from authority often further inflame the child.

For most children, their attachment anxiety is mild, and thus they keep it relatively hidden at school. Children avoid thinking about loss of mom or dad and, generally, aim to not talk about it. In the mind of a child, to speak of something makes it more likely to come true. Moreover, because the anxiety is threatening to them, they will seek to push away from their parent(s) so to distance themselves from the object of their anxiety. Basically, children tend to push away with an intensity proportional to the force of the attachment anxiety. In other words, the greater the separation anxiety, the greater the attempts to push away. The efforts in pushing away also make use of the tension built up from being in school all day. As a result, outbursts tend to occur in the evening at home.

Prior to pubescence, the child's perceptive awareness cannot create a systematic concept of anxiety apart from what they are experiencing. In other words, they cannot turn fear/nervousness into a belief system they can conceptualize and work within. Thus, they cannot answer *why* they are feeling nervous or uncomfortable unless they are in the midst of such an experience. In the majority of children, persistent anxiety (usually related to fears of separation or loss of parent(s)) gets routed somatically. Since the body is the sensory organ and irrevocably tied to conscious awareness, anxiety in children will manifest as physical symptoms—headaches and stomachaches normally. Preferably, children will externalize their anxiety onto their body or one step further—onto mom. When anxiety is being projected onto mom, then the child will be clingy, controlling, and relatively intolerant of negative moods from mom. They seek to make mom into a controlled, stable, positive reflection of themselves. Mom's reflection will be internalized as if they are responsible for her nervousness, and thus, such children take a controlling approach to their interactions with mom. Often, they will engage in more risky, daring behavior, hoping to demonstrate their capability and to prove to mom that she should not be worried. The false, reflective belief is in them being responsible for the anxiety they are experiencing from mom. The potential belief they are internally seeking to rebel against is their deficiency to deal with the dangers of the world. Thus, they tend to act out in ways which demonstrate their capability in doing things they believe mom worries they cannot. Often, this reinforces mom's worry, increasing her subjective need to take more control. Doing so, unfortunately, must be reflected by the child as a need to be controlled.

Most children of grade-school age do not have disabling anxiety because their inability to cognitively triangulate enables them to feel protected within their dependent relationship with parents. They may believe a tornado is about to rip through their house, but if they are sheltered by mom or dad (within the house) they believe themselves to be safe. The perceived ability for their parent to shield them is necessary for development to occur without the child perceiving all the potential threats within the environment. Prior to becoming mindful, children are unable to verbalize anxiety to any significant extent. They are unable to form the concept of anxiety separate from nervousness. Furthermore, since they cannot reflect on themselves, their expressions of anxiety tend to occur behaviorally and physically. As previously noted, headaches and stomachaches are the most frequent expressions of anxiety in pre-thinking children.

In children, compulsive behavior as a way to control their anger revolves around control of their environment. Predictably, play (what they do), possessions (what they have), appearance (what others see), and eating (what they take in) tend to be what compulsions center around. Compulsive behavior can first present at approximately eighteen months old but normally begins manifesting around three years of age. It represents the child's efforts to control their environment. These outward efforts are indicative of an inner effort to exert control within the brain. If there is a misbelief about one's anger being a problem, then the need for control is likely to be excessive. Predictably, there is a strong correlation between a child's previous experiences of instability within the environment and their anxious need for control in the present. Furthermore, spikes in compulsive behavior are frequently seen, especially when their parents are dealing with increased stress or there are impending changes the child has no control over. Routines and rituals throughout the day provide the structure to scaffold a child's exploration of new environments, and can help reduce the level of anxiety related to uncertainty.

A frequent cause of flare-ups of attachment anxiety occur when children are educated or told about certain safety related issues. For example, teaching children about *stranger danger* introduces a consideration into their perspective which does not exist naturally. It teaches them about grown-ups potentially wanting to steal them or do bad things to them. Since grade school-age children cannot conceive of the sexually driven behavior of adolescents and adults, the education is perplexing to their young minds. Thus, they have to use their imaginations to form an answer to the internal question each child has in reaction to the *stranger danger* message—why would someone want to do that? Even more poignant for modern children is the school based terror surrounding school shootings. Most grade-school age children across the country are informed about school shootings at school by their teachers or principal and thus get swept up in the anxiety of teachers and school personnel. Children of this age are without tether to contextual reality, and thus, they will think it likely could happen to them. For example, following the Denver, Colorado shooting at a movie theater (the Dark Knight), a first grade boy began refusing to go into his family's theater room for fear he would be shot.

In modern times, an enormous amount of worry is communicated through the efforts to keep children safe. Teaching children about the dangers of not crossing the street is something they can visualize and thus understand. They can see the cars speeding past, and thus identify the dangerous object. But to personify a danger—to make it a nameless, faceless person—seeds an idea in children which is not healthy for their budding concept of the world. In the rare case of a child who may be saved from harm by having such education, there are several more children who become disabled down the road from the paranoia blossoming into excessive social anxiety. While such children have other causal factors in their developmental soil which enable the paranoia to grow into a disablement, nevertheless, policy makers must attend to the developmental mindset of children at the point when children get exposed to frightening realities in the name of protection. Similarly, parents must be mindful of the ears of their children as it pertains to news—whether on television or being talked about—for children become attentive and curious when there is talk of real world peril. The risk is in paranoia getting imbued into the mind of a child who, because of their young age, can only apply it within their own limited context.

Though it is variable among young children, overall, their ability to understand inference and sarcasm is limited. Thus, adult talk or humor involving exaggeration ("you could have killed me") or sarcasm ("thanks a lot") will cause confusion in the child who interprets language literally. Usually by third grade, children have begun to understand this additional layer of communicative language. Before then, however, adults must be cognizant of the language being expressed around children. When dealing with attachment anxiety, it is worthwhile to consider how parents normally communicate their own physical or medical wellbeing. When a parent is acutely ill or in dealing with a chronic illness, how the parent relates to the condition or bodily state significantly impacts their child. Hearing of a parent's complex sounding diagnosis frightens a child, for they naturally assume such a denoted disease has terminal consequences. When a parent's illness or condition produces an inability to function (sick in bed, hospital), anxiety is created in the child. It is fundamentally different for the child to have a parent functioning while "under the weather" versus a parent in a non-functional state because they are ill. Most of the difference between the two can be controlled by the parent in their reaction to being ill and their overall portrayal of debilitation versus willfulness to maintain function. Parents, especially mothers, who have bouts of an illness which render them non-functional will intensify attachment anxiety in their children. Furthermore, the manner in which a child's parents react to physical illness will be passed on to the child who will react similarly. Thus, the constitution of the child is related to how he or she feels physically and is strengthened by parental under-reaction or hypo-reaction to the child's physical illness. This is not to be equated with neglect, for the parental assessment of the child's complaints or symptoms should produce an empathic interaction with the child. Such is necessary for the child to feel understood by mom and dad for how they are feeling. Otherwise, a hypo-reaction from the parent will not be internalized as reassuring.

In general, parents should be sensitive to their child's attachment anxiety, understanding how it underscores the child's behavior within the parent-child relationship. Parents who are non-empathetic to their child's attachment anxiety will often threaten abandonment or rejection in an effort to scare their child into behaving. What they do not realize, however, is the problem behavior is occurring in reaction to their attempts to control the child. Recall, a child with attachment anxiety will oppose being controlled since it makes them feel more dependent and less in a state of self-control. Thus, "scaring them straight" by threatening abandonment will ultimately increase the child's attachment anxiety. Even the punishment of taking away a child's belonging (toys, games, phone, etc.) is, from the child's perspective, a loss of something they identify with. Usually, the object is something which had been given to the child, so for the parent to maintain eminent domain over all things communicates the conditional nature of everything. Therein lies the rub—for more attachment anxiety is created when the relationships at home (parent-parent, child-parent) are conditional. When the security of attachment to people and things is conditioned on the subjective judgment from parents, then attachment anxiety gets exacerbated. Furthermore, parental divorce or separation brings such loss into experiential reality and thus heightens a child's fear of subsequent loss.

Children usually fulfill the expectations (not hopes) for them based on the reflective causality of how they are treated, not what their parents tell them. For example, if a parent nervously reminds the child to be careful, then the child will reflect causing the parent's anxiety because of a negative propensity or functional deficiency in them, and thus, they have to believe the reminder "to be careful" is needed. The fulfillment will be through carelessness. Excessive maternal worry is a problem due to the self-centered perception of children. Younger children especially believe they are causing the worry they see directed at them. Thus, they believe mom sees deficiencies or defects in them. If the maternal worry is directed toward safety and outside threat, then the child may place some causality for mom's worry on the world being a scary, dangerous place, and less on self-deficiency or incapability. When the time comes for the adolescent to become more independent, to take the necessary step away from home, they have to have confidence in themselves. Years of seeing a parent's worry, however, will have created a similar thought character in the teenager's mind as they relate to themselves. To become independent, the adolescent must take the worry off of the shoulders of their parent(s) and worry within themselves to a similar degree. For some, unfortunately, it's too much to shoulder in the context of them stepping forth into independence.

Anxious or overly cautious parenting, from the perceiving mind of a child, results in a weakening of the child's self-esteem and an increase in trepidation with the outside world. Children have a foggy picture of the future and a limited ability to anticipate potential danger. Moreover, they cannot appreciate the nature of the maternal instinct and do not understand mom has anxiety to some degree, independent of them. To children, only two explanations can form in their understanding of the parental worry they receive—either they have a deficiency of some sort, limiting their ability, or the world is a dangerous place. Both will increase anxiety in the child as they relate to their ability and sense of security going forward. Not until pubescence can they see the context of parental worry. However, they remain unable to understand parental anxiety existing apart from them causing it. The self-centeredness of an adolescent makes them reflect causing the reactions and occurrences around them. Until achieving independence, they remain tuned into the frequency of their parent's anxiety, and sense themselves to be the cause of it—why else would their parent be worried? Once puberty sets in and the mind can triangulate, then social anxiety comes to the forefront as the primary anxiety for children. The relatively sudden onset of being able to think about other people thinking about them, in addition to the volcanics of sexual attraction, produces a torrent of worry. The majority of anxiety which had been attached to mom and dad gets displaced unto the judgment from same age peers. Children with previous separation anxiety problems, in entering this period, tend to perceive others as disliking them, which they represent as rejection and then react with avoidance. These kids are usually very sensitive and have the potential to conclude others are mean to them and do not like them, thereby propelling their avoidance of socialization going forward.

Control

Since the purpose of growth is to attain independence, the desire for control is an imbedded characteristic of the human consciousness. Moreover, wanting more control has been the primary source of all human conflict. The desire for control develops naturally within each's individual consciousness as they grow into independence. There are a myriad of ways in which the human consciousness may seek to establish a sense of control. Control may be sought of oneself, one's attachment, one's body, or one's environment. How an individual fulfills their desire for control will significantly influence the experience others have of them. The level of desire for control will correlate with the proportion of themselves they believe needs to be controlled. This belief will occur in relation to their anger or toward a thought (e.g. loss, rejection). Thus, a certain amount of negative energy/feeling will be expressed through activity meant to increase their sense of internal control. Often, however, the negativity is absorbed by others who feel objectified in the process.

The human mind naturally seeks control in order to reduce anxiety or eliminate a sense of internal chaos. Uncertainty in the face of incessant environmental change is bothersome. The motor system takes effort to reduce fear by increasing outward control of the environment, including others. However, the net result is a passing on of fear since others will feel negated or distrusted. The effect becomes depleting or stifling to the individuality of others. Those who are a part of one's environment must ascribe to needing the control upon them or otherwise resentment will build. To need the control, they must have times where they become out of control or at least have instances where they regret not being controlled. Thus, a controlling approach to others precipitates their need to be controlled—which is stagnating to their growth.

A sense of psychological control is normally pursued by trying to minimize uncertainty. Thus, individuals will run thoughts around in their mind, creating *what if* scenarios in their head through the use of forethought. While doing so may be reassuring, thereby increasing their sense of control, in effect, they will have invested time and energy into potential negative scenarios. Increasingly, this will create a sense of approaching chaos, thus compelling a more intense effort to gain control. The quest for control is never satiated, however. It has no limits and no fulfillment.

Control is sought to the proportional degree to which one senses an internal lack of control. The internal milieu of one's mind, as thought interacts with feeling, involves a relationship where control of feeling is pursued. The more certain feelings are present which are believed to signal a threat, the greater will be one's pursuit for control. The error occurs in the perceived need for control, therein producing an internal rejection of an element within oneself. If the element had been integrated, then one would be able to recognize it as an aspect of oneself—arising from within—and thus enabling an appropriate channeling throughout one's personality. However, if kept disintegrated, then one will pursue control of the outside environment in order to generate the internal sense of control one believes is needed.

Relating to the environment to give an individual a sense of stability or control is most commonly done through compulsive cleaning and/or organization. A mechanical experience of cleaning or putting things away expresses the suppressive effort occurring internally. Since the physical environment is able to be objectified, as opposed to people, it is more easily controlled. Trying to control another individual, when the person is not seeking to be controlled, will invariably cause the individual frustration. Often, insult is taken as if incapability was perceived. Within relationships, control is sought of the other's behavior relative to oneself. Often, this occurs though manipulation of the other's emotion. Threats to break-up are tools to effect the other person, for one to get a sense of control through the other person. Controlling efforts, however, have a rejecting or degrading effect on the other person. When control is sought of another human being, there will occur a clashing of egos. Just as the ego longs for control, there is a relative intolerance to being controlled. Thus, a controlling relationship can only be sustained if the person being controlled believes, in doing so, the sacrifice is recognized and their efforts appreciated. Nevertheless, the control equates to an objectification of the individual, who, at some point, will need to be understood rather than controlled. Otherwise, as time progresses, a power struggle will likely take hold. Usually the struggle is lost by the individual who is more afraid to lose the other. Thus, the less attached individual normally garners the most control. Seen another way, the more one can objectify another individual, the less individualized "care" exists in favor of control begotten of the individual.

Control of someone cannot be truly loving since it is the antithesis of sacrifice. Negative emotions try to find expressive control through expression, thereby experiencing the effect the emotion has on the environment. When control of the environment is sought, however, one's growth gets stagnated. Intelligence is a growth process, and intelligent people naturally pursue a continual growth in their understanding of the human condition. This occurs through either the acquisition of knowledge or data (through learning) or by experiential insight. The latter requires one to have new or expanded experiences, and thus is incompatible with a pursuit of environmental control. The human desire for control is an attempt to oppose the uncertainty of life by trying to control outcomes. Doing so, however, detracts from one's experiential engagement with life. Thus, in doing so, one's ability to grow in understanding and insight is lessened.

As a child, when one believed they were protected by their parents—believing whatever was truly needed would manifest—one was able to live moment to moment within a sense of security. Returning to such a secure dyadic relationship with the world is not possible when one seeks to determine what they need and then control the fulfillment of such need. Rather, one must allow the world to manifest what is needed, trusting in the world to provide the proper experience for growth. Doing so roots one's perspective in the present and keeps one's thought mind openly attached to what is occurring in front of oneself, where one seeks to bring oneself to their present experience as best as possible. When the perceptive mind seeks to judge the present experience, then it is trying to relate the present experience to oneself—effectively, seeking to bring the experience internally. When the world is perceived as it is affecting oneself, then one is perceptively gravitating the world into one's internal feeling experience. Since one's feelings cannot truly be determined by the world, such a perspective is false. In fact, such a perceptive is inverted, for one's feelings are one's potential for growth. When not being actualized into growth/experience, then the feelings will cause one to subjectively feel anxious or restless. To then affix blame to the world (circumstances, experiences) gives the world cause of oneself, rather than seeing oneself causing the world. In externalizing blame, the cycle of anxiety, avoidance, and agitation continues.

Potential Energy

Potential energy is internal energy compelling expression. The expression occurs through transformation into kinetic energy. Kinetic energy is the energy of conception and action—of thinking and doing—and is necessary for conscious interaction with the outside environment. Kinetic energy is necessary for the internal creation of thought as well as the internal opposition to negative emotion. Willpower is made up of kinetic energy infused into the will and is sensed as an energetic drive. In other words, willpower is channeled potential energy properly integrated into the will. Energy which is not integrated will express itself in ways which undermine the individual's willed intent. Whether the trapped energy emerges all at once (outbursts of anger or sadness) or expresses itself more consistently (anxiousness, negativity), the energy has to be expressed. Moreover, when too much potential energy is trapped, excessive kinetic energy gets expressed into the body, producing symptoms of tension. The sensory experience of anxiety, thus, represents the internal expression of non-integrated potential energy.

Kinetic energy is naturally expressed into the environment and thus requires a mechanical or physical connection to the environment. The body is the bridge. Proper channeling of energy occurs across the bridge into the environment. Attempts to consume energy or power impede such channeling, thus leading to trapped potential. Effort to control the energy will manifest as worried thoughts or controlling behaviors, centered around not experiencing what is envisioned or sensed. Such a stance relative to this energy is in willed opposition of oneself and thus has to manifest destructively. The same energy, if transformed into effort for growth, has a constructive influence. This constructive influence demonstrates the growth promoting potential of anxious energy. Attempts to lessen anxiety, which do not enable creative expression within the world, come at the expense of connected activity and the growth contained therein—both of oneself and for those subject to one's output.

Conceptualizing sensory anxiety as an expression of non-integrated potential energy is the only explanation which accounts for its ubiquitous existence within individuals, where it occurs at varying intensity levels and takes on individualized ways of manifesting. Anxious energy is inherently uncomfortable because it represents impending change. The change is occurring outside of one's conscious intent, and thus, the anxiety is sensed negatively and given thought as if occurring from the world toward oneself. The mind naturally seeks to make sense of the anxiety by finding cause outside of oneself. Yet, in doing so, an individual finds reason to be anxious, thereby forming their subjective experience of life.

The conscious handling of anxiety is based on a belief about the feeling relative to fears of oneself. When consciously anxious, the mind creates reason for the anxiety so then willed effort may be directed toward securing oneself. Attaching it to outside cause—in the pursuit of *not* experiencing the uncertainty—unwittingly gives away control. This is because any willed effort from an individual is a commodity for others seeking to attach to such effort. Willed effort carries creative potential, and thus, for those who seek creative control of life, they require the ability to control the willed effort of others.

The more an individual seeks for the world to enable their security, the more their willpower must go toward attaching to people or possessions. Through such effort occurs the necessary self-expression, and yet, since their will is given to their attachments, significant growth does not occur. Attaining control of another's willed effort comes most directly and readily from within one's primary relationship as a result of the emotional attachment. In other words, an individual's will is given to another in order to avoid rejection or loss. Internally, within a relationship, one expects their willpower, in being directed toward the other person, to constructively manifest. Furthermore, the more willpower given, the more one expects a gain of security, and also the more sensitive one is to rejection or to *not* being enough. Put more simply, the more willpower put toward another individual, the more one is seeking for the other to fulfill them.

When energy is directed in order to *not* experience something, it creates a likelihood of such happening. When thought is formed from anxious energy, the conception finds what one seeks *not* to happen within the context of what is happening. Whether happening in the environment or within the body, the mind naturally perceives the anxiety in relation to a conceived source. Attaching the anxiousness to a source is the mind's attempt to gain control. In doing so, however, negative potential is seeded. The willpower which gets applied with the intent to *not* experience the actualization becomes the driving force for an individual's interactive behaviors with the world or their body. The effort, however, is based on a foreseen potential rather than anything actual. For most, the potential negatives are foreseen in relation to others—either loss of them or rejection by them. Unfortunately, imbuing them with such potential becomes the lamentable tragedy—by seeing the negative potential in another and relating to them based on such potential, the experience of them as such is much more likely.

All individuals naturally gravitate toward those who reflect them positively —meaning, those individuals who appear to see positive in them. However, for each, how those closest to them interact with their negativity is much more relevant for their growth and the eventuation of their positive potential.

The more another can enable an individual's anxious energies to undergo transformation into integrated kinetic energy, the more capability and overall growth takes place. Facilitating such a process requires providing them an understanding of their experience of fear, but not allowing such anxiousness to determine the reality existing in shared space. The outcome is, thus, an energetic expression without manifestation of the negative potential, and increasingly the ability to channel such anxious energy into positive activity within the world. Otherwise, control of the anxiousness is sought by finding outside cause for it—by creating it.

Anxiety (summary points)

- Anxiety is potential energy, purposed potential.

- When an individual tries to control, lessen, or avoid anxiety, they attach it to being caused by outside threat or physiologic conditions.

- When anxiety is accepted and understood as part of the uncertainty of life, then it is recognized to be part of growth, change, letting go/loss.

- If anxiety determines behavior, anxiety grows in intensity and experience narrows.

- Trying to control anxiety by attaching thought leads to worry about what is coming up, what could happen, what people think, etc.—creating negative experiences which are self-fulfilling.

- Anxiety attracts angry control.

Anger

Anger comes with birth and is expressed as wailing. Anger is disintegrated tension within one's motor system. Anger is energy in response to pain. When the energy is traveling through the efferent nervous system—through the motor system—it expresses itself into the environment. Verbal expressions of anger or frustration will not escalate into physical aggression unless the verbal route is impaired or is not effective. Physical aggression can be toward self, inanimate objects, or others. In children, it is usually toward parent(s). In adults, it is normally directed toward one's spouse and/or children. To direct anger away from others and give it expression in ways which are not destructive takes significant psycho-emotional maturity. Suppressing anger, or internally trapping it, is psychologically unbecoming to a child's self-esteem and early cognitive development. For children to become suppressive, their anger must pose a threat to the world as they experience it. Normally, this is because they have experienced their parent(s) being unable to tolerate their anger, reacting in a way where their security is threatened. Thus, the expression of anger becomes associated with a significant spike in attachment anxiety.

Anger is a negative feeling which arises as part of the human's natural reaction to life experiences. Anger is negative energy within one's human motor cortex in relation to the environment. Anger thus manifests in one's outward perception of others relative to oneself. The motor system uses anger to influence the environment—usually directed toward individuals. The intent to establish control in the face of a perceived threat often triggers angry action meant to re-gain control. Tension trapped in the motor system is internally felt as irritability and it colors the outward perception of others. Some of the tension will be expressed physically through neuromuscular tension, physical restlessness, and increased neurofrequency. Other, more systemic manifestations of tension will surface over time if excessive tension remains trapped in one's motor system (e.g. hypertension, gastric reflux).

A discussion of anger must abide by some some descriptive parameters—the first being—anger is a feeling, an emotion. Thus, anger itself is not a problem. Anger is inseparable from fear, in fact—anger and fear are of the same substance. Getting angry usually means one senses a threat. The threat could be perceived as coming from others or equally from within. Internal feelings of guilt, inadequacies, and negative self-judgments produce internally directed anger. Anger itself is not a problem. A person with an *anger problem* thus does not have anger as a problem. Rather, the problem is when anger gets control of the person. When one believes anger is a problem, then feeling angry is unable to be channeled into increased effort and intensification of focus, nor is it able to neutralize fear internally. Rather, it is externalized. Thus, to some degree, anger is always pointing back at such individuals, perceived as impending bad from the environment. Individuals who are regarded as having an anger problem invariably are willed to not be upset, for they are the most sensitive to being upset, and will see elements within their environment as causing their upset. Their effort to not be upset forces them to triangulate their upset, and thus, they are always putting out their upset. Others thus experience such individuals for who they seek not to be.

When do natural human feelings, in excess, become a problem? It is not appropriate to draw the line around the emotion itself as if its very substance, and thus its presence, is a problem. Rather, the problem, if one exists, will always exist in how the person relates to the emotion. Anger exploding unto the environment and unable to be controlled by the individual is a problem of anger dyscontrol. The expectation for adults to maintain control of their anger in public is a line strictly drawn by modern society. Most anger problems surface privately, within the home. Anger lives in the gut and breathes the air of other people, especially those closest to the heart. Most anger is built of thwarted passion. Children learn how to relate to their frustrated feelings by seeing their parent's handling of anger—what it entitles, how it's employed, and the shame (if any) in relation to it once it subsides. The more influence anger has within a child's environment, the more power the child will give to their own anger.

Since anger is a commonly shared emotion, the feeling itself cannot be a problem. Rather, if one believes their anger is a problem, then they will relate to the occurrence of angry feelings inside as a threat. To believe in a feeling as a problem within oneself tethers one's perception to the feeling having been inflicted or caused by something or someone within the environment. Thus, the more one believes their anger to be a problem, the more they will attach their anger to what they are experiencing. In other words, they will find fault around them, something to criticize. Being "made upset" is thus taken as an offense in and of itself, since such individuals expect those closest to them to relate to their anger with deferent consideration.

Within the child's environment, the amount and intensity of expressed anger imbeds itself in their developing personality. An individual's adult character will have a certain baseline level of anger, correlating with the amount of anger in their home while growing up. This is not the same as being angry, which is more specifically an interpersonal manifestation of anger. The ways in which anger may manifest or can be expressed are numerous. An important aspect of emotional maturity and healthy adult function is the manner in which an individual handles their anger, especially as it participates in the interplay of expressed anger in a binary relationship. For those who believe anger is a problem, when, as a young child, they expressed anger toward parents, the parental response was—either, in effort to make them feel better or in self defense. Both responses communicate the feeling being a problem and demonstrates a way of handling it. If the parent seeks to make the child not upset, then the anger is a problem and brings entitlement to be made to feel better. Going forward, the experience of upset then brings a sense of needing something or someone from outside to calm them down. Simply by having negative feelings, they believe they deserve to be made to feel better. Such an empowerment of negativity eventually traps them in an internal relationship with their potential for anger. When another does not respond to try and make them feel better, they will believe the individual does not care. Social discord is therein more likely due to believing others are uncaring.

If the parental response to someone's upset feelings (during childhood) was to get upset and either get angry or distant, then, as adults, they will respond similarly to something or someone they perceive causing them upset. They will have difficulty reconciling the thought of someone who supposedly cares about them making them angry. They expect others to relate to them in a way which seeks to minimize upsetting them, believing others are in regard of their angry potential. For others to do so, however, would require others regarding them with conscious fear. This then produces the experience for others of other having to "walk on eggshells." Less influence over others comes if others grow in self-confidence or lessen in fear. Then, the thought of not being cared about is created, potentially crystallizing into a belief acted out upon.

A good illustrative example is the male alcoholic who chronically drinks to manage tension which is potentiated as rejective anger within them (anger being rejected internally potentiates the anger to come forth rejectingly). Being angrily rejecting, however, is hurtful to those they seek not to hurt and thus destabilizes their environment. Such an individual will believe feelings of anger need comforting help from the outside. As a child, their feelings of anger, when expressed, were sought to be made better by mom. This created the need and sustained it. It is thus very difficult for them to perceive the alcohol as the problem in and of itself. Rather, the feelings of anxious agitation drive the use of alcohol in effort to self-medicate. Often, in such individuals, there is the belief of those closest to them understanding their affliction—their affliction being the negative feelings themselves—and thus, should be forgiving of them. When others do things which further anger them, a destructive lashing out can occur. Alcoholics, generally, compensate outwardly for their inner negativity through pleasingness, and thus conscious life tends to be exhausting. They tend to long for unconsciousness as a break from their conscious negativity. The alcohol facilitates unconsciousness, which is normally difficult for such individuals to achieve without a sedative.

The destructive eruption of anger is the emergence of the anger as a problem. Internally relating to it as a potential threat causes a welling up of the angry pressure. An eruption then creates, for others, the experience of anger as a problem. However, others do not tend to accept responsibility for causing it unless they truly could have prevented it. Enabling an individual to feel better is different than the individual being made better. The recurring cycles of reaction and remorse precipitate others feeling helpless, unfairly treated, and increasingly reflecting themselves as not being good enough. Others will then give up on making the person feel better—seeing it as a waste of effort unto a sink hole of negative feelings. Others will thus end up regarding the person as having a rather helpless anger problem. This then outwardly reflects the person's inner belief, further trapping them in the web of what they believe themselves to be.

Ironically, the belief in anger as a problem stems from its negative effect on others while at the same time being perceived as being caused by others. So to protect others from one's own anger as a problem is to distance or push others away angrily. Yet, the belief in anger as a problem tethers an individual to being unable to take responsibility for their upset. Along the same line, they will look for others to be considerate, and will expect pleasing efforts toward them when they are upset. Therein resides the dynamic of *push-pull* which is characteristic of the relationships for those who identify their anger as a problem. Put more simply, those who believe their anger is a problem will sense themselves caring for others through their internal suppression of their anger. They can thus consciously frame their "care" as inhibition of themselves, for what they did not do. Necessarily, at times, their anger emerges as a problem. Unfortunately, proving their anger to be a problem by manifesting it as a problem traps them in the misbelief, thus perpetuating the cycle.

An individual who believes their anger is a problem is bound to be in fear—either of themselves or of others. Generally, they are hypersensitive to conflict—often in a way where they are overly sensitive to hurting people's feelings. As such, they tend to be socially introverted, and characteristically their resting facial expression is less expressive than average. Furthermore, they will perceive no difference between *feeling* angry and *being* angry. Cognitively, the space has not developed. The conscious processing of one's angry feelings is similar to the conscious processing of hunger (as a feeling). Most people perceive no difference between *feeling* hungry and *being* hungry. A similar conscious inability to see the space between the *feeling* and the *being* occurs with anger when being processed as a problem. As such, anger has yet to be integrated, and thus is processed cognitively as if it is being inflicted. In relating to one's anger as a problem, all the efforts to control the anger or avoid triggers are futile without changing one's belief about the feeling of anger occurring within them. Good natured anxiety about oneself—namely, in believing one is a potential threat if made upset—causes hypersensitivity to conflict and a poor tolerance for frustration. Since life is inherently conflictual and challenging, the misbelief about anger will manifest with excessive distancing and isolation.

It is not uncommon to hear someone speaking about being made upset by someone else. In truth, once independent, no one can truly be made to feel (without there being physical contact). Rather, individuals attach their negative feelings to their experience, usually pertaining to how they represent being treated or what they had to endure. In doing so, they seek to externalize negative feelings existing within them as if the expression is legitimized based on their claims. Within a binary relationship, if the expression of anger from the other person is seen as a threat, then it will be reacted to in a maladaptive manner. To express upset feelings and be reacted to as a threat is an experience of rejection. The sensitivity toward upset feelings, if excessive, causes the other person to feel trapped. There occurs no pursuit of understanding but rather judgmental defensiveness. Therein, there occurs no sense of acceptance for the person who was simply expressing upset. For feelings to be kept unnaturally suppressed—because of a hypersensitivity to those feelings within another—is not conducive to growth.

A person who intentionally does evil is a psychopath, who may or may not feel angry when doing such deeds. They portray the difference between anger and hate. Anger, over time, will imbed into an individual's character, where others will experience them as an angry person, but not hateful. The more anger gets interwoven into someone's personality, the less angry they will consciously feel. Hate requires a judgment of an individual or a belief system through which significant anger is channeled. Hate may represent anger's sediment. Put another way, anger must settle onto something or someone, and if enough anger exists, it can easily emerge as hate. Bad behaviors should be differentiated from angry behaviors. Behaviors in the context of angry feelings must be understood differently than rule breaking and menacing pursuits. For example, cursing angrily as opposed to shooting squirrels, where the former is a defensive expression of disintegrated anger, while the latter is a willed behavior representing integrated anger manifesting as hate. Anger acting out does not make for a bad person. Anger needs to be taken at face value, understood as an emotional state—the same as fear, except occurring with intent.

The terms psychopath and sociopath were developed in the middle of last century in effort to give label to a type of individual who lacked empathy for others and whose conduct disregarded rules and was generally exploitive. The terms, however, were dropped from the official diagnostic manual over thirty years ago. Anti-social personality disorder is now the label applied to such adults. For children, however, the label of conduct disorder is used for those whose behavior is characterized by hurting others and violating rules. It is not uncommon for children who have been raised within unstable, abusive homes to have problems relating to authority figures and rules. Because of their early experiences with adults being undependable and acting themselves like mean children, such children are naturally uncomfortable with being controlled by authority (including following rules or laws). Both conduct disorder and antisocial personality disorder, as terms, cast a larger net than did the terms psychopath or sociopath. Thus, the diagnosis of antisocial personality disorder and conduct disorder have been applied to many more individuals. However, in doing so, the individuals who are most potentially dangerous—those who previously would have been termed psychopaths—are concealed within the broader diagnoses of conduct disorder and antisocial personality disorder.

A psychopath in the classic sense lacks the capacity for guilt. Moreover, such individuals have no fear of loss and, in fact, are attracted to loss (usually in the form of death). This combination of missing elements is exceptionally uncommon. When these two pieces of the normal human psyche are missing in a person, there will be noticeable signs by the time they come into elementary school. Moreover, during the grade-school years, such a child is less able to hide the cardinal behaviors: killing animals and fascination with fire. Such children have a compulsion toward hurting or killing, and they tend to prey on weaker or lower species. This aim reflects their desire to kill off weakness within themselves. Essentially, they are killing off any parts of themselves which demonstrate fear or dependence.

Children should identify with animals, especially domesticated animals (e.g. dogs), and thus, children should demonstrate signs of empathy in their interaction with animals—therein reflecting positivity toward a part of themselves.

Children have a severity of self-centeredness which opacifies their ability to see the emotional hurt their anger causes in others (when directed aggressively). They learn hurting others is wrong, and they will say it is wrong because "you get in trouble." Children do not recognize the inherent wrong in taking one's anger out on another. However, when it comes to anger toward their primary caregiver (usually mom), most every young child is sensitive and afterwards feels remorseful, if not frightened. This stems from the child's attachment anxiety—their instinctive fears of loss and the potential for rejection—where they fear driving their caregiver away. Thus, in children who have a significant amount of aggression, the more their primary caregiver is visibly insulted or affected by the aggression, the greater will be the child's resultant guilt and attachment anxiety. As discussed previously, when a child has heightened attachment anxiety, they are more likely to use anger for tension release and to push away. However, in doing so, if the child feels guilty for emotionally hurting their primary caregiver, then it becomes a cycle which doubles down on itself. The child can be caught in an aggression-attachment anxiety cycle with their caregiver, who feels similarly trapped. In such cases, therapeutic intervention is indicated.

Frustration is uncomfortable, painful to the psyche. At some level, for frustration to exist, there has to be an entitlement for it not to exist. Children usually get frustrated from their inability to control the world around them—especially individuals (siblings, parents, peers) who impede the child's ability to get what he or she wants. For the child, anger serves to gain control of the environment or gain control of themselves, and also enables a release of triggered tension. Anger expressed for the purposes of overpowering another tends to dissipate as the child gets older. By the time they reach adolescence, their anger will emerge defensively toward perceived threat or criticism more than being employed offensively. Pre-pubescent children do not have the capacity to consider others taking what they say differently than how they mean it. Thus, they will angrily threaten someone who is upsetting them. It is meant to be a show of power or force, such as "you better shut up or else." In their efforts to have a more powerful influence with their words, they often make threats where they are seeking to gain control by inducing fear. They have to learn certain things are always inappropriate to say—expressions which are off-limits even during times of emotional dyscontrol. These expressions, such as the threat to kill someone or bring a gun to school, then become like curse-words—rebellious and daring to say. Thus, curse-expressions, normally between peers (usually boys), are displays of bravery or toughness and help establish the social pecking order entering puberty.

A curse-expression should not be empowered by adults seeking to correct the behavior. In considering a hypothetical scenario of a 4th grader who threatens to shoot someone, where school officials respond by suspending the child plus requiring a psychological assessment prior to returning—by the school reacting in a frightened fashion, the fear shocks the child (who had been angry at a peer), and also makes the child feel powerful. Psychologically, they walk away feeling both more powerful and scarier than when they walked in. Moreover, it causes the child, who was simply too angry with another peer, to feel misunderstood and misrepresented. Thus, trusting the teachers and school authorities becomes more difficult. In the long run, the child will be more uncomfortable doing what school authorities ask of him. A cycle which builds on itself can occur, increasing the child's angry frustration in the process. An authority figure—whether a parent or a school official—cannot control a child or adolescent if scared of them. Fear is a force which should not be empowered—whether it's fear within a child (e.g. school avoidance) or fear of the child. Moreover, fear of causing upset to children, generally, empowers children when they are upset.

Entitled people are usually dissatisfied and resentful. The humble person tends not to be angry and exists in a state of less interpersonal discord than most. This is due to the fact that they do not have the same vigilance for others potentially being disrespectful or not recognizing their strength. They tend to feel grateful for whatever comes their way. Yet, if the humility goes too far, where shame enters the picture, then an element of masochism may be present, where the person believes punishment is deserved. In such people, they tend to gravitate toward people who like to externalize contempt and whose anger is dominating and devaluing—the sadist. Ultimately, a sadist gives and a masochist receives. A sadist makes and a masochist takes. Each is the flip side of the other. Each is born relative to the other from within a relationship which establishes the template of relationship dynamics. An alpha personality will seek the sadistic role, as they are aroused by being dominant. The masochistic individual is normally a self personality with an intensely critical internal element (alpha aspect), making them crave the catharsis of punishment. The extreme forms of such sadomasochistic relationships create the images most people have when thinking of sadomasochism. However, life has each person constructed in such a way where everyone should be able to relate to sadistic and masochistic desires. Therein, every binary relationship will have a balanced expression of each, where the alpha-individual manifests sadism inherent in the role in proportion to the self-individual's masochism. So while most people have a portrait of sadomasochism as polar extremes—starkly black and white—the reality is in the varying shades of gray which exists normally within all human beings.

The way anger is handled in a relationship is extremely important. What is the expectation each has for how the other person expresses anger? What is the expectation for the other in receiving their anger, in reaction to the anger? What is the significance of the other's anger? Is there an imbalance of sensitivity—where the individual is hypersensitive to the other's angry expressions but not to their own? Anger is an emotion which elicits a visceral response in people. Often, an individual sees the anger from another as representing something which in reality is different than what it represented within the expressing individual. Anger from one induces fear in another. Within long term relationships, anger usually represents a problem with the communication of feelings and expectations. Frustration with another person derives from feeling mistreated or misrepresented—usually both to varying degrees. In this way, anger forms like a shell around a person's core sense of individuality, aimed to protect. The shell of anger then dually serves to protect from further insult and to express or put out pain. However, in effect, with anger having so much rejective potential infused within it, the other person experiences not being liked or being degraded and will sense themselves rejected.

Anger is often purposed to release tension, especially in children. Without yet the ability to manage their tension through internal reasoning, children cannot implement a controlled release. Relaxation techniques are cognitive coping skills, and yet to employ them requires the ability to think. A lack of appreciation for the cognitive level of children is frequently evidenced by counselors who try to teach children to employ a positive voice internally to calm the anger down themselves. Unfortunately, until reaching puberty, the brains of children cannot have an internal dialogue, especially one which is therapeutic. Moreover, anger is energetic power, thus needing expression. Growing ways to channel it into creative or productive activity enables fulfillment of potential. Teaching children to reject anger by coping with it or escaping from it equates to teaching a child to divide themselves. Children cannot model the thinking of adults. They can, however, model the emotional behavior of parents. The manner in which children handle their anger will be characterized by what they see and experience. Moreover, the amount of anger present in a child tends to correlate with the level of disharmony in the parental marriage. Such anger stems from anger—they are the pieces which make up the inner child. The child then becomes an embodiment of the parental battle and cannot help but feel responsible. Being unable to control the situation, they can only act out the conflict. The road to peace must pass first through an internal harmony. However, without experiencing such between parents, the child is bound to the conflict to which their parents are embattled.

Anger from an adult is normally an agitated attempt to gain control over others or the environment. When one is striving to accomplish something which is being impeded, anger will emerge. At a very base level, everyone expects a just response from the environment. Effort and intent unto the world, done rightly, produces an anticipation for the effect being in line with the cause. This equates to entitlement for the world to respond as each believes it should. Most children do not wish to cause others hurt or suffering. When they do cause hurt, it is almost always during the surfacing of anger. The anger comes forth because they are not getting their way—whether their way is to protect themselves, get possession of something, or get control of the environment. The intention is not to hurt others in the process. The frequency of it happening however demonstrates how *mind-blinded* they are—meaning, their obliviousness to the perspective of another person. Recall, children expect mirrors in other people. To suspend how they are seeing things, so to take on another's perspective—to understand the hurt being caused to them—is essentially impossible for children because they are centered around their own first-person experience. They have a cognitive disconnect between their intended outcome (satisfaction of desire) and their effect on others. The cause and effect relationship with the world must be mechanical or able to be sensed. The understanding of another's mind requires imagination. If each person is to be considered unique (necessarily, based on experience and genetic combination), for someone to conceive of another requires imagining a different perspective. Naturally, children assume the only differences are those they can see, which is why their social focus is on physicality or appearance. In young children, who assume total mirroring from others, they expect others to know their want and align with their intent. The inability to control others as they would an inanimate object produces a base frustration which is usually the source of anger in younger children, and yet, is a necessary experience in the process by which children come to recognize the individuality of others.

The greater the dependence an individual has on another to get his or her desires met, the greater will be the relational tension. A child feels more confident and secure when they are able to meet their own needs. Being controlled means they are not in charge of their own activity. Anger will surface under such circumstances and is often used to push away in effort to protect their confidence and realize their potential. The other option is to internalize the anger and believe themselves incapable, thus needing their level of dependence. The latter leads to chronic self esteem problems and excessive functional dependence on others. If looked at from another angle, where parental control is excessive, the child is faced with the same dilemma —assume such care is necessary or oppose it.

Normally, individuals with significant obsessiveness are averse to loss of control. In the overwhelming majority of cases, the fear in losing control is due to the belief in their anger potentially being a problem. Thus, the compulsion for control is founded on a misbelief about the expression of anger. The intensity of the obsessive tension can be immense, whereby, in reaction to a perceived loss of control, rage may emerge. However, it is the mis-coding of anger as a problem which precipitates the welling up of angry impulses. Rather than having bits of anger expression within their normal activity—as part of the character of their interactions and efforts—the bits of anger are not integrated into their pre-frontal motor system. In children who are obsessive, rage fits can last hours. Looking at it another way, the outflow of tension in the form of anger can take hours until the child is depleted. The duration of anger outbursts in children is a good correlate to the child's level of obsessiveness. In an average child, the tension driving an outflow of anger will deplete after a few minutes. The intensity can be severe in a normal child but it tends to be fleeting like a firework.

Obsessive children, when very young, will commonly hit or bang their head during times of excessive frustration. This phenomenon is the same response as children smacking at their skin in effort to cope with pain from an acute abrasion. They are hitting where it hurts in effort to make the pain stop. They are unable to integrate the feelings, and thus, they consciously oppose them. Intense obsessive pressure is painful to the psyche and hitting their head is trying to make it stop. Normally, such children grow out of the head-banging behavior by acquiring other cognitive skills in dealing with building obsessive pressure. Such behavior illustrates how anger gets consciously directed toward the perceived source of one's pain. However, the only place anger is able to be appropriately applied, as nature intends it, is internally. There, it pairs with one's fear of the unknown, helping to neutralize it. Properly positioned as such, anger is an essential constituent of an individual's creative willpower. It enables them to take the necessary leaps of faith forward into new experiences, therein generating the proper expansion of awareness for growth in understanding to occur—for change to take place, for creation.

The use of emotional power to gain control over a situation by inducing fear will usually involve anger. Also, when a person feels impotent or worthless, they may seek to destroy what they are feeling powerless to effect. In order to understand an individual who is seeking to better control their anger, distinguishing between anger related to control versus anger arising from impotence is important. The former type must be pursued from the standpoint of letting go of control, as well as understanding the effect the anger has on the environment. Anger related to a lack of capability or helplessness must be pursued from the position of the individual being too self-critical. Though both types stem from fear, the former tends to be externalized unto the environment while the latter is blamed on themselves.

Nevertheless, the vast majority of people feel some amount of guilt when their anger comes forth, especially if taken out on others. Unfortunately, an increase in guilt often makes an individual more prone to anger, whether it is then taken out on others or expressed self-destructively. Thus, similar to fear, anger leads to more anger.

The relationship between anger and anxiety is the most relevant binary relationship within the human mind. The existence of fear within the human condition is due to the loss of connection at birth combined with uncertainty and the threat of loss/death. Intuitively, fear feels like a lack of something—a lack of confidence or a lack of security. It is thus natural for fear to look outward to find a source of relief or something for which to attach the fear, to give it a cause the individual can relate with—therein, gaining some control through avoidance or escapism. Such attempts, however, are always futile because the source is from a misbelief about themselves, leading to an internal rejection of some part of themselves. The attempt will be to attach thought to the anger (e.g. being threatened), blame the feeling on surrounding circumstances (e.g. work environment), and then seek to avoid instances of upset. In other words, a certain amount of time/energy goes into *not being* that someone. Unfortunately, if an individual seeks to not be of a certain character type, then necessarily they must be fleeing from a belief they are that type. The feeling (anger) is not the problem, but rather the thought about themselves as being potentially hurtful causes an avoidance of connecting to others, or they devote excessive time to activities purposed to increase their sense of control.

The character which comes forth in their attempt not to be of a certain character is equally as wrong since it is compensatory rather than unitary. A person's actual character can only manifest from the integrated whole. The compensatory character will always be driven by fear since the individual is rejecting a certain proportion of their willpower. Anger is the conscious manifestation of the individual will and is attracted to what the person consciously believes is the source of their pain. It seeks to control or neutralize the source of the problem. When an individual believes the source of their discomfort is something or someone outside of themselves, anger will surface and either gain control or reject. Either way, externalizing the anger into the environment (even just having angry thoughts) is an injection of negativity. Naturally, this gives anger a bad name. However, if directed internally versus fear, then it has a neutralizing effect on the fear. This is consciously appreciated when an individual takes a leap of faith—where belief and desire are pointing forward, and where both sensory fear and a thought fear of the unknown are pointing backward. In such an instance, their mind is balanced at the crossroads, and two options exist—jump or not. For an individual to jump, there are two ways in which to neutralize the fear keeping them from taking the leap. The first is for anger to internally surge toward the fear, seeing it as the source of the problem. This then provides a sense of internal confidence, allowing them to jump. The second method is to create a fear scenario outside of themselves which opposes the fear internally. For example, to believe not jumping would be upsetting to their friends. Doing so positions fear in opposition to the fear of jumping. Another illustrative scenario where the relationship between anger and fear is on display is with homework. Difficulty with comprehension triggers frustration —meant to provide a surge in focus and effort. However, if anger is perceived as a threat, then they will have difficulty organizing it into increased effort, and avoidance is more likely. Over time, such avoidance limits the individual's growth.

The attraction anger has to fear drives the frequently observed pairing of anger and fear. Within a unified psyche, as part of the whole, anger must play an important role as it relates to anxiety/fear. However, the role is impossible to appreciate without seeing what problems come about when an individual does not integrate their anger. When anger is taken out of the whole, anxiety or fear is left unopposed. Fear related to not being good enough or being rejected causes an individual to avoid new experiences. The outside world will be sensed as determining their life. Therein, to some degree, such an individual will live under a "black cloud." To restructure the internal framework so their anger is able to be expressed without damage to the world or to relationships takes introspective effort. To do so, an individual must begin with a commitment to unravel entitlements and address self-criticism. The most immediately beneficial step is for the individual to let go of protecting or controlling their internal space, or put another way—to accept themselves and focus on putting forth positive rather than combating negative. This then supports the directive—*spend your effort seeking to understand the other rather than trying to get the other to understand you.* The result will be twofold—firstly, a better understanding of another improves the ability to help them and lessens the expressed anger being taken personally. Secondly, from one side comes increased understanding, and from the other comes a sense of being understood—both powerful influences on relational wellness.

If anger is understood as the conscious experience of one's willful energy being trapped within the motor system, then its purpose can be more accurately represented. The life energy driving growth compels an individualized fruition of oneself. Striving to achieve within the environment and angrily seeking to push past one's pain utilizes the same directional energy. Thus, growth into the world always requires the vector of one's willful energy to be pointed toward becoming better, more *full*. Filled with *full* is the goal, and yet to accomplish such requires an acceptance of all parts of oneself in order to be fulfilled. Yet any fulfillment which is sustainable will be experienced as a blossoming of one's purpose unto the world, a becoming of love itself—a love which inspires growth in the world around oneself. When experiencing frustration, perceiving oneself as being "made to feel" causes one to be unable to use the surge in frustration for their benefit, for to overcome the necessary hurdles associated with life which are required for one to properly mature. If anger is not available internally, then one is more likely, for motivation, to depend on the judgment or encouragement of others. One will then have a sense of being determined by the will of others. This then precipitates increased sensitivity to others' upset—effectively empowering the angry feelings of others to be directed at oneself.

Anger is naturally attracted to what one perceives to be the source of pain. As part of the whole, anger balances internal fear related to the unknown, enabling internally willed leaps of faith throughout childhood and adolescence and then into adulthood—where one recognizes fear itself as the only obstacle. However, if anger is not yet integrated as part of oneself—as part of the whole—then internal fear is unopposed and outside anger (others' upset) is perceived as a threat. Thus, a certain proportion of one's willful energy gets routed outside of oneself and imbedded in the thought judgment of others, where one's time/energy goes toward avoiding causing upset in others or in dealing with one's own potential for upset. To the degree in which an individual denies part of themselves is the degree in which conscious anxiety will be experienced. Unfortunately, the greater a person's anxiety, the more the anxious sensory experience will be perceived as being sourced from the world somehow. The ability for them to see it as a consequence of self-rejection is impossible. Each individual with a disorder of their mental health is necessarily blind to the interaction they are having with life—where their sense of the outside world is infused with a proportion of their willpower in the form of anger, pointed at the source of pain—themselves.

Anger (summary points)

• Anger is kinetically purposed energy.

• When disintegrated, anger is trapped in the afferent sensory system, where it is sensed as outside pressure or stress. It causes cognitive clouding and a sense chaos. When it remains trapped in the afferent sensory system, anger is perceived as occurring from the world, and thus its expression will be destructive—either physically, environmentally, or in thought.

• When an individual believes anger is a problem, anger is experienced as happening to them rather than from within them. When believed to be a problem, the handling of anger impedes channeling. Attempts to control anger imbue it with negative potential, and thus, it remains trapped within the afferent sensory system.

• When integrated, anger exists within the efferent pathway, within the motor system, and thus is the source of internal motivation, positive willpower, and a drive to do. When channeled, anger takes kinetic purpose in the environment, thus propelling experience, accomplishment, and growth.

Depression
The word *depression* has been incorporated into general use language as a result of the exponential increase in depression being diagnosed clinically over the past two decades. The term is frequently used to describe how one feels. When someone is feeling bogged down and not happy, they are "depressed." When someone is stressed out and irritable, they are "depressed." When someone is in a state of mourning, they are "depressed." When someone is questioning the meaning of their existence, they are "depressed." As a clinical disease-state, depression historically represented a severe melancholic state where the physical lethargy and cognitive apathy became literally disabling. Although the formal diagnosis of depression—under the term *major depressive disorder*—requires certain criteria be met, the advertised availability of antidepressant medication and the prevalence of prescriptive treatment for depression has lead to increasing numbers of people subjectively struggling with depression being treated medically. Depression is most commonly a phenomenon of adulthood and is based on the individual feeling depressed. Children and adolescents, thankfully, do not have a similar propensity to articulate feeling depressed. However, with the rise in entitlements paid to those who are suffering, it is becoming more common to hear adolescents complaining of depression.

Depression has become part of the average person's vocabulary for a certain mood state. What people associate depression to mean depends on their experience of it, and depression can be quite variable in the way it presents and the causal factors underneath. Also, every individual's state of life must be taken into account to give context to the depression as occurring along the journey of life. A depressed state is frequently from the mind getting stuck in the mud of one's path. As one was living or as life was proceeding, one could go no further. A call to change is created by the psychological and physical stagnation. One has taken on too much, the horizon has vanished, things have changed, people have left, etc.—whatever it may be, a reconfiguration is often the secret strength and gift of depression. Whether the change needs to occur in one's environment, one's perspective, or in one's relationships, something usually has to change.

The hypothesis of depression being of biological cause, analogous to an infection or a chronic medical condition (diabetes), has alienated people from themselves. Doing so serves to dissociate the individual's conscious responsibility from the experienced symptoms. The problem this causes is two-fold—first, it misses the call to reflect on one's current state of being and one's current directional heading. Secondly, it infers that adults are stagnant entities, no longer compelled to grow. Therein, it misses the lifespan as one of continual maturation, of a potentiation of each individual. The meaning of symptoms is unappreciated without a context. Often, buried beneath the affliction is the call to change, to let go, to adapt to others, and to re-conceive of life—its meaning, one's meaning unto it and, in general, one's purpose for waking each day. Thus, one who "has depression" perceives the symptoms as imbedded genetically (or biologically imbalanced) into their experience. So instead of seeking to face the anxious signals and be themselves—to stop seeking to please others or avoid others' upset—they learn to live with it and force those around them to accept it as part of their character in general. They are blinded to their imbalance of psychological energies, relationship insecurities, and excessive self-centeredness. The latter feature, a base tendency in everyone, nevertheless causes increased likelihood for depression the longer it persists into adulthood.

Depression in a child is uncommon. When a child is depressed, however, it is readily identifiable by the loss of the characteristic enthusiasm from the child's countenance—the excitable expectancy of hope and wonder which fills their eyes. Children have yet to internalize a significant amount of self-contempt. Additionally, they do not have a triangulated rejection of themselves. Thus, they are more likely to have a *learned helplessness* type of depression. Such is the type of depression created in laboratory rats to study biological and behavioral aspects of depression. The *learned helplessness model* conceives of depression as being the result of feeling helpless to make necessary changes within the depressed individual's environment. The classic procedure to induce the laboratory depression is to place a lab rat in a tall bucket 3/4 full of water. The rat seeks to climb out but cannot. It dives down to the bottom several times in growing desperation to find a way out. A stopwatch records the time elapsing until the rat gives up and takes to drowning. Once this occurs, the animal is rescued by the technician and the time is recorded. When the same animal is exposed to the *forced swim test* again the following day, it gives up sooner. When back in the cage under observation among the other lab rats, its behavior is more withdrawn.

The *learned helplessness model* is applicable to children since they exist in a state of dependence. This is especially true for young children who, prior to the age when thinking begins (puberty), are in a dyadic relationship with the world. This means they cannot create a metaphorical escape, for their world is literal. This is protective for young children against depression since it makes them unable to judge their life negatively. They cannot internally create a depressive, lamentable representation of their lives. They have to be literally dealing with loss or the threat of loss, where the loss is significant (usually of their caregiver). Just as the lab rat swimming in the bucket requires the technician's help, so do children need their caregiver(s). If a child is unable to get their psychological or emotional needs met, they will escalate their attempts to get it. The desperation will come forth intensely, potentially through violent dysregulation of their mood and behavior. If their crazed attempts fail, eventually at some point they will give up trying. The acceptance of their helplessness is a depression. It is visible in their face as a sunken spirit and their personality gives sluggish engagement. Treatment has to be individualized to the child's attachment situation, working with all the psycho-social factors surrounding the individual child.

Depression becomes much more common with the onset of adolescence. Not surprising, once a child goes through puberty and is able to think about themselves relative to others—when internal judgment becomes prominent—they naturally become more reflective and socially conscious. There are two character qualities which exist in almost all adolescents who get depressed—they internalize criticism/blame and they suppress their emotion. When there is a high level of criticism and an excessive amount of negative emotion being held inside, depression is frequently the result. These individuals tend to feel excessively guilty when they externalize anger or aggression. Thus, they usually do not have outbursts of blameful anger externalized onto others (e.g. parent(s)). For most adolescents who have angry outbursts (usually at home), doing so helps keep the amount of negative emotion on the inside at manageable levels. Even though displacing anger onto others is immature, doing so keeps the risk of depression down. When a parent is unable to tolerate the negativity without a decompensation themselves, the child will seek to suppress their negative emotion secondary to guilt and fears of loss. Sometimes this precipitates depression from the lack of external outlets and diminished emotional security. Going through a depression is a normal part of separating from home, of becoming independent. The process is undoubtedly like an arduous break up for both adolescents and parents. A tremendous amount of preparatory distancing, psychological rebellion, and peer relational support is required to enable a successful separation, free of excessive mood issues. Nevertheless, a period of depression should be expected. Furthermore, when an adolescent is going through a *transitional depression*, they should receive supportive reassurance. Such a period can be priceless if it allows for education regarding the mental importance throughout life in being able to let go of emotional crutches, and thereby accept negative emotion as a component of change, of growth.

When an individual relates to their condition as an affliction, they will try to incorporate the depressive condition into their self-identity. Wrapping it into a victim mentality and believing themselves disabled from certain aspects of life (e.g. school, work) promotes chronicity of the symptoms. In other words, the more they incorporate depression into their identity, the more depression will be part of their personality. Moreover, periodic depression is unavoidable when stuck behind a maturational hurdle, behind which are the markings of a milestone. The criticism of their own fears and sense of weakness causes a buildup of tension. The excessive tension, if it remains trapped, produces mood problems—ranging from a lethargic, unmotivated depression to an irritable, explosive depression. Having a diagnosis which is medically recognized, labeled, and treated with medication brings some relief due to the patient feeling legitimized. Or, in the case of an adolescent angrily pushing away, a diagnosis further justifies a parental re-up of imposed restrictions—which the adolescent has been raging against. In people prone toward avoidance, often they will use the diagnosis to justify further avoidance, thus perpetuating the problem.

Depression surfaces differently in expresser-individuals as compared to those who are suppressive. For the expresser, a clinical depression will be associated with a painful loss—whether an actual loss (e.g. death of family member) or symbolic of a previous loss. An expresser-type individual will usually find ways to emotionally discharge negative emotion, thereby lessening the likelihood of getting depressed. Through their relationships, there occurs an expression of themselves. Thus, depressive symptoms in self-expresser adults are frequently linked to a rejection. Expresser-types in the alpha role will externalize the negativity unto those they are able to negatively judge or criticize. This guards against depression in such individuals, though they tend to be hypersensitive to loss. The alpha-expresser is more prone to a depression involving explosive irritability and blame (usually at home).

On the other hand, the suppresser-individual tends to manifest *classical depression* in which there is excessive negativity being internalized. This occurs from a combination of trapped tension and self-rejection, both of which are in excess during periods of depression. From a psychological perspective, these two forces together precipitate most periods of depression in suppressive individuals. Since an alpha-individual's judgment of themselves is tied to the way in which the outside world represents them, representational failings in such individuals involve a symbolic loss of identity. Self-suppressers tend to internalize the most guilt or self blame of the four personality types. The alpha-suppresser, of the four types, tends to hold the most negative emotion inside.

In assessing the character of an individual's depression, the emotional types can be divided into—*expressive* (irritable) and *suppressive* (displaying introjection). Expresser-personalities will usually manifest an expressive depression, while the depression of suppresser-individuals is normally suppressive. This latter type is a shut-down, withdrawn, apathetic depression where the mind struggles with guilt and a generalized sense of inadequacy. They castigate themselves for any expression of their negative emotion and their foresight trends toward hopelessness. In contrast, an irritable depression is more of an externalized depression—meaning, the hostile criticism and intolerance comes out in the individual's interactions. Restlessness is more likely than vegetation (the opposite is true for individuals with an introjective type of depression). Expresser-individuals seek to externalize their feelings and so, when depressed, the negativity needs expression. Thus, toward others, these people will be caustic and irritable and frequently come off as agitated. Children and adolescents, for healthy development, frequently must off-load or externalize negative emotion. This keeps the amount of negative or depressive pressure at manageable levels so as to not thwart their developmental growth. Thus, depression in children and adolescents is usually of the irritable type, even if they are bound toward becoming a suppresser-personality.

The psychological precipitant of depression can be sub-typed as either based on relational loss or self-loss. Loss of an attachment is often the precipitant to depression at any age. Expresser-personalities form more dependent attachments, and thus are more destabilized by a relational loss as compared to suppresser-individuals. Self-loss means an individual, internally, is rejecting of themselves. Normally, such individuals anticipate or suspect similar rejection from the outside world, which often drives excessive avoidance. Their self criticism is intense, and they believe themselves likely repugnant to others. These individuals are usually suppresser-personalities. They often negate emotions, including hope, and their preparedness for the worst ensures the horizon is always gloomy. Simply holding in too much negative emotion will precipitate an introjective type depression. Anxiety, existing as negative tension, thus goes hand in hand with depression.

When the motor system is unable to express tension in an organized, purposeful way, the tension gets diffused throughout one's afferent nervous system. Depressive symptoms will then dominate one's sensory system, projecting into one's connected experience of the world. In effect, one's creative potential, if unable to be expressed properly or somehow expelled into the environment, creates systemic suffering. A breakdown of one's body and a dimming of conscious excitability in relation to the outside world is observed. When tension explodes out of someone, it is usually because of a damning of disintegrated energy within the motor system, where too much pressure has built up. If the energy was integrated, then it would be subjectively sensed as power supporting the will, thereby getting channeled into willed activity. The damning effect comes from conflict regarding the potential effect one may have on others. Subjectively, an individual will sense internal agitation and likely perceive it as being because of whatever is happening around them.

If emotion is recognized as internal energy, then the organization of energy into one's motor system is intentional and purposed to generate effortful experience. Not doing so is a rejection of oneself, an avoidance of experience. Energy should not be purposed unto itself. This means one should not effort to feel better or to not feel a certain way. Doing so simply centers oneself around the negative feelings, and thus the negativity will grow in magnitude. One's aim is very determining to one's experience. Thus, rooting one's attention on what could go wrong or what appears wrong will ensure wrong is always magnetized into close proximity. If such negativity is reflected back unto oneself, then the energy will build up and a cyclical depression may occur, serving to express the self-punitive negativity.

Most everyone assumes life is evolving, and science has illustrated the importance of an organism's adaptation to life. On an individual level, the pressure to evolve is sensed as an inner drive. The ability to then adapt to changing conditions or modify one's perspective so to accommodate increasing levels of awareness is essential. To expect life to adapt to oneself will bring about worsening frustration. Taking responsibility for one's state of being (including for how one feels) often requires the swallowing of a bitter pill made up of self-criticism, remorse, and a sense of worthlessness. Yet, it is through doing so whereby people are able to shed aspects of themselves, thereby enabling emotional and psychological growth. When an individual comes into certain realizations about themselves or about life, a state of depression is expected once the process of change or letting go begins. Normal periods of depression are thus an inextricable part of one's journey through life. "Normal" people thus get depressed. In other words, getting depressed does not make someone abnormal. However, the more depression becomes represented as a problem through advertisements and awareness campaigns, the greater will be people's tendency to denote not feeling well as a problem rather than as a growing pain of character development. Periods of personal change involve letting go of old habits and concepts or giving up on certain ambitions or dreams. Having to sacrifice oneself for the betterment of another or to do what is best for the family or system in spite of personal desires is painful and challenging. Within the letting go of personal feelings or beliefs, there is often a palpable sense of inner hallow or emptiness and depression is common. It is hard for people to fundamentally change or take a significant growth step forward without undergoing a painful letting go of fears, attachments, or desires. A depressed period is a manifestation of the ongoing change, but the letting go must occur to completion or else the depression will worsen. With such a view in mind, the depressed person should be supported and treated in ways which do not disable or weaken.

The Case of Eeyore

Eeyore is the depressed donkey from Winnie-the-Pooh. Eeyore's outwardly occurring personality is depressed and well illustrates the character of an individual who struggles with classical depression. Furthermore, understanding how Eeyore relates to himself demonstrates the psychological underpinnings of depression. Eeyore perceives his sad feelings and lack of internal happiness to be his primary problem. His aim is to *not* be sad, and so he avoids things he believes make him sad. Spending time with friends enables him to feel card about, and so he feels better when with friends. However, he is sensitive to being a burden and tries to avoid causing upset. He believes he shouldn't feel so depressed and focuses on doing things to make himself or others feel better. Frequently, Eeyore, because of self doubt and a tendency to forecast things he doesn't want to happen, decides not to speak up or try new things. When alone, he senses himself worthless and rejected, and is quick to believe nobody wants to be around him. When he is around others, especially friends, he behaves in ways so not to cause hurt feelings, and seeks for others to regard him as "nice" and helpful.

When Eeyore's will is examined, his intent is to not internally feel depressed and rejected. To do so, his cognitive effort is rejective, and thus he only sees materialized negatives and only feels his own negativity. Trying to keep the negativity outside of himself is Eeyore's attempt to separate himself from the internal sadness which he believes is a problem. Ironically, interacting with his internal sadness as a threat prevents the necessary acceptance and subsequent integration which would allow him to overcome the sadness. If the sadness was integrated, then he would no longer cognitively reject it. The sadness would no longer be trapped in the afferent sensory system, and thus not be tethered to the world or trapped in his body. Rather, the energy would be available to his efferent or outgoing motor system, and thus would be part of his positively willed effort unto the world.

SYMPTOMS OF TRANSITIONAL CONSCIOUSNESS

The symptoms of one's consciousness nearing a transitional point can be momentous. A certain threshold of conscious suffering must be reached before a letting go occurs. For consciousness to become aware of itself as the problem, as needing to change, equates to a giving up on oneself. This necessarily induces significant psychic pain. Since one experiences oneself most readily through another, often, the realization occurs within the context of a relationship—through the experience of one's opposite. Invariably, consciousness must be at the end of its road, sensing nowhere to go, unable to effect the change in experience one senses so desperately needing. Though growth steps in consciousness occur throughout the lifespan, such shifts are most notable and dramatic during childhood and adolescence.

Adolescents

Humans come into the world as sensorimotor beings, fully dependent on the parental consciousness. Transitional steps into cognitive and emotional independence are expected as part of the maturational process. Furthermore, in recognizing approximately one-half of adolescents will transition into being suppressor-personalities and/or alpha-personalities, it becomes important to understand the symptoms of a transitional period so as not to mislabel it and to best support its progression. Transitional symptoms tend to draw parental concern as they outwardly manifest in the emotionally changing youth. The handful of years between puberty and later adolescence involve intense psycho-emotional changes as a result of the necessary identity formation while emotionally separating from parent(s). It is a time of self reflective development, where each is bound within his or her own standards, and thus in perception of others as beholding such standards as well. The transition involves a bridging between dependence and independence, where those who are going to remain as self-personalities must take on judgment and care of themselves, while those who will become alpha-personalities must take control of their "self." Both paths, in order for a healthy outcome, require the dependence of childhood to be left behind. Certain spoils get retained well into adolescence, for the parental safety net provides foundational reassurance and a release valve for tension (e.g. emotional fits in the developing suppressor-personality). Ultimately however, healthy adult relationships require individuals being emotionally separated from their parents. For the older adolescent, this is normally accomplished through the establishment of a transitional relationship.

Prior to an adolescent becoming independent from their parent(s), their conscious perception is one in which they feel emotionally determined by others (reflective thinking). Normally, most of the blame is directed at parents, teachers, and the system of authority—those perceived as standing in the way of their independent fruition. However, if home is too comfortable or accommodating, social anxiety too excessive, or if there is too much vulnerability associated with separation from parent(s), then the ego attachment may fail to dissolve. In such situations, the adolescent's ego drive, purposed toward independence, may recede in order to lessen the conscious tension. Specifically, desire and arousal diminish. Conscious beliefs and thoughts, though always changing, will consistently produce the same net result—no growth or movement forward. Prior to the ego decreasing its drive, conscious tension intensifies because of increasing tension between the growth impulse arising from the nucleus causing strain to ego attachments and fears related to loss or rejection within their perceived dependency on parent(s). As time elapses while stuck in this position, the ego drive diminishes, and increasingly the body will demonstrate joint pain and stiffness as well as a significant level of lethargy. Invariably, the ego relates to the conscious symptoms as an affliction—a condition—and uses it to consciously justify the diminished movement forward.

Change is difficult, and the difficulty with change increases with age. It is analogous to turning the wheel of a car—when not in motion, the tires are more difficult to turn. If standing outside watching someone turn the wheel of a car while the car is stationary, one will notice much more friction on the tires. However, if the car is in motion, then the turning of the tires gets less resistance from the road and occurs more smoothly, naturally. Similarly, when people seek to feel better or more straightened out, it will be more difficult if they are not moving forward or in the process of growing through activity. In other words, being active enables change to happen more readily, without so much resistance. Adolescents, because of their ongoing growth and development, are in a state of perpetual change. Thus, change occurs more naturally in adolescents—for they are cars in motion.

For emotional or behavioral problems in an adolescent to be conceptualized as an individualized condition misses the source. Adolescents are not yet psychologically or emotionally independent. Their moods and behaviors thus occur within the context of the relationship from which they seek to separate. Transitional periods during development generate increased tension due to the pressure to let go contained therein. Put simply, an adolescent consciously will stop pursuing approval from their parent in favor of being in control of themselves. This requires a shift in the relationship dynamic between the teenager and their parent(s). A power struggle will take hold if the character of the relationship does not transition supportively. Getting imbedded in a power struggle can be difficult to get out of for the parent. If the teen is unable to attain a sense of control, then they will consciously seek to feel powerful or influential. This is when the teen will seek for the parent to do things for them or get help from the parent in doing things they do not want to do. Seeking such influence over the environment comes across as attention seeking. Such adolescents will usually act out, frequently getting themselves in trouble in the midst of their effort to reflect having an influence over the environment. They cannot know what a positive influence of the environment looks or feels like, and thus, they are only able to reflect an effect through negative acting out.

When a teenager is only able to experience their negative feelings/behaviors impacting the environment (rather than their positive behaviors), then they are entrapped with their negativity also being their source of attachment. In other words, they believe people are interested only in their negative aspects. Anything the teen senses as positive about themselves will be kept on the inside. They will then need a functional outlet for their positivity to grow. A strength, gift, or talent becomes essential for them to believe in and put effort into developing. Otherwise, the relative lack of positive ability within the environment (home, school, athletics) creates a belief in needing the effort from others to help them in order to experience achievement. This will lead to excessive psychological dependence in order to function. Just *to do* anything they don't want to do takes prompting and pressuring from parents. To some degree, then, they perceive a need for such external influence in order to self-activate, in order for them *to do*.

The tension between a parent and their adolescent, because of the adolescent's incessant pursuit for more autonomy, gets acted out within the relationship. Adding to the volatility is the adolescent's increased awareness conjoining with an increased sense of vulnerability. This is especially the case if the increased independence was not realized through more autonomous capability being developed, but rather was thrust onto them because of a parental disablement or a loss of parent(s). Part of the intuitive nature of parenting is deciding how much autonomy to provide without providing too much (and thus triggering anxiety). Parenting the adolescent is analogous to having a fish on a line—which is being allowed to swim away. The goal is to have enough tension in the line so the fish does not feel untethered. But just as importantly, the goal is to not have too much tension—where the fish is spending energy pulling at the line or, even worse, having their head turned back around, facing the parent and fighting to get more line. Because of the stepwise, back and forth manner in which children and adolescents develop, a parent's effort to maintain a perfect amount of tension in the line is impossible. With younger children (before puberty), the parental experience is more aptly described as "the great un-hug." In other words, from birth until the child begins to think for themselves, the parent must gradually relax their hold. Doing so often requires conscious effort to counteract the urge to be protective or controlling.

Once a battle for control takes root, improved compliance is unlikely attained without changing the control dynamic. If an adolescent is fighting a parent for control, they are doing so because either they believe they have developed the capability to be more autonomous or the anxiety in being dependent (needing to be controlled) is too great, so they are seeking to push away. Thus, the teen, in fighting for control, is demonstrating a psychological or emotional need to feel more in control. Parents should seek to adjust so to enable them to sense more control. Usually, this can be accomplished by the parent stepping back and doing less directing. Giving their teen more control and autonomy within a controlled environment can help significantly. The parent controls the structure of the environment but the teen is given more autonomous control within the environment. The parent thus steps back from directing their teen's behavior and does more overseeing, ensuring the rules are being followed and expectations fulfilled. In effect, the parent goes from a director's role to more of a producer's role. The teen should feel more autonomy because they are being told to do things less, but the parent still maintains a sense of control through oversight. The parental position of control, however, becomes more dependent on rules being clearly delineated so the teen knows what is expected and the consequences for infractions. The more the parental control is based on the parent as a person exerting direct control, the more suffocated the adolescent will feel and the more contentious they are likely to become.

Negative feelings in a younger child are usually expressed through anger and crying fits. More relatable for adults is the sense of stress and anxious worry manifesting within adolescents. This is because the adolescent is seeking to psychologically and emotionally care for themselves. Thus, they seek to internally fill the shoes of the supportive parent as they regard their own thoughts and feelings. In other words, they begin parenting themselves.

The ability to parent themselves, however, requires space and time to develop. When the adolescent's wants/frustrations have been chronically given into, then they do not get the necessary experience in dealing with not getting what they want. Thus, they will have difficulty setting limits with themselves—increasing the likelihood of imbalance. Occasionally, those children who are overly worried about will demonstrate a lack of worry during adolescence. This is because psychologically they are delaying the development of the internal voice, as it would bring too much internal tension. By keeping the worry for them on the outside, their behavior, especially during adolescence, becomes more risky and consequential.

, Avoidance can be a grave mistake for the emerging adolescent if it becomes ingrained as their approach socially. An almost complete social withdrawal can result. Come high school, the sense of internal panic and social phobia can impair their ability to attend school. Many such adolescents turn to an alternative or home-based program for their education. Nevertheless, their social phobia frequently worsens, graduating into a fear of leaving the house (agoraphobia). Once this severity level is reached, reducing symptoms enough to get them back into the regular school setting is extraordinarily difficult. The most reliable sign of an adolescent not moving toward independence is in not pursuing their driver's license. A parent struggling with their teen's mood symptoms and isolative behavior can easily overlook their lack of ambition to drive. However, more than anything else, the effort toward getting their driver's license demonstrates the intention of becoming independent.

Frequently, while still bonded to home, an adolescent will engage in risk-taking rebelliousness to oppose the worry—almost to prove the parent wrong. But in reality, it is to prove to themselves they are capable. It is to lessen the worry they feel fated to take on, to leave much of it behind. Adolescence is a privileged time period for the teenager, for they are able to let someone do their worrying for them. They bask in the regressive perspective from childhood, where their actions are a problem only if they get in trouble or are scorned by authority. Teenagers who have been raised under a significant level of parental worry and/or skittishness often will gravitate toward the most rebelliously brave peers in order to siphon courage and thus balance the imbedded anxious insecurity. A delay in taking on autonomous function (including worry about themselves) often results from a lack of adequate self-esteem or inner security with themselves. Anxious parenting is frequently the precipitant, and thus, their relationship with the parental worry will grow increasingly discordant. If independence comes too suddenly or prior to the adolescent being ready, a spike in worry and physical nervousness is likely. Being unable to tolerate or persevere past this period compels a return home to re-secure themselves. Such is usually the scenario when the young adult takes leave from college because of homesickness or psycho-emotional difficulties.

If a parent's anxiety generates excessive functional support (usually with activities and schoolwork), perseverance and self-initiative become compromised. Both of these qualities are relevant to the normal process toward independence from home. The resultant self-doubt can be crippling for the adolescent. Their propensity to arrest their own ideas or decisions and engage in an obsessive loop of thought can be disabling. Seeking to feel prepared is characteristic of this style of anxiety, where much of the individual's thought energy is devoted to what's coming up. Such an individual fears embarrassment, to be surprised, to be caught off guard, and they frequently seek advisement and reassurance from parents or peers. They very much insist on knowing the situation before they react to it. Otherwise, they feel painfully out of control. In adolescents who have obsessive anxiety and a compulsive need to feel in control, they will query parent(s) excessively with *what if* worries.

For an adolescent, becoming an independent adult requires breaking themselves away from the worry of their parents. The adolescent must take the perceived worry upon themselves. Essentially, they must begin to worry about themselves as they were worried about. Most of adolescent rebellion, as it occurs in the home, is the teenager trying to oppose the legitimacy of the parental concern or restriction. They wish to leave behind as much of the negativity shown onto them as possible. For most of their developmental life, they believe themselves to be the cause of their parent's emotion, especially parental upset. Thus, they often hold on tightly to the hope of eventually being good enough to make their parents happy.

In conclusion, symptoms of childhood and adolescence are transitional in nature—meaning, they are produced by the developmental changes the child or adolescent is undergoing. The symptoms or problem behaviors are contextually inseparable from the drive to function separately, autonomously. Thus, proper understanding of the struggling child or teenager requires recognition of the relational conflict over autonomy. Prior to becoming independent, the adolescent cognition has a thought-feeling overlap where they expect to feel good enough in order to be good enough. In other words, the feelings are perceptively in front of the *doing* or the *being*. Letting the inhibitory feelings go allows them to activate independent of how they feel—a consciousness growth step which enables them to leave home.

Discussion Topic (self-cutting)

There has been a rise in adolescent cutting behaviors over the past two decades. However, the underlying reasons have eluded the general public. Moreover, the mental health system misrepresents it, and the emergency response handling of the self-injurious adolescent is misaimed at saving their life. The conception of self-cutting being a step toward killing oneself or a slippery slope toward suicidal acting out is erroneous. This is not to say an adolescent who engages in self-cutting may not kill themselves, but the self-cutting behavior itself is an immature coping mechanism aimed at suppressing their negative emotions. It is an attempt to get power and control of emotional pain and fear. When a whirlwind of sadness and anger is storming inside the adolescent who seeks to control it without letting it erupt unto others, they feel internally out of control. They naturally become inclined to transform such painful emotion into physical pain—pain which they are in control of causing. Usually they are upset with parent(s) and so control is an acutely central issue. Moreover, cutting gives a visual representation of the negative feelings they have inside. The behavior is a form of externalization and thus expression without losing control of the emotions. It also placates the need for punishment and thus expresses their guilt. Naturally, they feel better after cutting—calmer, more in control. The act stabilizes them, and thus, it is a coping mechanism. The cutting, in its pure form, is simply a fledgling attempt to control their emotion without expelling it onto another person. Often, the teen feels shameful and tries to hide it, as they should. They should recognize it as a weakness and thus seek to get stronger—emotionally and psychologically. Self-injurious cutting is a naturally occurring urge associated with the process of internalizing the source of anger—in effect, taking it out on themselves rather than on someone else.

If the cutting behavior becomes communicative or wrapped up in a push-pull dynamic with parent(s), then the cutting may take on more of an expressive function. As it does, it becomes more of a problem. For the adolescent, the initial onrush of parental concern feels good and its visibility is reassuring. However, the warm feeling turns into suffocation when the repercussions of scaring their relationship settles in. Namely, they face a decrease in privacy and autonomy and the concern from parents is sensed as rejection. Increased restrictions are frequently imposed, including not being left alone. This runs directly counter to the direction toward which their development points—toward independence. Though reassuring for a short period of time, there are consequences for falling back into the parental safety net. It weakens their esteem and increases their psychological and emotional dependency. Thus, there will be a return of distancing behaviors—attempts to push away through defiance and discord—and the cycle will continue. If the self-cutting continues in reaction to negative feelings toward the parent(s), it will be seen as manipulative. A parent will then experience the self-injurious behavior as an attempt to undermine parental control. Parents get debased in their effort to get control of their teenager, however, as their teen is taking control into their own hands (so to speak). The teen senses it as giving visibility to how their parent is making them feel. The fear their cutting generates, and the influence it achieves, gratifies some of the anger toward their parent(s). More importantly, it provides the adolescent a sense of power (influence) over the parent(s), and so they tend to maintain the cutting habit longer than would be expected based on the cutting being a coping mechanism. Self-injurious cutting, as an emotional coping behavior, well represents the magnitude of the transition from expresser to suppressor. It also illustrates well the repercussions in misunderstanding and thus mishandling of behavior which is emotionally driven and transitional in nature.

Bipolar Disorder

Manic-depressive illness was re-labeled bipolar disorder when the third edition of the diagnostic manual (DSM-III) came out in 1980. Then, with the publication of the DSM-IV in 1994, two types of bipolar disorder were formed —bipolar I and bipolar II. The purpose of the change was to expand the umbrella of bipolar disorder, to enable the diagnosis to be applied to a greater number of individuals. Once the new terminology took hold, the rate of bipolar disorder being diagnosed (and thus the numbers of total bipolar patients) began to increase and continues to rise. Partly, the rise is from the gradual fading of personality disorders from the minds of clinicians. Historically, the personality disorders were diagnosed in those who were unable to self-regulate their negative emotions and whose mood alternations would impair their function by infusing volatility into their relationships. Gradually over the past 25 years, academic focus has been on the disorders felt to be the most "biologic" or rooted in a patient's bio-physiology. The younger generations of mental health professionals have thus shifted their approach away from the personality and more toward making a diagnosis. A patient who previously would have been characterized (and categorized) by one of the personality disorders now is most likely to receive two or more diagnoses—an anxiety disorder and a mood disorder. The latter frequently being bipolar disorder.

In fact, the diagnosis of bipolar disorder has become popularized to the point where "bipolar" is now heard in the vernacular of young people. They use it to describe general mood lability or a teeter-tottering of mood. Normally, street-use of "bipolar" is for describing someone who outwardly flips into expressive anger hysterics without much forewarning. The intensity of the mood expressivity normally surprises those around such an individual, often leading to being branded "bipolar" by their peers. Usually, if the criteria for which to diagnose bipolar disorder are strictly applied, such individuals do not qualify to be labeled bipolar. However, by stretching certain criteria and excusing the discreet time period requirement*, clinicians are diagnosing bipolar disorder at a growing rate.

The distinction between the two bipolar types is not currently captured by the descriptive language of the diagnostic criteria. To assist clinicians in differentiating between the two, emphasis has been on severity differences. Bipolar I, being the more severe type, is supported by psychosis or a necessity for hospitalization during times of mania. Science likes to chop things into little pieces and then put them back together understandingly. Over the past decade, the proportion of psychiatrists who believe the two types are of a single condition has become the majority. Thus, when the new diagnostic manual for mental disorders came out in May 2013 (DSM-V), and bipolar disorder remained divided into two separate types, it confounded clinicians and researchers who believed the sub-typing would disappear. Fortunately, the situation is one where the intuition has been correct, as will be shown below.

In looking at bipolar disorder (I & II) through the binary personality model, a pattern of triangulation comes into view. More dramatic, however, is how the two bipolar types are distinguished from one another based on bipolar I being a pre-alpha-individual having episodic transitions to an unsupported alpha-identity, and bipolar II being a phenomenon of self-activation. The self-activation is most often seen from false-alpha-individuals, but can also be seen in other situations—to be elaborated on in pages to follow. Initially, the character of bipolar I disorder will be presented.

Bipolar I

To understand bipolar I disorder, the nature of the developmental transition into an individual's alpha-identity must be clearly understood. An arrest within a triangle of dependence with their parent (or caregiver) is observed in individuals with bipolar I disorder. Recall—for an adolescent destined (per gender role/identification) to be an alpha-personality, there must occur a transition point where they transition to the thought side of consciousness, thereby becoming thought dominant. The potential seems wired into the brains of individuals whose gender is that of the alpha-parent. In these individuals, the transition from pre-alpha to alpha occurs rather abruptly—similar to the onset of puberty. As previously detailed, this flip into their alpha-mindset is ignited by feeling out of control within the framework of pleasing dependence (self/child). There is a shift of consciousness from the self or feeling position to the alpha or thought position. Ultimately, they must give up on feeling accepted. Doing so provides them a sense of control they previously did not experience. They thus gain a sense of stability through the repositioning. By going from a perspective whereby they are reflecting on

---

*Time period requirements: Diagnostic criteria for diagnosing bipolar disorder (both I and II) require at least 1 week of mania/hypomania and at least 2 weeks of continuous depression.

thought to a perspective reflecting on feeling (and thus identified as thought), involves a fundamental shift in their perceptive reality. However, for the transition to be real (sustained, permanent), the individual must have an adequate amount of self-esteem imbedded in a reality-based form, as a foundation for their outward identity. In other words, they have to be something (thought) they can represent realistically to others and which can serve to sustain independence. A foundation of self esteem also is required, whereby excessively low confidence can impair the transition. For to transition, the individual must let go of their primary attachment from the self/child position, usually with parents—which is a two-way street. The fears of loss which must be surmounted in order to transition to an individual's alpha-identity are usually mirrored by the person's parent(s). For individuals stuck in the triangle of dependence, fears of loss are greater than average and grow more intense the longer they remain arrested within the triangle.

When there is a lack of the necessary identity formation, the pre-alpha individual will demonstrate a pattern of shifting identities, each without much basis in foundational reality—like a child thinking what they want to be for halloween. Effort spent imagining the future consumes an inordinate amount of their mental energy. They are consumed with thoughts of themselves. Since loss and eventual death are unavoidable, they have difficulty seeing anything positive or hopeful. Being overly focused on imagined outcomes makes every formed idea seem unattainable, and they usually avoid taking initial steps because of excessive insecurity. Part of this insecurity stems from an unformed self-representation, and the rest is tangled up in the dependency on parent(s). The dependent position feels safe and more emotionally secure. However, the attachment precludes the formation of an independent efferent identity. Without an independent identity ever being achieved, a person's identity is always conceived in triangulated form. This essentially means individuals of non-independent status cannot internally represent themselves in a way where they do not feel determined by their circumstances or environment. Others experience such individuals always making excuses for where they are in life or speaking unrealistically about their aims. They tend to do more hoping than doing, which demonstrates their dependent state of mind and the need for a transition to the thought (alpha) side of consciousness.

The build up of tension in the pre-alpha individual is unavoidable due to the stifling of potential. The pressure for growth can be appreciated whenever there is a sticking point, where the individual is not moving forward as they should. In such situations, there is a damning effect, where the pressure build-up seeps through as neurologic expressions of anxiety, physical symptoms, or panic. To manage this anxiety, a large proportion of bipolar I individuals consume alcohol in periodic excess. If the tension reaches a certain point, a transition into an alpha-identity can occur, allowing for expression of the trapped energy. The rush of energy which occurs, in going from a trapped state within their afferent sensory system to an expressive flow state through their efferent system is orgasmic, and also time limited. It is, by definition, episodic. Knowing it is time-limited triggers the impatience in individuals who are in a state of mania. The end of the episode involves a depressing return to the fears, insecurities, and relational shackles. However, because the alpha-identity is founded on a mental representation, the identity shift which occurs during an episode of bipolar I mania can be as dramatically unrealistic as what a child picks to be for halloween. Basically, it can be psychotic.

Increased difficulty becoming independent comes if excessive parental control/criticism, or loss, has undermined the foundation of self-esteem in the pre-alpha child. Confidence in their capabilities must build throughout development. In other words, the pre-alpha adolescent has to have an infrastructure of identity strong enough to support the transition into their alpha-identity. Excessive worry and criticism from parents compromises their confidence. Furthermore, as the transition into their alpha-identity begins, there becomes an observable power struggle between the pre-alpha child and the alpha parent. This partly serves to diminish their investment in ever being good enough for their parent. In pre-alpha females, the unraveling of the relationship with mom helps energize them to detach from the child position through the potentiation of their rejective energy. In alpha-male families, the power struggle with dad has the potential to do the opposite—where the son clings more tightly to the pre-alpha security in the child role with mom. Not identifying with dad, and yet having a close relationship with mom, usually reflects problems in the relationship between mom and dad (if a relationship exists).

A mother's level of difficulty with loss—whether emotional/attachment loss or the loss of control—is relevant to both Bipolar I males and females. Excessive anxiety is imbedded into the transition process from dependent child into independent adult. A contributing factor of equal relevance is a father in an alpha-male family who remains attached to his mother. Essentially, in such a scenario, Dad's path has caused a closed circuit, where there is no demonstrable path to independence. Numerous other factors increase the likelihood of getting stuck in the triangle of dependence. A self-mom, not uncommonly, puts the male child too prematurely into the alpha role because she has strong relational desires to feel pleasing and loved. Thus, an alpha-male's personality development can get arrested in a dependent triangle (where mom is a self-personality). If too emotionally needy, moms engender guilt for growing apart. In fact, an emotional decompensation in mom can easily arrest their effort toward independence.

Cycles of mania will serve to express self energy in fantastical form. Alternating cycles of depression characterize periods of return to the pre-alpha attachment from within the feeling (self) side of consciousness. Sometimes, steps which seem positive and grounded will trigger a momentous mania, resulting in loss of previous steps forward. To become independent, an individual must undergo a loss, and so a mild depression is common, if not expected. The phenomenon of an individual having to let go of home attachments in order to feel better means there will occur increased anxiety during the process. In other words, they will have to tolerate feeling worse before getting better. Furthermore, a depression can be expected once the child-based attachment is severed. With the threat of depression looming darkly on the horizon, and loss fears being too great, it is difficult for someone who is not independent to overcome the sadness without help from those they are dependent on. The anxiety which comes into a bipolar I individual when they seek independent function is intense. This makes sustaining jobs difficult, and working around other people is often very stressful. Bipolar I individuals tend to flee when stress comes into their world, usually through behavioral avoidance and/or denial. Without facing fears and overcoming them, there is a shortage of self-esteem. Without the self-confidence to take the necessary steps toward becoming independent, they rely on a manic, unrealistic identity in order to have the necessary release of psychological tension.

Because of the rise in numbers of alpha-females and thus alpha-female families, there are more adolescent girls struggling with transitional difficulties. In such families, the power struggle between mom and daughter grows intense during adolescence, where the battle for control disrupts the entire household. The adolescent will try to control mom by entitling self-appointed needs/wants. Because mom is the alpha, the daughter will not be able to transition in her relationship with mom, propelling the daughter to establish relationships outside the home. If there is a significant amount of anxious dependency on mom, then likely mom is a controlling worrier. Thus, an aspect within mom may feel more comfortable and in control if her daughter is disabled. For the daughter, there is security in being under mom's wing. When mood problems become relatively unbearable for the parent(s), the family often will seek clinical help for their daughter.

Providing a diagnosis confers knowledge of the condition, which naturally infers it is treatable. Moreover, an alpha-female mom, armed with the diagnosis and a treatment plan, with the best of intention, almost always increases the oversight of her daughter. Conceiving of their child as having a medical condition, disease, or illness, compels mothers into a nursing role. However, this perpetuates the power struggle. This recycles the battle for control and ties up each's energy—energy which, for the developing teen, should be directed as much as possible toward becoming independent. Further passage of time in a stagnant position causes the horizon to darken, and a gray scaling of life increasingly colors their surroundings. The depression of bipolar I disorder can be very dark and melancholic with a profound hopelessness tied to a sense of inevitable loss. Moreover, if they feel burdensome to others and believe themselves devoid of goodness to others, the risk of suicide becomes real.

The cognitive hallmark in bipolar I individuals is the shift which occurs from the feeling side of consciousness to the thought side in manifesting mania. When back within the feeling side of consciousness, the lack of realized independence disables an ability to separate feelings from thoughts of themselves. In reflecting off of positive feelings, they form thoughts internally which are unable to find support within external reality. Their tether to family dominates their mind in such a way where they cannot conceive of themselves separately. Their self-identity is too tied to their family, and so they cannot recognize any other way to be. They wish for their sacrifices to bring good fortune, and to some degree are holding out for the pleasingness of their youth to pay off. To give up seems tragic. However, without separating, they will be unable to develop a sense of independent control over themselves, and thus, will continue to exist as they are "made to feel."

Bipolar II

Bipolar II disorder is characterized by periodic bursts of *self-activation*—a term used for several decades to denote the psychological process of being outwardly oneself, directed toward a full actualization of oneself. For example, the toddler walking away from mom in pursuit of a ball or an adult seeking a graduate degree so to be able to take on more responsibility are both common scenarios of self-activation. In individuals who naturally identify as a self-personality, an expression of themselves is necessary for psycho-emotional stability. Usually, the expression comes in the context of relational or vocational strivings.

For bipolar II individuals, the periodic bursts of expression are usually required because the person is functioning in the alpha-role despite being a natural self personality (false-alpha). This constitutes the majority of bipolar II individuals, though the reasons for the false-alpha positioning are varied. Because their gender was not the gender of the alpha-individual in the family they were raised within, they do not possess the wiring to undergo the type of transition where the flip into one's alpha-identity occurs with a full repression (or rejection) of the *self*. Cognitively, they are reflecting on how they feel from the thought side of consciousness—and yet seeking to establish environmental control through a denial of their self element. The expression of the self energy comes in the form of self-activation and usually happens outside the home, symbolizing the internal split. Thus, in the person in the alpha role who is not naturally an alpha, there will occur a welling up of self-energy. Expression is required, but such expression is often in conflict with the alpha role, especially when the self-activation involves a significant loss of control. Episodic hypomania, in these individuals, can be visualized as an emergence of an activated self energy which has lost compartmentalization and overtaken their consciousness. Frequent irritability during periods of self-activation stems from an alternation in perspective toward others, where they are seen as an impediment or burden.

The consciousness change back to the thought side involves a self rejection, where life seems gray and somewhat hollow. When a self-personality occupies an alpha position within a binary relationship, then the relational expression of self cannot steadily occur. Rather, it is the person's internal alpha which gets expressed. The expressive energy of their self-identity is thus trapped. The energy wells up over approximately 1-3 weeks then triggers a hypomania. The hypomania is simply an outflow of self-energy and/or self-expression. Generally, an individual manifesting bipolar II symptoms can be understood as being in a relationship where the expression of self is unable to naturally occur.

Behaviors driven by self-desires are normally observed during hypomanic periods. Psychologically, there is a hope for reward or recognition (e.g. gambling, affairs, religiosity), and so there is often an enthusiastic expectancy for something good to happen. If impediments arise, then irritable reactions are more likely. There cannot be a delusional change in identity as with bipolar I since there is no activation of a representational alpha identity. Rather, any bizarre thinking is usually a mixture of false hope, poor judgment, and unreal expectations. By the nature of self-activation, a hypomanic bipolar II individual will demonstrate an anticipation for overvalued judgment or good fortune. Bipolar I individuals, on the other hand, expect to be the judgment and often present themselves as good fortune for others. In a similar fashion, the character of the depression draws a legible line between bipolar I and II. For those appropriately labeled as bipolar II, the depression will be a depletion of self-enthusiasm and a graying of experience, where the alpha-related duties return as heavy burdens and overall they feel weighed down again. The depression suffered by bipolar I individuals, in contrast, is characterized by a depressed identity and hopelessness regarding their future.

Being unnaturally positioned in the alpha role is normally driven by excessive relational insecurity from the self-position. Excessive feelings of being controlled or used arise within such individuals, as well as poignant fears of loss/abandonment. Often a complementary relationship with a parent remains intact, providing the false-alpha-individual an ever-present framework to fall back on. Relationship bursts from the self position are expressive and stabilizing for the false-alpha and thus, during times of hypomania, sexual acting out and other relational exploits are not uncommon. A more common method for stabilization is to have a binary relationship with their child/adolescent who they reflect as thought of themselves. This enables more stable function due to an ongoing expressive relationship for the false-alpha's sequestered self. However, as might be predicted, the child's eventual separation from home threatens the psychological structure and increases the possibility of bipolar symptoms emerging. If a bipolar I individual becomes independent or a bipolar II individual repositions their role in their primary relationship, the bipolarity diminishes. The cyclical flow of nature itself ensnares humans into a natural cycling, so mood cycling can never be totally abolished.

Recall, the natural expresser-self-personality requires externalization of alpha judgment (reflecting on thought from the feeling position), which is best accomplished in the context of a relationship. If a bipolar II individual in a false-alpha position has an extra-marital relationship (with an alpha-individual), the bipolar symptoms will abate. This results from having an outflow of self-expression, so the welling up of self-expressive energy no longer occurs. Just because the bipolar symptoms diminish does not equate to the individual being "better," since the self attachment often produces more anxiety. Thus, their cycles occur more from within the relationship—thereby being outwardly stabilized to some degree. The underlying insecurity propelling the false-alpha positioning becomes unveiled from the self position. Ultimately, their fears regarding loss of others (abandonment, rejection, tragedy) must lessen for there to occur significant and sustainable improvements. The cyclical nature of life, in combination with the human's dual minded consciousness, make fluctuations of mood, energy, and outlook an inexorable aspect of being alive. This natural bipolarity is mild and rhythmic. It is best observed in people who are in an independent state. Young adults are frequently propelled, because of their subjective instability, into complementary relationships. The stabilization many experience in getting into such a relationship is due to the binary structuring of the relationship, where each receives complementary support from the other. Because the cyclic phenomenon is present naturally in normal individuals, "abnormal" is thus a severity of normal—a magnification of something experienced within everyone. Where to draw the line then is a question with no clear answer. For simply by drawing a line (forming judgment) and calling one side normal and the other side disordered or mentally ill, the human species is seeking to judge itself. Thus, such lines will always be fought over.

Adult Growth

Changes in consciousness involve a discrete shift—a new "I"—akin to an update of a computer's operating software. Thus, an individual's current "I" will experience an impending separation from themselves. Because the energy coming at the individual is outside their consciousness, "I" can only regard it as a threat. The effort to establish control drives the desperate search for the cause. However, for "I" to explain the sensory experience of physical anxiousness, it has to explain it as a phenomenon sourced from the body—within the afferent sensory system. The only way for consciousness to reject the experience or separate from it is to perceive it as occurring within one's "me" aspect. Whenever consciousness is relating anxiously or rejectingly to feelings being physically sensed, then by the very nature of perceiving oneself, one is dividing themselves. The attachment of "I" to "me" is such where "me" is being protected or kept separate from "I," and needs to be broken in order to integrate "me." When "me" is integrated (perceived as letting go), emotion is experienced internally from an integrated position and thus is available as a source of positive power. The previous feelings of "me" therein get transformed into an internal sense of fulfillment, functional capability, and energetic effort of "I." When "I" integrates "me," there occurs a transformation of "I." The transformed "I" has a greater level of awareness and perceives or thinks fundamentally different than the previous "I."

When conscious beliefs about oneself in relation to others and beliefs about others in relation to oneself are conflictual with the truth of one's becoming, then the stage is set for potentiated energy to compel a shift of consciousness. Certain misbeliefs engendered during the reflective identity formation process of childhood are wrong. These beliefs, at some point, will prevent a further growth in conscious awareness since such would necessitate a restructuring of one's belief system. Doing so is very difficult for the human mind, and thus, individuals are more likely to engage in a defensive battle of right versus wrong, where they can keep themselves as "right" and others as "wrong." The staging of life necessarily requires a restructuring of one's perspective in order to mature appropriately. Generally, the stepwise growth of one's consciousness occurs as a de-centering of one's perspective. To de-center is difficult since it is experienced as a loss of self or a letting go of control. All the conscious efforts to keep one's perspective "right" or to avoid risk will come at the expense of self-development. Often, excessive inhibition due to a belief in outside threat or in one's incapability is a precipitant to contextual anxiety attacks.

The experience of *ego death* is a death of one's consciousness—one's "I"— and thus is terrifying. Desperation to avoid dying is all one can think about. The focus may become obsessive and disabling in its own right if one's consciousness does not take the growth step forward. The ego does everything it can to diminish the sense of dread, and one can quickly become buried behind worry and avoidance. However, the "cure" is in the letting go of oneself, where the feelings are not determining thought but recognized as a sign of impending growth. Consciousness is unable to change itself, which is where change is occurring. Thus, one must let go of trying to do things to avoid the feelings. For behavior driven by fear will be in the opposite direction being compelled by growth and will intensify the conscious awareness of the fearful feelings internally.

Transitioning to a willed consciousness requires a death of the physiologic consciousness, where an individual's consciousness no longer identifies with their internal space—where sensorimotor feelings no longer determine actions. The physiologic consciousness is driven to maximize pleasure and minimize pain. In contrast, the adult consciousness is such where the individual's actions are willed, independent of fear or desire. From the willed consciousness, the body is vehicularized—driven into life for a purpose which transcends the body itself. In order for an individual to go at life properly, they must will themselves. Thus, a primary attachment to one's afferent sensory system prevents a willed effort forward. The physiologic consciousness gives primary consideration to protecting and fulfilling the internal space, whereas the willed consciousness gives primary consideration to fulfilling space in front of oneself. The detachment process enables the potential to come into the efferent motor system. As it is experienced by consciousness, the detachment feels like death. From an experiential standpoint, consciousness feels the impending demise of oneself. A frantic desperation to get help is often undertaken (panic attack), and the more one focuses on their body, the greater will be their sense of needing medical intervention. Usually, the person presents for medical attention thinking they are having a heart attack. Medication given acutely provides the individual relief, and a basic workup rules out a cardiac cause. However, without an understanding of the experience, to where meaning may be ascribed, an individual is unable to integrate the feelings. When integrated, as energy, the feelings are infused into the individual's willpower and thus become part of their efferent output.

Panic

A panic attack is experienced as impending death of oneself. Consciously experienced, suddenly, one becomes struck with the stark certainty of one's imminent death or "doom." The conscious need to make sense of it and gain control of oneself causes most to believe their body is having a heart attack. Some will conclude they are going crazy or losing their mind, and therein become afraid they are going to kill themselves or become insane. The attack itself normally lasts for fifteen to thirty minutes, but the conscious remembrance of it and the fear of it happening again produce the most debilitation going forward. Consciously, one takes to fearing the fear—the pathognomonic feature of panic disorder. The panic attack happens to oneself from outside one's awareness and represents a dying of consciousness and impending rebirth of oneself. The sensory experience of panic is centered in the chest, where subjective dyspnea is accompanied by a rapid heart rate and other adrenaline based symptoms. Mentally, an individual experiencing a panic attack believes they are dying or losing control of themselves. The experience is a re-experiencing of the sensory experience at the moment of birth. Humans are born suffocating. Each's sensory system begins life as a sudden awakening to heaviness in the chest and a sense of panic in beginning to breathe. The separation or loss of physical connection with mom—as the causal event, and the subsequent physical closeness in response to the separation—establishes the emotional attachment. Growing up, however, necessitates letting go of such emotional needs. Doing so necessitates a quantum shift of consciousness and enables a growth step in perceptive awareness. Although being pressed toward a rebirth phenomenon, the "I" of consciousness experiences the shift as impending death. Only through an erasing of one's current self or "I" can there occur an updated "I" which is more fully potentiated.

Consciousness is like an operating system. A panic attack is like a signal indicating a software update is needed—the impending download of a new consciousness operating system (version). Consciousness cannot know what the update needs to be and cannot conceive of anything greater than oneself. The updating process must thus occur at night while one is sleeping. When one is having panic anxiety, the letting go to fall asleep process is much more difficult. Predictably, when panic anxiety is occurring, one has more trouble turning thoughts off and falling asleep. The experiential awareness of impending death debases one's sense of internal security, and thus falling asleep feels like falling into a black hole. Generally, the anxious energy infuses hyper-vigilance into one's arousal level. However, because the panic attack turns conscious attention onto one's sensory system, following an attack, individuals become their own worst enemy by attending to every aberrant sensation. When the fear of having another panic attack causes one to avoid doing things, the fear becomes empowered and thus worsens. In other words, the anxious hurdle just gets taller and more daunting. Ascribing meaning to the panic symptoms gives influence to the fear, leading one to become barricaded behind the anxiety. The necessary direction for self-fruition stands in the opposite direction, however. Heightening conscious anxiety often keeps an individual from taking the necessary steps forward, especially if the panic feelings are believed to signal a problem.

Most commonly, an individual struck by a panic attack is in a transitional phase of their life. Thus, to be able to step forward, a letting go is being demanded. Usually, the letting go involves an attachment to family or to outside judgment as the source of internal acceptance. At a conscious level, a giving up on protecting internal feelings is beckoned, where letting go of caring directly for their internal space is needed. For many, being motivated by fear eventually brings them to the point of fear on fear. At such a juncture, the need is to let go of their attachment to fear for the protection of themselves. No matter what the underlying cause for the panic, the nature of what is happening—the death/rebirth of consciousness—is the same for everyone. Outside support should be in reassurance of a positive outcome despite the negative experience. The only potential pitfall lies in attaching to the panic itself as a problem, thereby focusing more intensely on bodily sensations. When "I" focuses on physical feelings (e.g. adrenaline sensations), fearful energy gets directed into the body—into the afferent system—increasing the likelihood of physical symptoms related to tension (e.g. increased heart rate, lightheadedness, headaches). Thus, the character of response to a panic attack becomes a self-fulfilling prophecy, therein demonstrating the source of the problem—"I's" relationship with "me."

The outreach for help to get a sense of control—to enable the "I" to avoid the fragmentation or perceived death of oneself—finds an attachment within the medical system in the form of a diagnosis (panic attack, panic disorder) and treatment (Rx, therapy). In attaching to having a problem, a significant amount of attention and energy is spent fighting off what is actually a threat of impending growth or individuality. Intervening to reduce anxiety runs the risk of enabling avoidance behaviors to continue, whereby the individual does not take the necessary growth step. Rather than vilifying anxiety or giving it prophetic power, understanding the growing pains associated with the expansion of consciousness would demystify the panic symptoms for the sufferer. Consciousness cannot perceive itself and thus cannot recognize a symptom of itself. Not being able to pin down the cause of the feelings, and thus gaining no reflective control of the feelings, causes one to consciously feel threatened and insecure. Therein, individuals in the aftermath of a panic attack are often riveted to figuring out the cause in order to regain a sense of control and internal cohesion. They will become hyper-vigilant to anxious sensations within them, thereby increasing their overall anxiety. An individual's consciousness seeks to uncover the problem—believing they have a problem. Yet, therein lies the rub—they do not have a problem, but in believing they have a problem, they are being the problem they are experiencing.

The scenario following a panic attack is analogous to a young child who has a painful bowel movement. Most parents have experienced the situation where a child, because of mild constipation, has a painful bowel movement. This frightens the child and makes them fearful to re-experience what was painful and confusing. As a result, they will avoid going on the toilet. This, of course, worsens the situation since it will precipitate further constipation. The longer the child waits until going, the more symptoms they will have related to the constipation and the more painful will be the eventual bowel movement. Since the fear is conscious fear, the child's relationship with their scared feelings and the level of anxiety related to control are the driving forces for their behavioral avoidance. Parents, in such a scenario, are able to see the forest from the trees, and thus, they can provide the necessary support and reassurance to the child. If a parent was to reflect worried concern, thereby mirroring the child's fear, then a worsening of the anxiety would occur.

Along similar lines, if the worry related to the panic attack itself or having another attack does not find outside reassurance, then the anxiety will worsen. Fear generates its own momentum, giving birth to a progeny of individualized fears. Attaching a label to the panic experience allows people to realize the symptoms are not foretelling. They can at least recognize the sensations are produced by anxiety and not an impending death of their physical being. However, receiving the label of *panic disorder* does not provide an understanding. The label may determine medication treatments, and medication can help, but does not confer existence of a chemical deficiency or imbalance. Chemical treatments interact with the body and thus will affect individual's sensory experience. By reducing some of the more physically rooted feelings of anxiety, medication enables an individual to temporarily feel better. However, the substance of the panic—the anxious sensations themselves—are not the problem. Rather, the symptoms of panic are compelling a growth step of consciousness—to produce a layer less of egocentricity. If the step forward is not taken, then the anxiety will ultimately grow worse, representing excessive energetic potential trapped in the afferent system. Blunting the anxious feelings with medication is sandbagging a breeched levee. It is not the solution.

For the outside observer, identifying what someone needs to let go of is difficult. The sufferer, however, usually knows. There is often a child attachment still lingering based on the person's perceived need, which is a false belief about themselves, misbegotten as a child. Sometimes a fear of death itself is standing in a person's way of living. In other cases, people are consciously called to let go of their pursuit to feel loved, and others are called to let go of being in control. Without letting those go, an individual's ability to give of themselves for experience and growth is compromised. When a panic attack is properly recognized as a changing of consciousness, then the experience of impending doom simply represents the doom of an individual's current system of consciousness. It is a growth step, an update—an advancement or evolution of themselves. Having a panic attack should thus be met with congratulatory support—not for the pain of the experience, but because of the growth for which the pain portends.

EFFECTIVE DISORDERS

Self-centeredness

The characteristic most correlative with psycho-emotional suffering is self-centeredness. Not to be confused with selfishness or self-serving behavior, self-centeredness is a perceptive process where one, to a certain degree, perceives outside only as outside relates to how one feels on the inside. The ability to put oneself in the perceptive shoes of another and reflect back on oneself is a mental skill which requires a significant amount of developmental maturation. Children, prior to puberty, cannot suspend their point of view and assume the perspective of someone else. The development of triangulated thinking (pubescence) allows an individual to reflect on how others perceive them. The level of misperception in children, however, as a result of the self-centeredness, is substantial. In other words, a self-centered person's perception of others is based on how they reflect the other person to be relative to them. For example, a self-centered person frequently believes people do things purposefully to upset them, being unable to see the person's behavior as being unrelated to them. When simply experiencing others as they affect oneself, others are rendered two-dimensional. Judgment of others is thus based on how they make the judging individual feel. A truly open-minded effort to understand the point of view of another requires taking an outside in look at oneself. To do so, a certain level of identity development, and security in one's identity must exist. Otherwise, an individual will remain in their self-reflective bubble, controlling their experience and seeking mirroring. The older one gets, the more there occurs detriment from staying within one's own bubble. *Bubble-trouble* may be assumed to characterize the socially anxious or emotionally reactive adolescent. Although self centeredness is most blatantly problematic in teenagers, the level of self-centered thinking is integral in understanding a person's mood or anxiety symptoms at any age.

A person's frustration with the outside world or others is highly correlated with their level of self-centeredness. The expectation with advancing age is for one's level of self-centeredness to lessen. The more one focuses on others, without reflecting them toward oneself, the more one comes to understand others. In doing so, one gradually develops an increased sense of personal goodness and connectedness with others. Also, with the de-centering of one's perspective comes an increased sense of duty or responsibility to others. From an energy vector standpoint, the more self-centered, the more one is perceptively relating everything back unto oneself. During a child's development, this enables a buildup of capability and individuality. However, if it continues into adulthood, the self-centeredness causes increased mood volatility and contentiousness toward others. Existentially, much of life is in search to internally get what one is potentiated to eventually give forth. Thus, growing nearer to getting requires actualizing the giving, which is predicated on a de-centering of oneself—becoming less attached to one's internal space. In order to most fully give of oneself, one has to invert their self-centeredness. In effect, they must turn inside out. Their energy vector must point outward, and their consideration must be for the nurture of others.

Paradoxically, the less self-accepting someone is the more self-centered will be their conscious perception. The more self-centered an individual, the more they will be unable to perceive themselves creating their frustrations. They will experience others as revolving around them, and thus will frequently be frustrated by the behavior of others, perceiving the behaviors done to them or in relation to them. The more self-centered an individual, the more they believe everyone sees things the same way they do, and thus, the more they become enclosed in their own belief system. Others who see things differently will thus have to be judged as wrong or somehow deficient. Putting conscious effort into sustaining their belief system and proving themselves right—at the expense of others having to be wrong—necessarily leads to conscious negativity and isolation. Self-centeredness is not willingly relinquished by the developing consciousness. The desire to feel better about oneself, and more secure generally, drives the effort to connect with people. Since understanding and enjoyment of another person requires one's attention being fixed on them, through these connections, self-centeredness lessens. Furthermore, the begotten sense of connectedness is reinforcing to one's sense of self, and the fear of losing the connection helps limit self-centeredness as well.

The ego consciousness naturally perceives reflectively—meaning, consciously seeing others or experiencing things as objects relative to one's internal space. There is an initial inability to see others for anything more than objects to either consume or reject. In other words, the ego perceives through a lens of desire or judgment. Both lenses opacify the other person as an individual. Adolescence is a peak time for ego dominance since the ego is creating belief about themselves in order to provide a foundation for which to enable independence. When others do not reflect such a belief, they are usually rebelled against. Conflict is frequent due to the inability to relate to others in a way where the other person feels understood/respected. The more ego-dominant an individual's consciousness, the more difficulty they have in their interpersonal relationships. This is because of a perceptive intolerance for others when they do not provide what the ego wants—namely, to feel loved, to feel in control, and to feel powerful. Naturally, others will feel objectified, used, or manipulated. Furthermore, when getting to know someone, the ego aspect is only getting to know how the other person affects oneself. The ego will represent the other person as a resource, a tool, a support, or an externalization of itself. The latter phenomenon is common, where the ego denies an aspect of itself by projecting it onto another. The tendency is then to try and control the other person or keep control of oneself through avoidance.

The activation of the two-part consciousness initiates the recognition of an internal judge in everyone. With such recognition comes, for each, a preoccupation with what others are thinking about them. The adolescent years are consumed with thoughts of others, and yet, those thoughts do not extend beyond what others think about them. So in actuality, each is only thinking about themselves. Thus, the internal criticism existing inside each adolescent is projected into the potential minds of others who are in judgment of them. Since the other minds are similarly consumed, no one is actually judging the other. It is like each is inside their own bubble but cannot recognize others are similarly self-encapsulated and thus not in true consideration of them. Thus, the perceived judgment is indicative of their own internal self-criticism. If their level of self-criticism is excessive, then it may project too greatly onto others and potentially be an unsurmountable hurdle. In such situations, the adolescent perceives others being rejecting or critical, potentially believing themselves *bullied*. However, since others are similarly self-centered in their thinking, often a person's shyness or defensiveness is interpreted by others as the person not liking them, to which others react negatively.

The bubble which encapsulates a self-centered individual is protective, and the stepping forth process is a gradual one. The more fear someone has about another person's judgment of them, the more self-centered will be their perception. With fear, the mind naturally keeps a vigilance for what is believed to be threatening. Thus, others will be perceived through a lens which measures their level of potential threat, thus biasing one's perception toward the bad in others. The more fear, the more one seeks to feel better—more comfortable. This causes a desire to escape or get relief from the outside (environment, others). Such efforts will tether an individual's perception to how they are being affected or neglected, and they will judge others based on how they perceive being treated. People then get classified based on how they make the individual feel. This type of self-centeredness is natural during adolescence but presents problems if it continues too far into adulthood. With time, and the growth of responsibility which comes with age, a self-centeredness causes an excessive accumulation of burden and worry. Moreover, if one's perception is only able to see others as one reflects them to be, then others will be two-dimensional. They will be without depth. Over time, others will trend toward feeling disregarded and relationships will lack depth, though the self-centered individual will be blind to such.

In the effort to further understand another person, one's attention must focus on the other rather than on how the other is affecting oneself. For conscious attention to go from how one feels or how one is being treated to thinking more about another person's inner experience and perspective, is a cognitive milestone normally achieved in adulthood. For some, anxiety about criticism or being hurt keeps them rooted in their own thoughts and feelings. In doing so, they base their defensive behavior on what they perceive being thought or done by others, thereby enabling control of their world by maintaining a reflective bubble. By avoiding recognition of others' internal world, they are able to avoid having to consider things from the others' point of view. Excessive fear of judgment and/or emotional fragility usually keeps an individual remaining overly self-centered for their age.

It is normal for adolescents to reflect the behaviors and attitudes from peers back onto themselves, to which they attribute negative intention, thus believing themselves disliked. The self-centeredness of the age and the intense thinking about what others are thinking about them causes a perception of peers doing things to them purposefully. They will misinterpret a peer's action or take a comment wrongly which in actuality had nothing to do with them. The danger parents must help guard against is the adolescent forming a belief nobody likes them. In the face of an adolescent's intense complaints, dramatic reports of mistreatment, or feeling generally rejected, parents must remember the adolescent's impression is to some degree misaligned. For parents to empathize is appropriate, but to react as if their child is being bullied or mistreated will invariably fuel the fire. The situation is analogous to the *boo-boo scenario** and should be parented as such. The

---

*The "Boo-Boo" Scenario: A toddler falls and then, in realizing their physical injury, begins crying and runs to the parent. A show of empathy followed by unconcerned reassurance immediately calms the child, who then runs off and resumes their original pursuit.

parental reaction should be understanding but unmoved, whereby they reflect an optimistic outlook toward the situation.

Once an individual attains psychological and emotional independence, considering the individuality of others begins to occur naturally. However, if their perception remains reflective, and they continue to entitle subservience to their feelings, then others will feel used. Others experience being two-dimensional objects for the person's consumption. Such an individual is blinded by their own ego reflections and thus can be termed *narcissistic*. As a label, a *narcissist* comes with ill-defined lines, partly due to the developmental normality of narcissism. Thus, age must be taken into account. The older an individual, the more *narcissism* becomes an aberration and the more such individuals stand out. A significant proportion of young adult narcissists will, through life experiences, mature past their self-centeredness. They will come to more generally appreciate the individuality within people, and their relationships will grow closer from greater mutuality and true consideration of the other person. More on narcissism is contained within the section on personality disorders.

The self-centeredness of the adolescent perspective is in part due to the fragility of the identify formation process. An adolescent operates from a ready-state of defensive perception, creating a hypersensitivity to themselves. Their lack of solidified identity creates conflict between who they seek to be, who they are trying not to be, and who they believe they are. In general, at any age, having a conflictual relationship with oneself impairs the ability to escape a self-centered perspective, thus rooting such individuals in their reflective thinking. In other words, someone who is not yet internally unified will be triangulated internally with themselves, and thus, the world will only be a reflection of themselves. They will see everything and everyone outside of themselves based on which side others fall on—for or against, good or bad —therein demonstrating the conflict and the necessary sidedness of their perspective from within the conflict. Others will experience a sense of being objectified since they are not experiencing the conflict. Yet, despite others' efforts to avoid getting caught up within the negativity, not getting involved is very difficult. Thus, such individuals tend to experience volatile relationships until the point where they are able to realize the effect they have on others.

Victimization

In 1980, new mental health diagnoses were published with sharp criteria, developed so the effectiveness of treatments (medications, therapies, etc.) could be established through research. However, when Prozac (generic name fluoxetine) exploded onto the market in 1988 (officially released 12/29/87), prescriptions of antidepressants rose dramatically—ushering in two decades of pharmaceutically driven mental healthcare, and changing the societal perspective on anxiety and depression. Commercials began coming into family rooms advertising government approved medication for treatment of an "illness." Since the specific mental disorder (e.g. depression) is a *mental illness*, the advertisements were never technically wrong, but the conception created in the mind of the average individual was erroneous. Driving Prozac's popularity among prescribers was its non-lethality in overdose. In other words, it was not a potential suicide weapon. Most antidepressants predating Prozac, if taken in substantial amounts, could be fatal. Thus, the prescribing of antidepressants had been generally left up to the psychiatric specialist. However, with the development of Prozac (and subsequent medications of the same class), physicians at the primary care level began prescribing antidepressants, and for two decades thereafter, the prescribed number of antidepressants grew exponentially. Naturally, doctors tend to not diagnose a condition unless they intend to treat it. Thus, with medications in their arsenal to treat depression more comfortably, the number of individuals diagnosed with depression has steadily grown. Advocacy groups have added to the growth by promoting awareness of the diagnosis, and also by popularizing screening and risk-identification methods.

The current medical system conceptualizes the mind as being biologically determined. Neurologic structure, neural signaling, and levels of chemicals are believed to underlie mental symptoms. So when an individual has too much anxiety or emotional unrest, their inherited genetics are now being blamed as the underlying cause. The concept of being born anxious or depressed is not compatible with the human experience. Nevertheless, it has settled into the modern perspective because of the desire for passive, biological (chemical) treatments. Furthermore, it has been capitalized on by modern youth in their aversion to accepting responsibility and entitlement to feel happy. The conveniences afforded to people of modern times lessens their willingness to work. With a lack of will power, engaging in efforts to sacrifice and find balance are often regarded as too painstaking. A socio-cultural emphasis on achieving balance is incompatible with a cultural pursuit of excess. Children receive minimal exposure to the importance of harmonizing their body and mind through their activity. Happiness is popularized through glorification of excess. In doing so, envy has become an epidemic—for there is always someone with more, objectively more.

Modern society enables an individual to live simply, comfortably, without having to functionally support themselves. Basic resources are not being competed for, and a safety net of social services is in place. The pursuit of being judged as disabled has grown dramatically over the past fifteen years, especially for mental health diagnoses. Efforts to promote equality and get away from the inequality of outcomes have stripped modern youth of being able to take responsibility. The making of excuses for not meeting expectations has become commonplace. For example, the expression "that's just how I am" is commonly said to excuse oneself of the accountability to change. Most individuals who seek to empower their diagnosis will not take steps to minimize its burdensome or negative effect on others. When traits are physically inherited, identifiably so—such as an individual's appearance—there is intense effort to compensate for inherited traits the person does not like. In effect, they are taking accountability for their inherited appearance and making the best of it.

Treating the world based on how someone feels or what they want creates interpersonal discord. When the negative trait is used to explain how an individual outwardly acts or treats others, then the person is identifying as the negative trait. For example, to blame one's moodiness on being bipolar is to identify oneself as a person who is moody rather than apologizing for how one mismanages oneself at times. To do the latter is to recognize how one's moodiness negatively effects others, and thus should promote appreciation for others and humility for the burden it brings. Otherwise, the label is being used to excuse oneself of any responsibility unto others because of it. In fact, over the past two decades, mental health diagnoses increasingly have entitled certain spoils, including an overall decrease in accountability. Making excuses for how one has acted based on one's feelings is a characteristic of childhood, and should not be allowed to persist much past puberty. For example, Jack doing something to Jill because she made him mad is immature because it falsely attaches causality to someone else for his behavior.

Parents adapt to their children, and often expect the outside world to adapt to their children as well. With the modern hypersensitivity to hurting their developing self-esteem, children are treated as if they are fragile—their feelings are pampered. If the human child is believed to be determined by genetics, then the goal will be to minimize their distress. Then, by minimizing upset, the child, as much as possible, will unfold into a nearly perfect specimen. However, despite the separation at birth, the child takes almost two decades to come into a sense of true separateness. The character shaping influence exerted by the parents is profound, and yet normally occurs imperceptibly to the parents. By protecting against distress or environmental insult, the child is bound to believe they require such protection. They must then sense themselves as either frail or vulnerable or the world as dangerous or imposing. Since the parental goal is for their child to grow up into a good, happy, successful person, it is imperative to help them develop the adaptation skills for life, as well as a reasonable expectation for what life will present.

Modern parents, as a whole, are having more difficulty setting limits with their children. Modern media advertises happiness and Hollywood creates it. Thus, since life is difficult and the type of happiness advertised is not being experienced, parents often seek to compensate by trying to make their children happy. To make children happy is not possible, although trying to do so requires pleasing their desires, which unfortunately leads to spoiled discontent. Moreover, when the adolescent has to confront the world not being a push-button happiness kind-of-place, they are ill-prepared. Misaligned expectations will frequently cause a sense of being treated unfairly. The world, to such an individual, seems to oppose what they want from it, which they sense as unfair. They may feel victimized simply because their expectations were mis-set, and thus, the treatment they experience is mistaken. If they misinterpret others as being mean because of the relative difference in how they are responded to, then they may not be able to get over the interpersonal hump and establish mirroring relationships. Frequently, such children (middle-school, early high-school age) will mislabel others as not liking them, essentially blaming others for being unfair to them or mean to them. They are quick to see themselves as being bullied, and then seek validation for their sense of being victimized through excuse making, sympathy, and entitlement for restitution. In this way, they find empowerment in being the victim.

For happiness to be advertised it must be objectively represented. It thus gets paired with materialism and the infinite pleasures supposedly contained therein. Unfortunately, this tends to be a road which widens its hollow as one accumulates more material attachments. It becomes poisonous to one's perspective to see other people as having more of what one wants—to envy. People with victimization in their perspective toward the world tend to have an equal amount of envy. The more envy invested in their perspective upon others, the more competitive they will be with others, which generally comes across as selfish and critical. Since capitalism fosters a competitive interpersonal dynamic, the materialism often strains relationships.

The term *cinderella syndrome* was previously applied to describe the mentality of someone identifying themselves as being victimized by those they are dependent on. The term is biased toward girls, and so *cinder-fella* may be applied to boys or men of this sort. Regardless of gender, such individuals react in certain ways toward perceived mistreatment. They cannot identify themselves outside the context of the unfair treatment from those to whom their minds are tethered. As such, they lack the independent mindset to enable separate, goal-oriented function. This creates passive wishes for an interpersonal savior, a prince. They keep their savior wrapped in fantasy, safely inside their coveting self, and color those around them as neglectful and bad. Keeping good and bad so separate is evidence of a split internally between good and bad. For internal stability to be maintained in such individuals, good and bad have to be kept separate. In healthy development, the good and bad elements internally intermix in effort to harmonize—the goal being to form a stable internal sense of self. However, when there is mistreatment, neglect, or abandonment—too much bad—then the child will keep it psychologically separate from their sense of self. The problem is their perceptive life will always be good or bad, and shades of gray will be difficult to see. Interestingly, this psychological lack of fusion enables an individual to perceive themselves as a victim while victimizing others just as they were once victimized, all the while psychologically feeling entitled to do so as a victim. The problem resides in the lack of intermixing of good and bad, so a unified sense of self (some good, some bad) cannot form. Necessarily, their binary relationship maintains such a divide as well, and is thus characterized by times of feeling rejected (as if bad/unworthy) mixed with times of angry rejecting of others, sensing others as bad. The flip-flopping of the good and bad elements being expressed underlies the mood swings which can be intense. Also, the perceptive experience of others will be of two separate personalities. As such, participation in a true complementary relationship is impaired.

Because of their self-absorption, adolescents naturally have a *cinderella/ cinder-fella* perspective toward their parents. It tends to generalize toward any entity restricting their self-entitled autonomy. Additionally, the competitive social milieu creates, in the insecure mind of a teenager, a sense of being deprived relative to peers. Part of the ineffable annoyance for parents is the shameless narcissism of the adolescent. To get to do whatever they wish to do without having to take responsibility to sustain themselves, nor participate in the structure which sustains them, is unrealistic. Smartly, adolescents step lightly out of the house, wanting to minimize burdens. In their minds, the more they can exploit the resources at home without being tethered to home, the better.

As the teenager nears leaving home, a natural carsick like feeling comes with spending too much time at home. Being with friends and lovers and on the move is what feels fresh, crisp, and alive. It is a beckoning for their developing spirit. If anxiety or other circumstance impedes them from having connected experiences, then their spirit will be under-nourished. This will fuel a base sense of being victimized, since developmentally they are not flowing forward. Anytime prior to becoming independent, an adolescent is likely to feel victimized if they are not getting the necessary nutrients for growth—whether the needed growth is physical or psycho-emotional. During adolescence, the necessary nutrition (figuratively) is found outside the home, and their disposition becomes increasingly starved without peer relationships. Under-nourishment in this area often causes depression, irritability, and physical symptoms such as lethargy and gastrointestinal issues.

When someone cannot enjoy their interaction with life, they often will seek people, experiences, or objects to deliver happiness unto them. When the happiness they seek continues to elude them, either they give up on the entitlement for such happiness or they seek to discover if something is wrong with them. People are quick to question if a disorder or disease is preventing them from feeling the happiness they sense lacking. At this stage, individuals who continue to sense the need to feel better or believe they deserve to be happy, will often present for clinical assessment. Normally, as things currently stand, the medical system will endorse a disorder—whether primarily labeling the problem as an anxiety disorder or a depressive condition. This provides the person hope in the problem getting corrected out from under them. In other words, the wish is kindled for the feelings to be taken away without conscious effort. Such magical thinking stems from early childhood where mom could make things better by the warmth of her affection.

In effort to more directly fulfill themselves, each seeks to depend less on others and be able to control their own world. Desire presses one to grow up and become autonomous. Beliefs which support seeking happiness or comfort are an unavoidable by-product of these desires. The way parents pursue happiness will be the tools given to the child. When desires are unmet, the amount of potential upset and the amount of influence begotten by the upset, engender's the child's level of entitlement to be happy. Believing a sense of security is achieved through controlling the fixtures of one's environment as well as the reactions one gets from all the nouns of the world (people, places, and things) leads to continuous frustration. This is because the focus for every interaction is in its self-serving outcome or how it aligns with one's expectations or desires.

Take a playground full of children as an illustrative analogy, where each is being propelled by the same force—to express themselves and fulfill desire for fun. In their random running about, occasionally one child will run into another. When a child is run into, they will often react as if the other child did it intentionally. The other child feels run into as well, and so the reaction is similar. Most likely, each child will get defensive and react as if the other mistreated them. However, the more each blames the other, the less either will be able to learn from the experience. To believe it should not have happened, the fact it did creates a sense of being victimized. If each looks at themselves and sees how they could have been different (more aware of the surroundings, more in control of one's body, etc.), then they learn from the negative experience. In the analogy of the playground, if collisions with other kids continue to be experienced as intentional mistreatment, then the child will grow increasingly frustrated. The expectation is then for others, in recognizing the frustration, to make efforts to alleviate it. However, this assumes that others are responding to what the child does or does not want. The more the child believes others should attend to their experience, the more "mean" they will believe others to be since each is rooted in their own perspective. When there occurs a collision between two children, each's reaction will be perceived by the other as judgment. The ability to understand the other's reaction as defensive, intended to protect rather than to reflect judgment, takes maturation through experience. The high-school setting is consumed with everyone reflecting judgment off of others and clamoring for recognition of their feelings. While each believes the negativity from others is due to other's negative judgment of them, in actuality, the negativity is due to each feeling the other dislikes them or is a threat to their self- conception. To avoid collisions, an individual must regard others and the character of their impact on others, thereby taking responsibility for their own approach. A person is wise to focus on changes they can make to their approach rather than trying to effect change in those who react to them.

The character by which an individual judges the nouns around them is a very powerful predictor of how they will experience life. An individual must be accountable for the color of their judgment. Put another way, the more negative is their judgment, the more negative will be their experience. This sounds simple and intuitive, but it is not. For if someone wants to be happy then they must hold themselves responsible for perceiving things happily. To illustrate—imagine coaching a young kids soccer team. Perceiving them play —their uncoordinated efforts and frequent missteps with the ball—occurs through a lens of positive regard for their potential. They are seen for their becoming, for their individual growth intent. The perception does not center around the perceiving individual but rather centers around them. In the context of a primary relationship, holding the other hostage as it pertains to subservience of their negative feelings or desires often shipwrecks a relationship. The pleaser self-individual, in such a relationship, must either want to work off guilt or has self-shame due to a chronic sense of inadequacy. Otherwise, they will internally represent being mistreated and build up resentment. The individual whose empowered feelings are used to control the relationship will become increasingly consumed with how they feel about things and what they want. Thus, unless their perspective matures, they are destined for discontent. If an individual's judgment is rooted in the experience of mistreatment or bad luck, then the negative aspects of their experience will always be preferentially noted to validate their self representation as a victim. Basically, within the garden of life, they spot the weeds. The seeds for victimization are usually planted during childhood. As a child, such individuals felt their desires and efforts were devalued relative to mom's emotional needs, or one of the parents was abusive (usually dad). To some degree, being in a victimized state brought increased security in the form of love and attention—whether directly experienced or experienced second hand.

The increasing use of *post-traumatic stress disorder* (PTSD) as a diagnosis over the past decade illustrates an increase in clinical attention being paid to the psycho-emotional effects of trauma. The diagnosis is being more frequently given to patients whose anxiety and mood symptoms clearly stem from childhood physical, emotional, or sexual abuse. If the childhood history of individuals receiving mental health care is examined in moderate detail, the proportion of those having suffered abuse, molestation, or abandonment would be over 80%. For those who work with patients and their families, this number is not surprising. Thus, diagnosing an individual with PTSD from childhood trauma is a slippery slope with blurred lines.

An important aspect of human psychology for people to understand is how the experience of trauma is handled by the developing psyche. The younger the child the more a traumatic experience will profoundly affect their development. It may be likened to a young sapling hit with an axe—it will always bear a misshaped growth pattern. In comparison, an older, more established young tree can take the same strike from an axe, and while it will bear a scar, the direction and pattern of its growth is not altered. In fact, the more a traumatic experience can be remembered, the more it was processed at the time it happened. Early trauma or witness to trauma—which cannot be remembered due to the child's early age—is more deeply imbedded into the child's neurological hardwiring. Their sensory nervous system, as a result of the trauma, will have areas of hypersensitivity. Going forward, their ability to function securely within relationships is compromised. But most compelling and of interest is the phenomenon of a *repetition compulsion* regarding the traumatic experience. Basically, the traumatized human psyche is compelled to symbolically re-create the traumatic experience. Any trauma is going to exist in an individual's experiential memory with a certain amount of tension and uncertainty. The brain will seek to lessen the psychic anxiety surrounding the experience through the repetition compulsion. To do so, the individual (usually without awareness of doing so) brings about similar scenarios in attempt to gain mastery or an internal sense of control. The individual may play the traumatized role or the trauma inflictor role. A child identifies with both parents, so if they experience trauma through the witness of domestic violence, they often will engage in similar scenarios with siblings or peers. Usually, however, the child will act out the violence from the role of the aggressor versus the abused parent (usually mom). In doing so, the child is able to reduce the fears of getting abused like mom through identification with the aggressor (dad). However, the guilt experienced usually brings about more attachment anxiety, increasing the tension, which then gets released through aggressive distancing versus mom, and the cycle continues.

A traumatic occurrence, as it is memorialized in the brain, has a significant amount of anxious energy attached to it. The brain's internal dealings with this charged experience are twofold—to keep structured control over the experience (repression, neurologic inhibition), and secondly, to lessen its energy or electro-chemical potential. The latter aim is accomplished through expression, which takes a myriad of forms depending on the person's age, character, and environmental influence. Children, who are not yet able to triangulate their thinking, are limited in their psychological capability to process a traumatic experience. Their ego defense mechanisms are few, and those available to them are, from the adult perspective, unsophisticated and immature. Mostly, children will seek to *act out* or behaviorally engage in a role-playing re-creation of the traumatic event or experience, thus producing the repetition compulsion.

The phenomenon of acting out trauma is most starkly observed in the occurrence of sexual abuse or molestation of a pre-pubescent child. In such a scenario, the child is of an age where there is no physiologic underpinning for the child having sexual awareness or a sex-drive. Thus, for a child to display sexualized behavior, it has to be assumed they were introduced to it from the environment. Exposure can be relatively innocuous, as is common with media or internet exposures. Similarly, a child witnessing sexualized interaction or intercourse between parents is not an uncommon experience for a child. Even more common is a child's witness to parental masturbation. With passive sexual exposure, there is no trauma for the child. Thus, the level of anxious impact in such a passive experience will be minimal. Without anxiety imbedded in the experience, a child's psyche will not have urges toward expressive re-enactment. In such scenarios, no fear existed for their own safety or wellbeing, and there was no significant sense of being out of control or endangered. Thus, the child will not have anxiety (potentiated energy) compelling them to think about or re-experience what they witnessed. For an experience to be considered traumatic, either it must create a panic level of fear or the child must feel out of control.

In a situation of a child acting out sexually, their first instance of doing so should be interpreted as "playing house," and thus understood as an effort to act like the grown ups who the child saw having sexualized interaction. Any scorning for the behavior creates an intense impression, and so the likelihood of a recurrence is minimal. It may be assumed, in the case of continued acting out, the child is having a compulsive urge to do so, which suggests a likelihood of having experienced sexual trauma. Usually the child will either engage in the behavior alone—doing to themselves what was done to them—or they will take the perpetrator role toward another child. The adolescent or adult who, as a child, was sexually abused or molested often experiences an urge to perpetrate when they become the age of the perpetrator who molested them. Moreover, the urges will be directed toward children of the age they were when they were abused. In this way, the re-enactment seeks to expel anxiety by being in the dominant position. The aim here is toward the achievement of mastery, to gain a sense of control over a traumatic experience which remains active in their psyche. Acting the trauma out with another individual engenders or passes on the trauma, and is inappropriate. Expressing anxiety and intense feelings related to the trauma in a healthy, appropriate way (e.g. psychotherapy) can be very beneficial. In contrast, doing so by propagating the trauma toward another usually causes more guilt than relief of traumatic tension.

The line between what is and what is not sexual abuse receives no meaningful debate, as there is little to no gray area. In contrast, the line for what constitutes physical abuse is more blurred. Moreover, severity of physical abuse does not line up directly with severity of trauma, as numerous other psychological variables are at play. For example, whether the abuse is predictable or not is significantly impactful, as is the abuser's intent (punishment, cruelty, anger, hate). Understandably, the presence of others who are being similarly abused (e.g. siblings) can normalize the abusive treatment, lessening the profundity of the traumatic impact. The age of the child, duration and severity of abuse, and relation with abuser are the elements which determine how the child then outwardly manifests the trauma.

Prior to reaching the age where they are able to mentally reflect on themselves, children cannot conceptualize themselves as victims. They can feel the abuser was wrong, and they can be scared of it happening again. However, they will not be able to create an identity of themselves as a victim. Their propensity for optimism generally, and their consciousness tether to the present, keeps their mind from judging themselves or making triangulated conclusions of their experience. Thus, it is important to not engender a sense of being a victim even when the child encounters undeserved or accidental injury or mistreatment. Helping the child find their strength requires parents reacting to their child's woes and wailings as if the child is tough enough to deal with whatever it is they are upset about. If mom is protective of the child toward the child's father, it will create internal conflict and a hypersensitivity to mistreatment from peers and teachers. If a child's father is critical and ambitious, and the mom is sensitive and very empathetic, then she may be quick to feel sorry for her child. Feeling sorry for one's child, however, is never appropriate to display. Pity, like worry, always weakens.

Creating a thought of potential trauma for the child by exposing them to a potential threat is priming them to be traumatized. A threat will sew a seed of fear which previously did not exist in the mind of the child. Though it is not associated with an experience, nonetheless, it brings forth the idea. Egregious examples of this are the *school shooter drills*, where young children, who would never imagine such a thing happening to them, are introduced to its potential reality at school. The young child's level of self-centeredness makes them unable to understand the unlikelihood of such a disaster happening to them. Furthermore, an inability to comprehend the drill occurring in the context of disaster preparedness makes each child feel like a "sitting duck." This position then precipitates thoughts of being victimized, and the subsequent build up of anxious energy tends to get expressed or acted out at home.

A hypersensitivity to being mistreated usually accompanies the outward perception of those who believe anger to be a problem. Such individuals usually guard against both causing upset and being made upset, driven by the belief in their potential to hurt others. Thus, they believe in their potential to victimize others, and yet, reflectively they perceive others victimizing them. The phenomenon of an individual, who others feel victimized by, perceptively experiencing themselves as victims, evidences how the relationship an individual has internally manifests through the character of relationship they establish with the world.

The Victim Center

Within everyone is a place built on a victim foundation, framed by all which has been done wrong to them. Inside this victim center, mistreatment is given memorial. The victim center houses frustration which wells up throughout the day, collecting angry remnants of themselves which are being suppressed out of fear of being rejected. The anger which is kept within the victim center is sensed as having been inflicted. Inside the victim center are walls memorializing the suffrage—the wrongs committed against them—reflecting reason for the victim identity.

Behaving to please others or in avoidance of causing upset equates to being false. Being false in order to avoid rejection is an illusion of security. From the victim center, rejection is utilized to separate or disconnect from the threat being perceived. Not being themselves—for the purpose of not being rejected or hurt—prioritizes not experiencing part of themselves rather than seeking to be themselves. Doing so traps energy or power in the victim center, resulting in an internal feeling of emptiness which fills with gnawing frustration. A sense of having been robbed of their potential is then begotten within the individual's thought of the world.

The template for the victim center's existence is the hunger—food—consumption triangle. Thus, the tension trapped within the center is non-integrated and felt within the stomach area. The character of pressure and emptiness which is experienced is illustrative of the center's positioning relative to hunger in the stomach. To thus reflect not getting something from the world or others is natural. However, the resentment which builds leads to surface upset and a propensity to reject those closest to them.

The frustration, when trapped within the center, is sensed as having been inflicted, and thus, when being expressed, an individual senses giving back to the world what was done to them. Yet, no actual rejection occurred. Such was wrongly perceived based on the individual's internal rejection of themselves. Thus, the angered expression is the victimizing move. Although such behavior is happening under the illusion of being a victim, truly, such behavior victimizes. It is a lamentable aspect of the human mind—bound to see the rejected aspects of oneself in others. Thus, the victimizer believes they are the victim as they are victimizing. The bully believes they are being bullied as they are bullying.

For an individual to not appreciate their effect on the environment means they are primarily relating to their own effects (feelings), and thus, they can only sense the environment for its effect on them. To gain awareness of their thoughts as determining the internal effects which they then bring to the environment is thus liberating. However, such an awareness threatens those with an active victim center because it forces them to take responsibility for their feelings. Awareness is avoided by individuals who are securing themselves via rejection, since negative feelings internally trigger their defensive rejection outwardly.

The more fear which is attached to the potential rejection by others, the more others are given control over the individual's will—resulting in behavior driven to not experience rejection. However, because the behavior is based on an active rejection of themselves occurring internally, the sense of rejection is inescapable except for when they are rejecting outwardly. This accounts for the false sense of security enabled by not giving others control of their behavior, as well as the sense of power they experience from the willed use of their rejective energy. The power of rejection—the energy—under normal conditions, is pointed at themselves in effort to not lose control of themselves. The opposed positioning relative to themselves uses willpower to control this rejective power, thereby undermining their sense of internal power or physical energy. Fatigue and bodily symptoms of trapped tension (headaches, acid reflux, pain) manifest as a result, especially in those with active victim centers.

The experience of life is thus, to a large degree, an experience of what an individual is or is not doing to themselves. To sustain a rejective relationship internally, and thus, in keeping the outside world positioned as a threat, attaching to the judgment from a higher power is often stabilizing. When an individual seeks to avoid part of themselves, they must be perceiving negative feelings as an insult rather than as an adaptation to effect the cause. As an insult, the internal effects become the perceived threat, thus positioning them relative to their feelings in a way where such feelings weaken the individual's will rather than empowering it. Simply put, to process negative emotion as a threat weakens an individual's sense of being able to effect change, and makes for a maladaptive handling of the emotion.

Personality Disorders

The personality disorders were given separate classification in 1980 within the Diagnostic & Statistical Manual-III. Since then, a slow suffocation has occurred in favor of the disorders which are more easily applied to subjective symptoms. Moreover, the disorders promoted as being hereditary or "biological" gained in popularity as medication treatments for mood and anxiety disorders increasingly came to market, further diminishing clinical attention paid to personality disorders. The clinical focus gradually shifted to Axis I diagnoses, allowing the pharmacologic treatment to thus be dictated by evidenced based medication treatment. The sentinel difficulty in diagnosing personality disorders has been the quickening of modern day healthcare, where a spot-diagnosis (diagnosis made on the spot) is expected. By definition, to diagnose a personality disorder requires forming an understanding of a person's personality in the context of their current and past relationships. Doing so becomes a "can of worms" for any clinician who is pressed for time and looking to make a diagnosis so to dictate treatment. Another impediment to diagnosis and treatment of personality disorders comes from the disorder itself. A person's personality is their way of relating to the world relative to themselves, and underlies how they see themselves relative to the world. A person with a personality disorder will seek help for how they feel in a way which is disordered. While this may be used to shed light on the diagnosis, dealing with it is difficult, especially in a non-specialized setting. Within their relationships, there will be unintended discord from others feeling disregarded, and from the person's hyper-reactivity to perceived rejection.

Within the Binary Psychology model, *ego-blindness* is the common denominator in defining a personality disorder. *Ego-blindness* is a condition where one can only experience others for how others relate to them or make them feel, and where all motivation comes from the ego seeking to feel more secure, more power, or more love. Within their outward relations, such individuals are only able to reflect how someone is relating to them based on how the person is affecting their feelings. Their primary relationship is with how they feel. In other words, their "I" of consciousness is locked in on a reflective perception of others—thus, always sensing others as causing the defense of themselves. All thoughts about others will be as others think, feel, or relate to them. Unfortunately, as they imbue others with the characteristics they fear within themselves, insight is unbecoming.

When one is primarily regarding how they are being treated or made to feel, their perception of others will be two-dimensional. Since one cannot know oneself except through an experiential understanding of another, to focus one's attention on oneself through others is simply a triangulation of oneself. The experience of others, thus, will be such where one feels de-individualized or used. This becomes off-putting unless the other person is similarly reflecting, thereby forming a mirroring relationship. Such mirroring relationships are characteristic of adolescence and become more disordered as one ages. The personality disordered individual will necessarily run into difficulty within a complementary or binary relationship. This is because of the necessary sacrifice of either feeling or thought in establishment of a complementary union. To play both sides will make the other person feel inwardly excluded and outwardly used. The double-standard between how they treat those they are closest with and how they expect to be treated is such where two separate perspectives can exist depending on which justifies their behavior. Since their primary relationship is with themselves, they can always blame others or the environment for negative feelings they experience and which are used to justify their behavior. In tethering their negative feelings to others, personality disordered individuals are dependent on others attaching to such feelings. Thus, they will either be making others feel negative (fear, guilt, inferiority) or expecting effort from others because of their negative feelings.

Adolescents must be recognized, by their very nature, as having a disordered perspective of themselves relative to others and others relative to themselves. With a primary focus on their feelings and/or their desires, they organize their perception to explain how they feel or what they want. Their primary reality is how they feel relative to themselves. The world is then constructed to explain such feelings. However, the more someone believes upset feelings to be a problem, the more they must perceive victimization at the hands of either the world or their body (illness). Trying to feel good enough or secure within themselves, thus involves trying to escape the bad feelings. When someone attributes cause for their negative state to something outside their control (or beyond their ability to grow past), then the individual will be externalizing their problem.

When others are being pleasing to them, the personality disordered individual will reflect being respected, loved, admired, or suspicious. They attribute a positive reflection of themselves as causing the other person's behavior. On the other hand, when another is being upsetting, then the personality disordered individual's perception of them revolves around the upset, as if the other person intended to cause such upset in them. In other words, they characterize the other person as "bad" if they feel badly, and characterize themselves as "good" when the other person is being positive. Being consciously focused on their own reflection in others means two things —first, the individual has yet to feel good enough about themselves, they have yet to grow up. Secondly, they cannot know others beyond a *like* versus *don't like* representation. The all good or all bad way of relating to others is illustrative of the self-serving character of ego judgment. Recall, ego judgment is an internally represented value judgment which has no basis in an understanding of the person being judged.

Since personality disordered individuals are able to reflect the positivity shown unto them, others can get trapped in believing themselves very much liked. However, once conflict arises, the one-sidedness becomes apparent. Individuals who are very capable self-personalities are susceptible to this mirroring effect, essentially blinded by their own positive, giving effort. They reflect being recognized—and thus valued—for their effort and pleasing intent. In order to love another person, understanding the other person is required. For each, it is very important to understand the other person's individuality—their depth of character, their insecurities, and how such fears manifest. For being misrepresented precipitates a sense of estrangement.

The most lamentable characteristic of the personality disordered individual is their blindness to themselves. The manner in which they experience others treating them is simply a reflection of themselves. Thus, they are always experiencing themselves without realizing it is them. It may be analogized to someone shaking a tree believing it beholds the fruit they need. As the tree fails to drop the expected fruit, frustration grows and the person shakes more vigorously. Finally, from the tree falls an acorn, hitting the person squarely atop the head. Assuming the individual is personality disordered, then they will perceive the situation as them having been mistreated. They cannot see the tree as never beholding the fruit they sought, nor the effect they had on the tree which precipitated the experience of the acorn falling on their head. They will convey the experience in a way which vilifies the tree and seek for others to mirror a similar experience of the tree. Sadly, if the person could have recognized the tree gave of itself by dropping the acorn, then the sense of mistreatment or misfortune would diminish.

Since ego-blindness is normal during adolescence, an ego-blind adult should be regarded as developmentally arrested, thereby creating the potential for curative space through maturation. Otherwise, ego-blindness becomes another label without conferring information regarding what is needed. From the outside looking in, the presence of an ego-blinded consciousness is not readily distinguishable, but can be easily identified through relational experience with the individual. The relational experience with such an individual will be one-sided—where their thought cannot form independently from how they feel, and thus, the other's individuality is never truly recognized. The ego-blinded individual will use anger to gain control by exploiting the anxiety of the other person. Usually, this occurs by making threats to either harm or abandon the individual. In having an effect, they feel powerful and in control. They are blind, however, to the degrading effect on the other person who, despite outwardly giving over control, may be detaching themselves underneath. Eventually, this enables them to break from the relationship with the ego-blinded individual—a difficult task normally, since the ego-blinded individual invariably will become vindictive and hateful through the separation process.

When the ego-blinded individual experiences someone pulling away, they will often say cruel things in order to see if the person still cares. They seek to see emotion. They cannot recognize the individuality or personhood of the person they are hurting. They can only see the emotion as being relative to themselves. Everything they experience is mirrored unto themselves. In such individuals, thoughts subserve internal feelings which are blamed on the world. Rather than their feelings translating into effort and thought being intended forward, the ego-blinded individual expects the world to effort unto them—to care about how they feel. They expect genuine care to come unto them, but can only genuinely care about themselves.

When one behaves primarily in effort to not *feel* a certain way, then one's personality is *neurotically disordered*. Alpha-personalities account for the majority of this type. When one behaves primarily to not *be* a certain way, then one's personality is *dependently disordered*. This type is constituted by self-personalities. For both types, their relationships will be impeded by a feeling-thought relationship inside them which excludes other people's reality. The feeling-thought connection internally prevents them from having to reflect themselves. In other words, it keeps them from being able to see themselves through the other. They can only see the other through themselves.

The *dependently disordered personality* type is classically represented by the borderline personality, where fear of losing the attachment dominates their relationships. The parasitic need for the other person is rooted in fear of themselves—of being alone, of one's aggressive potential, and thus is a reflective relationship. Such individuals are unable to consider the other person beyond the other person's potential to abandon them. The behavioral acting out in the context of a threatened abandonment is thus maniacal and often necessitates external controls being applied. Usually, such controls involve the mental health system. The dependently disordered type of individual is much more familiar to the system (compared to *neurotically disordered personality* types), and thus are regarded as more problematic. In such individuals, their insecure or aggressive thoughts will trigger a cascade of fears and emotional acting out. They then have an inability to reject the thoughts, believing they need reassurance, and thus, they believe they have no choice but to express them.

The *neurotically disordered personality* is consciously contrived in order to compensate for another aspect of themselves, and thus, the descriptive parameters must involve the duality. Their interaction with others on the outside will be compensatory or in effort to balance what they believe or fear to be true on the inside. Thus, their outward personality is moulded to be the inverse of the problem trait. This affixes the person in a dualistic psychology, where growth or change of either part threatens the balance. Change is associated with a lack of certainty or the inability to control the outcome. Thus, life itself, as a result of the inexorable change, becomes a threat to their conscious stability. The interactions with others will be in order to fulfill their representation or get what they believe they need. New endeavors are avoided and there is no motivation to grow. The motivation comes only from what is forced upon them. Such individuals then form the belief that if others would comply with their judgment and meet their expectations, they would be stable and content. By definition, this externalizes blame for how they come forth.

Subtypes of personality disorders were initially constructed through a psychoanalytic framework. However, the shift to a more diagnostic approach beginning in the 1980's has lead to the current confounding of different personality disorders. Subtypes other than borderline personality disorder, narcissistic personality disorder, antisocial personality disorder, and dependent personality disorder, are rarely applied clinically. The aforementioned four are still utilized occasionally and have relevance to understanding certain individuals. The following framework is in effort to enable a more meaningful application for diagnosing personality disorders.

The four personality disorders noted above can be divided into dependent type and neurotic type, where borderline and dependent personality disorders go under the dependent type personality disorders (self-personalities), and narcissistic and antisocial personality disorders are categorized as neurotic type personality disorders (alpha-personalities). If the individual's binary mind is not emotionally or psychologically independent, then they are categorized under the dependent type heading. If they are completely dependent without shifts into a distancing, aggressive self, then dependent personality disorder is best applied. Diagnosing borderline personality disorder is appropriate then for the dependent type personality who shifts back and forth between clinging and pushing away. Individuals who are independent, but who cannot, in their relationships, step beyond the internal reflection of themselves, are categorized under the heading neurotic type personality disorders. Antisocial personality disorder and narcissistic personality disorder are thus categorized under the neurotic type heading. While less noticeably needy, and thus less likely than a dependent type personality to fall on the system or present dramatically for help, the disordering impact within their relationships is undeniable and equally as maladaptive. Those of the neurotic type are more comfortable being independent, however, and their difficulty is primarily within a binary relationship. This is due to their inability to sacrifice what they want or how they feel without experiencing themselves getting used (antisocial) or put down (narcissistic) in the process.

Topic: The Rapist

The scale of potential problems which may arise from an individual blindly mirroring themselves is illustrated by the occurrence of rape. A rapist will often blame their sexual desire on the victim, as if the victim intended to cause such feelings. Then, when their bullish advances are resisted, they experience anger. This marks the point where a sudden shift occurs, palpable to each. The rapist, though experiencing the upset internally, sees the source externally. This induces their sympathetic fight response which is the rape itself. The victim's own natural sympathomimetic response to the sudden surfacing of the rapist's anger is to take flight. However, their flight physically is blocked and so they take flight from their body. The dissociation from their body, by dampening the sensorial experience of the assault, is protective, to some degree, for the victim's psyche. The rape itself is invariably aggressive and a means to an end. Once ejaculation occurs, then the aggressive internal experience of the rapist subsides. Once this happens, the victim is merely an object the rapist wants to discard. The victim seeks to escape the situation as quickly as possible, and usually does so quietly to avoid further insult. The rapist will go forward believing the victim either got what was secretly wanted or, if not, then the victim got a deserved lesson regarding being a "tease." Clearly, from the victim's perspective, neither thought is correct, and thus the rapist's belief about the situation is wrong. However, from the perceptive standpoint of someone who is a rapist, the world is intentionally agitating. They cannot perceive their perceptive experience is largely a result of the world's defensiveness toward them. Angry thoughts can cascade obsessively, and their interaction with the world, generally, is filled with an underlying contempt. Normally, they are avoidant of potential conflict with men, and yet, they believe themselves under-appreciated. Most rapists are unable to consider themselves unto others, but rather are stuck in the reflective experience of themselves. Thus, they can only experience others as others relate to them. They are quick to feel taken advantage of when their efforts are not rewarded. They expect care from women to come in the form of subservience to their feelings. The objectification occurs in the fulfillment of their perceived need—which, in the case of a rapist, is desire admixed with anger—both which get the entitled alleviation in the process. The psychology of the rapist is illustrative of the disordering and dangerous potential in reflecting the world as being responsible for one's desires or experiential feelings.

CONCLUSION

Change

To meaningfully effect the declining mental health of our culture, mental healthcare must transition out from its present position within the medical system and into a system which nurtures growth.

The medical system treats problems which arise at the materialized or bodily level. Understandably, the sciences have sought to stay objective, thus binding scientists, in their quest for further understanding, to study measurable or observable phenomena. However, taking such an approach to mental health occurs in ignorance of the mind. By taking a mind-blinded approach to mental health, scientists have sought to reduce mental derangement into a physiological phenomenon, such as a chemical imbalance. The aim has thus been to find the cause for mental health disorders within the physiology of individuals who have been diagnosed with a disorder. The belief in such is then predicated on a predetermined nature or make-up—the hunt for which has lead scientists to focus on the human genome. However, no bio marker has been found of true significance—nothing physically or genetically which can explain mental symptoms or account for a specific disorder. Moreover, unlike physically founded diseases, no mental disorder can be found post-mortem. Rather, every mental health condition occurs from within the dynamic life experience. In other words, mental health problems are conditions of living, of being.

For everyone, life is felt through the body and intended upon by the mind, therein generating experience. The mind exists as the perceiving entity within consciousness, which maintains an awareness of being alive. The mind exists relative to the body, and thus relative to life impressing upon the body. Through recognition of the mind as an entity, an understanding of the relationship occurring between mind and body can then be pursued. Clinically, by taking the focal point off of the body and focusing instead on the mind, the mind's processing of bodily effects becomes relevant for understanding mental disorders. If bodily phenomena occur for all individuals—where bodily effects (feelings, impressions, potential for loss) are not limited to those individuals with mental disorders, then the handling of such effects must be implicated as the precipitating cause of an individual's disorder. To illustrate—a smell is a bodily effect which is similar between individuals, but the meaning or thought given to the smell is from the mind. Thus, the initial impression or effect (the smell) occurs the same for everyone, but the experience of the smell becomes individualized based on the mind's processing or perception of the smell. This perceptive step is initially either accepting or rejecting—where a rejective handling would perceive the smell as a threat, thus producing a noxious experience of the smell as happening to them, generating a physiologic fight or flight response. The build up of tension is then used to push away from the smell—either by taking flight from or fighting away the perceived cause (source of smell). Oppositely, an acceptive processing of the smell has it perceived as part of the environment, where the individual is able to either willfully become more attentive to the smell—thereby amplifying the awareness of it—or else assign irrelevance to the smell, allowing it to fade from perceptive awareness.

When the mind is rejecting certain bodily effects, an energetically equal amount of conscious attention must stay attached to the effects, thus trapping the individual in the experience of such threat. Anything perceived as a threat —including a negative feeling occurring within an individual's body—receives meaning in the form of thought and power in the form of energy. Ironically, despite an individual's intent to not experience what is being perceived, the rejective effort infuses life into the threat. In other words, effort directed toward (x), even if the effort is to control or eliminate (x), infuses energy or power into (x), thus amplifying the experience of (x) as a threat. For an individual who is caught up in trying to not experience negative bodily effects (anxiety, anger, sadness, loss), the medical system, by taking a similarly rejecting approach in effort to "help," actually gives life to the perceived problem. Furthermore, such an approach depends on a materialized substance (medication) existing outside of the individual—for which they are bound to believe they need. Unfortunately, forming such dependencies is counter to the direction of growth.

The mind changes through growth, where steps are taken which lead to less identification with the bodily experience, thus generating a more mindful consciousness. Such growth occurs through a letting go and acceptance process, which is very difficult, rather than through alleviation or separation from part of oneself. However, the essential importance of such growth occurring through life is best noted within those who do not grow—who spend their energy and focus trying to not experience what they have yet to accept within the life experience, which is always a projection of what they have not accepted about themselves. Such individuals center their daily intent around feeling well rather than being well, where the potential to change is pursued so to feel better rather than to be better. Effort to feel better then occurs at the expense of growth, because growth happens from a willed effort to be better. Such effort is necessarily forward facing and requires a giving of self—akin to the effort required when playing sports or doing artwork. For an entity to support growth, it must provide a structure which enables growth. Then, such growth depends on the willed effort of those who seek to be better within the provided structure. Such structure must be built to support the positive potential in those striving to be better rather than being set up to limit their negative potential. In fact, the more a system is built to prevent negative, the more those seeking to be better will feel compelled to either defend themselves or else keep part of themselves hidden or separated. In contrast, a system oriented to see the positive potential in everyone does so with structured expectations for such, and seeks to support the fruition of each's potential through nurturing the positive. The inherent flaw in a system which seeks to prevent negative is in the system's reflection of rejection to those it seeks to support. Moreover, the message it delivers to individuals is misguided—by make believing in a positive life experience being found though the avoidance of negative—as if not experiencing bad is the same as having a good experience, or not being bad is somehow equal to being good. Since the medical system centers around treating bodily problems, it is already built to combat or prevent negative. Thus, the inclusion of mental health within the medical system is being done in ignorance of the individual and cultural impact in doing so—where, increasingly, individuals are relating to only themselves—only to how they feel—where they can only see the world through the lens of how they feel about it or for what they perceive needing from it. Unfortunately, this comes at the expense of what each is able to put into life, therein limiting growth to a proportional degree. Moreover, this lack of fruition—when an individual's potential is wrapped up in trying to fulfill themselves—produces a continual sense of something missing.

The System's Weakening Of The Will

The medical system's rejective approach to negative feelings, by providing chemical alleviation, is undermining growth and potentiating dependence on both the chemicals provided and the system itself—the entity providing such chemicals. Without understanding how the mind causes the problems an individual experiences through their body, we have been only able to focus on the body itself—in attempt to understand and eradicate the symptoms being experienced as a problem. The effort to materialize the case has come in tandem with a materialization of chemicals to treat the problematic effects being experienced within the body. The mind naturally ascribes material need to sensory experiences arising from the body which are rejected—those an individual is willed to not experience. Thus, the more an individual's will is directed toward not experiencing negative effect, the more they will need to depend on an outside remedy.

When the will is determined by feelings (desires, emotions, fears), then it is not free, for it is reacting to effects within the body. When reacting to the body, then the mind perceives outside stimuli or internal need as causing oneself, thus being determined by conditions. Framed another way, when the human will is directed toward not experiencing negative effects/feelings, then it remains bound to the protective relationship with the body, which includes effort to fulfill perceived emptiness or lacking. A free will has accepted the potential for negative effects, essentially having let go of effort to not suffer, thereby coming into positive being, where the will is free and forward facing. As such, the creativity of the will is applied positively, and thus impacts the environment in a growth promoting way.

The free will within everyone, once it has been attained, cannot be given away without attaching an expectation for something in return. Doing something for someone of one's free will is significantly different than if the doing for someone is willed toward fulfilling or protecting oneself. Doing things with the intent of being pleasing to another or gaining their approval amounts to a giving away of the will—which produces a sense of being ineffective. Put another way, unless an action is freely willed, the nature of the action is consumptive or protective. Such acts are bound within the human triangle of attraction and repulsion, wherein a sense of self is both sought and protected. This triangle arises from the will which remains bound to the body. A freely willed individual, rather, operates with a will which is no longer attached—it has gained independence—and thus cannot be threatened by life, for it only seeks a full expression of itself.

Becoming freely willed is thus only possible when the mind is no longer internally willed—whether to fulfill, protect, or control. The effort to internally fulfill oneself comes atop a sense of something missing, while protection occurs of a self-image which is created and maintained internally. The willed effort to control oneself internally is made toward one's anger, which depends on a misbelief about one's potential to hurt others when angry. Letting go of the effort toward internal fulfillment, protection, or control is thus a necessary step in becoming freely willed. The supreme difficulty in doing so stems from the destruction of consciousness—the changing of mind—which is experienced as an impending rejection, death, or loss. The willed opposition to the change necessitates an attachment—

someone or something which is needed to enable the ongoing rejection of the potentiated change—to enable an escape, to feel better. However, the expense is paid through not being better, where there occurs no growth in capability or understanding.

The more power afforded to how one feels in determining what is done or not done, the more likely one will attach to needing to feel better in order to be better. In other words, when the will is aimed at not being negative, one cannot conceive of themselves being positive in the face of feeling negative. Based on feelings occurring within the body, the mind can internally reflect needing something. However, feeling a need is subjectively perceived and not true. Yet, to experience the lack of need requires the individual to will themselves through the feelings—to reprioritize the will in such a way where what is done or not done is based on a willed purpose outside of themselves. Otherwise, the will is intended toward one's subjective state.

By trying to alleviate negative effects occurring within the body, the medical system has communicated a need for such through conceptualization of the individual as having a problem. Younger individuals especially much prefer the thought of themselves *having* a problem rather than themselves *being* the problem. "I have a problem" versus "I am the problem" is a fundamental line which gets drawn, where the former gives the problem to the body, while the latter ascribes the problem to the mind. The belief in having a problem is preferred by people when they believe help is begotten as a result. To pursue a fix for oneself by ingesting a chemical is willed toward not experiencing the negative effects which one's mind perceives as a threat to one's sense of intactness. Attempts to change body chemistry produce temporary changes in the effects, thus providing an experience of alleviation. However, such benefits are not well sustained and tend to perpetuate the misbelief of needing to ingest something to counter the negative effects.

Seeing Both Sides

Two positions of consciousness exist within the adult human mind—the feeling position and the thought position. Feelings and thoughts are distinct entities. Though they overlap, a feeling does not carry thought and a thought has no feeling. The human mind begins as sensory or feeling awareness reflecting off of the outside environment. During childhood, the environment is thought. The other side of consciousness—through an internalization of thought—becomes independently active around the time of puberty. This creates the two-part consciousness, enabling the individual to internally give thought to their feelings or to give feeling to their thoughts. Interaction between the two, within the individual consciousness, produces the thinking awareness which characterizes the adult human mind. The seat of consciousness, one's observing "I," in order to think, must reflect off of the other side, thereby creating a concept of oneself relative to the environment. Since there are two potential positions within the two-part consciousness, one's "I" must be rooted as either feeling (self) or thought (alpha). One's seat of consciousness, thus, has two possible points of view—either as feeling interacting with thought (self), or as thought interacting with feeling (alpha). If one's "I" of consciousness identifies as feeling, then one will perceive thought outside of oneself. One will seek to know oneself through thought. Internally, one's reflections will consist primarily of thoughts. However, one who is identified as feeling forms their self conception (as it flows outwardly) based on their effort and intent—the care they bring forth. From the feeling side of consciousness, the belief in oneself and what one believes about oneself are based on one's functional ability. From the flip-side, where the "I" of consciousness is identified as thought, one perceives feeling outside of oneself. From this position, the reflective process occurs off of feeling (desire, energy, movement, emotion) in forming thought. Thought is given to outer feeling. Internally, focus is on how one feels or on how others are feeling. From the thought position, one identifies with their applied judgment, their reputation, and seeks to reflect respect and loyalty. From this position, one seeks to know oneself through feelings.

From the thought side of consciousness, where one is bound to reflect on feeling, there are two possible sources of feeling. The primary focal point can be positioned either on how one feels (physically, emotionally) or on how others feel. During development, the initial focal point is invariably on one's own feelings since one transitioned into the thought position to take control of the feelings. Where from the feeling side of consciousness, for individuals destined to identify as thought, being attached to the thoughts of others in deriving one's sense of value and security is unsustainable. Transitioning to the thought position detaches the sense of oneself from the approving thought of others, taking control of one's feeling-self in the process. The initial goal is to feel stable and in control. However, perceiving one's feelings as being determined from outside of oneself (from the environment or others) tethers one to process the feelings through either control of the environment or avoidance of situations or people. Irregardless, if an individual's own feelings are the primary focus as they interact with the world, then they are only coming to know how the world feels to them. Getting to know how things feel relative to themselves traps them in a world of their feelings. When thought is formed directly from internal feeling, the world can only be experienced as an expression of such feeling. The world cannot become known independent from the individual's own feelings about it. The natural direction of growth, throughout adulthood, is away from one's own internal feelings as the primary focal point and more onto the feelings of others. From the feeling side of consciousness, one must reflect on thought. Just as with those from the thought side of consciousness having to reflect on feeling, those from the feeling side have two sources of thought for which to reflect on—internal thought or external thought. Internal thought includes memories, images, and words. External thought is contemplative of something or someone else. Then, within this external thought world, one can either be in regard of the world (people, places, things) relative to oneself or oneself relative to the world.

Both the source and the cause of negative sensory phenomena for a baby are due to elements outside of their seat of consciousness or motor effort. The remedy comes from the parent (e.g. feeding), begotten from the outside through consumption. Or it can come in the form of alleviation if something causing the discomfort is removed (e.g. taking off wet, cold diaper). Negative feelings are thus initially tethered to outside thought (parent) for remedy— for structure. The thought structure for the consciousness processing of uncomfortable feelings is necessary for normal neurodevelopment to occur. Normal development maintains the direction of increasing connectedness with the world—a growing ability to mentally communicate and to physically interact. Consciousness initially handles a feeling or sensory signal by processing it through a binary bifurcation where it is routed either as a *problem* or *no problem*. When alleviation is provided from the outside, in the context of the child's upset, the feelings get attached to the outside (similar to hunger), and thus the upset is expressed in order to receive what is needed (similar to food). Such a feeling will then be coded as a *problem* requiring conscious attention and outside alleviation. Once the child is able to form motor intent (to see something in the environment which triggers a desire), then upset feelings will occur secondary to the child not getting what they want. If their upset continues to find outside alleviation through the parent, then they will continue handling such feelings as if the feelings should not be happening and need outside alleviation. Not until a change in processing to where the feeling or emotion is routed *no problem* is the child able to tolerate frustration enough to be parented. Once the child is able to communicate, their upset feelings should no longer be employed to get their way. In such a scenario, the child who believes their upset is a problem will expect the upset to have influence over their parent. In effect, the upset is occurring like hunger where they believe they need something in order to manage it. Thus, escalating anger in a child is simply them intensifying their effort to demonstrate upset—as if the upset should speak for itself. In undergoing the initial processing division, any feeling, emotion, or sensation routed as a *problem* will attach itself to an outside cause and then an outside need. As a result, the feelings get perceived and trapped within the afferent or incoming sensory system and thus triangulated—whereby, the body or outside environment is experienced as producing the negativity.

When the parent, serving as thought, enables the child to feel better, then the child will be relatively stable. However, the stability is enabled within the dyadic dependence on the parent. As a child grows more able, they begin to form their own desires relative to the environment. Inevitably, they will have to face their parent upsetting them relative to their desire within the environment. This is an important juncture since the source of making things better (parent) becomes the source of frustration. Aggressive anger toward the parent is likely to surface, and the reaction by the parent must not involve getting angry, sad, or anxious. Parenting with emotion keeps a child's negative feelings from being normalized, and keeps the child in an unnaturally dependent position in order to manage their negative feelings. Once socialization begins, a child may become discordant or avoidant if negative emotion is being processed as a *problem*. The cause for every negative feeling being processed as a *problem* will get attributed to something or someone outside of themselves. Therein, they believe in an entitlement to feel better, sensing themselves as a victim. A child may perceive others as having intended to upset them, and thus increasingly come to believe in a world where others are mean and potentially victimizing. This early development within a child's consciousness leads to eventually believing their feelings are a problem and thus need to be controlled. Therefore, at the onset of thinking, they will typically "flip" into the thought position in an attempt to garner control over their problematic feelings. Although this transition leads an adolescent to believe they will feel better, it often leads to an extreme rejection of their already negative feelings, and thus anxious symptoms become exacerbated. What follows is the intensification in the belief of needing outside help to feel better, typically in the form of alcohol/drugs/addictions/parents/healthcare system.

Within the two-part consciousness, if conflict is occurring, then disharmony prevents internal security and acceptance. But mostly, it keeps an individual's consciousness rooted internally—affixed to their own feelings and reflections, and thus unable to truly regard the world outside of themselves. Being stuck on themselves, where the world is simply as it effects them, blinds their awareness to themselves relative to the world. When the world is related to as if one is hungry and the environment is a dinner buffet, then eventually, after enough consumption, an individual's appetite will diminish. To generate interest thereafter takes a special entree, something greater than they have already experienced. Nothing looks good and there occurs a conscious apathy in relation to what's out there. Often, as a result, such individuals will turn to drugs in order to enliven their experience.

Seeing Problems

Feelings or sensory experiences cannot be a problem. Sensory awareness is life, and life is subjectively experienced. Feelings are part of being alive. Everyone has feelings, including the negative feelings—anger, fear, and sadness. Because feelings are common to everyone, no feeling can itself be regarded as a problem. The feelings may signal there is a problem, and may be regarded for such experiential information, but the feelings themselves cannot be the problem. The difference in cognitive processing, and thus perception, of feelings which are believed to be a problem versus those which are not regarded to be a problem is significant. Perceptive effort to uncover and eliminate the source of a problem feeling is fundamentally different than the perceptive handling of a feeling that, while uncomfortable, is not believed to be a problem. When not believed to be a problem, a space exists between what happens on the outside and how one responds emotionally. Without this space, one experiences being *made to feel* by others or circumstances. In other words, negative feelings are perceived to be happening to oneself— analogous to hunger—as opposed to being sensed as occurring within oneself. Put another way, problem feelings are rejected, and thus, energetic potential inherent within feelings is not sensed by the efferent or outgoing consciousness—the will—as power within. As such, emotion as *energy in motion* is not purposed positively by the will.

Universally, people do not perceive any meaningful distinction between *feeling hungry* and *being hungry*. Put another way, there is no consciousness space between the feeling (x) and the being (x) when (x) pertains to a physiologic state. However, when (x) involves one's psycho-emotional feelings, then there should be conscious space existing between what happens on the outside involving one's afferent nervous system and how one responds, which is an efferent action. For example, consciously recognizing the difference or space between feeling upset and being upset means the internal feeling does not equate to an outward being of the feeling. In other words, rather than believing the environment is determining one's feelings and subsequent being, psychological control of one's feelings in response to the environment gets established. Consciousness then takes responsibility for feelings which can be transformed into purposeful output through the efferent system. Taking responsibility for feelings is different than taking blame, for there is no blame in having the feelings. Returning to the internal gas analogy, the occurrence of gas inside oneself is an unavoidable byproduct of life. If the gas is seen as a threat, then consciousness will not develop an expressive relationship with it, but rather will take a rejective approach. However, this will cause more systemic impairment. Similar to psychological feelings, a rejective approach will thus not open up space for which consciousness can develop understanding, control, and proper expression for the feelings.

A large proportion of "mentally ill" individuals have not yet become emotionally independent. Their dependence will be from the dyadic relationship as a child, and thus certain feelings never take on thought other than signaling a need. In believing certain negative feelings are problematic—anger, anxiety, sadness—individuals maintain an attachment they believe they need—either to their parent or to alcohol/drugs/addictions. The manifestation in those who have not yet become emotionally independent is usually more behavioral, and occurs within the context of their primary relationship. "Mentally ill" individuals who have established independence generally demonstrate an erroneous belief in needing to remain in control of certain feelings—usually anger. The belief in needing to exert control over their emotions drives excessive forethought, stress, and relationship distancing. However, the effect is a welling up of negative tension which increasingly threatens expression. Any expression will be consciously overwhelming, often coming forth explosively or dramatically, and thus further solidifying the belief in such feelings or emotions being a problem, to which they seek escape. Mental illness from the feeling (self) position will be experienced by the suffering individual as a thought problem. A problematic, erroneous thought (loss, rejection, abandonment) is being given attention and effort. In other words, a negative, erroneous thought is being "cared" about. When a negative thought is attached to and thus given feeling (self), experiential reality is generated. Since the thought is normally based on a fear of losing an attachment, mental illness from the self (feeling) position most often occurs within the individual's primary relationship(s). Furthermore, the primary entity providing the person's externalized thought (spouse, parent, boss) must be taken into consideration in assessing the person's "illness." From the thought position (alpha), mental illness is not a problem of an individual's sensory feelings or emotions themselves, but rather is rooted within their thought handling of the feelings. Misbelief about the nature of a feeling occurs on the thought or motor side of consciousness. The "illness" thus stems from a belief in certain feelings representing a problem and thus needing rejective handling.

The human consciousness cannot see itself as contained within the whole. Rather, the human consciousness perceives oneself as the whole. There is no natural inclination toward realizing one's role within the whole. The drive which comes naturally is to fulfill oneself—to objectify the world and everyone in it based on the fulfillment of one's conscious desire or need. The human consciousness expects the world to manifest one's intent. Put another way, the human perception naturally structures its thought or understanding around feelings or sensory impulses. Beliefs are formed by attaching the environment, as thought, directly to feeling, thus forming early knowledge as if one's conscious feeling is the center of the universe—as if the feeling was the a priori event which caused everything else. The human consciousness, once it develops the internal ability to give thoughts to feelings or to give feelings to thoughts, becomes truly individualized. Then, one must go forward in order to come to know oneself, to realize oneself.

The phenomenological occurrence of passing on fear through defensive perception evidences the interconnectedness of humans. What an individual defends within themselves will be imbued into the other through the defense itself. This allows them to conceive of how they are coming off to others when defensive. Though unable to see oneself, an individual can recognize how they are being mis-perceived and thus running into relational frustrations. When consciousness makes a negative feeling the sentinel problem, then the individual will perceptively construct the world in order to explain the feeling. The feeling will be attached to people, places, or things so to give consciousness a way to organize the feeling and thus consciously control it.

Doing so, however, externalizes the negative feeling, thus giving it to the world. In doing so, such individuals consciously believe elements within the world are making them feel negatively. Forming thoughts about themselves or the world in order to explain their negative feelings is an inversion of thought consciousness, effectively keeping them trapped with their negative feelings. If an individual takes a step further and believes there is conscious intent from others to cause their upset, then a significant break from shared reality may result through such a portal of paranoia. Ascribing intent to others for causing their feelings makes others into two-dimensional props set relative to the scenario constructed of their own thoughts.

Seeing The Light

Life energy compels individualized growth, pushing for a total individualized fruition of each. Striving to achieve within the environment utilizes this directional energy. Thus, growth into the world always requires the vector of willful energy to be pointed toward becoming better, more "full." Filled with "full" is the goal, and yet, the achievement of each requires an acceptance of all parts of themselves. Any fulfillment which is sustainable will be experienced as a blossoming of one's purpose within the world, a becoming of oneself, and a fully potentiated giving of oneself. Energy is unidirectional prior to entering each individual. It is moving forward. Energy is time, always moving forward in the same direction. Once entering the individual, a certain amount must go into sustaining vital functions which need energy to operate properly. Having energy flow into an individual's thought consciousness then activates awareness of the environment, essentially materializing an experience of individuality.

The interaction one has with the world, including others, can either be giving or taking. Often, the taking process is veiled as a reaction to what is being demanded by the circumstances one perceives. However, when one's goal is to interact with the environment (or those within it) so to feel better or more secure, then the net result will be consumptive or rejective. Growing into one's independent individuality is necessarily a consumptive and rejective process. The transition into maturity requires a shift in perspective whereby the world is no longer regarded as it pertains to oneself, but instead the world is perceived as one is unto it. For this shift to occur, there must occur a letting go of the primary effort toward one's internal space—either to fulfill it or protect it. The call is to potentiate one's internal space. The longer one goes in life seeking to get the world to fulfill oneself, the greater will be the frustration with life. Too commonly, individuals blame their dissatisfaction on their circumstances or those around them. Spewing criticisms or chronic complaints eventually brings about isolation, as others will be naturally repulsed. Often, this perpetuates a cycle of rejection the individual cannot perceive as stemming from what they have put out, and thus re-enforces their externalized negativity. If one is going to see the negative in the environment or in others, then one's life will be filled with either discord or excessive anxiety.

The adaptation to life involves growing better able to independently and purposefully handle one's feelings. To manage oneself within the world, where one senses fulfillment, requires having creative power. One has to eventually learn to grow the world. The creative ability comes in the combining of one's energy/time with one's thought. While most perceive the outside world as dictating their thought, growing into an awareness of one's capability to look at things differently, to change the thought, is a milestone of immeasurable benefit. The space where change occurs is between oneself and the world. Thought negativity or rejection toward the world is based on centering the world around oneself. Thus, the potential shift in perspective is born out of a de-centering of oneself. In other words, for to center oneself around the world, and perceive life outside through the lens of one's potential toward it, is a shift in thought structure. Dong so enables one to see the bright side. Then, the world experiences one bringing forth such brightness.

Stability and power are found through the bonding of opposites. Whether it is the right bonded to the left, the self to the alpha, or the proton with the electron, life itself is a bonding of opposites. Love is the glue to the bond. Love does not reflect since it is universal, and thus can not be rejected. Efforts toward oneself are counterproductive to the bond. Love cannot feel itself, but it can experience itself. Thus, feeling loved has little to do with the individualized fruition of one's love. Experiencing love requires one to first overcome their gravity—their fears and self-entitlements. Much like the airplane accelerating down the runway, consciousness must reach a critical speed before it can be raised from the ground. Just prior to lifting into the air the plane is doing all it can to go fast enough. Yet, as it is, despite all effort otherwise, it cannot take flight. For flight to take fruition, it needs an adjustment in the angling of its wing. Once this occurs, the plane lifts into the air. Though its skyward effort must continue, it now occurs more naturally and freely— without the effort needed to overcome the attachment to the ground. Similarly, consciousness is attached to itself, and thus is bound by its own misbeliefs, blinded by the reflection of one's own image.

Instances where one consciously intends to cause hurt of another, not in defense, but in offense, are rare, and usually are directed toward siblings. Nevertheless, for one's anger to organize into thought and then into offensive intent to cause hurt or upset feelings is cruelty. An act of cruelty usually scares oneself, forming a counter judgment and a belief of being potentially "bad." Consciousness will attach the cruelty to the feeling of anger, therein seeking to avoid situations or individuals which cause upset. Hypersensitivity to being perceived as mean or critical drives one to be overly nice and accommodating to others in defense. However, doing so is laborious since it is not done out of love but rather out of fear, and thus is mentally exhausting. Love will thus be conceived of as a feeling of control and security, and one will put effort into minimizing the internal sense of frustration. The lamentable tragedy of the situation, however, is most of the positive energy (willful effort) goes into opposing oneself. Judgment of another relative to oneself is a slippery, dangerous slope. For the overwhelming majority of interactions, inconsideration is as far as an offense may be taken. To cross the line where another person's intent is judged, causes erroneous conclusions and, for the individual being judged, a sense of being targeted or attacked. Judgment of another person based on the feelings or thoughts the person elicits within oneself is immature and should not be part of the adult perception.

When an individual cannot regard themselves as being potentially hurtful, then there will be no compensatory avoidance of being hurtful. A falsified persona conceived as "nice" will not exist. When an individual is unified, then bringing themselves fully to the present moment becomes possible. When unified, an individual is able to comfortably and expressively bring themselves to the world in front of them. Security is derived from what they are able to bring to the world. They do not have to depend on what the world gives them or how they are judged. They recognize the quality of their life will be from the quantity of themselves given to the world. They are wise to not pre-judge what a quality life should be, thus allowing the world to teach them through their own internal qualification of themselves relative to the world. In other words, if an individual is living correctly, and properly giving of themselves to the world and those around them, then life will give quality to their being.

The Free Will

The Free will within everyone cannot be given away without attaching an expectation for something in return. Doing something for someone of one's free will is significantly different than if the doing for someone is willed toward fulfilling or protecting oneself. Doing things with the intent of being pleasing to another or gaining their approval amounts to a giving way of the will, which produces either a sense of being ineffective or used. Put another way, unless an action is freely willed, the nature of the action is either consumptive or protective. Such acts are bound within the human triangle of attraction and repulsion, wherein a sense of self is both sought and protected. The triangle arises from the will which is still bound to the body—to the individual's "me." A free will, rather, is the will which has gained independence. A free will is thus unattached, unable to be threatened by life, and only seeks a full expression of itself.

When the will is determined by feelings (desires, emotions, fears), then it is not free, for it is reacting to effects within the body. When reacting to the body, then the mind perceives outside stimuli or internal need as causing oneself, thus being determined by external conditions. Framed another way, when the human will is directed toward not experiencing negative effects/feelings, then it remains bound to the protective relationship with the body, which includes effort to fulfill perceived emptiness or lacking. A free will has accepted the potential for negative effects, essentially having let go of effort to not suffer, thereby coming into positive being, where the will is free and forward facing. As such, the creativity of the will is applied positively, and thus impacts the environment in a growth promoting way.

The more an individual is freely willed, the greater will be the emanation of light. Thus, when two individuals are freely willing their positive effort into a relationship, the growth of the entity is exponential. Oppositely, when either individual's will is given away within the relationship, then the relationship is either consumptive or protective—neither of which potentiates growth. In other words, for either individual to be seeking to secure or fulfill their internal space, such occurs at the growth expense of the relationship. If one of the individuals within the relationship is primarily attached to their own internal space, then they will judge the other individual through the lens of input rather than output. Output occurs from an individual into the space between, where the relationship is formed. Input, rather, occurs as a reflection of the other person's effort relative to oneself. Perceiving the relationship as such, input gets false equated to output. Unfortunately, focusing on another's input blinds an individual to their own lack of output as a result. Relationship success, as a general rule, requires both individuals to prioritize their own output—for each to focus on what they put out—what they do for the relationship, rather than what the relationship is (or is not) doing for them. Relationships being experienced from a self centered point of view produce a distorted reality of the other person, as well as a misconception of the relationship. Relationship health is compromised as a result, and excessive energy will have to be spent in effort to maintain intactness—to not break up. However, such effort comes at the expense of positively willed energy being intended toward growth into the space between.

Seeing Growth

As a method of assessment—identify the element being rejected—either a feeling or a materialization of attachment. The rejected element will be trapped in the afferent nervous system and thus expressed physically—either through rejective expression into the environment or within the body (illness, symptoms of tension). Tracing the rejected element being expressed starts with the individual's subjective sensory experience within their affective sensory system, and then generally throughout the body. The tracing continues from the body into materialized attachments such as food, people, or objects—wherein the element is expressed or compensated for. A clinical assessment must identify whether the individual's perceiving consciousness is reflecting initially on feeling to form thought (alpha cognition) or reflecting on thought to form feeling (self cognition). For an individual operating from the alpha perspective, a feeling is most feared. If a thought belief about a feeling is wrong, then the cognitive processing of the feeling will misattribute the feeling to the environment. Thus, the individual forms the thought concept of being victimized or unfairly burdened. In other words, the individual perceives being caused to suffer. The more the alpha cognition consciously focuses on their feelings, the more they will perceive the environment as having negative feelings for them. Then, things other people do are more likely to be seen as intentionally upsetting.

Any feeling being coded as a threat gets attached to and thus brought into experiential reality as a problem. Any conscious attention on the feeling magnifies it. Then, giving thought form to the feeling increasingly gives it experiential awareness within the environment. To be "better" requires a shift in focal point—off of one's own feelings and onto the feelings of others, where the intent is to give outward thought to produce positive feelings in those around oneself. Being surrounded by positivity enables one to reflect being loved, in control, or powerful. For this is to happen, however, it is imperative to let go of the effort to internally feel love, control, or power, for oneself, at the expense of others or the environment. To do so is exceedingly difficult, but it is through such toil where one grows the strength to detach from one's own negative feelings, and therein learns to transform such feelings into seeds of positivity sewn outside of oneself. The first step in being able to do so involves turning one's conscious attention away from one's own internal feelings or thoughts and seeking to realize oneself separate from the feelings or desires one is having internally. It is imperative to come to the point where one recognizes the desires and feelings are meant to enliven one's experience, and should not determine one's thoughts. Feeling is meant to combine with thought to produce experience and growth. However, to do so requires another—someone or some entity to give of one's attention to, toward whom one's effort may flow. Otherwise, consciousness will be trapped in its own bubble, where self-fulfillment is impossible, for one cannot love oneself as one seeks to feel loved. To satiate the longing for acceptance each is born with, one must grow into being able to give what is sought. Otherwise, consciousness is in a state of defense or separateness, perceiving life reflectively. In other words, one remains trapped in the mirror. Only through the giving of oneself does the space open up for one to have a true experience of acceptance. For the self-personality, thoughtful love is the ideal position for their consciousness to occupy relative to another. An alpha-personality, on the other hand, should consciously fulfill a belief system constructed of loving thought.

A notable feature of life is the frequency in which a "leap of faith" is required. Stepping into new experiences is unavoidable because of the indefatigable forward progression of time. New experiences keep the mind having to assimilate new information and thus growing in understanding of oneself and the world. Plentiful are times where an individual wants to do something but fear of the unknown compels them in the opposite direction. The necessary leaps of faith will not come from a surge in positive thought, but rather from a surge of internal adrenaline (fight), which binds the fear, enabling them to push past it—essentially lessening the conscious perception of fear and thought insecurity. Thus, they are able to step forward into their belief. When anger is sought to be rejected from an individual's character, or avoided, then it is not internally accessible so to oppose the fear and enable the faith step forward. In order to step forward then, an individual must have a fear scenario from the outside which is vector opposite to the internal fear holding them back. For illustration, consider someone getting up on a diving board for the first time—where upon reaching the edge they are afraid to jump. In order to jump without having a willed surge of internal adrenaline, the individual must create a fear scenario for if they don't jump—for example, being thought of negatively by their friends for not jumping. Jumping then in fear of being rejected for not jumping, while enabling them to jump, does not grow internal self-esteem as much as if an individual pushes themselves past the fear.

An individual who cognitively reflects on thought to form their feeling—which is then given in the form of effort and desire toward another or the environment—is a natural self-personality. When such an individual presents clinically for help, it may be assumed they are reflecting off of their own negative thoughts. Such thoughts will be ideas of rejection or loss—of being unloved or not good enough. The effort from the self-personality is to impress or to reflect acceptance. In doing so, such individuals try to achieve certain thought reflections, and thus are seeking to create positive regard for themselves. When the self-personality puts their effort and desire toward an internal thought being kept private, then the thought takes on more reality in the person's reflective perception of the environment. In believing part of themselves unacceptable or likely to be rejected, they will try to keep it separate. However, in doing so, there becomes a personified formation of thought which does not express itself with the rest of their personality. As a result, tension gets trapped within the sensorimotor system. The tension then infuses a sense of agitation within the individual's perception, wherein others are colored as more rejecting. The individual then expresses themselves negatively in a way where it leads to an experience of rejection. Loss fears then become actualized, creating a sense of being out of control. A desperate clinging or an angry distancing will then ensue in effort to secure themselves. Often, the self-personality individual emotionally personifies the problem within a binary relationship. Thus, especially for patients who are self-personalities, approaching treatment from within the context of their primary relationship is essential for treatment success.

If an internal feeling is used as the starting point to characterize the environment's affect on oneself, then the thought is a formation of feeling in relation to the environment. If one focuses on how they feel internally to form thought about the world or others, then the judgment is only a reflection of oneself. To have an experience which generates understanding, one's thought mind must be outwardly focused and open to understanding. When the individual two-part consciousness forms thought based directly on how one feels, then there can be no actual understanding of another. Others will experience being wrongly judged and unable to "get through" to such an individual. Thus, such individuals rely on loyalty founded on moral or ethical law or consequences they can impose. Otherwise, they have to consciously try to bring themselves positively to others. To do so, however, the starting point for doing cannot be their internal feelings—meaning, their sensory system should not determine their action. The starting point, rather, must be on others, with the intent of providing positive regard so to have a positive effect.

If an internal thought is the starting point to which an individual gives their effort, then an obsessive imbalance can occur rather quickly. An individual who is identified as feeling (self-personality) will effort themselves toward an externalized thought. If the individual creates their thought reflectively, then it is a formation of their feelings and is not true. Thus, an individual cannot legitimately say, "You don't love me" to someone based on internal feelings of being unloved. Doing so externalizes an internally formed sense of potential lacking. At a basic level, people create their own experience based on thought attachment to negative feelings. To the extent an individual expresses or energizes such a thought into the environment determines the magnitude of the derailment from shared reality. Rather than forcing one's own thought into interpersonal space, the effort should be toward understanding the thought of others or some aspect of the world outside of themselves. Thus, an open-minded effort outside of oneself is necessary in order to grow in understanding.

For the psychological sciences to disregard the binary nature of the human mind in favor of individualized labels (judgments) misses the forest from the trees. Moreover, approaching individuals, who are seeking psycho-emotional help, as diseased or individually disordered—through a process of labeling them and then trying to "control" their symptoms with chemicals—perpetuates the problem. When someone feels psychologically lost and emotionally unstable, they are usually needing a change of consciousness—a growth step of the mind. A misbelief about one's feelings or emotions—whether it be sadness, anger, or fear/anxiety—as being a problem binds the mind to find explanatory cause outside of them. If the belief became corrected—whereby the negative feeling, though uncomfortable, is not processed as a problem—then the energy would be integrated into the individual's efferent activity, and sensed as positive potential within them.

The healthcare system should be seen as the thought which seeks to cure problems in patients. Generally, individuals who reject their negative feelings are seeking to confirm how they feel is a problem. Thus, the healthcare system is perpetuating the problem by treating the negative feelings as a problem. If the mental health system corrected itself, then it would gradually be eliminated. The concept of mental illness would fade from public consciousness. However, the current conflict within the two-part consciousness—between feeling and thought—has brought increasing numbers of people forth who find the feelings associated with life unbearable. Up to this point, the mental health system has been trying to make sense of the "illness" as if the "illness" is outside an individual's consciousness—as if the sensory experience is being determined by the body—like hunger. So naturally, "foods" in the form of medications have been increasingly sought to manage feelings. Such an approach roots the patient in having an illness—an affliction—and thus is non-sensical to envision growing past. Yet, if the symptoms stem from a conflict between feeling and thought secondary to a misbelief about feelings, then it cannot be sourced from the body. Moreover, focusing on a patient's bothersome feelings—where medication treatment is in effort to make them feel better—affixes the focal point wrongly. Therein, rather than focusing on the actual problem point, providers unknowingly participate in the rejective approach to feelings.

Comprehending the importance of connecting with the present moment comes through the recognition that only within the present moment can someone realistically attach to life outside themselves. For it is within this state of connectedness where someone can have a true expression of themselves, and where their energy/feeling flows outside of themselves, thereby having a constructive effect within the environment. Imagine everyone has, whenever awake, a firehose from which feeling/energy shoots forth. The outflow is constant and unable to be turned off while awake. The hose flows toward whatever is focused on, and thus each's own focal point is all which can be controlled within the scenario. Energy/feeling can only flow out of an individual's experiential orbit when two conditions are met—it is occurring within the present moment and their focal point is outside of themselves. If they turn their focus on their own feelings, then the hose will flow into their sensory system and their feelings will become more intense. Likewise, focus on internal thought scenarios (past or present) will cause a welling up of thought pressure or sense of mental stress. Focus on their own body will induce anxious hypersensitivity to physical sensations. Finally, a focal point fixed on the image of themselves in the mind of another is the same as focusing on themselves.

Assuming one's focal point is correctly positioned on something or someone outside of oneself, then two possible approaches exist in relation to the something or someone. One may either construct or destruct. One may either see the positive or the negative. One can either make or break. When one gives criticism or negativity, the effect will be depleting or constrictive to those within the environment. Oppositely, a constructive intent seeks to have a positive impact. To do so, one must see the environment for what one can bring to it, and regard others for what one can bring to them. Purposing one's outflow in order to establish more control over the environment is primarily regarding the environment as it relates to oneself. Rather than trying to create within the environment, effort to control the environment is in order to compensate for one's anxious feelings or negative thoughts. When creating, the environment becomes an expression or extension of oneself. Thus, when one compensates, life becomes increasingly dissatisfying. For wellness, the handling of one's negativity must occur within one's dynamic being, thus being channeled through a digestive process, whereby the feelings are sought to be understood and properly expressed. It is analogous to the digestion of food, wherein the digestive process enables absorption of the nutrients which then get turned into energy and expressed through the maintenance and activity of one's system. One's emotions, similarly, when understood for what they are and for what they signify about one's current state of being, become naturally diffused into one's effort and intent. As such, one's creative potential flows into efferent, willed output.

If symptoms or problem behaviors can be recognized as a mismanagement of energies in the context of thought creativity, then changes in an individual's internal thought relationship with their feelings can lead to a fundamental shift in the handling and thus conscious perception of their feelings. Furthermore, the ability, through positive thought, to create positivity outside of themselves for which they can step into, is the proper path. However, the entrance to the path is blocked by each's native desire to get or feel for themselves, to control their own fulfillment from the world, or to not experience what is feared. Expressing negative feeling and expecting a positive result should be limited to childhood. Becoming *grown up* is thus marked by taking responsibility for oneself—for what one puts out, for what one does, for mistakes made, and for the correction of oneself.

The revolutionary nature of Binary Psychology occurs by way of understanding the binary or two-part consciousness. Stepping back from the disease model of mental health enables an escape from the myth of mental illness. Within the two-part consciousness exists the mind-body relationship in a triangulated context with the world. Consciousness itself is produced by the interaction of feeling and thought—the fusing together of feeling and thought to produce experiential awareness. The interaction between feeling and thought is thus decisive in forming the individual perceptive experience. As sensory information is processed within this triangle, with the life impulse for growth vitalizing each's way, an individualized consciousness intends into the world. Through life, a growth of consciousness is compelled. The growth of consciousness requires an expansion of two elements—understanding and awareness. A greater understanding of the nature of life, and an awareness of one's full outgoing potential comes through willed experiences. Increasingly, as consciousness expands, the creative aspect of consciousness infuses into one's awareness—whereby one senses the creative nature of one's perception. The judgmental, logical aspect of consciousness—which relies on experience and rational observation—has been the dominant form of consciousness throughout human history. The positional perspective within the two-part consciousness which forms judgments and seeks to be in control will necessarily be biased against a loss of control of the self or the emotional aspect of consciousness. However, the loss of control is due to a misrepresentation of the emotion, subsequent misperception of its meaning, and resultant mishandling of it. The conscious processing of certain feelings depends on the encoded belief about the feeling or emotion. Thus, the error occurs along the bridge between the two sides—the bridge connecting sensory feeling with thought representation—where these two entities meet, where consciousness is born.

The Binary Psychology Triangle

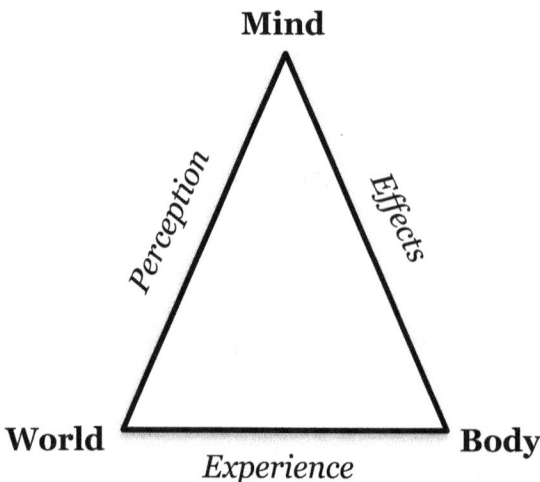

Mind

Perception

Effects

World

Experience

Body

The power of the mind is able to be recognized when its role in assigning cause to bodily effects (impressions) is understood. The perceived world is naturally the cause of negative effects, such as anxiousness, where reason for the anxious effects is found (e.g. lion attacking). The mind will perceive the world to explain what is being felt, thereby generating experience. In other words, the mind separates from negativity by materializing outside cause, whereby rejective action is then taken versus the cause. A false sense of stability is gained through rejecting potential negative, where feeling better is begotten through the expression of the negativity which was preexisting. Negativity which is blocked, controlled, or avoided becomes trapped within the mind-body space—where such rejected energy or potential gets expressed through deleterious physical symptoms or negative emotions.

The mind initiates willed action. Any action requires the body to be the vehicle for which to move—to do, to impress change upon the environment—to create. Thus, any action beholds an intent relative to the environment—where the intent is based on the mind's desire relative to the environment. If the environment is perceived as a threat, then naturally the mind's intent will be to reject the source of potential negativity. Since the negativity is sensed through the body, the mind attaches to an outside, environmental cause, where the mind can exist in a third-person or separated position relative to the body and the environmental cause. In other words, the mind is able to perceptively detach from the body whereby the reference point then becomes the environment happening to oneself rather than oneself happening to the environment. For an individual to happen to the environment, the mind has to be in connection with the body. Otherwise, a reflection of rejection occurs, where then energy is trapped within the mind-body space in the form of tension. Such trapped tension then gets expressed as either physical rejection or rejection of connection. Either way, cause of the the individual's state of disconnection will be perceived as happening to them as a result of the environment or from the effects occurring within their body. As a rule, when an individual is relating to negative effects occurring within themselves, they are bound to either express the effects (negative emotions) or perceive cause within or need from the environment. Otherwise, the mind—the "I"—is the cause, wherein the individual perceives being the cause of their own effects. At this juncture, to change must be an "I" change rather than a feeling or "me" change.

Within the mind-body connection, an individual may impress their energies into a willed effort to have the desired impact unto the environment. Action necessarily requires a mind-body connection, whereby the potentiated energy within the body is actualized within the environment. Doing so causes a sense of vulnerability since the mind and body—being in a state of connection—is unable to be defensive. Defensiveness, rather, invariably comes from a disconnected state. When defensive, no matter what an individual does, they cannot take responsibility for doing so—rather, the individual perceives themselves reacting to effects from an environmental cause. The cause is seen as the source for the action taken whenever the intent for the action is to not experience something. For instance, an action by an authoritarian body, when done in protection of someone, occurs with the goal of keeping something from happening. In such a scenario, the responsibility for the action is given to the potential for negative, with the goal of the negative not happening. However, since such an action does not have a positive goal, its utility will erode and increasingly be exploited for intentions retailed to individuals seeking to control or avoid each other.

Illustrated differently, the teacher who is most moved by their student's complaints will nurture the most discord between students. An action which is not toward something actualized, but rather is made in order for a potential negative to not materialize, gives power to such negative potential. Such action is a double negative, where positivity is illusory and unable to be achieved—therein forming an imbalance.

The current attempt to understand the nature of consciousness is being lead by theoretical physicists. At the atomic level, where the fundamental particles exist in a state of binary relativity, physicists have had to confront the effect human consciousness has on whatever system or element being observed. In trying to predict the behavior of nature, scientists in the early 1900's assumed nature existed independently, and operated according to Newtonian (mechanical) principles. At the atomic level, however, their mathematical principles did not hold up—they were unable to account for the behavior of atomic particles. Quantum physics was thus formed, and eventually lead to the present dilemma wherein the world of potentialities is being explored. Within the uncertainty of what may be, the human consciousness exists as a determining part of what occurs. However, in trying to qualify the human consciousness, it has been broadly defined as one's feelings/thoughts/ideas, and is a similar entity across humans. Yet, in a way similar to the relevance of a subatomic particle's direction of spin, the human consciousness occurs in two possible states or positions. Since the thinking consciousness requires two parts in order to triangulate awareness, there occur two naturally occurring positions. An individual will either be positioned as feeling/energy moving toward outside thought, or they will be positioned as thought regarding feeling/energy outside themselves. Classically, paradigms of thought have been constructed from the thought side of consciousness. However, since the thought side of consciousness cannot perceive itself, it cannot judge itself. From the thought side of consciousness an individual can only feel themselves. Thus, attempts to understand the human mind, including consciousness itself, have fallen short. Since the two-part consciousness occurs as a relationship between two elements (feeling and thought), understanding the mind can only come from a superposition. Understanding the nature of something as a whole can never be fully achieved from a position within the whole. Effort to understand something by objectifying it within the thought mind occurs in attempt to gain a sense of control. The objectification itself will then cause the potentialities to collapse into the individual's experienced reality, and their consciousness will perceive it as having happened, rather than recognizing how they made it happen by seeing it as such.

Over the past one-hundred years, insights within quantum physics have shown the judgment of the observer has a determining effect on the behavior of light. To investigate something objectively is, thus, not possible. Though the scientific method has become more refined, and standards for research studies more rigorous, nevertheless, the effect of judgment (the hypothesis) on what is seen or observed is unable to be controlled. In other words, phenomenon are inseparable from the observation or recognition of the phenomenon. The rational, thought mind seeks to know, to objectify, to reduce uncertainty through organization of sensory phenomenon. Yet, each individual cannot perceive their own expectation in what they are observing, or their causal effect on what they are experiencing. The less a person recognizes where they are precipitating their experience, the more they will perceive the experience happening to them and outside their control. The less someone's subjective reality aligns with the objective reality of the material world or the subjective reality of others, the more conflict or frustration occurs within their interactions. The crucial insight this brings for psychologists and philosophers is in the role human consciousness plays as part of the creative process. What the human consciousness perceives as reality is the initial brushstroke of creation. People, generally, must recognize their "take" of the environment has a determining effect on the environment (including others).

When an individual's experience with their parent(s) involved their parents seeking to please them or make them feel better, then an entitlement to be happy or pleased will be imbedded in how the individual perceives life. Such an individual will be critical toward others or the environment. This is because of the belief in happiness being obtainable through cleaning away the negative elements, as if happiness exists on the other side. However, such a belief is untrue, and is actually opposite to what is needed for the pursuit of happiness. Happiness involves finding the good in everything, rather than the bad, which can only come to fruition through the understanding and acceptance of the bad. Judging the world negatively as it treats oneself is opposite to judging oneself as one treats the world. Through the latter approach, an individual can intend themselves positively unto the world, and in doing so can increasingly distance their consideration from the world's treatment of them.

Gaining insight as to how humans should approach life cannot be acquired through human judgment. Insight is found, rather, in characterizing nature. Nature rewards creative effort by manifesting the thought behind it. The world opposes being blamed and seems to not care about how someone feels relative to it. Nature seems to believe every individual is equipped with all they need and nothing they don't—where each individual, as a whole, has the potential to be perfect. But for someone to come into fruition of themselves as such, certain corrections must occur. Despite being propelled for themselves, and in regard of life relative to themselves, each must come to purpose their life within the world. The world gives based on what it receives, not based on relative judgment. To judge the world is a rejection, and rejection gets in the way of each's experience within the world. Judgment can only occur relative to an individual's feelings or thought desires, and prevents judgment of their efferent being. The human perception senses contrast and is naturally divisive, thereby producing the experience of separateness and individuality. Thus, the human experience will always be for each to accept themselves, to embrace their role within the whole, and to grow in understanding of creation. In doing so, each's sense of connectedness with life grows as their perspective becomes de-centered or more outgoing. The ability to give light to the world comes through acceptance of the darkness rather than through effort to avoid or reject negativity.

A Metaphor for Living

The most useful metaphor of life, for which a person may conceive of life and frame their direction, is to see the world as their dance partner. Three principles hold inexorably true within the partnership—within the dance. First, the world compels a full individualized blossoming of each individual, where there occurs an ever expanding realization of who one is within the dance. Secondly, the world regards each as having everything they need. Each individual has all the necessary pieces to solve the puzzlement of their life. There exist no extra pieces, but a lifetime (or more) may be required to get them all properly aligned. The third and final principle is that each person, in their dance partnership with the world, makes the first move. If their first perceptive move is to reflect off of their own feelings, then the world will give them cause for such. If the first move results in a sense of being determined by the world, then the person is making their first perceptive move unto themselves. Though they will perceive the world causing them to be as they are, in truth, the world is manifesting, for them, an experience of themselves. In other words, a person's life experience (the dance) takes the form of the relationship occurring within them. Each beholds the power of creation within them, and yet, to willfully create requires a full giving over of oneself, where the believing mind pushes past the feeling body. Doing so is making the first move.

The world is bound between the two poles within each individual, where it serves to buffer the process of unification. During the human lifetime, within the world, each is given an opportunity for potentiation of themselves, wherein a balance between the two poles may be reached. The balance, then, enables them to unify through integration. Attachments within the world enable each individual to stabilize themselves during the dfficult experiences which characterize life, but are also the bridges by which people grow more unified. What each seeks internally from life will be what each ultimately grows to give unto life. Each's experience from the world will be primarily based on whether they have sought to brighten the world or brighten themselves. Each is constructed as a battery—powered by a positive pole and a negative pole—where the positioning of the poles is significant. For if someone primarily seeks internal positivity (or a lack of negativity), then they must position the negative pole externally. In other words, to seek internal positivity, the world becomes negatively potentiated. Oppositely, if the negative pole is internally centered, then an individual can relate to the world as the positive pole. As such, an individual may grow into the world—into increasing positivity—where their effort flows in support of their intent toward growth. However, in order to do so, all negativity must be accepted on the inside. Each is called to lay down their sword of rejection, to let go of their defense. Only then may the sword be used to make the world a better place.

— Brian P. Lahey, M.D.

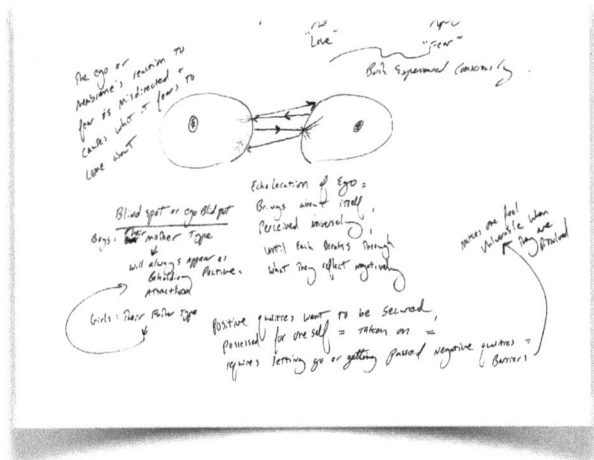

Dr. Brian P. Lahey, M.D. is a board certified specialist in both child/adolescent and adult psychiatry. He also specializes in treating opiate dependence, as well as working with couples looking to grow their relationship. Dr. Lahey is currently in private practice, seeing patients. Increasingly, his efforts are toward implementing systemic changes within homes and schools.

Other works by Dr. Lahey:

Of Mice & Children: Learning to Think & to Love (2016)
Emotional Intelligence Curriculum
The Mind Diet (M.D.)

Blog: Mind Over Matter
blog.upandupsolutions.com

"Newspapermen eating candy, had to be held down by big police. But someday, everything is gonna be different...when I paint my masterpiece."

— Bob Dylan

www.ingramcontent.com/pod-product-compliance
Lightning Source LLC
Chambersburg PA
CBHW080605270326
41928CB00016B/2929